Rea

NEW STUDIES IN AMERICAN INTELLECTUAL
AND CULTURAL HISTORY
Jeffrey Sklansky, *Series Editor*

Reading the Market

Genres of Financial Capitalism in Gilded Age America

PETER KNIGHT

Johns Hopkins University Press
Baltimore

Johns Hopkins Paperback edition, 2018
2   4   6   8   9   7   5   3   1

Johns Hopkins University Press
2715 North Charles Street
Baltimore, Maryland 21218-4363
www.press.jhu.edu

The Library of Congress has cataloged the hardcover edition of this book as folllows:
Names: Knight, Peter, 1968– author
Title: Reading the market : genres of financial capitalism
in gilded age America / Peter Knight.
Description: Baltimore : Johns Hopkins University Press, [2016] | Series: New
studies in American intellectual and cultural history | Includes bibliographical
references and index.
Identifiers: LCCN 2015047643 | ISBN 9781421420608 (hardcover : alk. paper) |
ISBN 9781421420615 (electronic) | ISBN 1421420600 [hardcover : alk. paper) |
ISBN 1421420619 (electronic)
Subjects: LCSH: Finance—United States—History—19th century | Finance—
United States—History—20th century. | Journalism, Commercial—United
States—History | Capitalism and literature—United States—History. | Finance
in literature. | Finance in art.
Classification: LLC HG181.K63 2016 | DDC 332.0973/09034—dc23 LC record
available at http://lccn.loc.gov/2015047643

A catalog record for this book is available from the British Library.

ISBN-13: 978-1-4214-2521-4
ISBN-10: 1-4214-2521-1

*Special discounts are available for bulk purchases of this book. For more information,
please contact Special Sales at 410-516-6936 or specialsales@press.jhu.edu.*

Johns Hopkins University Press uses environmentally friendly book materials,
including recycled text paper that is composed of at least 30 percent
post-consumer waste, whenever possible.

Valerie Kay Knight (1940–2014)

CONTENTS

ACKNOWLEDGMENTS

This project has racked up debts that will take a lifetime to repay. Writing this book, however, has also made it apparent that, at its best, the academic community still operates as a gift economy rather than as an exchange economy. For making the sometimes impersonal and abstract process of research more personal, and for proving that not all insider networks are sinister, I would like to thank all those who took part in the Culture of the Market Network, funded by the United Kingdom's Arts and Humanities Research Council (AHRC), in particular my co-organizers Sven Beckert, Christopher McKenna, and Julia Ott, as well as Jean-Christophe Agnew, Joyce Appleby, Edward Balleisen, Marieke de Goede, Justin Fox, Alissa Karl, Leigh-Claire La Berge, Jessica Lepler, Jonathan Levy, James Livingston, Stephen Mihm, Rowena Olegario, Martin Parker, Mary Poovey, Jeffrey Sklansky, Richard White, and David Zimmerman.

For generously taking time to share inside information with me, I am grateful to Steve Fraser, Walter Friedman, Richard R. John, Marina Moskowitz, Caitlin Rosenthal, Brook Thomas, and Caitlin Zaloom. I am also indebted to the organizers and audiences at seminars and conferences I have taken part in, especially the École Normale Supérieure de Cachan (ENS Cachan); the National Museum of American History Colloquium; the Centre d'Études et de Recherches sur la Vie Économique des Pays Anglophones, part of the Centre for Research on the English-Speaking World (Cervepas/CREW) at Paris III; the British Association for American Studies; Lancaster University; the University of Copenhagen; the University of Edinburgh; Leibniz University (Hanover); and the Research Colloquium on Crowd Dynamics and Financial Markets at the Copenhagen Business School. I would like to thank the MA students in my Fictions of Finance class, and all my colleagues in English and American Studies at the University of Manchester, especially Laura Doan, Hal Gladfelder, and David Matthews, as supportive heads of department.

I owe a debt of thanks to Jeff Sklansky, as the series editor, for his initial enthusiasm; Bob Brugger, at Johns Hopkins University Press, for making a speculative investment in this project; the anonymous reviewers of the manuscript, for their thoughtful suggestions for improvement; and Kathleen Capels, for her meticulous copyediting. A portion of chapter 2 appeared in an earlier form as "Reading the Market: Abstraction, Personification and the Financial Column of *Town Topics* Magazine," *Journal of American Studies* 46 (2012): 1055–1075; and a section of chapter 4 was first published as "Edith Wharton and Inside Information," in *Class and the Making of American Literature: Created Unequal,* ed. Andrew Lawson (New York: Routledge, 2014), 147–61. I am grateful to the presses for permission to include the revised versions here, and the respective editors and reviewers for their perceptive comments.

Personal generosity is one thing, but for hard cash and institutional support I would like to record my gratitude to the Leverhulme Trust, for a Study Abroad Fellowship; the Warren Center at Harvard University, for hosting me; a Baird Society Resident Fellowship at the Smithsonian Institution; and a Gilder Lehrman Fellowship at the New-York Historical Society. I would like to thank the staff and librarians of those institutions, as well as those at the New York Public Library and the Baker Library at the Harvard Business School. For conversation and hospitality while on research trips to the United States, I am grateful to John Plotz and Lisa Soltani, Judith and Paul Plotz, and Gus and Davina Porter.

I began this project in the basement of libraries in the United States, consulting long-forgotten financial advice pamphlets and novels, but by the time I came toward the end, much of what I needed had been digitized. I would therefore like to acknowledge the importance of the Internet Archive and other institutions that have preserved and made this material available. Although reading the outpouring of Gilded Age financial literature on my computer at home was far easier (and racked up far fewer air miles), there are some things that virtual scholarship can't produce, such as a serendipitous meeting with Michael Zakim in the reading room of the New-York Historical Society.

My heartfelt thanks are extended to Andrew Lawson, who generously provided an incisive reading of the manuscript. I would like to thank everyone involved in putting on the "Show Me the Money: The Image of Finance, 1700 to the Present" exhibition, above all my co-conspirators, Paul Crosthwaite and Nicky Marsh, whose intellectual companionship has meant so much to me. This book would probably have been finished much earlier if I had not gotten sidetracked into our collaborative ventures, but I am eternally grateful that I did.

Thanks also are due to my parents, for their unfailing support over the years. This book is dedicated to my mother, Valerie Knight, who sadly did not live to see it completed. My deepest debt is to Lindsay and Elspeth, who have counted the cost of too many lost weekends and evenings I spent reading the market.

Reading the Market

Introduction

Finance is a subject which the liveliest writer may well despair of making popular, since the mere sight or suspicion of it alone is enough to cause every reader, except the dullest, to close the most promising volume.

Henry Adams, "The Legal-Tender Act" (1870)

There is no more interesting or exciting serial story than the stock-ticker tells, from day to day, to those interested in the stock market, or one that often excites more joy or sorrow, or carries with it more weal or woe, prosperity or ruin.

Henry Clews, Fifty Years in Wall Street (1908)

In the opening chapter of *The Pit* (1903), the second book in Frank Norris's unfinished epic trilogy on raising and selling wheat, the young Laura Dearborn attends her first opera in Chicago. She is annoyed that the men in the audience are disturbing the aesthetic purity of the drama with their constant whispering about the day's events at the Chicago Board of Trade. "It was terrific, there on the floor of the Board this morning," one of the voices asserts. "By the Lord! they fought each other when the Bears began throwing the grain at 'em—in carload lots."[1] Yet all of a sudden, Laura comes to see that the financial wranglings at the Board of Trade are not a dull, workaday distraction from the operatic performance she has come to see:

> And abruptly, midway between two phases of that music-drama, of passion and romance, there came to Laura the swift and vivid impression of that other drama that

simultaneously—even at that very moment—was working itself out close at hand, equally picturesque, equally romantic, equally passionate; but more than that, real, actual, modern, a thing in the very heart of the life in which she moved. (34)

On the way home from the theater, Laura is amazed to find that the financial district is still buzzing with energy:

> The office buildings on both sides of the street were lighted from basement to roof. Through the windows she could get glimpses of clerks and book-keepers in shirt-sleeves bending over desks. Every office was open, and every one of them full of feverish activity. The sidewalks were almost as crowded as though at noontime. Messenger boys ran to and from, and groups of men stood on the corners in earnest conversation. The whole neighborhood was alive, and this, though it was close upon one o'clock in the morning! (39–40)[2]

In contrast to Henry Adams's despairing sense that the "mere sight or suspicion" of finance is enough "to cause every reader, except the dullest, to close the most promising volume," *The Pit* both revels in and is repulsed by the dramatic action of the nation's stock markets. Finance, for Norris, is a matter of romance as much as realism.[3]

In *The Pit*, the love plot and the business plot begin to be entangled when Laura falls for Jadwin Curtis, an arch-speculator of Napoleonic charisma who attempts to corner the market in wheat futures. At first sight, the novel works to humanize the opaque operations of the market. Through the sheer force of his personality, coupled with his seemingly limitless buying power in the Chicago Board of Trade, Jadwin attempts to bring the entire market under the control of his individual, mighty hand. The personal battles of the brokers, however, are dwarfed by the picture of "the market" as a sublime, impersonal force: "The market was in a tumult. He fancied he could almost hear the thunder of the Pit as it swirled. All La Salle Street was listening and watching, all Chicago, all the nation, all the world. Not a 'factor' on the London 'Change who did not turn an ear down the wind to catch the echo of this turmoil, not an *agent de change* in the peristyle of the Paris Bourse, who did not strain to note the every modulation of its mighty diapason" (328). Norris's novel about the romance of finance was serialized in the fledgling *Saturday Evening Post* and became an instant bestseller on its publication in book form in 1903, selling 95,000 copies during its first year. It was turned into a Broadway play in 1904, and in 1907, D. W. Griffith directed *A Corner in Wheat*, a silent film based on the novel and Norris's short story, "A Deal in Wheat," which had explored similar themes. The novel also inspired "The

Pit," a board game produced by Parker Brothers in 1903. This "frenzied trading game" achieved enormous commercial success by promising "exciting fun for everyone."[4]

In the decades around the turn of the twentieth century, fiction writers, financial journalists, and market apologists likewise began to insist that—for better or worse—the world of finance provided excitement and intrigue worthy of high literature. Money "is the romance, the poetry of our age," a character ruefully announces in William Dean Howells's novel, *The Rise of Silas Lapham* (1885), while the Wall Street grandee Henry Clews declared that "there is no more interesting or exciting serial story than the stock-ticker tells."[5]

In the Gilded Age and the Progressive Era, Americans began to spend an increasing amount of time thinking and reading about financial markets. Nonetheless, according to most historical accounts, the vast majority were not yet actively involved in investment or speculation. The American economy was still primarily an agricultural one, with the percentage of the labor force in industry not overtaking that in agriculture until the eve of World War I; likewise, a market for industrial stocks did not emerge in any significant way until the 1890s. Although the historical data on participation in the U.S. securities market is patchy, most accounts agree that by 1900, only a tiny percentage of Americans held investments in the legitimate stock market. Even as late as World War I, the estimated number of Americans who owned stocks or bonds was only 0.5 percent of the total population. This was not least because, in most cases, the minimum trade of 100 shares on the New York Stock Exchange (NYSE)—$10,000 if the stock was trading at par—coupled with a minimum margin (deposit) of 10 percent, meant that well into the twentieth century, dabbling in the stock market remained only for the upper classes.[6] Moreover, the financial sector contributed only 2 percent to the overall U.S. economy in the 1870s, rising to 4 percent by 1920.[7] If participating in the stock market was impossible for all but the wealthiest Americans in the late nineteenth and early twentieth centuries, and it constituted only a small part of the wider economy, then why did its "feverish activity"—"picturesque," "romantic," and "passionate," but also "real," "actual," and "modern"—loom so large in the cultural imagination? And why did the turn to finance matter? *Reading the Market* attempts to answer these questions.

The standard historical narrative is that popular involvement in the stock market did not really take off until the 1920s, enabled by the increase in surplus personal savings and promoted by a public relations campaign, mounted by the NYSE in particular, that aimed to make share ownership appear not merely democratic but positively patriotic, cashing in on the success of the federal government's promotion of Liberty Bonds in World War I. This popularity was short lived, however, as the crash of 1929 scared off many ordinary investors until the 1950s, with the real increase in involvement coming from institutional investments, such as pensions, in the 1960s and 1970s.[8] This story is broadly correct, but, like the figures for stock market participation cited above, it leaves out several important elements that help explain why the market became an object of such dread and fascination around the turn of the twentieth century. First, Americans had already become caught up in the patriotic fervor of bond holding with Jay Cooke's promotion of Union bonds during the Civil War. Second, the development of new financial activities, such as derivatives trading (in the form of commodity futures), demanded a new way of thinking about the nature of value. Third, many Americans were involved in speculative activity that took place outside the New York Stock Exchange and the Chicago Board of Trade (CBoT). Up to 1890, more securities were traded on the Boston exchange than on the NYSE, for example; in addition, there were many other kinds of financial speculation besides the officially recorded data on stocks and bonds of firms listed on the main exchanges.[9] Although prestigious institutions like the NYSE and CBoT made strenuous efforts in the late nineteenth and early twentieth centuries to restrict popular participation in financial speculation by increasing the barriers to entry, their campaigns were not entirely successful. New York's Curb Market and Consolidated Stock Exchange, along with smaller stock and produce exchanges dotted around the country, dealt primarily in secondary trading on securities listed on the NYSE, or in less-prestigious (and often more dubious) securities not listed on the main exchanges, usually purchased in smaller lots, which made them accessible to the fabled investor of limited means.

In terms of numbers of participants, the legions of bucket shops that sprouted up throughout the United States in the 1890s and early 1900s were more significant than their legitimate counterparts, including second-tier exchanges and over-the-counter trading. Bucket shops were small brokerage firms, often with several branches, that allowed clients to bet small amounts on the rise or fall of stock and commodity prices. They promised a taste of the excitement of speculation for those unable to participate personally in the NYSE or CBoT, due either to limited means or being far removed from the action. Bucket shops were able to offer low margins and small lots because, in most cases, punters were merely betting against the house, rather than purchasing any actual securities. Some bucket shops were out-and-out scams, with bettors fleeced by being fed fraudulent quotations over a delayed wire feed. The hundreds of thousands of bucket shop speculators, therefore, do not show up on any of the official statistics of securities ownership, because they did not technically own any shares.[10] Yet the volume of business conducted by the bucket shops far exceeded that transacted by the legitimate exchanges: by 1889, for example, bucket shop clients were estimated to be betting on the equivalent of 1 million shares per day, seven times the volume traded on the NYSE.[11] In addition, thousands of more ordinary Americans were enticed into what they thought would be lucrative speculative deals by confidence artists, who advertised what would turn out to be fraudulent brokerage services, specious investment advice, and other financial scams. In 1902 alone, an estimated $200 million was lost in dubious investment schemes and other get-rich-quick con tricks.[12]

Even if they were not technically owners of securities traded on the legitimate exchanges, bucket shop clients and those responding to the welter of newspaper advertisements for speculative schemes considered themselves to be financially involved in the market, with its fickle fortunes determining theirs. Long before they began to show up on any official statistics of popular participation in the NYSE and CBoT, ordinary Americans became entangled in the market, both in reality and in their imaginations. Some thought they were investing for the long term, but others were merely keen to enjoy the fruits of speculation that they felt were being unfairly hogged by the "insiders" on the nation's exchanges. Indeed, some of the very farmers who condemned the Chicago Board of Trade's speculation in "wind wheat" (as they termed the "fictitious dealing" in futures contracts for grain that far exceeded the actual crop that was being grown) were themselves betting in the bucket shops, convinced either that buying agricultural futures would help hedge against the risks of uncertain harvests, or—more likely—that they, too, deserved to get rich quick.

This imaginative engagement with the stock market cannot, however, be explained entirely by the rise of a financial netherworld outside the lofty confines of the NYSE. Judging by the ubiquity of market reports, Wall Street fiction, and other accounts of finance during this period, many more Americans became emotionally invested in the stock market long before they became financially invested, whether in a legitimate fashion or otherwise. The idea of finance in general, and the stock market in particular, exerted a fascination—part desire, part dread—decades before the NYSE engaged in a concerted public relations campaign in the 1910s and 1920s to educate the public and present share ownership as a patriotic duty. Indeed, this vicarious encounter with the market arguably helped pave the way for that later democratization, even in cases where the overt tenor of the reading material warned about the dangers of "outsiders" getting mixed up in speculation.

This book explores the many ways in which Americans learned to "read" the market in the Gilded Age and the Progressive Era. For much of the nineteenth century, the stock market was regarded as inconsequential at best and immoral at worst, with numerous sermons and diatribes condemning speculation as no better than gambling. Likewise, the Brahmin view of the stock exchange as a den of thieves was only confirmed, in their eyes, by the distinctly unsavory cast of robber barons, whose antics repeatedly featured on the front page rather than the business page of newspapers. From the other end of the class spectrum, Populist writers also condemned the stock market for the way in which it seemed to undermine the republican conviction that economic value should result from labor, rather than speculation with other peoples' money. From the 1880s onward, however, numerous novels, short stories, investment-advice guides, brokers' newsletters, newspaper columns, illustrations, and magazine articles were less immediately concerned with attacking the stock market than making sense of it, rendering its mechanism and patterns legible for their readers. Speculation was increasingly viewed as legitimate, but even condemnations of the market helped render it legible and thus call it into being.[13]

This book provides a taxonomy of how Americans made sense of the market in the last decades of the nineteenth and the first decades of the twentieth centuries. In this historical moment of rapid industrialization, finance had not yet come to play the central role in the American economy that the crash of 2008 made manifest. Yet it was during this period that many of the ways of organizing and representing the financialized economy were still in a state of flux, before they came to be taken as natural and inevitable economic facts. As Marieke de Goede argues in her influential "genealogy of finance," it is vital to "reread the historical controversies and political struggles that slowly and contingently produced meanings that are in many instances unquestioned today." Doing so allows us to challenge the technocratic inevitability of the triumph of financial abstraction by attending to the "political debate, confusion, contingencies, and reversals" in a formative period of financial capitalism.[14]

In my study of the genres of financial capitalism, I consider popular understandings *of* the market, as well as emerging representational technologies produced *by* the market. In this respect I am following in the footsteps of *Genres of the Credit Economy*, Mary Poovey's pioneering study of writings produced by and about finance in the wake of the financial revolution in Britain.[15] My approach is also informed by Andrew Milner's account of genre as a variety of what Raymond Williams calls "selective tradition."[16] In this view, genres are best understood not as categories to which particular texts and artifacts belong—or fail to belong—according to a set of externally imposed criteria, but rather as forms, constituted immanently, by the practitioners themselves, through their affiliations with or dissociations from their predecessors. This book therefore analyzes the forms of knowledge produced in and by financial capitalism as they began to constitute a particular, identifiable way of organizing the world and explores their genealogy, their operation, and their consequences.

In light of this structuring focus on genre, the following chapters examine the market report and the wider growth of nonspecialist financial journalism and fiction; the development of popular investment-advice manuals, in addition to primers on how to decipher the chatter of the stock ticker; charts, diagrams, cartoons, and other illustrations that attempted to capture not merely scenes within particular stock exchanges, but the idea of the market itself; the confidence trick, the market tip, and varieties of inside information that seem to offer a shortcut to elucidating the market's mysteries; and conspiracy theories in both fictional and factual works, as a way of making sense of the system of finance as a whole. Some of these cultural forms (such as Frank Norris's novels) are comparatively well known, but others (such as investment-advice manuals) are less familiar, dismissed by economic historians as inaccurate, by intellectual historians as trivial, and by social historians as irrelevant to the story of class struggle. One aim of this study, therefore, is to bring them to light, in order to recognize the importance of what might be termed a vernacular epistemology of finance and investigate how the dominant modes of financial knowledge are neither natural nor inevitable.[17] There is now a considerable body of scholarship on the emergence of the professionalized discipline of economics during this period, but comparatively little has been written on how a lay audience grappled with economic ideas in general or how, in particular, ordinary Americans built up a mental picture of the market. "The print culture that helped people make sense of money through financial advice," Lendol Calder notes, still "awaits its historian," despite the fact that "concerns about money, how to get it, how to save it, how to invest, multiply, and spend it have likely sold more books in the last two hundred years than any other subject after religion."[18] Yet these works of popular finance did not merely describe how to speculate; they also contributed to the discursive and political struggle over what form money should take; the meanings of new financial operations, such as futures trading; and the role of finance in the wider economy.

Those struggles have largely been forgotten as the representations, instruments, and institutions of finance that emerged in their wake have long since become naturalized.

Semiotics of Finance

Reading the market had to be learned. As Americans were increasingly forced to do business with strangers during the course of the nineteenth century, they had to develop skills in assessing the situation. At first this involved learning to interpret subtle clues and signs to verify that a stranger was trustworthy. As John Kasson argues, in an urban market society characterized by increasing social mobility, Americans turned to various forms of "the semiotics of everyday life" to render the labyrinthine chaos of the city and the market legible. Etiquette writers, novelists, detectives, and others tried to solve the problem of distrust in a market society by making social types recognizable, including the "pretentious Fifth Avenue parvenu" and "the feverish Wall Street speculator."[19] At first, reading the market involved interpreting the new social identities created by it, but later in the nineteenth century, as David Henkin has demonstrated, it also started to involve deciphering the more impersonal visual and verbal signs that proliferated in urban centers and began to constitute an emerging "financescape" that required new guidebooks.[20] Henkin shows, for example, how Americans had to learn to read the welter of banknotes that began to circulate promiscuously in the second half of the nineteenth century, many of which were either drawn on banks whose reserves could not underpin the notes they issued or were outright fabrications.[21] Even the counterfeit-detector books, published to aid customers in deciphering whether a particular note was spurious or not, were themselves sometimes fakes, setting up a potentially infinite regress of interpretation.[22]

In a society increasingly reliant on "paper profits" and "fictitious capital," ever-more-vigilant reading becomes both a necessity and a liability. As David Zimmerman notes in his study of panic fiction from around the turn of the twentieth century, "the stock market offered a thrilling read—literally," with crowds of investors across the nation poring over market reports and the stock ticker. The market itself, Zimmerman continues, is "constituted and sustained by these acts of reading": it is "composed of readers who are intensely aware that other investors are reading the same material at the same time and that their collective interpretations and predictions will have an effect on the market."[23] Speculators try to second-guess not only how those other readers are reading the market, but how they, in turn, read other market readers, and so on, into the potentially infinite chamber of echoes that can lead to a self-sustaining financial panic.

The outpouring of figurative writing and visual imagery about finance helped Americans read the market, in the broad sense of understanding how finance functioned in general, and how the nation's stock exchanges worked in particular. But a great deal of print in the last decades of the nineteenth century was dedicated to reading the market in a more literal sense. The money column in newspapers and periodicals, along with investment newsletters and advice manuals, provided a regular barometer of the financial markets, reporting and interpreting the endless fluctuation of stock prices churned out by the increasingly ubiquitous stock ticker. In addition, the emerging profession of technical, or chart, analysis attempted to render legible what it deemed to be the deeper patterns of market movements by abstracting them from the minute-by-minute tide of price variations coming over the ticker. Reading the market thus increasingly meant viewing price-data charts, with their now-familiar sublime and inhuman imagery of mountainous peaks and troughs. In a twist, however, on what today is termed behavioral finance, the abstract digest of prices was itself often endowed with human characteristics, as if the rise and fall in prices was not a result of fickle investor sentiment, but the emotional instability of the market itself.

The scene of market reading also began to change. Many illustrations of the placeless and abstract market that began to fully emerge in the last decades of the nineteenth century continued to focus on the crowds at the center of the frenzied action on the floor of the stock exchange. A significant number of images, however, depicted isolated individuals far removed from the maelstrom of the exchange, engaged in an intense reading of prices emerging from the stock-ticker machine. The constant churn of the ticker tape turned Americans into fixated and frequently anxious readers of the market, whether in person or vicariously, through consuming fictions of finance. For example, Edward Neufville Tailer, a New York City clerk who became a successful businessman, recorded in his diary not only the daily weather, but also the financial meteorology of changing stock market prices, along with frequent visits to his broker, many times merely to see what was happening on Wall Street.[24] Even for those not anxiously checking the daily rise and fall of their actual investments, like Tailer, the stock market—as a proxy for the larger role of finance in people's lives—was anxiously watched in the Gilded Age and the Progressive Era.

Market Performance

What the various genres of financial capitalism explored in this book have in common is that they do not merely provide a detailed accounting, whether financial or moral, of the stock market, but instead constitute technologies of representation that actively shape the market they seem so naturally to depict. Some are literal devices for recording market data, such as the stock ticker, but I also consider financial journalism and financial fiction, seeing them, for instance, as communication technologies that also help produce the world they describe. Scholars of social studies of finance have begun to examine the rhetorical and performative construction of financial markets. They have attacked the value-neutral claims of orthodox economic theory, arguing that economic theories are not merely reflections of what is already out there, but instead legitimate and even actively create the economy they supposedly describe. Donald MacKenzie, for example, has provided a compelling demonstration of how technical financial models (such as the Black-Scholes formula for pricing options) are *performative* technologies that reshape the very financial markets they seem to neutrally ob-serve: the more traders use the model, the more prices converge on what the model predicts.[25] In this study, however, I argue first, that it is not just the detailed models of financial theory that shape the market, but a much broader range of discursive practices, institutions, regulations, and conceptions, including the idea of the self-regulating market; second, that those forms of market culture are themselves shaped by financial activity; and third, following the work of Judith Butler, that the "performance" created by those representations is not inevitable and final, but is open to wider cultural contestation.[26]

Some of the readings of the market explored in this book are of specific stock and produce markets, most prominently the Chicago Board of Trade and the New York Stock Exchange. Many depictions of these exchanges in fiction, journalism, and advice manuals act as financial Baedekers, introducing the strange customs of these exotic locations to the armchair traveler. Such accounts tend to focus on the specific personalities and even the particular architecture of each location, often taking in the view from the visitors' gallery. This volume is not, however, a study of the consolidation of and turf wars between the nation's stock and pro-duce exchanges, although many of the primary sources it explores are caught up in that story. Instead, it tells how geographically specific financial marketplaces, in which the desires and intentions of particular individuals played themselves out, were nevertheless part of a larger and more abstract "financescape" that seemed to be governed by a logic that no one, including the most powerful spec-ulator, could control. Even those accounts that focused on specific markets and their triumphs, tragedies, and personalities began to conjure up the idea of the market as a single, coherent entity, an abstract idea that existed over and above its specific physical incarnations. The depictions of financial activity examined in this book began to create what might be termed a Wall Street of the mind;

and indeed, "Wall Street" was often used as a verbal and visual shorthand for the entire financial system, with the NYSE in particular serving as a synecdoche for the market as a whole, the capital of Capital.[27]

This book examines the origins of the notion that the market has a life, a mind, and even a will of its own, or, at least, operates by its own logic that has very little to do with the fundamental values of individual corporations or broader, underlying economic factors. In short, during this period there emerged the glimmerings of the idea that beneath the surface drama of daily events, whether in the citadel of the New York Stock Exchange or in a humble local bucket shop, there was a larger system at work, a system that, in significant ways and to an increasing number of observers, seemed to move by its own mysterious volition and coordination. In earlier decades, Americans had already grappled with the social, political, and metaphysical problems of paper money, the fungibility of value, and the impossibility of taking strangers at face value, but it was only during the Gilded Age that a truly placeless and faceless market emerged, whose abstractions, in turn, were made legible through personification. To be sure, the liberal notion of the market produced by all this fevered reading was, as the epilogue will discuss in more detail, still a far cry from the neoliberal mantra that "the market knows best," which came to ideological prominence in the 1980s. Nevertheless, we need to recognize the significance of this much earlier conceptual shift that transformed actual stock markets into the abstract notion (and linguistic shorthand) of "the market" that could be observed through different optics and various locations.

The specific stock exchanges that came under the lens of public scrutiny or were dreamed up in the fiction writer's imagination might be vilified or romanticized, but, in either case, an abstract yet animated image of the market emerged from these representations. Even the stock ticker and price charts, which seemed merely to provide an objective register of the market, created what Audrey Jaffe has called a "vivified abstraction," a concrete projection of collective affect that was endowed with intentionality and then internalized, as if it was a natural expression of individual emotion.[28] In *The Pit*, for example, Jadwin deludes himself into thinking that the market is merely his plaything. Like a Napoleonic general, he is able to conquer it:

> Then at last the news of the great corner, authoritative, definite, went out over all the country, and promptly the figure and name of Curtis Jadwin loomed suddenly huge and formidable in the eye of the public. There was no wheat on the Chicago market. He, the great man, the "Napoleon of La Salle Street," had it all. He sold it or hoarded it, as suited his pleasure. He dictated the price to those men who must buy

it of him to fill their contracts. His hand was upon the indicator of the wheat dial
of the Board of Trade, and he moved it through as many or as few of the degrees of
the circle as he chose. (332)

The novel goes on to suggest that price fluctuations in the stock market are not
ultimately the result of human manipulation, but instead are the inevitable consequence of the sublime economic force of supply and demand. The invisible
hand of the market, we are led to believe, trumps the once-mighty hand of the
individual speculator. Jadwin thus insists that he is not able to control the market;
it controls him: "You think I am willfully doing this! You don't know, you haven't
a guess. I corner the wheat! Great heavens, it is the wheat that has cornered
me! The corner made itself. I happened to stand between two sets of circumstances, and they made me do what I've done" (283–84). In Norris's novel and in
other depictions, the market, despite being a human creation, is naturalized as
a sublime and self-regulating force that is indifferent to human concerns.[29] As
de Goede has argued, the task of a historical genealogy of finance should be to
denaturalize the "truths" of economic knowledge that have come to be taken for
granted.[30] If recent writers have attempted to demystify the "myth of the rational
market," which had come to be taken for a timeless and objective truth, with the
dominance, since the 1980s, of the efficient market hypothesis (EMH), then one
task of this volume is to demystify the logically prior notion of the market as an
entity that is both abstract and yet curiously animated.[31]

Furthermore, the idea of the market that was constructed by the discourses
and practices of investment advice and technical analysis in the late nineteenth
and early twentieth centuries was increasingly autopoietic, a self-referential hall
of mirrors in which the quoted prices no longer seemed to reflect real-world
economic conditions, but increasingly responded and referred to patterns that
are peculiar to the market itself.[32] Nonetheless, many mainstream financial commentators, such as Charles Dow, continued to insist that stock market prices
reflected fundamental economic values, which were the surest guide to future
movements: "The best way of reading the market is from the standpoint of values. The market is not like a balloon plunging hither and thither in the wind."[33]
Dow himself, however, helped develop precisely the kind of financial journalism
that made reading the market an obsessive nation pastime; and the Dow Jones
Industrial Average, his pioneering stock market index, likewise contributed to
the idea of the market as something resembling a single, albeit complex, living
organism, whose temperature could be taken by the use of economic indicators.

For the most part, the emerging profession of economics ignored the realm of stock market investment and speculation, in part because it was keen to distance itself from these folk forms of financial knowledge and activity. When these early economists talked about "the market," rarely did they mean the stock market. The marginalist revolution, however, which began to take hold from the 1880s with the work of economists such as Stanley Jevons in Britain and John Bates Clark in the United States, has much in common with the idea that causation in the stock market is endogenous rather than exogenous: that panics, for example, might result from the market reacting to its own movements, rather than to real-world events or conditions. The key marginalist insight was that value, and therefore price, are not an effect of an established order of worth (whether God-given, or, as political economy had insisted, man-made), or even an indication of the amount of labor involved in producing a commodity, but are instead a result of market sentiment. This view bolstered the conception of the market as an autonomous, self-contained, self-referring system of signs.

The Financial Turn

Although professional economists at the time were slow to recognize the significance of finance in shaping the nation's economic destiny in the Gilded Age and the Progressive Era, the repeated financial panics that radiated outward from Wall Street and the other urban financial centers brought home to many ordinary Americans the extraordinary power of the stock market to hijack and derail the wider economy, coupled with the concentration of power in the hands of the financier class. Randy Martin has documented the "financialization of daily life" in the twenty-first century, showing how financial practices and ideas have insinuated themselves into the nation's inner psyche, since a reliance on capital markets has become a defining feature of economic life.[34] Even in the nineteenth century, many Americans came to think of their lives as being intimately shaped by new financial structures and assumptions. Jonathan Levy, for example, has demonstrated how, in the course of the nineteenth century, many people were becoming increasingly subject to the risks of the volatile economy, with the irony being that they turned to financialized solutions, such as life insurance, to alleviate the problems caused by the market itself.[35]

Recent historiography on the development of capitalism in the United States has likewise begun to place finance at center stage. Earlier muckraking historians, such as Gustavus Myers (in the 1900s) and Matthew Josephson (in the 1930s), had focused their attention on the venality of the robber barons when telling what they saw as the true story of the rise of American industrial might. Since the rise of business history, pioneered by Alfred Chandler in the 1960s, economic historians have tended to downplay the importance of finance in general and the stock market in particular. Yet after the crash of 2007, finance is once again of vital importance in debates about our current economic crisis. A number of recent historical studies have therefore begun to look again at the first Gilded Age, bringing the story of bankers and brokers to the forefront and, in the process, challenging the Chandlerian view of business history as the inevitable, technological progress of economic efficiency and improvements in management structures.[36] The (re)turn to putting the institutions, mechanisms, and personalities of finance at the heart of capitalism is crucial if we are to understand the deeper roots of our present situation.

The emphasis so far, however, has tended to be on the economic and political aspects of finance, with less attention paid to the conceptual and representational developments underpinning it, or to the way that financial ideas circulated in the wider intellectual life of the period. In contrast, the present study focuses on the everyday world of finance, taking its cue from work in economic sociology on the embeddedness of seemingly abstract and impersonal economic transactions within the broader cultural and social sphere. In a discussion of the emerging field of inquiry that is becoming known as the New History of Capitalism, Jeffrey Sklansky identifies four ways of analyzing capitalism that this intellectual project could profitably explore: as "a form of selfhood or way of being, a system of representation or way of seeing, and a framework of trust or way of believing," as well as "a system of power or way of ruling."[37] Where other recent works have concentrated on the political and economic institutions of financial capitalism, my book examines, from a cultural studies perspective, the ontology, epistemology, and phenomenology of everyday financial culture, both factual and fictional. The ways of being, seeing, and believing explored in this cultural history of finance, however, have very important consequences for capitalism's ways of ruling during this period, as well as for the possibilities for resistance to them. For example, whether the collusion of vested financial interests constituted a conspiracy—and how to represent it, if it did—vexed Populist and elite critics alike.

My claim, then, is that the conceptual adjustments that financial capitalism requires and entails are equally as important as its economic, political, and institutional arrangements. What distinguishes "finance capital" (a term that was first introduced by Rudolf Hilferding in 1909) from industrial capitalism is that profit is increasingly derived from financial instruments, rather than production, and finance becomes the master, rather than the servant, of the economic welfare of the nation.[38] In his revisionist history of the transcontinental railroads, for example, Richard White shows how the robber barons who dominated the industry made their fortunes less from the much vaunted application of modern management techniques than from the—frequently corrupt—manipulation of speculative securities.[39] Even in the flourishing industrial economy, with its rapid expansion of mass production, urbanization, and transportation, the engine of wealth creation was driven as much by financial speculation as by the manufacturing of material goods. In the new world of finance-driven capitalism, value begins to break loose from its moorings in physical commodities, tangible assets, or actual production and instead seems to become free floating, with wealth created seemingly out of thin air in the emotional rollercoaster of speculative sentiment in the emerging securities market. Yet that market was not as entirely weightless and self-referential as some critics have imagined: in the decades around the turn of the twentieth century, powerful groups of financiers and their coterie were indeed able to manipulate fictitious values via privileged access to and control of the credit system and money markets.[40]

An increasing apprehension about the endless fungibility of value nevertheless cast an increasingly long shadow over mental life in the nineteenth century.[41] The debates over the money supply that reached a crescendo in the 1890s, for example, revolved as much around the metaphysical nature of floating values as the political interests of the debtor versus the creditor classes. William James, for example, memorably compared the relativity of language and truth with the way in which a credit system of money no longer requires a solid underpinning to weld sign to referent: "Truth lives, in fact, for the most part on a credit system. Our thoughts and beliefs pass so long as nothing challenges them, just as bank-notes pass so long as nobody refuses them. But this all points to direct face to face verification somewhere, without which the fabric of truth collapses like a financial system with no cash basis whatever."[42] Paper money, credit instruments, futures contracts, the self-referentiality of stock market prices, inexplicable panics, the sudden rise and dramatic fall of speculative fortunes—in short, the increasing abstraction, dematerialization, and deterritorialization of finance—all contributed to a sense of its fictitiousness, which, in turn, led to efforts to call attention to its unreality and to reground the idea of value in something concrete. It is for this reason that *Reading the Market* attends to the fictiveness of finance, both in invented tales and factual writings about the market. Wall Street fiction—not merely a passive reflection of an existing economic reality but part of the cultural armature that helps create it—is here studied alongside the fabricated financial values produced by the stock market. Fictions of finance helped make sense of the strange new world of the make-believe nature of finance.[43]

Abstraction and Personification in the Age of Corporate Personality

My principal argument is that in the Gilded Age and the Progressive Era, the market was viewed as both impersonal and personal, abstract and concrete, often in quite contradictory ways. The evidence explored here suggests that we therefore need to rethink the story of the development of capitalism in nineteenth-century America. In particular, I wish to revise three influential accounts of economic life in the United States from the nineteenth to the twentieth centuries. First, that there was a transformation from a moral economy, based on the logic of gift and expenditure, to a capitalist one, based on exchange and accumulation. Second, that there was a mechanization of trust during the period under discussion, with trust in systems replacing trust in individuals. Third, that financial capitalism brought about an increasing abstraction in social relations.

In *The Great Transformation*, Karl Polanyi argues that nineteenth-century Britain underwent a profound shift: from a traditional society governed by personal relations of reciprocity and redistribution to the birth of the modern liberal state, with its impersonal and implacable logic of the self-regulating market.[44] Although Polanyi recognizes that markets had existed in earlier historical periods, the "market society" that emerged in the wake of the Industrial Revolution brought about a thoroughgoing transformation in economic epistemology. In a market society, the ultimate motive for all endeavor is profit, and the only form of value that really counts is price. Yet the rational calculation and self-interest at the core of neoclassical economic theory are not, according to Polanyi, timeless traits of human nature, but are instead produced by the economic system they supposedly underpin. In his counter-to-orthodox economic theory, Polanyi drew on the work of anthropologists, such as Bronislaw Malinowski, who, in the first half of the twentieth century, had begun to be fascinated by the idea of alternative forms of "primitive" human societies that seemed to be organized by reciprocity, obligation, and kinship rather than by self-interested greed and the anonymous encounters of the market; in short, they suggested that a gift economy (or moral economy, in E. P. Thompson's formulation) had been replaced by an exchange economy.[45] Like Polanyi, these anthropologists argued that a more human-centered form of economic organization had existed in the past, but it was in danger of being wiped out by capitalist modernity, which viewed society as atomistic, rather than caught up in chains of mutual obligation and networks of kinship.

In a similar vein to Polanyi, Roy Kreitner has shown that the utilitarian picture of human nature developed by neoclassical economics in the nineteenth century was not timeless and inevitable, but was actually an effect of the forms of society that it seemed so naturally to create: "The imagined individual of theoretical contract discourse begins as an abstraction describing real-world persons, natural and corporate, who engage in contractual activity. But this image does not stop at description. Instead, it transforms the objects it purports to describe. The 'inner image of reality' [in Georg Simmel's phrase] is transformed as it sheds the characteristics of communal connection, passion, anxiety, beneficence, trust, in favor of precision and cold calculation."[46] What Kreitner's and other accounts of contract law have in common is the notion of a broad transition from a personalized to an impersonal understanding of economic obligation, a shift, in the classic phrase of Sir Henry Maine, from status to contract.[47]

In addition to these broad metanarratives of economic and legal development, several studies of late nineteenth-century America have focused more specifically on what might be termed the mechanization of trust in the corporate era. In doing so, they draw on the work of Niklas Luhmann (himself building on the ideas of Simmel), who argues that in modern capitalist societies, interpersonal trust is replaced by trust in abstract and anonymous systems, including legal, regulatory, and scientific institutions.[48] Luhmann suggests that trust in modernity becomes structural, rather than personal or psychological, and is one of a number of complexity-reducing strategies for coping with a situation in which people are increasingly reliant on overwhelming amounts of technical knowledge that they cannot possibly hope to master personally. Luhmann's notion of trust can help explain, for example, the development of contract law in nineteenth-century business as a way of providing reassurance when dealing in the marketplace with anonymous strangers, some of whom might well be inscrutable, not to mention the new possibility of having to deal with huge corporations that are distinctly impersonal. Rowena Olegario, for example, has argued that the development of credit reporting in the second half of the nineteenth century provided the requisite trust that could grease the wheels of an expanding national economy, in which dealing with strangers was becoming the norm, by relying on more-objective and impersonal measures of trustworthiness (such as objective financial worth and the likelihood of repayment) rather than more-traditional and subjective evaluations, based on a personal connection or traditional moral or ethnic prejudices.[49] Likewise, it is possible to understand the emergence in American commerce, around the turn of the twentieth century, of the money-back guarantee, fixed prices, and uniformly branded packaging as a response to the problem of trust in an impersonal marketplace, rather than merely as the result of improved economic efficiency and technology.[50] In a similar vein, historians have recently begun to focus on what we might call the late nineteenth-century technologies of identity verification and other sciences (and pseudosciences) of detection, such as phrenology, the rogues' gallery, fingerprinting, and, in a related development, anticounterfeiting.[51]

The final narrative that this volume draws on, but also reconsiders, is the common observation that economic life in the course of the nineteenth century was marked by increasing anonymity, impersonality, and abstraction. The dangers of economic and social interactions with strangers worried many writers, not least because the potential separation of face value and true worth meant that any encounter in the marketplace might leave one vulnerable to a confidence trick or to other forms of fraud.[52] Many commentators were likewise alarmed by the vast size and correspondingly implacable impersonality of the new industrial combinations. By century's end, despite these corporations coming to count as legal persons in the eyes of the law, they were popularly reviled as "soulless." In his classic work, *The Philosophy of Money* (1907), Georg Simmel argued that in a capitalist society, money leads to the interactions between people becoming ever more impersonal, because of its promotion of rational, calculative, and abstract thinking, since money is taken as the universal measure of value. According to Simmel, money's logic of generalized equivalence invades all areas of social life. A market society increases personal freedom but, in doing so, dissolves traditional bonds and kinship ties and changes the way people think and feel, introducing abstract calculation into all realms of life. In Simmel's influential account, in modern capitalist societies, money thus serves as an objectified and impersonal form of trust that erodes the localized and personal aspects of trust. It grinds down differences and makes all commodities, labor, and land commensurable. Money, Simmel notes, is "interchangeability personified."[53]

Although there are many significant differences between these various accounts of the coming of economic modernity, I am concentrating here on the key features they have in common. Each offers an important corrective to economic orthodoxy, not least in their insistence on the historical contingency and embeddedness of economics in particular social and political formations. My study builds on this tradition of alternative sociological and cultural interpretations of financial capitalism. The culture of the market explored in this book, however, suggests that we need to qualify these influential narratives. First, the accounts tend to assume that the "great transformation" is a one-way process that leads inexorably to increasing abstraction and anonymity. While the story of a world turned upside down by the material and cultural dimensions of capitalism in the nineteenth century provides a powerful explanatory framework, it nevertheless blinds us to the possibility that this development might be cyclical rather than unidirectional, and that the transition might have been more contested and contingent than previously imagined. For example, in his account of the "long twentieth century," Giovanni Arrighi argues that the epistemological and social upheaval brought about by the shift from productive to financial capitalism is not confined to our current era of globalization. Instead, he insists that it is a cycle of hyperaccumulation that has happened repeatedly over the course of the last five centuries of capitalism, albeit each time with greater intensity.[54] In a similar fashion, Mary Poovey suggests that the "crisis of representation" brought about by the introduction of paper money in Britain happened not once, but repeatedly, accompanied by a series of anxious attempts to make sense of the philosophical ramifications each time.[55] James's specter of "truth collapsing like a financial system" repeatedly haunts the popular culture of finance throughout the time period covered in this book. It is for this reason that the overall organization of *Reading the Market* is synchronic rather than diachronic, even if each chapter charts out the changing fortunes of each mode of representation that it analyzes.

The transition in the Gilded Age and the Progressive Era to increasingly impersonal, systemic, and abstract forms of trust was likewise more complicated than most accounts have allowed. For example, as Scott Sandage has demonstrated, credit-reporting agencies operated as much through networks of personalized spying as they did through the anonymous and abstract logic of statistics, with the two modes of attaining information operating hand in glove.[56] We can also discern the persistence of the personal in an era of impersonal abstraction in the efforts to humanize the "soulless corporation" in the early decades of the twentieth century. In his pioneering guide to "financial advertising," for instance, the advertising agent E. St. Elmo Lewis recounts the story of an old lady who demands to know the name of the teller she encounters in her bank:

> The old lady typified the feeling of the world. We want to know the man, the individual, the personality with whom we are dealing. I hear the banker say, "Yes, but the bank is a corporation, an aggregation of individuals who represent other individualities and it can have no personality." Probably he will quote that ancient and moth-eaten jest, a corporation has no soul, as proof conclusive that it has no mind or body. He will tell me that the whole tendency of the day is away from personality in banking. . . . So long as friendship is a part of business, as it is; so long as enmities and misunderstandings are possible, as they are; you will have personalities.[57]

Although Lewis presents the desire to personalize the soulless corporation as a natural tendency ("we unconsciously reach out for that personality which lies back of all corporate unities"), Roland Marchand and other historians have shown that the idea of a corporation having a "soul" did not come naturally, but was the result of concerted public relations campaigns and legal wrangles.[58] In his influential account of modernity, Anthony Giddens joins Luhmann in highlighting the importance of the mechanization and systematization of trust, but, in addition, he observes how consumers and citizens need to think of and interact with faceless bureaucracies as if they were individuals.[59] Even the notion of money as a force for abstraction par excellence has been challenged, with Viviana Zelizer, for example, documenting the many everyday practices of money handling that involve marking out as special—personalizing, in effect—what might otherwise seem merely impersonal and entirely fungible.[60]

My central proposition, then, is that the rhetoric of personalization and personification was vital to the transition to financial capitalism, both for its apologists and its critics. The autonomous, sublime, and self-regulating market is the creation of a particular set of mystified and mystifying market discourses that rely on the tropes of personification and personalization. These discourses attempted to counter the impersonal abstractions of the market, but at the cost of confirming its totalizing power. The intertwining of a gift economy and an exchange economy was central to the development of financial capitalism in the Gilded Age and the Progressive Era, because it legitimized the impersonal abstractions of finance by personalizing them. Yet, in doing so, it also made them legible and thus more amenable to criticism. Even after the seeming triumph of abstraction, then, the impulse to personify remained.[61]

As Mark Seltzer notes in his study of the logic of naturalism, at the same time that people were increasingly being turned into machinelike *things* in the reifying regime of factory life, so, too, were inanimate objects and business collectives increasingly being treated as *people* through sentimental personifications. Seltzer is concerned specifically with the "double movement" by which "the privilege of relative disembodiment that defines the citizen of liberal market society ('abstract universal personhood') is correlated with the making-conspicuous of the body in consumer society."[62] My interest in this volume is in the more general double movement by which economic ideas were abstracted and, in turn, humanized. My argument therefore concerns the personal *within* the impersonal, and the concrete *within* the abstract. The rhetorical trope of personification attributes human emotions and intentions to transpersonal entities—such as the very idea of the market—and, in doing so, considers them as if they were larger-than-life persons or gods or, in the related image of anthropomorphization, as if they were animals. At the same time, however, personification serves to abstract away from the individual and the particular characteristics of the people that make up those entities. The trope of prosopopeia thus both personalizes and abstracts at one and the same time, creating an inherently unstable rhetorical accommodation to the "great transformation" of capitalism around the turn of the twentieth century.

As the epilogue discusses in more detail, the first Gilded Age laid some of the conceptual foundations of the more ideologically concerted fetishization in our current Gilded Age: of financial markets as divine but irascible gods ruling over us mere mortals. *Reading the Market* explores the rhetorical strategies of containment and adjustment—"modern cosmologies," in Elaine Freedgood's evocative term—that helped Americans explain and accept the development of financial capitalism in the late nineteenth and early twentieth centuries.[63] Many of these strategies revolved around imagining a personal connection and intentionality within the abstract process of finance, or envisioning the abstraction of finance *as if* it were a person. Older forms of knowledge were used to make sense of newer modes, and, in doing so, both were subtly transformed. As Robert Wiebe notes in his classic study of the transition of the United States from an agrarian to an urban, industrial, and, above all, market-oriented society: "As men ranged farther and farther from their communities, they tried desperately to understand the larger world in terms of their small, familiar environment. They tried, in other words, to impose the known upon the unknown, to master an impersonal world through the customs of a personal society."[64]

This book explores a range of vernacular genres of economic epistemology and practice in five chapters. The first chapter examines the development of the market report, in the postbellum period, seeing it as one of the most important ways in which Americans learned to "read the market." It tells the story of how the money column changed from being merely a feature of specialist financial journalism to a mainstay of popular newspapers and magazines, using the *New York Herald* and *Harper's Weekly* as two case studies. Through a detailed examination of the financial pages of *Town Topics*, the preeminent society magazine of fin-de-siècle America, the chapter also shows how the image of the stock market created in those pages was both the abstract, price-allocating mechanism that neoclassical economics was beginning to theorize *and* a realm of gossip and intrigue. Market reports, the chapter concludes, helped create the very market they supposedly described.

The second chapter considers the stock ticker as a more literal and mechanical mode of market reading, which, like the market report, performatively constructs the market it seems to objectively record. The ticker, in theory, made the stock market more legible, transparent, and efficient, enabling the "perfect competition" of nascent economic theory. In both the reality of its usage, however, and in the way that it was described in the emerging genre of popular investment-advice manuals and biographical accounts of traders, such as Edwin Lefèvre's classic narrative, *Reminiscences of a Stock Operator*, it never fully achieved this. The ticker indeed made possible an anonymous and placeless market that unfolded simultaneously in all corners of the nation (and, increasingly, the globe). Yet the physical location and personalities of specific stock markets—the New York Stock Exchange especially—continued to loom large in cultural imaginings of the market in general and, in particular, in the rash of instructional guides on how to read the ticker that began to be published around the turn of the twentieth century. Moreover, the machine that supposedly promoted anonymity and abstraction in the market was itself often personified, just as the investment guides that sought to introduce seemingly scientific, technical analyses to ordinary speculators continued to invoke more-mystical forms of interpretation.

The third chapter asks how Americans pictured the placeless, abstracted, sublime market around the turn of the twentieth century. What were the visual analogues that were used to make it legible, and in which different representational modes was it portrayed? The chapter examines how a particular idea of the stock market was constructed in paintings, cartoons, guidebooks, photographs, and architecture, before going on to consider the way in which popular-magazine illustrations of the period tried to represent a market that was becoming increasingly unrepresentable. Personification was vital to this endeavor, but new forms of abstraction also emerged in novel representational technologies, such as the charts, diagrams, and indices that were beginning to appear in the financial press and other guides to interpreting the market. The chapter argues that these innovative technologies did not merely visualize the market as a whole (or the economy, which later theorists took as their object of analysis), but, in doing so, they also helped construct those realities.

The fourth chapter discusses the surprising persistence of the reality and the imaginative appeal of confidence games and inside information in a historical moment supposedly characterized by an increasing anonymity and abstraction in economic affairs. Beginning with a reading of Herman Melville's prescient novel, *The Confidence-Man* (1857), the chapter argues that the con trick works through a mimicry of contractual forms of encounter, appealing to status in the age of the contract. Although the confidence game became industrialized around the turn of the twentieth century, I show how it continued to operate through a personalized appeal. In extended readings of the work of William Dean Howells and Edith Wharton, the second half of the chapter demonstrates how inside information remained crucial to the cultural imagination of Wall Street, suggesting that a personalized gift economy was not replaced by an impersonal exchange economy, but became fused with it.

The final chapter focuses on conspiracy theories about finance around the turn of the twentieth century, in a range of cultural forms: from Gilded Age satirical cartoons and muckraking investigations, to Frank Norris's novel *The Octopus*, to a diagram of interlocking corporate directorships produced by the Pujo Committee's investigation in 1912–1913. Conspiracy theories melodramatically claim to discover individual intention behind historical events, and they are usually contrasted with supposedly more sophisticated accounts that find either contingency or structural forces at work. In the case of the conspiracy-minded imaginings of individual agency in the age of the trust that are explored in this chapter, however, the impersonal system of finance is presented as if it were the result of a personal conspiracy of powerful individuals. These conspiratorial accounts create a personification of an abstraction, seeing system *as* conspiracy. Populist and Progressive conspiracy theories, then, are not merely the misguided delusions of those unable or unwilling to come to terms with modern economic conditions. Instead, they are a potentially creative, if also contradictory, way of bringing together the notions of structure and agency.

Together, these chapters tell the story of the uneasy resistance against and accommodation to the abstractions of finance through vernacular genres of economic knowledge. These ways of reading the impersonal market worked by making it personal.

CHAPTER ONE

Market Reports

What, then, should be our guide in speculation? What are our sources of information? For without some hint or inkling of the future of stocks how can one trade intelligently? Let us consider the courses of information at the disposal of the trader. First, there is the "market tip"; second, the "inside tip"; third, newspaper stories and gossip; fourth, news bureaus and market opinions by professional opinion makers and professional tipsters; fifth, statistics as to earnings, financial condition, business condition, etc., of the various properties whose stocks are dealt in; sixth, money and financial conditions of this and other countries.

> A Wall Street "Piker," "Confessions of a Stock Speculator" (1907)

The financial writer must work hard in dull times, because it is so hard to write, and when the market is active because there is so much to write about.

> Edwin Lefèvre, "The Newspaper and Wall Street" (1904)

Of all the genres of financial capitalism, the market report in mass-circulation newspapers and magazines has arguably been the most influential in teaching a lay audience how to read the market. It provides a daily barometer of the economic climate, a set of numbers and diagrams from which the concerned citizen is meant to discern the lulls and storms of the global fluctuations of finance, providing a routinized, collective projection that is depicted as both cause and consequence of national mood. Yet it must be remembered that the market report is not a timeless, natural, objective snapshot of economic reality. Like the weather forecast, it is a historically and culturally specific representation, the outcome of a contingent and contested struggle over what is to count as economic reality—not least the suitability of the weather as a metaphor and even a causal explanation for price fluctuations.

This chapter discusses how the view of the market created by the financial page in newspapers and magazines in the second half of the nineteenth century in the United States was the result of a mixture of technical innovation, journalistic creativity, rhetorical construction that combines scientific precision and folk wisdom, and—it goes without saying—market forces. Whether in specialist publications aimed at businesspeople or in the financial pages of mainstream newspapers and magazines, market reports that moved beyond the bare bones of lists of what were termed "prices current" began to reshape how both professionals and laypeople imagined the market. By revealing the supposed natural laws of economics that explained the movement of prices on the one hand, or by attributing price fluctuations to secret manipulations by the big operators dominating the nation's stock and produce exchanges on the other, the money pages in the nineteenth century began to reconfigure both professional and popular knowledge of financial capitalism. This chapter begins by outlining the emergence of financial journalism in the United States, distinguishing between market reports written for business professionals and those aimed at lay readers. It then looks in detail at three case studies from the latter half of the nineteenth century, arguing that the emerging popular financial press constituted a particular kind of performative technology that pandered to a need that it helped create. Financial journalism for the lay reader, I will argue, contributed simultaneously to the condemnation and the normalization of speculation. It did this by presenting "the market" simultaneously as an impersonal abstraction, governed by natural economic laws, *and* as the product of gossipy, personal relationships. An older and more personal interpretation was not replaced by a newer faith in the objective power of numbers to represent the market, but was fused with it. People explained the abstraction of financial markets by personalizing them; but this had the effect of letting the system itself off the hook, since the class interests of elite financiers were obscured as they were turned into melodramatic gossip.

The Revolution in Financial Information

The market report began in sixteenth-century Europe, when merchants began circulating lists of prices current (of commodities and exchange rates), along with the details of the arrivals and departures of shipped goods. This kind of commercial knowledge had previously been closely held by insiders and shared only within a network of personal contacts, but the invention of the printing press made possible the widespread dissemination of what had traditionally only been transmitted by word of mouth or individual correspondence.[1] This was the first stage of an "information revolution" that compressed time and space in the world of commerce, although, until the advent of the telegraph in the 1830s and the subsidiary development of the stock ticker, with its near-real-time broadcasting of quotations in the 1870s, these records of prices were always already out-of-date. The pioneering organizers of the Antwerp Exchange in the 1540s realized that they could not only profit from selling the information in printed form, but that in making the data widely available, they would boost commerce in the city. The lists functioned as advertisements for the range of business that could be conducted in the Exchange. By the seventeenth century, Amsterdam was publishing a weekly commercial paper in four different languages, setting the benchmark for prices throughout Europe. The circulation of published lists of prices current across Europe and through the international circuits of trade thus did not serve merely to record the existing, internal workings of the exchanges; by enabling the free flow of commercial information, they helped create and make more efficient the very possibility and visibility of an international market that exceeded the transactions conducted locally at particular marketplaces by individual merchants.[2]

Although London had published printed sheets of prices current since the early seventeenth century, its financial press was invigorated after the accession of Prince William of Orange in 1688, accompanied by an influx of Dutch merchants. In the eighteenth century, London witnessed the rapid expansion of financial newssheets specializing in four areas: commodity and stock prices on the exchanges; rates for bills of exchange; details from the customs house regarding imports and exports; and marine lists (such as *Lloyd's List*, first published in 1692) that tracked shipping cargoes. In fact, precisely because the financial newspapers made available information that previously could only be gathered in person at the exchange or the customs house or from a network of personal correspondents, brokers could now work out of an office or even a coffeehouse, such as Lloyd's, that subscribed to the financial sheets, knowing that they were not necessarily missing anything by not being on the floor of the exchange in person. London, as the center of Britain's commercial empire, became the market for all kinds of commodities and stocks traded across imperial circuits of enterprise. It comes as little surprise, therefore, that the first financial newspapers in the United States only emerged after the American Revolution, with the growing need of its citizens to share information and set prices locally.

It was not until the nineteenth century, however, that the market report, in a number of related developments, began to move beyond mere lists of prices current. First, the four types of specialist financial sheets began to be collated into generalist business publications, followed by the publication of the various prices current in mainstream newspapers. In the 1830s in the United States, nonspecialist newspapers began to include not only lists of prices current, but also a brief commentary on market activity, often a short leader written by the financial editor.[3] Publications such as the *New York Herald*, for example, pioneered a more personalized tone in their money pages. The evening edition of the New York papers that were published after the close of the Stock Exchange was known as the "Wall Street edition," while morning papers, such as the *Sun*, had the most-popular reflective money columns. The 1840s saw the emergence of periodicals that, although aimed at a specialist business audience, were nevertheless keen to integrate detailed commercial information with wider moral, political, and economic commentary. Up until the mid-1880s, the few stocks traded on the stock exchanges (the Stock Exchange and the Curb Market in New York, the other regional exchanges, and the over-the-counter trade) were predominantly those of the railroads, and the front pages of the newspapers were no strangers to lurid tales of the financial skullduggery of robber barons, with speculation by the bulls and bears thus functioning as a form of spectator sport. The many flotations of giant, new, public corporations around the turn of the century likewise attracted much popular interest, but by now, with the proliferation of stock tickers and bucket shops, members of the public were no longer necessarily merely spectators in the drama. Toward the end of the century, middle-class magazines, such as *Harper's Weekly* and the *Saturday Evening Post*, began to include financial columns, along with illustrated, melodramatic short stories and serialized novels about business and finance by writers such as Edwin Lefèvre, Frank Norris, and Harold Frederic. Following earlier attacks by midwestern newspapers sympathetic to the Populist, agrarian attack on futures trading in the commodity exchanges, in the Progressive Era, magazines such as *McClure's*, *Munsey's*, *Everybody's Magazine*, and the *Independent* began to publish articles criticizing Wall Street practices, such as wash sales and stock watering, as well as the proliferation of bucket shops.[4] After the turn of the twentieth century, there emerged more-specialized popular magazines, aimed at investors of modest means and bucket shop speculators, such as *Financial World* (established in 1902), *Moody's Magazine* (1905), *Ticker* (1907; later renamed *The Magazine of Wall Street*), and *Commerce and Finance* (1912), as well as reports circulated by the emerging profession of technical analysis.

The muckrakers hoped to use publicity to bring to light financial fraud, but it was often publicity in the newspapers that helped fuel fictitious stock promotions in the first place. As chapter 4 discusses in more detail, some market reporting was actually a scam: at times, newspapers were in the pay of financial promoters, who used the publicity to manipulate stock or grain prices, while seemingly neutral and informative market letters and investment guides were, in reality, manipulative advertisements designed to bring in more customers to the bucket shops that produced the letters. For example, an article by an anonymous and rueful ex–Wall Street "piker" in the *Independent* in 1907 asserted that although some honest newspapers merely gave objective reports of financial facts and conditions, others merely pretended to do so: "The majority of financial writers for newspapers are personally interested in the market, and their comments are colored by their own market position. Again, a number of newspapers— either the entire paper or the financial columns thereof—are controlled by the market giants, and their market comments are designed to further the plans of these men. Therefore, when one reads the columns of the newspapers he cannot fathom the motives behind them; accordingly, as market guides they are unreliable and even dangerous."[5] Likewise, Henry Clews, in his retrospective look back at his fifty years' experience on Wall Street, complained about "the 'points,' the 'puffs,' the alarms, and the canards," put out by financial news agencies and the morning Wall Street news sheets "expressly to deceive and mislead" the gullible public.[6] By the early twentieth century, then, the American public had a surfeit of financial information and advice to choose from, although not all of it was necessarily accurate or objective. The proliferation of fraudulent financial reporting during this period thus gives a new twist to the argument that the market is performatively constructed by the genres that seem to describe it: at times, the manipulated representations of the market in the financial press resulted in would-be investors creating the very market conditions conjured up by the fake descriptions. The most notorious and extreme case of life coming to resemble art was the work of Thomas W. Lawson, a media-manipulating stock promoter who later became one of the most vociferous muckraking protestors against the abuses of the system. His account (in both fictional and nonfictional form) of an imminent market panic helped fuel the very cataclysm that his fantastical writing predicted.[7]

Every Man a Speculator

The increasing visibility of popular financial reporting is puzzling, however, since the level of public interest did not immediately match the reality of stock market participation. If (as we saw in the introduction) the demographic of share ownership on the legitimate exchanges was restricted, the fascination with Wall Street, part fearful and part admiring, nevertheless pervaded popular culture. In real terms, there might have been few actual outsiders engaged in speculation on the NYSE, but the *perception* that there were provoked much anxious commentary in the financial press. Indeed, popular market reports were often couched in the rhetoric of an unequal battle between bulls, bears, and lambs. The vital question was whether more-easily accessible financial information and greater transparency in corporate reporting would be enough to solve the problem of the informational asymmetry that put ordinary investors at such a disadvantage. Were financial reports the solution to the problem, or did they make it worse, because they gave outsiders the deluded impression that they, too, were now insiders?

In the decades on either side of the turn of the twentieth century, the figure of the vulnerable investor of modest means became central to debates about the legitimacy of the stock market. On the one hand, financial reformers insisted that small investors were significant in number and should be protected from the manipulation of insiders, as well as from the dangers of fraudulent overcapitalization of corporations, through the active intervention of the government in regulating new stock offerings and requiring public incorporation of the stock exchanges themselves. The U.S. Senate's Industrial Commission, investigating the "trust question" in 1900–1902, identified the outside investor of modest means as central to the developing idea of an American industrial democracy. The hope was that ordinary citizens would be able to own a modest stake in the newly formed industrial trusts, reinventing the dream of proprietorial democracy in the age of corporate capitalism. Along with academic economists such as Jeremiah Jenks, Richard Ely, and John Bates Clark, the commission argued that, without full transparency of financial information, outside investors were investing merely on blind faith.[8] After the Wall Street panic in 1907, the Hughes Commission in New York State went further, recommending a number of measures designed not merely to enforce corporate financial transparency, but also to actively protect vulnerable outsiders, such as tightening control over quotations and forbidding trade in potentially risky, unlisted securities that made no financial disclosures at all. Likewise, in 1913, the U.S. House of Representatives' Pujo Committee recommended "complete publicity as to all the affairs" of listed corporations on the stock market.[9]

Wall Street professionals, on the other hand, insisted that the best way to promote the American values of democracy and independence was for the market to be left free and unfettered, with caveat emptor as its guiding principle; it should not be up to the government to save the "lambs" from their own folly. The professionals argued that instead of protecting *inexperienced* speculators, any reforms should be aimed at discouraging *unqualified* investors. The Hughes Commission, though, hedged its bets and also recommended doubling the NYSE's margin requirements in order to discourage small-time speculators, following the distinction, first made by U.S. Supreme Court Justice Oliver Holmes in his landmark 1905 ruling on bucket shops, between "speculation which is carried on by persons of means and experience, and based on an intelligent forecast, and that which is carried on by persons without these regular qualifications."[10] The reformers complained that the market was being manipulated by professionals, putting the wider public off of investing; in contrast, the governors of the New York Stock Exchange insisted that the market was indeed best left to professionals, the only ones able to properly shoulder the risk and maintain a liquid market.[11]

It must be remembered, however, that many more people engaged in stock market activity in the late nineteenth and early twentieth centuries than the figures for official participation suggest. For one thing, the ubiquitous presence of bucket shops allowed Americans of modest means (clerks, in particular) to have the vicarious thrill of speculation, even if they were not technically purchasing actual stock in corporations—although some undoubtedly thought that they were. Despite ongoing legal attacks led by the New York Stock Exchange, bucket shops spread prolifically throughout the nation from the 1870s up to about 1915, when the legal campaign waged by the principal exchanges to protect their price quotations as intellectual property finally triumphed. One answer to the mystery of why popular financial journalism flourished far in advance of actual mass investment in the stock market is that many Americans were, in fact, involved in speculation, albeit in a way that does not show up in the scant historical evidence we have for active participation in the nation's formally constituted exchanges.

Another part of the explanation is that the money pages of popular publications pandered to the public's desire for the *simulation* of speculation, even for those who were not placing bets in bucket shops. The abundance of popular guides to speculation and financial journalism suggests that ordinary Americans were emotionally—if not literally—invested in the market *before* the rise of popular share ownership with the take-up of Liberty Bonds in World War I. They craved a daily or weekly fix from the nation's financial soap opera, seeking investment advice even when they had nothing to invest. As Mary Poovey explains in the context of early Victorian Britain, "the new City columns treated the financial world as a distinct culture, which writers strove to make interesting even to readers who did not need to know about international exchange rates or economic theory." In explaining the market's perplexing ways to lay readers, Poovey argues, popular financial journalism also served to normalize the chaotic fluctuations of the markets.[12] Part of the ideological function of the "new financial journalism," moreover, was to make the market seem of vital, daily importance to casual readers, even in those times when panics, corners, and booms were not making the headlines. It helped create an imagined community of market watchers, persuading them that it was their duty to check the money page obsessively and to identify emotionally with the rise and fall of prices that, as the new marginalist economics was beginning to argue, were an aggregation of investor perceptions, rather than the objective, underlying value of the corporations.[13] Popular market reports, as we will see, anthropomorphized the rise or fall in prices as the vital signs of the body politic, a metonymic transposition from the supposed psychological disposition of individual brokers on the floor of the NYSE to the mood of the market as a whole.[14]

The Commercial Sublime

The diverse array of financial publications outlined above can be divided into two broad camps. On the one hand, there were newspapers and magazines aimed at a lay audience that began to include financial information among their general-interest articles. On the other hand, there were publications aimed at business and finance professionals (both those who aspired to be a professional and those who wanted to think of themselves as such), which often tried to embed the reams of technical information amassed in tables and lists into more-general discussions of political economy. Before examining in detail three case studies of financial journalism for a lay readership, it is worth briefly contrasting the cultural work performed by those publications that were written for a professional readership. Their outlook was usually conservative, with an emphasis on the objectivity of statistics and economic laws, part of the larger goal of trying to convince both the public and would-be regulators that the market was not the plaything of insider cliques, but an impersonal, scientific mechanism managed by seasoned brokers and traders for establishing fair prices and redistributing risk, fulfilling a socially useful function. By appealing to a specialist audience of bankers, brokers, and businessmen (or would-be members of those professions; young clerks were often the implied readers), the publications also served to reinforce a sense of collective identity for their readers as part of an emerging cadre of financial professionals, in pointed contrast to the more-visible public image of the financier as a robber baron.

New publications—such as *Hunt's Merchants' Magazine* (established in 1839); the *Bankers' Magazine* (1845); the *Commercial and Financial Chronicle* (1865); the *Financier* (1884); and, of course, the *Wall Street Journal* (1889)—were high minded and aimed mainly at the business community and the upper classes. Their claim, epitomized by Charles Dow of the *Wall Street Journal*, was that they provided a "faithful picture of the rapidly shifting panorama of the Street." The desire was to create "a paper of news and not a paper of opinions," trading on a mixture of impartial and impersonal reporting that combined narrative and statistical overviews of the condition of the market.[15] The claim of the professional business press, in short, was to bring a new objectivity to the presentation of Wall Street as an institution governed by natural laws, instead of fraudulent, personal influence.[16]

William Buck Dana's *Commercial and Financial Chronicle* (1865), for example, was self-consciously modeled on Walter Bagehot's weekly newspaper, the *Economist*. It endeavored to explain for a small but influential readership what Dana believed were the underlying, immutable laws of economics, which were providentially ordained. It was not just descriptive, but didactic; its aim was to teach its readers to interpret correctly the data it provided. Thus anything that interfered with the natural order of supply and demand in a free market was to be condemned. The economy, for example, was figured as a vital force, an organism unto itself, with capital supplying the blood circulation to keep the whole thing moving. The journal nevertheless recognized its role in promoting the commercial progress of seemingly external influences, such as business cycles, and even psychological factors, such as investor confidence. Like other conservative financial publications of the nineteenth century, it supported a broadly Adam Smithian, laissez-faire approach to commerce, along with a Social Darwinist outlook.[17]

What is striking about specialist business publications, such as the *Chronicle*, *Hunt's Merchant's Magazine*, and the *Banker's Magazine*, is that they were not content merely to provide an objective, statistical description of the market; they also felt the need to explain its workings to their audience. Poovey has argued that in the eighteenth century in Britain, writing about the market in particular, and economic value in general, divided inexorably into two strands, with literary writing increasingly defending the cultural value of imagination in contrast to the commercial value of factual information. As Elizabeth Hewitt has demonstrated, however, the specialist business press in the earlier part of the nineteenth century in America strove to keep together the genres of fact and fiction by creating a "literature of commerce." *Hunt's Merchant's Magazine*, for example, was marketed not at specialists in a particular trade or financial activity, but included all commercial enterprises, combining sections on specific industries with articles of general interest. It consciously brought together statistics with an analysis that had a literary bent, arguing that American business was itself a new art form, an expression of a national economic sublime. Its aim was "to educate its readers in the practical details of the modern marketplace and simultaneously to offer itself as commercial epic."[18] Although these dry, professional periodicals included a surprising number of fictional and personal accounts of finance, the moral of the story was inevitably that the banker must remain dispassionate and objective, refusing sentimental attachments or personal responsibility for the inevitable human tragedies caused by the operation of economic laws. Although the financial press, aimed at professionals, thus deployed a personal rhetoric, it merely served the propose of reconfirming that the market was impersonal and impartial.

The Philosophy of Commercial Affairs

In contrast, the money page of mass-circulation publications explicitly aimed to humanize the abstractions of finance in its leader article, which provided an explanatory framework for the lists of prices that were, for many readers, inscrutable and illegible—in some cases literally so, as they tended to be printed in tiny typeface. In 1904, the broker and Wall Street writer Edwin Lefèvre wrote an article in the *Bookman* validating the craft of popular financial journalism, which had begun to take shape in the last quarter of the nineteenth century. Lefèvre argued that, unlike college professors and those who write for dry economics periodicals, the financial journalist must have "knowledge obtained at first hand, of the men whose personality so dominates the financial markets that it is very hard to disassociate the men from the events."[19] The focus on personality, rather than objective economic facts, was precisely what the specialist and academic presses complained was wrong with popular financial journalism. What distinguishes successful financial reporters for Lefèvre, however, is that "they are men who are able to deduce from dry statistics facts of interest to human beings." Lefèvre thus sees the money page as fulfilling a socially useful role in teaching the ignorant public how to think about Wall Street: "They are beyond question an educational force, and it is not their fault that we are hysterical as a nation and that the public goes to extremes in its stock market opinions and no less so than in its judgment of the financial leaders."[20] With the panics that regularly shook the wider economy in the nineteenth century, it comes as no surprise that the general reader would be interested in learning more about finance in those times of dramatic events on Wall Street. Yet the financial pages of general-interest publications endeavored to make the vicissitudes of the stock market of vital interest to readers, day in and day out. "The financial writer must work hard in dull times," Lefèvre states, "because it is so hard to write, and when the market is active because there is so much to write about."[21]

The outline of the larger historical transition that took place over the course of the nineteenth century, from the recording of prices governed by Providence or impersonal economic laws to the kind of reflection on the human drama behind the fluctuation in stock quotations that Lefèvre recommends, is foreshadowed in embryonic form in 1835, in the very first two editions of James Gordon Bennett's *New York Herald*, the pioneer of popular journalism in nineteenth-century America. The first edition was significant in that it understood the importance of including a substantial money page, but that page merely contained a list of prices current, based on Bennett's fact-finding strolls along Wall Street. For the second edition, Bennett—who was writing the whole paper himself—recognized that a list of prices on their own would not suffice; he had to make sense of them for his readers. It is therefore intriguing to note that Bennett's first discursive "Money Market" column in the *Herald* was on the dangers of speculation, and it put forward a conspiracy-minded explanation for the fluctuations in prices, laying the blame on a "secret conspiracy of our large capitalists."[22] Despite being a former teacher of economics, Bennett was willing to countenance rationales that involved individual manipulation rather than abstract economic forces, unlike the editors of more middle-class business publications. His duty, as he later explained when improving the "ship news and commercial departments," was to make the raw figures talk, even for businessmen: "The spirit, pith, and philosophy of commercial affairs is what men of business want. Dull records of facts, without condensation, analysis, or deduction, are utterly useless. The philosophy of commerce is what we aim at, combined with accuracy, brevity, and spirit."[23] Bennett here sets up the terms of the debate for the function of the market report for the remainder of the nineteenth century. Should the facts and the figures be allowed to speak for themselves, as if the market itself had a voice, with the financial page the concern only of the professional trader? Or should the journalist endeavor to humanize the abstractions of the market, to make the "philosophy of commerce" part of the wider drama of ideas, with all the ideological baggage that the genres of conspiracy and melodrama bring with them? By focusing on the "spirit, pith, and philosophy of commercial affairs," popular financial journalism in the second half of the nineteenth century strove to make the mysteries of the market engrossing and intelligible to its readers, including those who were not necessarily Wall Street regulars, but only by turning it into melodramatic conspiracy that tried to find a hidden agency behind structural forces. It achieved this partly by adopting a stance that combined a quasi-anthropological distance from the exotic customs of Wall Street with a gossipy appeal to readers, as if they were insiders in this tribe. But the price they paid for this personalizing approach was to divert attention from considering the vested interests of finance as a system; and, by making the fortunes of the market a matter of personal affect and identification, to transform ordinary Americans into vicarious spectators of finance, which, in turn, helped legitimate the importance of finance to the wider economy, even as it led to Populist attacks on it.

We can see some of these rhetorical maneuvers at work in the *New York Herald* in the late nineteenth and early twentieth centuries.[24] Before giving the list of prices current, the market page gave a summary of the previous day's activity, not of the aggregate economy or diverse markets in general, but the floor of the New York Stock Exchange in particular. The column tends not to focus on long-term trends or underlying economic explanations, but instead uses the format of a daily diary, coupled with a focus on the manipulations of insiders, to give a sense of immediacy and familiarity to the market.[25] The column gives outsiders the view from the inside of the Exchange, as a battleground of bulls and bears in constant struggle. Readers are made to feel that the columnist knows the major players intimately, but that he is on the side of the readers, condemning insider manipulation. One April day in 1883, for example, we learn that "the bulk of to-day's transactions is to be correctly attributed to the Board Room members," while three days later, it is reported that "outside of the Board Room nobody did anything; inside of it professional traders had the swing of business."[26] The column reports financial rumors but is not always able to give the complete inside story: "People identified with Vanderbilt interests," readers are told, "intimate that there is foundation for the telegraphic report of a new scheme to build a transcontinental railroad from St. Louis to San Francisco. Specific information, however, is refused."[27]

Although the column is remarkable for its comparative lack of philosophizing about the causes of market movements, from the 1880s onward it nevertheless constantly argues that the market would be better off if outside investors helped rally the market into action, to prevent it from becoming merely the plaything of professional traders: "It is almost nauseating to again be obliged to repeat the fact that the ups and downs of prices are entirely ascribable to manipulation of Board Room traders. There is no public, no anybody, except professionals, that takes the least interest in stock speculation."[28] In contrast to the condemnation of amateur speculation by the exchanges, the money page in the *Herald* insists that the market should be democratized, albeit merely for the sake of bringing some excitement to the dull periods of trading. The market report also strives to appear neutral and objective, but is clearly—like most of its readers—far more in sympathy with the optimistic bulls than the pessimistic bears.

The tone is chatty, witty, and informal, full of the latest colloquialisms and bon mots doing the rounds of the Exchange. "The boot was on the other leg today," we are informed. "Prices which had every indication yesterday afternoon of going to the 'demnition bowwows' [i.e., the damned dogs] turned suddenly upward this morning, and, with the exception of a pause now and then, tended toward higher figures."[29] In addition to this kind of jocular phrasing, the column's richly figurative language tends to make the market seem familiar and homely. In considering the previous day's activities, for example, the columnist imagines himself as a farmer or shopkeeper, weighing up produce: "'Hefting' it after an avoirdupois fashion, the general market may be described as being heavy and weak."[30] Like a crop, the market begins to "droop" as the sun approaches its "meridian values" (i.e., before the Board Room members broke for lunch); like a stubborn mule, the market needs "a rap over the head" from the bulls before it retreats, "beaten and disgusted." The market is also likened to a horse race, with the rise in prices held back as if by the heavy going: "Looking over to-day's stock market sporting men would say that the advance in prices was so heavily handicapped by the bad weather that little or no improvement in them was either probable or to be expected."[31] Likewise, "the week opened with much strength as to a rising scale of prices, but at the same time with a feeling of impending apprehension that the advance had been 'going the pace' too long and too rapidly."[32] Or the market is itself depicted as a horse, firmly under the control of the inside manipulators, with ordinary speculators (the imagined readers of the column) being pulled along unceremoniously:

> The great operators have the stock market so thoroughly in hand that they are able to start prices off upon a gallop or pull them up upon their haunches whenever circumstances afford good reason to do so. As for speculators generally, who, so to speak, are inside of the coach, their feelings are in nowise considered. Whether prices move briskly upward or briskly downward, the passengers in the current speculation stand about as even a chance of being dumped into the ditch of lower prices as of being landed upon the platform of higher ones.[33]

The market is also frequently described in medical terms, as if it were not just an animal, but a *person*: "The upward movement, which had grown almost strong enough to 'go it alone,' has again been knocked off its pins."[34] "The spasm of improvement noticeable on Thursday and Friday," readers are informed, "seems to have passed away and the market has relapsed into its old collapsed condition. What is worse, the public has had another scare and is now more timid than ever."[35] Noting that "prices were passably strong at the opening and heavy and dull at the closing," the columnist asserts that "the market has got back into the old rut" (a farming metaphor, retooled for psychology and, in turn, used for finance), and that the public—in opposition to the professionals—was, only a week previously, willing to help "extricate it from the Slough of Despond."[36] The mood and psychological status of individual traders becomes confused with that of the market as a whole. On 12 February 1890, for example, under the heading "A Dull Morning Followed by a Rattling Afternoon," readers were informed that "a report that Mr. J. Pierpont Morgan had been stricken with apoplexy was circulated on 'Change." It turned out that the rumor was wildly exaggerated, as Morgan had only been suffering from "la grippe." Here, the fortunes of the market seem to turn on the health of one man, who not only embodied, but, as the Pujo Committee later alleged, personally controlled the entire market, without ever setting foot on the floor of the Exchange. When the columnist concludes a report with the declaration that "the market closed feverish and weak," readers are left to wonder whether the market's woes are merely an allegorical projection of Morgan's health, or whether they are directly caused by rumors about his fever.[37]

The column repeatedly blurs talk about the mood of individual brokers with a figurative account of the mood of the market. After a July Fourth weekend, for example, we learn that, "with the exception of the stocks referred to, the list was stagnant and more or less 'groggy'—a condition by no means extraordinary in view of the extended holiday and its patriotic and spiritual accompaniments."[38] On 26 February 1881, we are told first that "in the morning the stock market opened in a weak and feverish condition," and immediately after that "there were anxious and frightened faces by the score at the Stock Exchange."[39] In a fairly straightforward way, we can surmise that the market is feverish because the traders are frightened, but the order of the sentences suggests that the causal direction is the other way around: the brokers are anxious *because* the market itself is feverish. The individual mood of market actors comes to be figured as an aftereffect of the emotional turmoil of the market, which is itself imagined as an individual. In a similar fashion, the column frequently draws on the literary trope of the pathetic fallacy, blurring, in its rhetoric, the causal linkages between the internal mood of investors, the mood of the market, and the state of the weather.

"There was dull weather out of doors and equally dull business within," we learn, "and between the two the market remained sluggish."[40] Likewise, "with the hot weather and the half holiday which brokers vote themselves on summer Saturdays, it was no wonder that business should have been dull on 'Change to-day and utterly devoid of excitement."[41]

The most common emotional description used in the *New York Herald*'s money page is not excitement, but dullness. Even more than the columnist's annoyance at the market being controlled by professionals, he becomes exasperated when, day after day, little seems to happen. On an April Monday in 1883, unremarkable weather is blamed for producing a dull market; the report for Tuesday begins by stating morosely that "today's stock market was dull and dismal"; and by Wednesday, the writer is beginning to despair, insisting that "to-day's stock market was so dead, so dull, so utterly wanting in everything worthy of attention that it is simply a waste of space and printer's ink to make notice of it in this column."[42] Prices hold steady during the summer, with the headline on 6 July announcing "A Dull but Very Firm Market." The headline on 7 July is forced to proclaim that the market was "The Dullest for Years," followed by "The Stock Market Dull and Weak" on 8 July, and "A Stubborn Dullness" on 9 July. By 12 July, the writer is once again despairing that there is nothing to report: "Today's stock market was dull and steady. A really good sensation would have been cheap at any price, but none was afforded. . . . So far as the day's business was worthy of record, the least said of it the better."[43]

In part, this obsession with dullness is a consequence of the writer's conviction that the outside public needs to become involved in speculation; only they can stop the market from becoming a tedious plaything of the professionals. Yet it is also a result of the need to make a report every day, to find something of interest for readers who have little or no direct involvement in the market. The thinking is that even if it is dangerous for would-be speculators or out of step with economic fundamentals, a lively market is better for the casual observer than a dull one. Instead of offering a long-term view, in which temporary fluctuations of prices are shown to be mere blips, the popular money page, with its daily dramas (or insipidity, from a lack of them), invites the reader to identify completely with the vicissitudes of the market, to ride the emotional roller coaster with no end in sight. Making the quotidian ups and downs of stock prices matter to readers of the *New York Herald* is also a result of its presentation of the market: simultaneously a remote realm in which financial titans do battle in a scale that dwarfs humble individual investors, and a familiar place that can be made sense of through homely metaphors. This figurative exchange between the structural abstractions of political economy and concrete popular representations ended up serving the needs of financial capital, rather ordinary people.

The "World of Finance"

Where the *New York Herald* pioneered a rhetorical style of financial journalism that sought to add human interest to its daily tables of economic figures, the ten-cent, middle-class weekly magazines that began to be published toward the end of the nineteenth century dispensed with the lists of prices altogether, concentrating instead on including financial information and advice as part of their roster of topics suitable for a genteel audience. Although the approach of the magazines' main editorial pages was often a muckraking condemnation of sharp practices, such as wash sales and stock watering, and a Progressivist call for regulation, their financial columns often served to normalize and even glamorize the heroic actions of Napoleons of finance. *Harper's Weekly* provides a good example of this contradictory stance.

The principal editorial page in *Harper's Weekly* regularly discussed economic matters. For example, it counsels against the silverites in the gold-standard debates leading up to the 1896 presidential election, and likewise warns that a William Jennings Bryan victory in 1900 would be bad for business. Despite its broader interest in political economy, the magazine only instituted a dedicated financial column in August 1899, entitled "World of Finance." Beginning in March 1900, the column is attributed to A. K. Fiske; the broker and financial journalist Edwin Lefèvre took over in October 1901, continuing until 1903; and, after a hiatus, the investment banker Howard Schenck Mott revived the column in April 1908, now as a full-page spread. The "World of Finance" section takes its place alongside other topics the magazine's imagined reader needs to know about, from the bicycle craze to the war in Cuba. Unlike the daily New York newspapers, as a weekly magazine, *Harper's* cannot give its readers the same sense of being immersed in the daily ebb and flow of market activity. Instead, it provides retrospective summaries, along with broader reflections on stock market trends and economic principles. The relationship between the immediate events being reported and the lessons to be learned are, however, at times unclear. Instead of a moral being drawn out of the material at hand, it can begin to seem as though individual episodes are reported merely as a pretext for the larger didactic point the writer wants to make.

Although much of the "World of Finance" is still concerned with the minutiae of advances and declines and manipulations, one constant is its political stance, which combines a reformist call for transparency with a conservative reluctance to regulate private business. "It is to be regretted," the column opines, "that the industrial corporations do not make regular statements of their operations such as are made by most of the railroad corporations, though there is a good deal of force in their contention that they would thereby be furnishing information useful to their rivals in business."[44] In addition to this call for Progressive financial reforms, which would nevertheless be voluntary rather than mandatory, the aim of the page is didactic. Its goal is to teach lay readers how the stock market works, not so much in the name of objective reporting or for the purpose of exposing its evils, but, ultimately, in order to persuade the public to participate. The column does not just report on the market for spectators; it gives advice on how to become involved: "With due care in the selection there are many opportunities presented in times like these on the Stock Exchange, and the man with funds to invest will not be slow to see them."[45]

As part of that act of persuasion, the money page in *Harper's* tries to show that financial fundamentals and economic laws, rather than investor psychology or insider manipulation, are the real operative forces behind stock market movements. A column summing up the year 1900, for example, concludes that "the end of the year finds us in a strong position industrially, commercially, and financially, with a much better prospect for continued prosperity than appeared at the beginning."[46] Likewise, the money page repeatedly emphasizes the "economic maxim" that "continuously idle money is a practical impossibility. If it cannot find profitable employment in ordinary business channels, it is bound to seek investment channels."[47] The column thus also insists that the stock price of many companies is a fair reflection of the value of their assets and earnings, even if it is forced to acknowledge that some of the giant combinations recently created were (in the jargon of the day) overcapitalized.[48]

Howard Mott, in particular, perseveres with a rhetorical insistence on economic laws as the true underlying cause of market events, even when it might begin to seem otherwise. For example, he begins one entry by noting that it is a feature of the American national character to have all or nothing, with a tendency to go to extremes, and the market in property values follows this psychological trait. Yet he nevertheless maintains that the movement of prices is more a result of economic rather than psychological factors, which were becoming more prominent in accounts of panics around the turn of the century: "So our property values fluctuate with the same violence as the general estimate of them. I do not mean to say that the question of property values is wholly psychological. Far from it. Indeed, I expect to show, before you shall finish this page, that natural forces are controlling."[49]

Sometimes a more complicated interpretation is required, when the fundamentals seem to tell a contrary story:

> To the lay mind the rising stock market of the past two months or more is a remarkable paradox. Rising prices for stocks appear logically to demand increasing corporate earnings; yet ever since last October corporate earnings have been declining, and during most of the period there were no noteworthy indications of a revival in business. It is quite evident, however, that last year's panic depressed the prices of nearly all securities far below their intrinsic values, as those values would be determined under normal business conditions. The very sense and meaning of a speculative market is that it anticipates future rather than existing conditions.[50]

Although the "lay mind" might be forgiven for thinking that a rise in stock prices should reflect the earning power of a corporation, the more-sophisticated analyst should understand that prices have already factored in an anticipation of future earnings—an idea of market perfection that became dominant with the development of the efficient market hypothesis at the tail end of the twentieth century. In a refrain that has been repeated in different guises in boom times ever since, readers of the *Harper's* column are also told that the remarkable new fundamental economic conditions mean that traditional standards of valuation are no longer adequate: "The stock market has, for some time past, been suffering from a curious sort of deadlock. Advocates of a rise have abounded, while there have been not a few believers in lower prices. It has been repeatedly pointed out in this column that the extraordinary conditions of industrial and commercial prosperity and the even more unusual magnitude of financial operations and readjustments of corporate capital have necessitated not, indeed, utter disregard of precedents, but rather new standards of comparison."[51]

Harper's money page sometimes acknowledges, however, that market movements cannot always be explained in terms of economic fundamentals. Instead, manipulation by insiders is to blame. Like the *New York Herald*, *Harper's* repeatedly laments that "trading in stocks seems to have become an unpopular pastime with the general public," suggesting that "the lack of outside interest in speculation" is a result of "the relapse of the stock market into tiresome 'professionalism.'"[52] At times the writer feels able to account for what looks like manipulation in terms of the economic laws of supply and demand: "A flurry in money at the close of the past month revived the suspicion again that there had been manipulation for the benefit of the banks and trust companies who had funds to lend. There may have been some 'jockeying' by the money-lenders but the high rates could not have been brought about unless there had been a real scarcity of loanable funds."[53] But more often, the column rails at the lack of involvement by the general public, which, in its view, leaves the market vulnerable to manipulation by a clique of insiders: "The dullness which has prevailed in the stock market of late is obviously the logical consequence of the lack of outside interest in speculation. As a matter of fact, the public at no time since the panic of last May put a sudden and disastrous stop to the speculative craze has evinced any decided disposition to forget its wholesome lesson."[54] And, in another column, "Irregularity was the principal characteristic of the trading in stocks last week. Outside interest in speculation continued at a low ebb. This left the market in the hands of the professionals, who are prone to govern their actions by technical conditions, and to respond readily to rumors of all sorts."[55] If no new capital is being channeled into productive use by the market, then the only explanation for market movement the financial writer can find is that there must be intentional manipulation by a clique of insiders pulling the strings. Yet if the tacit aim of the column is to encourage outsiders to enter the market, the rationale given in each case seems to undermine that conclusion. In the first example cited above, the writer ironically affirms that there is a good reason why the public might be wary of getting their fingers burnt again: when the public does invest, it can lead to a "craze"; yet when it stays away, the market is sown up by insiders and lapses into "dullness." In the second quotation, the problem is caused not by gullible outsiders who misread the market, but by "professionals" who ignore economic fundamentals, because they are so caught up in obsessively tracking the technical and psychological noise of the market itself.

Unlike other Progressive Era attacks on speculation as a form of gambling, the money page in *Harper's* is keen to persuade readers that participating in the market is sensible; yet, at the same time, it warns them that the market is manipulated by a small clique of insiders. With "more holders of stocks and bonds [than] ever before known," the column insists that, even if the only active speculators are professionals, the "daily fluctuations of listed securities attract an extensive passive interest"—not least, I might add, in the proliferating market reports in the popular press.[56] If the number of nonprofessional participants in the stock market is increasing, the magazine sees part of its duty being to warn would-be speculators to act cautiously, because of the possibility of confidence tricks: "Although the better class of investors are unwilling to increase their holdings at the present moment, promoters of fictitious companies are offering long lists of stocks whose flimsiness is concealed behind columns of advertisements."[57] The column thus simultaneously takes a paternalistic stance to tyro investors in its warning against seductive stock promotions, while also assuming a patrician view that it speaks for the "better class of investors," who are savvy enough not to get caught up in the market at present. There might be problems with stock promotions, the column suggests, but the best cure is not regulation, but for outside investors to become smarter. Speculation might be a disease or a flirtation, but that does not necessarily mean that the public should stay away from it: "The germs of speculation have been spreading lately, and it seems that very slowly the public is again receiving into its system the fever of stock-buying. One hears more 'tips' and rumors of 'deals' nowadays than in many weeks. . . . The public has been strenuously wooed in one way and another for a period of six months, but until recently there had been no encouragement given by it to the attentions of the syndicates with stock to sell. Now matters indicate the development of an interesting flirtation."[58]

At times, therefore, the "World of Finance" column suggests that reading the market's signals requires adopting a hermeneutic of suspicion, because nothing is as it seems, and the intentions of traders cannot easily be assumed from the visible evidence of activity on the floor of the Exchange: "The stock market from time to time shows weakness, but it is distinctly traceable to the operations of the professional speculators; and on the next day it displays strength, because the same professionals are buying back stocks sold on the previous. And as always happens when the trading is of this 'professional' character, 'sentiment' changes with the fluctuations in prices, being depressed when stocks are falling, and hopeful when they are rising."[59] The movement of the market is now to be thought of not simply as a reflection of abstract economic fundamentals, with the price of corporate securities solidly based on the underlying value of its assets; nor is it the case that the price is a warranted representation of future value, as suggested earlier; nor even is it a result of broad and impersonal popular-investor sentiment. Instead, the implication is that the canny market reader must recognize that the price signals have been deliberately manipulated through wash sales by a small group of professional traders, in order to look like a genuine market movement. The trick is to discover malign intentionality beneath what has been made to look like impersonal, structural forces. Readers are thus taught that rising prices do not necessarily provide a realistic reflection of increased productivity, because the market might merely have been manipulated, in order to make unsophisticated outsiders think that such is the case. Even though its focus on economic fundamentals makes *Harper's* closer in tone and outlook to the financial press, which is aimed at business professionals, it nevertheless instructs its lay readers on how to identify the hidden hand of market manipulation behind what, at first sight, seems to be the invisible hand of supply and demand.

Town Topics

My final case study, *Town Topics* magazine, is not chosen because it was the most influential financial publication of its era. Indeed, if it is remembered at all in the historiography of America's Gilded Age and Progressive Era, it is never for its money pages. Yet the magazine is worth exploring in some detail, because the rhetorical convergence between its gossip pages and its money section drama-tizes the way that popular financial journalism both abstracted and humanized the workings of the market, and brought a financialized logic to its analysis of society manners. In the same way that the gossip pages helped create the very idea of "society," while at the same time policing its indiscretions, so, too, did the financial column conjure up "the market" for its readers as simultaneously an impersonal, self-sustaining, self-regulating entity, and as a thoroughly personal arena of gossip and intrigue that needed continual surveillance.

In 1885, the brothers William and Eugene Mann took over an existing publi-cation called *Town Topics* and turned it into the most influential and widely read society-gossip magazine in the country. The driving force behind the rise of *Town Topics* was Colonel William D'Alton Mann. He had had a long and varied career before he took on the magazine. He claimed to have served as a cavalry officer in the Civil War, and he was a confidence man and schemer who had been, at one time or another—or represented himself as—an engineer, hotelkeeper, inventor, entrepreneur in the oil industry, tax assessor, newspaper publisher, candidate for Congress, and millionaire inventor and manufacturer of luxury railway sleeping cars.[60] By the time Mann took over *Town Topics*, he was in the process of losing most of his millions with the failure of the Mann Boudoir Car Company, but he continued to live liberally, lunching magnificently at Delmonico's restaurant each day, and each weekend during the summer season hiring an entire Pullman car to take the staff of the magazine to his country retreat—whether they wanted to go or not. By all accounts, Mann and most of his employees lived in a perma-nent alcoholic haze, but somehow they managed to concentrate enough each week to put together an issue of *Town Topics*.

The main feature of the magazine was a column called "Saunterings," tak-ing up roughly twelve pages, about half of each issue. It was written by Mann himself, under the pseudonym of "The Saunterer," and was based primarily on information supplied to him by an army of society insiders, servants, and spies, such as a clergyman and a telegraph operator in upscale Newport, Rhode Island.

Some of the information came from anonymous tips, often from those harboring a grudge. The column, consisting of a series of short but sometimes suggestively connected paragraphs, covered society events such as balls, dinners, and coming-out parties in New York and fashionable watering holes, as well as noting new styles in dress, décor, and food. Many of the entries were seemingly bland or even quite complimentary about their subjects, but, read in the right way, they verged on salacious gossip about prominent society figures and their misdeeds. The reports were often (in newspaper jargon) "blind": they did not mention the actual names of the people involved, but they either included telltale clues, easily recognizable by those in the know, or were placed close to another, quite innocuous item (the "key") that *did* give the names of the participants, leaving readers to make their own inferences.

In addition to the gossip column, the magazine also contained other regular features on diverse subjects. The full title of the publication was *Town Topics, A Newspaper of Society, Fashions, Drama, Music, Art, Books, the Club, Racing, Yachting, Military, Flowers, Household, Etc.* In part, the inclusion of these genteel and fashionable topics served to make reading gossip more respectable to an imagined middle- and upper-middle-class readership, particularly women. The short fiction pieces were mainly sentimental stuff, and the book and art reviews were not especially noteworthy, although the magazine's later spinoff publications—*Tales from Town Topics, Transatlantic Tales,* and *The Smart Set*—did publish early stories by Theodore Dreiser, Sinclair Lewis, O. Henry, Jack London, and Stephen Crane.

Reforming the "Four Hundred"

For those men who presumably were worried about being seen to indulge excessively in the genteel arts, not to mention gossip, *Town Topics* also included a regular section on Wall Street. Because Colonel Mann was, at first, tied up in the legal wrangles involving his railway-car company, his younger brother Eugene originally edited the magazine. Eugene had studied political economy in France and Germany in the 1870s, before studying law and working for the Northern Pacific Railway Company. It is no surprise, therefore, that he was keen to include a section on financial matters, and from 1897 to his death in 1902, he wrote the Wall Street coverage himself.

One of the puzzles about *Town Topics* is who its readers actually were and why they read it. The magazine's masthead proclaimed that it was the "newsiest, brightest, wittiest, wisest, cleverest, most original, and most entertaining paper ever published." Even if that is somewhat exaggerated, its formula of combining society gossip with reports on the arts and Wall Street was very successful.

When the Mann brothers took over the paper in 1885, the circulation was only 5,000; but by 1891, it had risen to 63,000; and the Colonel claimed that by 1900, it had reached 140,000.[61] Like other early society publications, in its less-successful previous incarnation *Town Topics* had merely listed, without commentary, participants in formal balls and dinners, just as newspapers had, at first, merely published stock prices, before the emergence of the money-market column that sought to turn market activity into a coherent narrative, complete with human interest. Although society gossip had long been a feature of American journalism, it was, for the most part, dully factual at best and fawning at worst, and, in the pre–Mann brothers years, *Town Topics* was no different.[62] The revamped version of *Town Topics*, however, was a revelation, with its witty and wry attacks on the foibles of the upper class, and salacious and very knowledgeable gossip threaded in among the traditional reports of society happenings, along with other sections on the arts and business.

Colonel Mann insisted that the purpose of the magazine was not to flatter, but to expose the excesses of the pseudoaristocracy. He claimed that his work was in keeping with other muckraking journalism of the period, which had faith in the power of publicity to shame the idle, unproductive rich (who live off their Wall Street investments) into mending their ways:

> I have long been convinced that the 400 of New York is an element so absolutely shallow and unhealthy that it deserves to be derided almost incessantly. . . . There are a few conspicuous individuals who are constantly figuring as "leaders" of the fashionable lot, and there are others that are constantly pushing and clawing to get recognition and publicity, and to these I am merciless. I have iterated and reiterated that one inflated and preposterous man was a jackass, and that a vain and jealous old lady, who persists in being at the head of the court, is undeserving of the courtesy and tenderness that gentle and true womanhood commands from me, as from nearly all men.[63]

Mann's true mission in running *Town Topics*, according to a reporter from the *New York Times* who interviewed him, "was neither mere lucre nor the satisfaction of any personal vanity. What he wants to do is to reform the Four Hundred by making them too deeply disgusted with themselves to continue their present silly way of life."[64] Yet for all Mann's reformist piety in attacking the social elite, the magazine was written as if it was to be read exclusively by those in the innermost sanctum of society. Admittedly, the Saunterer's column makes mention of somewhat more people than the very narrow list of the four hundred guests that society leader Ward McAllister had famously declared could fit in Mrs. Astor's ballroom. Nevertheless, it maintains the illusion that society is a very exclusive realm, and that the readers of the column must be part of that select band in order to know what the gossip is about. Whether the column is full of intimate details, or whether it is mildly indignant at lapses of good taste, it always creates the impression of being written by and for those on the inside of high society. Although society figures were supposedly the subject of Mann's attack, they almost certainly did read the magazine, even if they would not admit to doing so, with the magazine finding its way "into almost every cottage in the Park [Tuxedo Park, an elite, Gilded Age resort in New York], as it did into the cottages, villas, and mansions at Newport." It was read, according to the son of the etiquette-guide writer Emily Post (herself a victim of Mann's scandal mongering), "upstairs, downstairs, and backstairs."[65]

The irony is that a circulation restricted to the Four Hundred would not make good business sense, so the rapidly growing readership presumably consisted not only of the innermost circle of high society, but those who delighted in mocking the scandalous behavior of their supposed betters, as Mann proclaimed. Although reliable evidence of the actual readership of the magazine is scant, it is, however, arguable that it also appealed to the vanity of those who wanted the illusion that, by proxy, they, too, were part of the inner sanctum of society. Like the market reports in mass-circulation newspapers and magazines, the gossip pages made the daily intrigues of the wealthy come to seem of vital importance to ordinary readers. The trick, then, was to present society as extremely exclusive, yet make readers feel as if they were included, and *Town Topics* played on the contradictory desires for privacy and publicity, secrecy and transparency, that made fashionable society tick. As Maureen Montgomery notes in her study of the contradictions on display in Edith Wharton's New York, high-society women courted publicity from the press in the promotion of their leisure-class activities, but the price they paid was an increased scrutiny by the gossip magazines of the boundaries of proper feminine conduct.[66] The complicitous gossip pages thus both condemned and sustained high society. In this way, as Eric Homberger's study of Mrs. Astor's world makes clear, the society column helped forge the very notion of the "society" it claimed to merely reflect, a world whose exclusivity had to be acted out in the full glare of public attention in order to promote its appeal.[67]

The financial page, I want to suggest, had a similarly conflicted attitude toward its subject. Like the other market reports discussed in this chapter, the Colonel's supposedly muckraking financial gossip helped sustain the very markets it appeared at times to criticize, and, in the process, obfuscated their operation. *Town Topics*' money section is both inclusive and exclusive, sycophantic and admonitory, a champion of the reformist call for the glaring light of publicity in financial affairs, yet a purveyor of inside information and an implicit supporter of the view that the New York Stock Exchange should rightly remain a private gentlemen's club. We can see these conflicting approaches, for example, in the name changes of the various columns making up the financial pages of *Town Topics*. One of the two regular money columns was originally called "The Game of Speculation: With a Glance at Dealers and Victims," suggesting a standoffish tone of disapproval. By the 1890s, mirroring the broader decline of militant Populism and the rise of a more reformist Progressivism, the column adopted a tone that was not so much an attack on speculation as the confidential advice between a trusted broker and his privileged client. It changed its title to "Whispers of Wall Street," drawing attention to the gossipy content of the piece. At one stage, the subtitle was "The Record of the Financier's Rambles," echoing the magazine's main attraction, "Saunterings." The subtitle of the primary editorializing column became "Hints for Bulls and Bears," as if it were a confidential etiquette manual for those new to the club. It appeared under the signature of "The Room-Trader," suggesting that this piece was truly written by a participant insider, while "Whispers of Wall Street" was signed at first "The Financier," and then "The Rounder," echoing the financial page's dual focus on the serious and the dissolute aspects of Wall Street.

"A Very Shocking Break in Society"

As in so many other accounts of this period, both factual and fictional, the fluctuations in prices of stocks are described in *Town Topics* in mock-heroic terms, a perpetual and *personal* struggle between the bull and the bear factions, with the focus on the dominant personalities of the exchanges. The story of a particular deal in Richmond Terminals, for example, is presented as a "hard-fought battle": "The General, flushed with the brilliant advance that he had made, was lavish in his gifts to his friends and admirers."[68] The market is often seen to be under the personal influence of a masterful player, a bold and energetic character: "You have doubtless concluded that Mr. Gould is at the back of this market, and I think that such a conclusion, if arrived at, will be proven a fact ere many days have passed. . . . I know for a fact that both Cornelius and William K. [Vanderbilt] are opposed to the payments of any such large amounts to stockholders."[69] There is thus a contradiction at the heart of the financial pages of *Town Topics*: if Wall Street was a rigged game in which the bulls and bears engaged in private battles, and the only sure outcome was that the lambs got slaughtered, how could you persuade more outsiders to invest, in order to help fuel the engine of a lively market—first in railroad shares and then in the public flotations of corporate stocks and bonds—during the Great Merger Movement of the late 1890s and early 1900s?

One solution to the problem was to insist that Wall Street, in general, was a democratic, rational, safe place for savvy investors to place their money, because it operated through aggregations of prices whose movements were impersonal, while, at the same time, to report on the market in detail, as if it were the gossip of an exclusive gentlemen's club—which the New York Stock Exchange, with its resistance to external regulation, in reality remained.[70] That is what the financial page of *Town Topics* did: it combined a broad editorial stance in favor of conservative speculation, transparency, and professionalism with an insider's gossip of tales of "the Boys" on the floor of the Exchange getting up to collegiate pranks. In this way, *Town Topics* makes visible the links between the personalized language of gossip and the abstract rhetoric of the stock market as a vast, price-processing information machine, a connection that, as we have seen, is visible in other popular accountings of the market during this period. Popular financial journalism like *Town Topics* thus provided an imaginary resolution to the problem of asymmetrical information in stock markets by rhetorically making outsiders feel like they were insiders. The resolution remained in the realm of the imagination, not least because the actual members of the NYSE jealously guarded their monopoly on price information. In the 1880s and 1890s, they mounted a series of legal challenges against the telegraph companies that were providing ticker feeds to bucket shops, as well as launching public relations campaigns aimed at convincing the public that investment remained distinguishable from speculation, if it was left to the professionals.[71]

Although the financial pages in *Town Topics* were there in part to make the gossip pages seem more respectable and offer something for the husbands of the women who were undoubtedly the gossip magazine's main audience, there are closer connections between the two sections than one might at first think. Elegant, authoritative, jaunty, and urbane, the two reports from Wall Street are very much in tune with the brisk reports of the society column, with both sections occasionally issuing stern reprimands for behavior deemed to be beyond the pale of accepted norms. For example, readers are informed, in a refrain that, as we have seen, is familiar to most financial journalism of the period, that "the general condition of the stock market during the past week has been decidedly dull and uninteresting."[72] Or readers learn that "there was nothing very sensational in the stock market last week; but the steady strength that was exhibited in all the leading stocks showed very plainly how the cat is going to jump. The

Southern stocks were undoubtedly the feature of the market, and General Logan opened his campaign in Richmond Terminal in brilliant style, making a move of 11–1/2 per cent in three days."[73]

It is important to note that *Town Topics* included not just neutral, factual reports of market activity, or even general editorial pronouncements on important issues, but columns offering what looked like specific investment advice. The "Room-Trader," for example, refers to his column as a "survey," but he also gives a simulation of intimate, personal investment advice whose selling point is its supposed accuracy: "Since I last wrote, I have sold a few of my Richmond and West Point Terminals at a profit of four points, and now intend holding the balance. . . . Without any prospect of a settlement of the Transcontinental difficulty, with the absolute certainty that the company is in urgent need of new steamers, and with the undeniable fact that there will be no dividend on the stock for many weary months, perhaps for years, to come, I cannot consistently ask you to buy it around its present price."[74] Yet it is only an imitation of personalized advice, made to seem intimate and individual for a mass readership. The irony of popular financial journalism is that, in theory, broadcasting market information should have cut down on speculation, because it introduced a level playing field between all investors and reduced opportunities for arbitrage, even for those at a geographical distance from the heart of the action in the nation's exchanges. Instead, the newspapers and magazines offered a *simulation* of privileged information in the form of tips and rumors that, by being broadcast widely, necessarily failed to provide individual readers with a unique competitive advantage. In fact, soon into the Mann regime, *Town Topics* established a separate Financial Bureau, offering investment advice by letter and telegraph to subscribers, which was advertised as a more exclusive, personal service. In effect, the *Town Topics* Financial Bureau promised to deliver what the gossip column only gestured toward, namely, inside information and trading advice based on well-placed intelligence. Its regular advertisement assured readers that its "sources of information are more complete, more from the 'inside,' and hence more accurate than those of any other paper or institution in the country."[75] The Financial Bureau thus functioned as both a supplement and a rival to the magazine's financial pages, putting idle gossip and speculation onto a professional footing.

Like the Financial Bureau, the columnists emphasized their insider status, thus underlining their accuracy: "My information, which comes from a direct and official source in Boston, is to the effect that the directors [of the Chicago, Burlington & Quincy Railroad] will probably declare a dividend of 1–1/2 per cent at their June meeting."[76] Although the financial reporters were always keen to point out their supposedly privileged access to the exclusive club of Wall Street insiders, they also took a pious stance in favor of exposing market swindles to the harsh light of publicity, just as the society pages both indulged in gossip and took a muckraking editorial position against social misdemeanors. "The day for making bogus statements has passed," the magazine announced, going on to insist that "chicanery, thanks to exposure, is being relegated to the background."[77] Likewise, it was not speculation per se that was at fault, but the few bad apples that were giving the Exchange a bad name: "I have had, in times gone by, and shall probably in the future again have to call attention to the despicable methods of some unscrupulous Wall Street operators. The shaking down and pounding given by the 'manipulators' of the Whiskey Trust, that resulted in ruin to so many, are fit subjects for consideration now that the 'deal' has been consummated, and that the insiders are once again to take the public into this confidence."[78] In the same way that etiquette guides and society columns served a disciplinary function in regard to women's conduct (the former dealing with idealized theory, and the latter with sometimes less-than-perfect practice), so, too, did investment-advice manuals and gossipy market reports fulfill a normalizing role in the theory and practice of market behavior.

Although the financial section of *Town Topics* at times takes a similarly outraged, muckraking stance as the Colonel's editorializing against the Four Hundred, it also indulges in the same frivolous banter as the gossip column. For example, the tone and language of society repartee is occasionally used wittily in financial advice: "Those who have an inclination to go short for a big turn, had better follow the advice to persons about to get married—'don't.'"[79] Conversely, the language of speculation is used metaphorically in the gossip pages to describe the rise and fall in the social stock of particular individuals in the marriage market:

Chicago is nothing without a sensation. This time it is not a break in wheat [i.e., a sudden fall in the price of wheat at the Chicago Board of Trade], but a very shocking break in society. The sixteen-year-old daughter of Mrs. H. O. Stone has gone and done just what, after all, has not so greatly surprised the knowing ones. . . . Her clever mamma was outwitted in a plan for matching the fatly larded millions of the late pork packing potentate with the yardstick millions of the still present Marshall Field. The insurance business captured the prize destined for dry goods, and mamma has avenged herself by dramatically cutting her graceless daughter off without a shilling.[80]

Personal gossip is also admitted into the supposedly more austere pages of the financial column, usually not for its own sake, but for what it explains about the movements of the market. On the one hand, financial woes are intimated to be the source of society scandal in the "Saunterings" column, for instance: "How the mighty have indeed fallen. Poor E. Berry is a blueberry now; but manages to be cheerful. The Pollocks, who cut a wild but brief swath here two years ago, have nothing left of their inheritance of $300,000 each, but its memory; I could name a few dozen others, who, even last winter, lived at the rate of $200 a day, with occasional plunges in the 'Street,' costing from $5,000 to $40,000 each, who now are stripped and credit less with no hope that Fortune will smile again."[81] On the other hand, domestic difficulties reported in the "Saunterings" column are rumored to be the cause of business problems:

> Scarcely a week ago, a callous commercial telegraph company passed over its wires the news that a very well-known Wall Street firm was about to be reorganized on account of the withdrawal of one of its members. The firm promptly denied the statement, but obstinately refused to furnish official endorsement of its denial.... At the same time Cadley began to talk mysteriously in clubdom about poor Mrs. Z., who was going to sue her husband for divorce; and that Mr. Z. had levanted to Europe while the family pot was cooling down; and that Mrs. Z. was packing up to move out of her apartments at the Saxony.[82]

Thus, in *Town Topics*, Fifth Avenue is shown as working the same way as Wall Street, with the reputations of individuals on the rise or fall, and the financial markets are portrayed as a mirror image of high society, governed by the same human passions and peccadilloes. Insights into the domestic arrangements of brokers, for instance, are claimed to shed light on financial dealings that would otherwise remain murky: "There are a number of rumors afloat to the effect that the financial firm of which Harry Hollins is the head will soon be dissolved.... There does not appear to be any actual certainty about the dissolution of the partnership, but the fact that Mr. Yznaga has gone to Europe, and the report of some trouble in his domestic relations, have in all probability given credibility to the story."[83]

There is a similar convergence between the personal and the financial in some of the short stories included in the magazine. For example, a four-act, satirical minidrama titled "Ebb and Flow," placed just before the financial section, recounts "the weird way in which money will circulate."[84] It is a parable of how personal connections become impersonal, and vice versa, and revives a familiar eighteenth-century trope of tracing the circulation of a coin in order to follow the course of a debt.[85] A married woman catches her lover, Percy Doolittle, about to write to a Jewish moneylender for a thousand dollars to pay off a debt he claims he has accrued from unwise bullish speculation on Wall Street. Noting that her husband, a stockbroker, has recently received a windfall from Wall Street by being bearish on the market, she promises to get the money from her husband to lend to her lover (she will claim it is for charity). In Act II, Doolittle is seen to give the thousand dollars to a different lover, only half-jokingly in exchange for the promise of a kiss. Act III reveals this second woman handing the thousand dollars over to her French hairdresser, supposedly to open a shop. In the final act, we learn that the Frenchman has taken the thousand dollars to the stockbroker husband for a reckless financial speculation. In contrast to the "Romances of Real Life" in *Hunt's Merchant's Magazine*, the logic of this story is that the impersonal abstractions of money as the "general equivalent" mask the complex networks of personal and financial obligations that fuel a credit economy—and which a gossip-cum-finance magazine is ideally placed to expose, albeit not at a structural level. Unlike the more familiar separation of business and romance plots in the sentimental fiction of the period, "Ebb and Flow" presents the two realms as fundamentally the same.

Making the Market Personal

Along with other accounts in the business press of the late nineteenth century, in *Town Topics* the market occasionally is figured as a vast, anonymous machine—increasingly global in scope—in which price movements are no longer under the control of a master manipulator, but are instead the aggregation of countless transactions that are in themselves random, yet, to the trained eye, nevertheless reveal meaningful patterns. At the same time, however, the market is presented through the synecdoche of the colorful cast of characters populating Wall Street. These individuals are represented as both the actual market-makers on the floor of the Exchange and as stand-ins for the market itself, anthropomorphized as a single, coherent entity, a hive mind with a distinctive character of its own.

Even when the gossip is not connected to the world outside Wall Street, the financial pages of *Town Topics* are dotted with snippets about the uproarious doings of "the Boys" on the "Street." For example, the "Whispers of Wall Street" column tells a story about a waggish broker sending a rat in a box to a fellow trader who dealt in Richmond Terminals, designated on the ticker tape by the initials R. T., and hence jokingly known among traders as "rats." In the same way that the Four Hundred comes to represent society itself, so, too, does the New York Stock Exchange (and the related commodity exchanges) function as a stand-in for the whole of the market. The complexities of finance in the age of industrial capitalism are reduced to, but also portrayed as, the personal goings-on of a private gentlemen's club: "The members of the Produce Exchange held a regular jubilee on Monday evening, and attended Nat Goodwin's performance of the 'Mascot' about 250 strong. Bob Clapp, resplendent in a magnificent dress suit, and accompanied by Wallace, occupied a stage box, and among the audience I noticed 'Jumbo' Goldsmith, 'Plunger' Miller . . . and a number of others."[86] More usually in the popular financial reporting of this period, descriptions of the New York Stock Exchange as a private club were harnessed to a critique of the lack of democratic accountability in the nation's financial center, but *Town Topics* combined an editorial call for reformist transparency with a rhetorical appeal to readers to consider themselves privy to the inside gossip of the club. As with its society-gossip pages, *Town Topics* maintains a hypocritical stance that both condemns and glamorizes the intrigues on Wall Street and in the drawing rooms of Fifth Avenue.

Knowledge of the market, *Town Topics'* financial page suggests, is based on personal, inside information, but the impersonal market can also be understood as if it were an individual. The anonymous writer is thus always keen to assert his personal friendship with those he regards as the key players. We learn, for example, of a chance meeting with Chauncey Depew in Delmonico's restaurant: "Within a very few hours I met my friend Chauncey M. Depew. . . . After finishing his midday lunch with apparently little effort, the President of the New York Central and Hudson River Railroad Company favored me with his views upon the market. Depew is very far-seeing. His friends are among the millionaires and savants of the two worlds. Everybody who knows 'Chauncey M.' admits that his magnetic powers are irresistible, and I believe he owes much of his knowledge to his ability to mesmerize his subjects."[87]

The financial section of *Town Topics* serves as a permanent enticement to outsiders to think that they are sufficiently on the inside to indulge in speculation, part of the rhetorical work that made it seem a perfectly respectable activity, rather than a form of gambling. Other editorials in the magazine, however, warn against brokers who actively advertise for business, a practice that was prohibited under the patrician rules of the New York Stock Exchange, which wanted to distinguish what its members saw as their respectable business from bucket shops and other less reputable institutions that dealt with investors of modest means: "So long as the candle burns within the legitimate precincts of Wall Street and the vicinity of the Stock Exchange, and the moths, well knowing the inflammable nature of their plumage, will insist upon singeing it, I have no fault to find with those who furnish the flame. But when a broker and a banker [Henry Clews] . . . deliberately goes about lighting his speculative tapers all over the city and employing agents to shoo unknowing and unsuspecting moths into their blaze, I moved, out of sheer pity, to raise a voice of warning."[88] As with the contradictory logic of the society pages, which both eagerly publicized the activities of society figures but then held them up for public scrutiny, the financial pages constituted an ongoing advertisement for the excitement of the stock market yet condemned brokers who courted publicity. The implicit invitation in the money section is that by reading the columns, you will become an insider, but this is coupled with the same warning that peppers the advertisements for the *Town Topics'* Financial Bureau, namely, amateurs and outsiders should be wary of speculating in the market: "The average investor will not put in an appearance until stocks sell ten or twenty points higher. It is when brokers' offices are full of customers, and everyone is loaded up with stocks and still anxious to buy more, that it is time to be cautious."[89]

Market Abstraction

For all that the market is presented in personalized rhetoric as a small and exclusive club, *Town Topics'* financial pages also insist, in moments of editorial piety, that it is governed by impersonal economic laws, akin to the weather or other forces of nature that can be predicted, if not actually controlled. Despite its interest in gossip about the big players, the money section affirms that the market is not under the control of individuals, and explanations of market events are to be found in fundamental economic conditions: "One fact must not be ignored, and that is, the market no longer depends upon what any one man is doing. It does not matter whether Addison Cammack, S. V. White, and T. W. Pearsall are bulls or bears, or whether Jay Gould, Russell Sage, or others are neutral. An effort to stem the rising tide of speculation would be about as ineffectual as an attempt to control the waves. The market is governed in the long run by natural causes. Temporarily, sentiment may prevail, but the upshot is invariably the same—reason dominates."[90] Despite the admonition against "sentiment," the financial pages of *Town Topics* are almost permanently on the bull side of the market, a stance that is based sometimes on an admiration for the cool-headed leaders of the bull faction, but at other times on an optimistic faith in the inexorable tide of American industrial progress, with one columnist, for example, patriotically declaring: "For the next two years, write me down as a believer in everything American—from the home-made pie to the subsidized railroads and their valuable land grants."[91] Despite this brief recognition that the "free" market is the creation of governmental legislation, institutions, and subsidy, *Town Topics* followed common practice in ideologically figuring the market as an unstoppable, impersonal, natural force:

"It is of no use—nothing can thwart, much less overthrow, the great and powerful combination of natural and consistent circumstances that must make this country prosperous beyond all calculations. . . . The tide of immense prosperity shall sweep over the entire country."[92] The impersonal and personalized visions of the market here become mutually self-serving, naturalizing the market by making its very strangeness seem as homely as apple pie.

In a final convergence between the language of society gossip and the rhetoric of the market, the stocks themselves are personified, acting out dramas that are only too familiar to readers of the gossip column. In a fudge between real human actors and personalized entities, the price of Canada South stock, for instance, is described as "acting in a very suspicious manner."[93] Or, for example, St. Louis stock is described as if it were a gentleman sauntering around town, withstanding attacks from rapscallions: "The St. Louis acted admirably. The weakness of the other market could not throw them 'off their pins,' but they stood erect and defiant, and helped rally the market, whenever the other stocks convalesced and were strong enough to place themselves under the new leaders."[94] Perhaps most significantly of all, the market in *Town Topics* is sometimes presented not merely as a coordinated and coherent abstract entity, but as if it were an actual person. "The market," the Room Trader writes, "reminds me of a man that is halting between two opinions."[95] In this way the aggregated, anonymous, and psychologically varied individuals that make up the interconnected circuits of the credit economy are abstracted and reified through the imagination of a single, coherent, placeless market, which is then reindividualized by proxy through talk of the market as having moods, whims, and opinions. Whatever the moralizing stance of *Town Topics'* editorials, the trope of personification thus contributes to this period's broader legitimation of the market as both eminently intelligible and yet still inscrutable.

The Real Business of *Town Topics*

All was not what it seemed in the business operations of *Town Topics*. The rumor among those in the know in the 1880s and 1890s was that the magazine was not much more than an extortion racket, a piece of gossip that eventually saw the light of exposure in a court case in 1905–1906.[96] The magazine ostensibly turned secret information about the wealthy into a commodity by selling magazines at ten cents per week to the curious masses, yet at the same time it conducted a cartel among the cognoscenti to keep the choicest items from reaching the open market. It turned out that if the magazine uncovered some embarrassing gossip about a prominent member of society, it would blackmail that person to suppress the story, and his or her name would then appear on Mann's "immune" list. If people paid handsomely enough, they would find their names mentioned in the gossip columns in glowing terms. For all Colonel Mann's bluster about bringing the light of muckraking exposure to the peccadilloes of high society, behind the scenes he was more than happy to bury the story for a price, an example of the very corruption he claimed to abhor. Some enterprising members of Mann's staff—it was never proven in court that they were acting under Mann's instructions, although that is likely—developed a further scam: anyone they had dirt on was persuaded to take out a subscription for a lavish, sycophantic volume that would record the "Fads and Fancies" of prominent New Yorkers. As the court case that exposed the scam made clear, there was never really any intention to publish the volume.

In the real business of *Town Topics*, just as in its coverage of social and financial events, the personal and the impersonal mingled promiscuously together, becoming mutually self-serving. Colonel Mann, for all his affected Old World and pseudo-Southern manners, was always keen to dress up the bribery as a legitimate business exchange, albeit presumably with an eye to any future legal case. In return for burying a story, he would "sell" shares in the magazine at vastly increased rates, although it was not always clear whether any actual shares changed hands. (Imagine the delight of muckraking critics when it turned out that the very businessmen who had complained about the intrusions of the press turned out to be part owners of one of the most notorious gossip magazines.) Instead of accepting a bribe pure and simple, Mann's other main trick was to disguise it as a business loan, albeit a loan that was more like a gift, because there was never any attempt by Mann to pay it back. Of course, it was only the semblance of a gift; at heart, it was really just a commercial transaction like any other. If the magazine and its subjects claimed that belonging to the innermost sanctum of society was not a question of money, but a quality of refinement that money could not buy, then its system of blackmail demonstrated that something seemingly as priceless as a person's reputation had a dollar value after all, understood by both blackmailer and victim alike.

Conclusion

Like many of the other genres of financial representation explored in this book, the market report did not provide a realistic account of an objective reality, but instead helped conjure into being the idea of the market as a single, coherent entity. Over and above the specific political positions the various publications took up in the debates in the late nineteenth and early twentieth centuries about the validity of speculation and the need for reform in the nation's exchanges, popular financial journalism served to create and naturalize the market as a "vivified abstraction," in much the same way as the half-sycophantic, half-judgmental gossip magazines helped to sustain the idea of high society.[97] As we have seen, popular financial journalism allowed readers to imaginatively participate in the trials and tribulations of speculation, and it came to make the market's numbers seem like an indispensible barometer of both national and individual moods. Unlike the focus on seemingly objective financial data and economic laws that were the staple of publications aimed at business professionals, the Wall Street pages of mass-circulation newspapers and magazines honed in on personalities and hidden intentions in their effort to humanize the abstractions of finance, thereby providing an explanation for the fluctuation in prices that contrasted with the numerical formulations of both technical analysis and fundamental analysis. But they also presented a split vision of the market, combining the view from up close on the floor of the exchange with a bird's-eye view from afar of the impersonal workings of the invisible hand; moreover, these different optics became combined, such as in the repeated, uncanny personification of the abstract market itself. The popular market report thus relied on a persistence of the personal touch in a historical moment in which the general equivalences of money, commodities, and statistics were eroding a traditional concern with the local and the particular. This seemingly retrograde insistence on reading the market in personal terms was not necessarily unwarranted: full financial disclosure was not yet compulsory, and trading on inside information was not made illegal (and certainly not rigorously enforced) until the New Deal reforms of Wall Street in the 1930s.

CHAPTER TWO

Reading the Ticker Tape

It takes years of study and actual experience at the tape to become a good tape reader. There are numerous ways of judging the market from the tape, and if one becomes expert he will be so sensitive to the various currents, tides, and eddies, that he can detect them instantly—just as a good pilot can see in advance of the "landlubber," when a squall approaches, and can judge the meaning and probable effect of every little puff of wind or change or sky.

The Ticker (1908)

Alongside the market report in mass-circulation newspapers, the genre of vernacular financial advice in the late nineteenth and early twentieth centuries helped to teach the layperson how to read the market in general, and the stock ticker in particular. The flood of guides to investment helped bring into being the very idea of the market as a coherent and predictable entity, and the subsequent increase in participation in it, based on those guides, in turn helped create the market in their image. The popularity of guides offering an education for outsiders in the ways of Wall Street thus served to normalize the operations of finance for the reviled and revered investor of small means, who was beginning to participate in the bucket shops, if not in the actual stock market. The promise of these popular guides to investment was not merely to make the market legible through purportedly objective accounts of the ways of the nation's stock and produce exchanges, but to make money for the reader, through a mixture of predictions, tips, strategies, maxims, stories, personal histories, and advice on how to turn oneself into a cool-headed speculator. As with the market reports in newspapers and magazines, these investment-advice manuals began to appear in considerable numbers, even before the incipient democratization of shareholding after World War I, and were as much a stimulation of popular curiosity about the stock market as a response to it.

Guides to the stock market during this period took on many guises, including manuals for would-be speculators, official histories of the New York Stock Exchange, biographies of the "kings of fortune," novels and short stories set in Wall Street, magazines outlining the principles of technical analysis regarding stock-price charts, and seemingly informative pamphlets provided by stockbrokers that were, in fact, scams. This chapter will begin by surveying the variety of this advice literature, concentrating on the period 1880–1910. These market guides draw on a set of tropes, narratives, and axioms that date back to at least the financial revolution in eighteenth-century Britain, with Thomas Mortimer's *Every Man His Own Broker; or, A Guide to Exchange-Alley* (1761) usually identified as the first volume that aimed to explain the workings of the stock market to the uninitiated, rather than merely condemning it out of hand.[1] What is distinctive about instructional manuals on reading the market in the Gilded Age and the Progressive Era, however, is that the very idea of what counted as the market began to change with the advent of the stock ticker and the subsequent development of technical analysis and chartism (as the practice of predicting future market movements from the immediate prior history of prices is now usually termed). As the second part of this chapter documents, reading the market came to mean reading the ticker tape, with its abstract procession of numbers and symbols, along with the charts that further abstracted the endless flow of prices printed on the tape into seemingly intelligible patterns of cycles, reactions, and averages. According to these emergent forms of popular financial advice, making sense of Wall Street was now less a matter of having privileged access to the cliquish intrigues on the floor of the Exchange (as implied by the frequent recourse to gossip in the market reports explored in the previous chapter) than of turning oneself into a coolly calculating decoder of the impersonal, disembodied, standardized price variations recorded by the stock ticker. This was far removed—both literally and conceptually—from the tactile inspection of the actual produce being traded or first-hand knowledge of the corporation's activities, and also distanced from sensing the mood of the market through personal interaction on the floor of the exchanges. As the final section of this chapter will discuss, the rational abstractions of the ticker tape and stock charts, however, together with the seemingly scientific and impersonal financial predictions they enabled, continued to employ a rhetoric that presented the technology of the market, and the market itself, as if imbued with a humanlike agency that was decidedly irrational, uncanny, and supernatural. My argument is not that the kind of market reading enabled by technical analysis has rightly been dismissed for its affinity with voodoo finance, nor even that tape and chart reading have been unfairly maligned for such associations, which are seemingly at a tangent to their main concerns. The conclusion of this chapter is that traditional, vernacular modes of market reading did not inevitably give way to properly modern and professionalized forms of financial knowledge. It was not simply a case of folk and technological varieties of economic wisdom operating along parallel tracks and appealing to different audiences (though un-doubtedly that was at least partially true). Instead, the newer methods of scientific analysis—supposedly operating at a level of statistical abstraction far removed from the intrigues of individual market actors—*incorporated* many elements, in both rhetoric and content, of a premodern financescape that attributed a myste-rious sense of human agency, via the logic of personification, to the market and its mechanical registers.

Learning to Read the Market

Nineteenth-century Americans of the middling sort gained what little knowledge they had of the workings of Wall Street from many diverse sources, ranging from first-hand involvement, as the victim of a bank defaulting, to sermons warning against the stock market as a form of gambling and from fictional accounts of panics and swindling to official governmental reports on the dangers of specu-lation.[2] Up until the 1870s, most published discussions of Wall Street showed a Brahmin distaste for its immoral ways, equating all stock market speculation with gambling, and thus attacking not so much the wealth derived from playing the market as the lack of productive labor required to get it. In addition to the condemnation of speculation to be found in midcentury sermons, newspaper editorials, Broadway satires, and cautionary tales, the sensationalist genre of city mysteries included sections on the dark arts of Wall Street in their pseudo-guidebook portrayals of New York, in titles such as George Foster's *New York by Gaslight* and Thomas De Walden's play, *The Upper Ten and the Lower Twenty* (1854), while George Francis Train's *Young America in Wall Street* condemned, through a series of letters to an imagined reader, the gaudy values of the city's elite whose wealth was founded on speculation.[3]

The message of such works was clear: engaging with the stock market, whether through investment or speculation, was not only financially risky, but led to depravity. The few guides from the antebellum period that did not instantly condemn the entire realm of business, but endeavored to take it seriously, were written mainly for an educated, middle-class readership (or those clerks who as-pired to become so) and either provided instruction in business ethics and habits or aimed to educate its mercantile-class readers in the underlying principles of political economy, rather than explaining the specifics of investment as such. For example, in 1856, Freeman Hunt, the founder of *Hunt's Merchant's Magazine*, published a collection of "Maxims, Morals, and Miscellanies for Merchants and Men of Business" on topics such as "How to Prosper in Business," "Effects of Ostentation on Credit," and "Self-Reliance, the Main Spring of Success." When the stock market is directly discussed, his warning is clearly to stay away from it: "Don't Leave a Legitimate Business for Financiering," one chapter warns. In a similar vein, Edwin Freedley's *Practical Treatise on Business* includes sections on "The Habits of Business," "Getting Money," and "How to Get Customers." Despite a chapter insisting that "Business Pursuits [Are] Not Incompatible with Moral and Intellectual Culture," however, Freedley's compendium of business advice also includes a chapter on "How to Get Rich By Speculation."[4]

The postbellum genres of success literature for the go-ahead generation of young men continued to offer familiar paeans to republican manliness and hard work, albeit unwittingly recognizing the importance of luck as much as pluck.[5] James D. Mills's *The Art of Making Money*, for example, provides sober introductions to topics such as business ethics and the nature of credit and promises that the art of making money is in every American's grasp. "Success is not the effect of accident or of chance," Mills claims, "but the result of the intelligent application of certain *fixed principles* to the affairs of every-day life" (emphasis in original), and he therefore proposes to instruct the reader in the "correct application of true business principles to the opportunities which are within the reach of all."[6] Although he recognizes the necessity of putting idle capital to work, he warns against speculation as merely another form of gambling and gives a detailed account of the operations of the Gold Room as if he were an ethnologist reporting on an exotic tribe.

When not directly condemning it, many novels, stories, and nonfictional accounts of Wall Street from the 1880s onward began to humanize the financial economy, simplifying its complex interactions by attributing price movements to a manipulation by all-powerful titans who conspired to corner the market. Although not designed as practical guides to investment, they nonetheless served to instruct readers not merely by making the jargon, mechanics, and personalities of Wall Street familiar, but by reassuring them that speculation—at least in the hands of professionals—was not inherently wicked. Unlike George Foster's *New York by Gaslight*, James K. Medbery's *Men and Mysteries of Wall Street* presented the enigmas of the financial district as something that could be explained and made less mysterious by a knowledgeable guide. This quasi-anthropological primer combined an insider's account of the quirks, customs, and japes of brokers and speculators with a detailed description of the mechanics of investment in its various forms. Similar compendious volumes appearing in succession—such as William Worthington Fowler's *Ten Years on Wall Street*, Matthew Hale Smith's *Twenty Years among the Bulls and Bears of Wall Street*, and Henry Clews's *Twenty-Eight Years on Wall Street* (later expanded to become *Fifty Years on Wall Street*)— provided a far less judgmental portrait of Wall Street than earlier accounts.[7] Although they condemned some sharp practices of the "king operators," they indulged their readers' appetites for dramatic tales of the legendary corners and pools organized by the "celebrities of Wall Street." "All along the pathway of the street," Matthew Hale Smith opined, "are noble characters who stand like light-houses on the tall, rocky cliffs, unchanged and unmoved by the agitation, turmoil, and ruin, that play around their feet."[8] Despite seeming to provide ammunition for those reformers who felt that the protection of vulnerable investors is best achieved by educating the public in the specifics of stock market activity, these compendia of Wall Street lore nonetheless tended—in part by sheer repetition—to legitimize the stock market by lionizing its larger-than-life "characters."

As we saw in chapter 1, however, by the 1870s, newspapers and magazines targeted at a lay readership were beginning to provide not merely a factual account of Wall Street activity, but to offer instruction in the arcane practices of the nation's stock and commodity exchanges. Tumbridge & Company's *Secrets of Success in Wall Street* (1875) is an early and—in comparison with more insistent promotions later in the century—restrained example of a neutral guide to the workings of Wall Street that turns out to be not all that it seems. In addition to a brief summary of stock market devices, such as puts, calls, spreads, and straddles, the guide helpfully includes satirical newspaper cartoons, along with photos of the brokerage premises, showing not only the solidity of its furnishings, but the clubability of its customers' trading room. The overall aim is to make speculation appear normal and businesslike: "Persons unacquainted with Stock Speculation may become perfectly familiar with the intricate machinery necessary for its operation by a careful study of these pages," the guide explains. "They will also attain a knowledge of financial matters useful in any pursuit, and may be the means of their making many safe and profitable investments; even those who have had an interest in stocks will find information and hints unknown to them before, which will greatly aid and increase their gains in future operations." In return, however, the guide concludes, "we solicit a share of your patronage."[9]

As chapter 4 documents in more detail, offering a free guide to the ways of

Wall Street as a promotion for a brokerage business became increasingly common. Advertisements placed in the Sunday editions of New York newspapers by "bankers and brokers" promised informative handbooks to potential customers.[10] For example, a typical Sunday in 1903 in the *New York Times* included advertisements from J. L. McLean & Company, who offer "our new Eighty Page Illustrated Wall Street Guide"; W. E. Woodend & Company, who urge readers to "send for our weekly Market Review"; Joseph Cowan & Company, who recommend to prospective customers their new book, "'Reveries of a Trader,' with side notes on successful speculation"; and Henry B. Clifford, "Bankers and Brokers of 10 Wall Street," who offer their booklet, "Fortunes That Grow in a Night." The most prominent advertisement, however, is from Haight & Freese, who were by far the largest operators of bucket shops in the United States in the late nineteenth and early twentieth centuries, with branches throughout the nation. In the preface to a revised and expanded 1898 edition of their *Guide to Investors*, they claim that the previous edition of 100,000 had sold out. Even if this figure is exaggerated, it is clear that free booklets such as Haight & Freese's reached a far larger and more diverse audience than their more traditional counterparts, issued by recognized publishing houses.

The manner of address of Haight & Freese's guide is explicitly populist, not because it presents a muckraking condemnation of the corruption of Wall Street, but because it makes an appeal to ordinary Americans, indicating that they, too, can have a slice of the profits that up until now have been confined to the financial elites: "Our manual is designed for the benefit of THE MILLION of busy people to whom the subject is of interest, but who require to have lengthy, tough details correctly explained and 'boiled down' for immediate and easy consumption." Far from viewing speculation as the fleecing of unwitting investors of small means by Wall Street manipulators, the booklet speaks to a republican ideal of independence of thought and a traditional belief in self-improvement, commenting that "when so instructed upon every detail (which before perusal of our MANUAL may have appeared to him like a mystery), the general reader will be in a position to operate with confidence upon his own judgment." Being familiar with the ins and outs of speculation is thus not a danger, but a duty: "It has become a necessity for all classes to be so informed if they are to have a fair chance of securing a portion of the immense profits which, year by year, are distributed by means of the rapidly accumulating number and value of Exchange securities."[11]

Although Haight & Freese suggest that their aim is merely to equip small investors with information about Wall Street's confusing ways, so they can make their own investment decisions, other guidebooks explicitly acknowledge that some novice investors may welcome "help" in figuring out which securities to buy—even to the extent of leaving that decision entirely at the discretion of the broker to whom they have entrusted their money. Many legitimate brokers during this period, however, note that they are reluctant to take on discretionary accounts, ostensibly because they can endanger friendships, even if the investments go bad through no fault of the broker. Other investment guidebooks counsel against discretionary accounts for the would-be investor of small means, because they can lead to irresponsible speculation with other people's assets, at best, and the fraudulent appropriation of a client's money, at worst. But many of the financial-advice booklets offered gratis to potential clients were aimed precisely to entice tyro speculators to lodge their savings with a broker, for him to use as he saw fit.

The rhetorical appeal of many of these fraudulent promotional brochures was, ironically, for potential customers to cultivate independence of judgment, not so much in choosing individual stocks (after all, that was what a discretionary account would do for them), but in choosing which broker to trust, given the unsavory reputation of Wall Street in the public imagination. The explanation that John H. Davis & Company gives is typical, in its insistence that the lack of trust is a result merely of ignorance about the mechanics of finance, an information gap that this booklet offers to plug, in a spirit of seeming philanthropy. "If there be any less confidence felt by the general public in this dealing with stockbrokers than with those in other branches of business," Davis explained, "it grows out of a lack of knowledge as to the rules and customs governing financial transactions, and the sole object of this little book is . . . to supply, in part, at least, the lacking information."[12] Having generously but disingenuously volunteered to provide the lay reader with a free education in the ways of Wall Street from the viewpoint of a supposedly well-informed and experienced insider, Davis's guide merely notes that "you should exercise the same good judgment as in your other business matters, by selecting a broker of standing and established reputation." There is an ideological legerdemain at the heart of these guides. On the one hand, they promise that an "Everyman" can be a speculator; on the other, they make clear that the stock market relies not on democratic access to capital, but on social capital. The coercive power of liberal individualism makes participation in the market seem necessary, yet the system was still heavily rigged in favor of the insiders. William E. Forrest (who distributed "Hoyle's Market Letter") also makes gestures toward the language of republican simplicity and plain speaking in his guide to Wall Street. Yet this guide hypocritically promises to protect the "lambs" at the very moment that it is trying to fleece them:

In putting forth this pamphlet the Author has no scheme to work. He has tried to give, in plain language, the facts, or some of them at least, about the game in Wall Street. He has made no effort at style in writing. Simple English and the 'calling a spade a spade' is what he has striven for. He does not set up to be a reformer. He accepts human nature as he finds it. He hopes that this little work may save a 'lamb' or two from the sacrifice. . . . Possibly, if the public learn something about the game, they may avoid making fatal mistakes. If the public should learn to play the game so as to win, that in itself would do more to break it up than anything else could.[13]

Like many other guides targeted at the investor of small means, Forrest's *The Game in Wall Street, and How to Play It Successfully* combines its more abstract pontifications on the nature of the stock market and the rationale for price movements with handy rules-of-thumb for would-be speculators, such as: "Hint Number One: After prices have been *declining for four or five months* and then come, comparatively speaking, to a standstill, simply moving up and down over a narrow range, *do not be tempted to take the bear side of the market*. . . . Hint Number Two: After the market has gone on for some time in the manner above mentioned, there will come a day or two of almost complete stagnation in the market. . . . Then you can buy stocks with safety and hold them for a good rise" (emphasis in original).[14] Forrest makes contradictory claims for the kind of knowledge that his guide imparts. On the one hand, he avers that speculation is a science, and that "one ought not to play this game at haphazard." He recommends "keep[ing] an accurate record of the fluctuations in prices," but he does not agree that the prices of stocks are governed by rigid laws of supply and demand. Instead, he insists that "these fluctuations are not due to chance but are *the result of design*" (emphasis in original), and learning to interpret the charts of market fluctuations will enable a person to have "a fairly good idea of what the pools are doing."[15] If speculation is a science, it is because price movements are governed by the reliably predictable human nature of the greedy pools of bulls and bears battling for control of the market. On the other hand, the knowledge to be cultivated by the amateur speculator is like the knowledge of an expert card player, who understands both the rules of the game and the psychological traits of the expert players: "When once this point [that the accumulation and distribution of stocks is orchestrated by pools of powerful investors] is clear in your mind all the mysteries will become plain to you. The game in Wall Street is a GAME OF HUMAN NATURE. The pool generals are men who study crops and politics, both domestic and foreign, and legislation and finance. They know when the time is ripe to start a bull or a bear campaign, and when they can afford to end it. . . . The cards they use are both 'marked and stacked,' and they take no chances."[16]

In reply to a potential objection that prices are governed by physical laws of nature, Forrest insists that "the factors that you mention as determining the prices of stocks have an undoubted influence, but, as you will see before you finish these pages, these commercial factors are not *the* determining influences directing the course of the stock market" (emphasis in original). The people who "run the game," Forrest insists, "allow for these factors and arrange their plans in accordance with them, but the general course of prices in the Stock Exchange is determined by human intelligence and not by chance or natural conditions."[17] Although amateurs cannot hope to go head-to-head with the market makers, given their expert understanding of both the wider economic landscape and the inside scoop on manipulations, readers are led to believe that they can nevertheless use their knowledge of human nature to turn speculation into a game of skill, rather than one of chance.

In a similar fashion, despite the title of A. N. Ridgely's *The Study and Science of Stock Speculation*, it offers advice not so much on the scientific foundations of finance as an insider's account of "the game, and how it is played." Asserting that 90 percent of transactions are speculative, and of those speculations, 90 percent are manipulated, Ridgely promises to instruct purchasers of his ten-cent pamphlet in the methods of the market manipulators (who "leave nothing to chance"), so they are not conned by these individuals.[18] Women and amateurs are warned to steer clear of this treacherous world, but the daring would-be speculator can glean enough of an education from the pamphlet to arm himself against the pitfalls of speculation. Ridgely warns against others who charge a high price for tips, but he insists that financial letters, if honest, are worth it. His advice is mainly based on an amalgam of market fundamentals, common sense, and Wall Street lore, but he is also willing to throw inside information into this contradictory mix, as well as chartist techniques, such as "Catching the Turns" and "Limited Pyramiding." Like other guidebooks for the general public, Ridgely is not doctrinaire in his account of investment methods, but instead, in a spirit of pragmatism, offers an eclectic mix of approaches.

Lewis C. Van Riper's *The Ins and Outs of Wall Street*—another promotional booklet of dubious legitimacy liberally advertised in the Sunday newspapers—combines a seemingly objective guide to finance for the layperson with an explicit call for readers to invest their funds with him for speculation. In contrast to the purists of chartism, Van Riper appeals to the pragmatic authority of hard-won experience, rather than any scientific laws of investment. He confesses that he came to Wall Street in 1888 but lost all his money in unsuccessful speculations, and therefore decided to stay and study how to recoup his losses. Although Van Riper's book is precisely the kind of promotional scheme for discretionary trading that more-respectable authorities (such as the Hughes Committee) warned against, he takes a dig at would-be speculators who, unlike those training to be lawyers or doctors, do not "read only those books written by those learned in the profession," but instead "read the Sunday newspapers and all of the flashing advertisements." The problem, as he sees it, is that "there are no standard works on speculation written by experienced, successful speculators," thereby insinuating that other guides are based merely on theory or a moralizing stance, written by those without direct involvement in the market. He insists instead that "speculation is a profession" and that the brokers on Wall Street are marked out by their "strict integrity and honest dealing," in part because their deals on the floor of the Exchange are conducted with "a nod of the head or motion of the hand" that is just as binding as a bond or a mortgage.[19] Van Riper is unequivocal and unapologetic that he is a speculator, not a broker, but he regards it as a scientific profession and thus is very particular to distance himself from both bucket shops and those who furnish market tips for a fee. In the Wall Street pecking order, it would seem, there is always someone else less respectable who can stand in as a negative analogue to underscore the author's claim to propriety. Appealing to the bullish sentiment of most amateur investors, he maintains that speculation is not mere gambling, because the real value of American industry is indeed increasing.

A speculator, Van Riper informs his readers, must learn to read the signs and symptoms of market movements, combining (in a wayward clash of metaphors) the skills of the weather forecaster and the physician: "Wall Street may be said to be the financial pulse of America, and it is the first to scent a coming storm." Speculative values are presented as natural phenomena, governed by the laws of nature, having "their ebb and flow just as surely as the tides of the ocean."[20] As "proof" of the accuracy of his predictions, Van Riper reproduces selected market reports from the *New York Evening Sun*, together with a gloss on how his market advice was subsequently borne out by market events (the gloss remains necessary, because it seems that the market cannot entirely speak for itself). Yet for all its helpful maxims and seemingly objective advice, *The Ins and Outs of Wall Street* is ultimately an advertisement for customers to place their funds under Van Riper's management and share in the profits—and presumably also the losses, although these are not mentioned. It comes as little surprise to learn that Van Riper had previously been implicated in a "racing information bureau" scam, and was "keenly sought" by detectives in 1900, along with other discretionary-account traders (such as John MacKenzie), after customers claimed that although they had been informed that their investment had made a profit, they had been unable to get their money. Detective McCluskey noted that "as a preparer and distributor of catchy, fool-trap circulars . . . [Van Riper] has no equal."[21] In 1920, Van Riper was finally imprisoned for five years for using the mails to sell fraudulent stock promotions, as well as for running a bucket shop.[22]

J. Overton Paine's booklet on *Speculating in Wall Street in Margins* came in a handy pocket size and was likewise written for potential bucket shop customers. Its tone is one of informal, manly camaraderie, like that used in reports on sporting endeavors. Full of the latest slang, it offers instruction via anecdotes taken from the author's own experience. It makes the intriguing argument that speculation will allow the humble provincial to feel connected to the pulse of global commerce: "Just pause and reflect up on this for a moment! Do you not feel interested in the possibilities of speculation? Judiciously conducted operations in Bonds, Stocks, Cotton, and Grain upon moderate margins enable one to invest a small sum so that it will yield very large profits; it also puts you in touch with the financial and commercial interests of the world." Paine tells how he began to see through the wiles of market manipulators, and the booklet shows how the small investor can likewise resist being fleeced. "It was at this time [1899]," Paine recalls, "that I conceived the idea that the 'Flower' tip to 'Buy B.R.T., for 200' was a dodge to catch the poor outsider, and I began to wage war against the 'Flower Crowd.'"[23] In addition to the authority of direct experience, the booklet includes testimonial letters from bankers and brokers that give it a gloss of respectability, but ultimately it is a direct promotion for placing funds with J. Overton Paine & Company, a bucket shop operation.[24] Given the dubious nature and legality of bucket shops (many of which were not much more than betting parlors masquerading as brokerages), it is with breath-taking chutzpah that Paine condemns advance-information bureaus, admonishing readers that "speculators and investors should seek more information from their brokers, in lieu of tips sent out by irresponsible news agencies and the 'tipsters' of Wall Street, if they expect their accounts to show satisfactory results."[25]

Henry Clews & Company's *Investment Guide* was also issued in a convenient pocket-sized format, but, unlike Paine's anecdotal promotion, it contains merely sparse digests of essential market information on railroad and industrial stocks and bonds. It is written not for the amateur speculator, but for the businessman who merely requires accurate information, rather than guidance (or, perhaps more accurately, for those who liked to think of themselves in this way).

Confirming its appeal to a professional audience, a testimonial from the *Journal of Commerce and Commercial Bulletin* is included in Clews & Company's guide, describing it as "one of the most compact and useful hand-books for investors issued in Wall Street. . . . All the essential facts as to earnings, expenses, capitalization, dividends, etc., of the important railroads and industrial corporations are selected and condensed with excellent judgment into a compact little manual of over 100 pages, which can readily be carried in the pocket or kept for reference in the pigeonhole."[26]

Positioned somewhere between the lively free guides distributed by untrustworthy brokers, and the deliberately dry ones issued by their more sober counterparts, are those guides that aimed to present a more unbiased overview of market mechanisms (particularly in the light of the new discipline of technical analysis), but targeted for a lay audience, rather than a professional one. For example, William Harman Black's *The Real Wall Street* is written specifically for the novitiate. Black was a lawyer, not a broker, and his book is designed to teach readers the basic elements of finance by following each stage of a stock market transaction as a mininarrative.[27] To do this, he gives generic names to each of the actors involved—such as Mr. Long, and Sellshort & Company—and thus personalizes the sequence of events in the buying and selling of investments. It is noticeable that Black does not moralize about the stock market or impose a distinction between sober investment for the long term and short-term risky speculation, but instead details the mechanics of purchasing securities, and even includes copies of the various forms employed by brokers, in order to familiarize outsiders with the logistics of share dealing.

Unlike the earlier genre of city mysteries, H. M. Williams's *The Key to Wall Street Mysteries and Methods* is not a gothic extravaganza of vice in lower Manhattan, but is a user-friendly guide for the public on investment and speculation, with no moral distinction between the two.[28] Williams adopts an informal tone, addressing his readers in the second person, and using confessions of his own costly experiences on Wall Street to illustrate his points. Like other unrepentant traders who have relied on particular tricks of technical analysis, he insists that he would have made more money not by adopting different strategies, but by following the advice laid out in his book even more closely. Novice speculators fail not because of the inherent riskiness of the market, but from ignorance, he contends, especially in a failure to understand the wiles of market manipulators. Like many others, Williams compares speculation with astronomy and weather forecasting, noting that scientific principles in all three disciplines now permit a transition from superstition to modern modes of rational and probabilistic prediction. Yet for Williams, successful speculation remains as much an art as a science, achieved, like other professions, such as medicine, through both education and on-the-ground experience. The book thus combines general reflections on the nature of speculation—most notably in an extended allegory about the path to Successville not being easy to navigate—with specific schemes for trading, based on tape reading and chart analysis.

John F. Hume's *The Art of Investing* was compiled from articles he had originally written for *Popular Science Monthly*. He had signed the magazine articles under his own name, and they had attracted "considerable correspondence." So, for the book version, he published under the appellation "A New York Broker," because, like H. M. Williams (apparently also a pseudonym), Hume, as a member of the New York Stock Exchange, presumably did not want to risk breaching its rules on advertising. In the book, "somewhat in the nature of a supplement, has been added a chapter on speculation," he notes. The additional section explores in more detail the mechanics of the New York Stock Exchange and warns, in particular, about the dangers of watered stock. Although an insider, he is critical of speculation when carried to excess: like a cuttlefish, whose dark ink stains the water surrounding it, he explains, the "Wall Street monster . . . by the example of its few conspicuous successes and its general demoralization, so impregnates the atmosphere of the whole country with the speculative mania, that thousands and thousands can not resist it."[29] A revised version of Hume's book was later reissued by market analyst John Moody's publishing company and credited Hume by name. Renamed *The Art of Wise Investing*, it includes the chapter on speculation from Hume, as well as a new first part, which sets out general advice on how to err on the side of caution in choosing securities. This version insists that there is a clear distinction between investment and speculation (the former is concerned primarily with safely preserving one's principal, while the latter chases a higher rate of return, potentially at the risk of losing one's capital). The guide aims to teach readers how to choose investments carefully and, the author (presumably Moody) insists, is "the concrete result of many years' experience and study of Wall Street conditions and methods." The work acknowledges that it possibly errs on the conservative side, and it repeatedly invokes the goal of "safety." Although would-be investors are advised to consult a reliable broker, the book also insists that they should learn for themselves how to identify sensible investments. Moody warns against merely following "fixed rules," exhorting instead that every security should be judged on its own merits. Moody insists that doing one's own research is vital, and he therefore recommends to readers *The Anatomy of a Railroad Report and Ton-Mile Cost* by Thomas Woodlock (editor of the *Wall Street Journal*), which is written "so that the uninitiated as well as the expert can understand" it.[30] He also praises the fledgling industry of corporate and financial statistics, with the volume, in effect, serving as an extended promotion for Moody's Bureau of Corporation Statistics and its *Manual of Statistics*.

Overall, the aim of *The Art of Wise Investing* is to encourage readers not to rely on stock market authorities, but to take responsibility for their own investment decisions, not least by buying Moody's other publications and services. The irony—as the popularity of the free investment guides and market letters suggests—is that readers might well have bought his book precisely in the hope of gaining handy rules-of-thumb for the "uninitiated" on how to invest. Instead, researching the endless potential pitfalls before buying a particular security threatens to become a full-time occupation, turning an amateur into a professional. Likewise, although the book aims to promote the idea of conservative investing as a safe alternative to risky speculation, it presents the stock market as such a minefield of potential complexity and deception that the seemingly clear distinction between investment and speculation begins to dissolve. Indeed, the author even warns that "there is such a thing as going too far in the matter of prudence," with the alarming result that "the investor may pay too dearly for safety."[31]

Thomas Gibson's *The Pitfalls of Speculation* was also issued by Moody's publishing house. It, too, does not see a problem with speculation per se, only with speculation conducted in the wrong way. Based on "a careful examination, covering a period of ten years," it decries following mechanical rules as much as it warns against chasing insider tips, unsubstantiated enthusiasms, and blind luck. Unexpected swings in the market are not caused by "manipulation and trickery," but are the result of the vast majority of purchases by the public (the "lambs") being made at the wrong time. In contrast, the "shrewd minority" are able to "foresee" market movements and take advantage of them to accumulate profits.[32] Gibson advocates applying "intelligent" business methods to speculative investments, which in part involve developing "clear thought and sound judgment." Since "speculation is a safe business when business methods are applied to it," the message is that readers would be crazy *not* to take a plunge: "So great are the opportunities offered by speculative changes, that, with proper methods and self control, the poor man cannot afford to overlook them."[33]

In the first decade of the twentieth century, Samuel Armstrong Nelson published several advice books on the stock market. In them, he expanded the ideas that Charles Dow had begun to develop in his editorials in the *Wall Street Journal* into a full-fledged investment strategy. In *The ABC of Wall Street*, Nelson compiled fifteen of Dow's editorials, covering topics ranging from "Trading in Cotton" to a "Dictionary of Wall Street Words, Names, and Phrases," and from "The Daily Work of a Broker" to "Calculating Bond Values." The tone is sober and factual, and the volume combines disparate elements—for instance, tables of "Lard Fractional Profits" with illustrations of the exterior of the Chicago Board of Trade. In the preface, Nelson states that he thinks the lay reader merely wants an objective and nontechnical account of how Wall Street works, rather than specific trading strategies or market tips:

> The editor presents this little volume to the American public in the belief that it will fill a demand. He has been asked many times for just such information as the book gives. He has endeavored, briefly, to present in an A B C way the methods of the men and the mechanism of Wall Street. He has tried to avoid statistics and details that are too technical for those other than the initiated. . . . This is in no sense a book treating of "How to Speculate Successfully," for much nonsense and very little common sense has been written on that subject; nor is it a history of Wall Street, for such a book would of necessity be much larger; nor is it a book for the busy men of Wall Street, who know, perhaps better than the editor, all the facts herewith presented; but it is what it purports to be—the A B C of Wall Street.[34]

Nelson admits that the manipulation of the stock market "is a scientific game in itself, . . . the successful rules of which can only be explained by those who have had the experience."[35] It is possible, he notes, that the notorious stock operator James Keene "would tell how he does it if you wrote and asked him—but the chances are that he would not." Nelson warns against "those gentlemen (?) who with suspicious frankness tell you in the advertising columns of the daily press that they can see through stock movements and manipulation with the aid of 'charts' and 'systems' [and] would bankrupt the Bank of England if they had the opportunity." Their services, he continues, are "as worthless as those of a fortune-teller."[36]

In contrast, in *The ABC of Stock Speculation*, Nelson—presumably responding to consumer demand—directly addresses the question of whether it is possible to make money by speculative trading, and whether there is, after all, some value to the "charts" and "systems" he had earlier ridiculed. He offers a whole chapter on the various emerging technical strategies of tape and chart analysis, such as the book method, the theory of double tops, the law of averages, and—his own preferred method—Dow's theory of action and reaction in stock prices (a "law" which states, for example, that a "secondary market movement" will be three-eighths of the "primary movement").[37] The problem, as Nelson sees it, is not so much to predict the market as to develop a trading strategy that actually delivers reliable results. At the very least, he advises, charting prices can alert outsiders to whether prices are being manipulated by insiders. Although he concurs with the basic assumption of technical analysis—that recent prices are indicators of future ones—he insists that a trading strategy must also develop an understanding of the underlying fundamental value of particular securities and of market conditions in general. Like other guides, such as Pratt's *The Work of Wall Street*, Nelson's *ABC of Stock Speculation* advocates learning to read not just the immediate trend of prices coming over the ticker tape, but the broader direction of the economy as a whole that, he insists, is not random and chaotic: "The best way of reading the market is from the standpoint of values. The market is not like a balloon plunging hither and thither in the wind."[38] For Nelson, what distinguishes speculation from gambling is that it involves an element of skill, unlike those who blindly "take a flyer." In his guide, the specifics of technical approaches, based on chart readings, are tempered with pages of more-generalizing axioms that distill the collective wisdom of Wall Street, coupled with advice on achieving the right kind of attitude for successful trading.

In *Bonds and Stocks: The Elements of Successful Investing*, Roger Babson, a former broker who pioneered chart analysis as a profession, offered advice similar to that of Nelson.[39] Babson suggested that, more than luck, successful speculation requires education in the laws of the market, which, like aspects of other professions, can only be achieved by careful study. The would-be investor should therefore pay attention not only to the surface noise of the stock exchange, but to the deeper causes of market movements, which, Babson insists, are not the result of accident or chance. Babson's book, like his other publications and market-analysis services, focuses on the power of the chart to present a clear-eyed overview of the underlying direction of the market and represents a self-consciously modern approach to speculative investing.

In addition to the work of professional market analysts like Moody and Babson, who emphasized the regularity and predictability of the price movements made visible through the tape and the charts, in the first decades of the twentieth century, academic treatises, congressional reports, and partisan histories, as well as official publications encouraged by the Committee on Library of the New York Stock Exchange, likewise focused on the scientific nature of the price setting carried out by the cadre of highly skilled and honorable members of the NSYE (usually viewed in pointed contrast to other exchanges and bucket shops).[40] Led by R. T. H. Halsey, the Committee on Library took on the role of public relations for the NYSE, and it redeployed the language of Populist and Progressive critics to argue that ordinary Americans should be allowed to trade in the "free and open market" without regulatory interference. The U.S. Senate's Industrial Commission and New York's Hughes Committee similarly argued that what was needed above all was transparency of information, so investors of small means could make prudent investment decisions.[41] The NYSE apologist William Van Antwerp, responding to a suggestion from one of the witnesses interviewed for the Hughes Commission—that the proliferation of stock tickers was, in itself, a prime cause of unwise speculation on the part of the ignorant public—argued instead that that ticker "is essential to publicity" and is a safeguard against manipulation, part of the arsenal of modern information sources that makes the stock market a democratic place.[42]

The Stock Ticker

In contrast to Van Antwerp's pseudo-populist faith in the objective, transparent, democratic ability of the stock ticker to turn the market into a level playing field for all investors (where manipulation would be impossible), many of the more vernacular guides to speculation outlined above provide specific instructions on how to decipher the potential manipulation of prices by learning to read the market and its opaque signals. Moody and Hume's *The Art of Wise Investing*, for example, insists that speculation involves learning to read financial instruments with something akin to a hermeneutic of suspicion: "Read it all, the little type as well as the big type, the endorsements, the coupons and all. Don't take someone else's word for it. Examine the seal, the signatures, even the embellishments."[43] Black's *Real Wall Street* includes a chapter on "Reading the Market Page in the Newspapers," while Babson's publishing company offered an entire book on *How to Read the Money Article*.[44] Publications such as Henry Hall's *How Money Is Made in Security Investments* emphasize the need to learn to read the "cautionary signals," to decode "the signs" that are legible in market prices, while Van Riper's *Ins and Outs of Wall Street* insists that Wall Street "is the barometer of the nation, but in order to read this barometer accurately we must study carefully its code of signals and learn the meaning of each market movement."[45]

From the 1870s onward, guides to the stock market increasingly equate reading the market with reading the ticker tape and the charts that digest its record of fluctuations. "Nothing, outside of newspapers," Black notes, "is so universally read as 'the tape,' by which is meant the paper ribbon upon which the 'ticker' prints its continuous bulletins."[46] Thus Williams's *Key to Wall Street Mysteries* includes a detailed introduction to different strategies of trading, with a section simply called "Reading the Tape." With the emergence of chartism in the last decade of the nineteenth century, publications, such as Nelson's *ABC of Speculation*, included whole chapters on a variety of "Methods of Reading the Market," while the *Ticker* gave precise instructions on the skill of tape reading, many elements of which are still cited today in guides to day trading for the lay investor.[47]

With the introduction of the stock ticker in the late 1860s, the general public were barred from the floor of the New York Stock Exchange, making it impossible for nonmembers to observe market transactions in any detail while they were taking place (as we will see in chapter 3, the view from the visitors' gallery could only provide a general impression of the frenzied crowd on the floor of the Exchange, rather than direct knowledge of particular transactions and prices). As Alex Preda argues in *Framing Finance*, however, the development of the stock ticker permitted a new vantage point for the activity of Wall Street, allowing tape readers to observe from afar individual transactions taking place on the floor of the Exchange in near real time, through the medium of printed symbols on the tape. The stock ticker, Preda concludes, "contributed to a radical abstraction and reconfiguration of the visual experience of the market."[48]

The stock ticker was pioneered in 1867 by Edward Calahan, of the American Telegraph Company, with Thomas Edison producing a more reliable version in 1869. The ticker was a development arising from the telegraph, having two wheels that could be controlled automatically: one printed the letter abbreviation of the company whose stock was being traded, and the other the price and volume of that stock. Apart from its increased speed and range of transmission, the ticker's automatic printing also made it more economical than the existing electric telegraph, which needed a skilled operator at either end. Prior to the invention of the stock ticker, messenger boys would run from the NYSE to the neighboring brokerages in the Wall Street district. With data supplied from the floor of the stock exchanges in New York and Boston, and the commodity exchanges in Chicago and elsewhere, tickers were installed in stockbrokers' offices, and even in some private individuals' offices, beginning in the late 1860s.[49] After the turn of the century, ticker use mushroomed, with tickers supplying a steady stream of financial and general news not just in legitimate brokerage offices, but also in bucket shops and upscale restaurants in Manhattan. The number of tickers in operation in this period is disputed, not least because of the discrepancy between licensed tickers in legitimate brokerages affiliated with the NYSE and the far larger number employed in bucket shops. Looking back from 1927, the *Magazine of Wall Street* estimated that there were 1,200 tickers in 1902, while E. C. Stedman's edited history of the New York Stock Exchange claimed that there were as many as 23,000 subscribers in 1905.[50] The popularization of the ticker did not, however, proceed inexorably. From the 1870s to about 1915, the stock and commodity exchanges engaged in a legal struggle to prevent bucket shops accessing, via the ticker, what they argued was proprietorial financial information.[51]

The stock ticker transformed financial information. As Preda notes, prior to the ticker, price quotations were slow, inaccurate, not standardized, and sometimes even forged. Summaries of price quotations that were printed in market circulars were always immediately out-of-date, and also often meaningless, because they were given without reference to price variations. Before the ticker, brokers were connected to their customers either in person or, more usually, by letter. The correspondence often combined personal and business matters; its aim was to establish a relationship of trust, rather than convey rapidly fluctuating prices. The advent of the ticker, therefore, created a shift in the nature of trust: whereas the status, character, and personal connections of the broker had previously conferred authority on market information, people began to place their trust in the impersonal technical accuracy of the ticker machine and in the professional authority of the emerging networks of brokers, market analysts, and exchanges that sought to maintain their social status, along with their monopoly over price data, by persuading customers of the need for their services. With the invention of the ticker, the site of speculation was increasingly removed from the face-to-face action on the stock exchange floor, with traders instead adopting a more impersonal engagement with the market as an idealized entity, rather than as an actual, embodied, physical space in Wall Street.[52]

Scholars working in the social studies of finance have advanced the argument that technologies of finance—including economic models and the practices of market specialists—do not merely provide a better lubrication for the wheels of financial machinery, but actively shape how markets develop, how people come to represent those markets, and even the very sense of subjectivity of market participants. Contributing to this field, Preda thus argues that the stock ticker cannot be thought of simply as a more efficient way of transmitting price information. It is, rather, a form of "socio-technical agency," part of an assemblage of technologies, discourses, and practices that reconfigure the very market that the ticker is purported to represent more accurately. The ticker, Preda suggests, encouraged an abstract understanding of the market, coupled with a disciplining of its economic subject into habits of rational calculation and unceasing concentration on the endless flow of prices. The streaming ticker tape thus prompted a form of reading the market up close, followed, in the first decades of the twentieth century, by the fledgling cottage industry of technical analysis, which produced charts enabling a view of the market from afar. The tape created a new sense of the market as a continuous, uninterrupted flow of rising and falling numbers, instead of a staggered series of semiprivate agreements on prices formed in the open-cry auctions of the exchanges.

In the "modern" financial-advice literature from the turn of the twentieth century, the stated aim is not to gain inside information through personal connections with the powerful cliques supposedly pulling the strings of the market, but to turn oneself into a recording machine, much like the ticker itself. The goal is thus to eliminate emotion and personality, in order to become totally in tune with the mechanical rhythm of the market, which is viewed, in an of-the-minute metaphor, as an electric motor: "The market is like a slowly revolving wheel: whether the wheel will continue to revolve in the same direction, stand still, or reverse depends entirely upon the forces which comes into contact with its hub and tread. Even when the contact is broken, and nothing remains to affect its course, the wheel retains a certain impulse from the most recent dominating force, and revolves until it comes to a standstill or is subjected to other influences."[53] As is the case with this quotation, some of the best expressions of the attributes required of the would-be tape reader are to be found in the *Ticker*, established in 1907 by the financial journalist Richard Wyckoff (writing under the pen name "Rollo Tape"), who was allied to other early chartists, such as Roger Babson and Samuel Nelson. The magazine (the forerunner of the *Magazine of Wall Street*) was aimed at the autodidact speculator of modest means and was designed to promote and democratize the new discipline of technical analysis:

> A little group of men, of which the writer made one, were discussing the attitude of the so-called public toward speculative and investment matters a few days ago and in the course of the conversation one gentleman, who is connected with a prominent stock exchange house, remarked on the growing astuteness of small investors. . . . "It is remarkable," he said, "how widespread education on topics of this kind has become. Every man of ordinary intelligence knows something about the tariff, the monetary question, the rebate system, and the inflation of corporate stocks. Twenty, or even ten years ago these things were matters to be understood only by politicians or students of economics."[54]

In *Studies in Tape Reading*, Wyckoff used choice extracts from the *Ticker* to produce a book-length, composite theory of tape reading and chart analysis, which had been set out piecemeal in the magazine:

> The Tape Reader evolves himself into an automaton which takes note of a situation, weighs it, decides upon a course, and gives an order. There is no quickening of

the pulse, no nerves, no hopes or fears. The result produces neither elation nor depression. There is equanimity before, during, and after the trade. The Scalper [someone who looks to take a quick profit] is a bob-tailed car with rattling windows, a jouncing motion, and a strong tendency to jump the track. The Tape Reader is like a Pullman coach, which travels smoothly and steadily along the roadbed of the tape, acquiring direction and speed from the market engine, and being influenced by nothing whatever.[55]

Wyckoff elaborates further on the qualities of concentration needed by this new breed of scientific speculator: "By proper mental equipment we do not mean the mere ability to take a loss, define the trend, or execute some other move characteristic of the professional trader. We refer to the active or dormant qualities in his make-up; viz., the power to drill himself into the right mental attitude; to stifle his emotions, such as fear, anxiety, elation, recklessness; to train his mind into obedience so that it recognizes but one master—the tape."[56] Even a bucket shop drummer like Van Riper concurs that a successful speculator should "drop all sentiment, pay no attention to news gossip, points, or tips, but merely become a machine with sufficient power to execute your orders according to market movements."[57]

In these how-to-speculate guides for the common man, predicting market movements is presented as a mixture of practical know-how and hard science, rhetorically reclaiming it as a respectable and democratic form of business activity, free from the taint of immoral and irrational gambling. Speculative finance is thus legitimized, because it no longer seems to involve succumbing to animal spirits or to a sinful desire to get something for nothing.[58] Instead, the speculator figures as the epitome of cool, detached manliness, influenced by no one, embodying a rational subjectivity; someone whose mastery of the market enables him to attain a sense of individual sovereignty, even in the age of corporate capitalism, which seemed to some commentators to make a mockery of the traditional republican value of self-reliance. The ideal speculator delineated by these guides is indeed a man. The bucket shop promoter John B. McKenzie's *Bulls and Bears of Wall Street*, for example, declares: "Women make poor speculators. Without the assistance of a man a woman in Wall Street is like a ship without a rudder. Those members of the fair sex who read these statements may take exception, but I assure them that I can pay no greater compliment than by saying she does not possess the qualifications necessary to the successful operator. . . . With all due respect to the modern woman and her ability in the world of commerce, in addition to being too impulsive and impressionable, she does not possess the mental equipment of her brothers."[59]

According to these accounts, tape-reading individuals can regain their own economic destiny by predicting the future, not through providential divination, or even a deep-seated understanding of political events and economic trends that might cause prices to change, but through familiarization with the microscopic patterns of price fluctuations themselves. In the view of many of these guides, speculation is not gambling, but informed prediction, based on a study of recent trends in prices on the tape, following the dictum that "what has happened in the past is the best guide to the future."[60] Tape reading, Wyckoff asserts, is "the science of determining from the tape the immediate trend of prices. It is a method of forecasting, from what appears on the tape *now*, what is likely to appear in the future" (emphasis in original).[61] Far removed from the turmoil of the trading pits, the dispassionate tape reader has a supposedly objective viewpoint that is, ironically, seen as even more privileged than the insider's view of a member of the NYSE, because it is safely removed from the distracting noise and personalities of the actual traders on the floor of the Exchange. Tape reading, according to these guides for the lay investor, affords a bird's-eye perspective on the sublime vastness of the financial market, and even the whole economy, with Wyckoff, for example, comparing the tape reader to the general manager of a store, overseeing all the information produced by each part of the business, in a fantasy of total surveillance, combined with an internal division of labor within the brain of the trader that equates with the reorganization of a company in the age of managerial capitalism:

> A Tape Reader is like the manager of a department store; into his office are poured hundreds of reports of sales made the various departments. He notes the general trend of business—whether demand is heavy or light throughout the store, but lends special attention to the lines in which demand is abnormally strong or weak. . . . A floor trader who stands in one crowd all day is like the buyer for one department—he sees more quickly than anyone else the demand for that class of goods, but has no way of comparing it to that prevailing in other parts of the store. He may be trading on the long side of Union Pacific, which has a strong upward trend, when suddenly a break in another stock will demoralize the market in Union Pacific, and he will be forced to compete with others who have stocks to sell. The Tape Reader, on the other hand, from his perch at the ticker, enjoys a bird's eye view of the whole field. When serious weakness develops in any quarter, he is quick to note, weigh, and act.[62]

The fantasy sketched out in these manuals of tape reading for the lay investor is not merely seeing the financescape as a whole by attuning and disciplining one's channels of perception to the rhythms of the ticker. In contrast to many of the early chartists, who were keen to emphasize the need for their expert services to make sense of the seemingly overwhelming mass of data, guides to tape reading instead held out to the amateur speculator the dream of becoming the master of the entire information-processing machine of the market.

"I Didn't Like the Way Sugar Was Doing Its Hesitating"

So far we have seen how financial advice was transformed over the course of the second half of the nineteenth century: from a series of Brahmin warnings to the common man about the depredations of Wall Street, to assertions that speculation should no longer be the preserve of the elites. At the same time, more-official accounts of the stock market in general, and the New York Stock Exchange in particular, deployed a similar populist register that promoted the independent judgment of investors and the transparency of financial information, even if, at the same time, they continued to insist on the exclusivity of their expert knowledge and their monopoly over the prices set by the Exchange. Moreover, the rapid adoption of the stock ticker meant that would-be speculators did not merely have access to ever-more-detailed and democratically available financial information, but, by training themselves to become dispassionate and focused readers of this economic barometer, they could, in theory, learn to see the underlying patterns of market movements that, chartists argued, were not the result of external factors (such as secret cabals or investor psychology), but the internal mechanism of the market itself. The second part of this chapter will reexamine this account of a slow shift to abstraction, impersonality, and rational calculability that supposedly helped make speculation seem sensible, arguing instead that popular guides to Wall Street, in both factual and fictional registers, presented the market in general, and tape reading in particular, as a supernatural practice, as much as a natural one. The financial imaginary during this period, I want to suggest, is continually haunted by the glimmerings of an uncanny, humanlike intentionality behind the invisible hand of impersonal market coordination.

In addition to revisiting some of the examples of financial advice outlined above, I will turn to Wall Street stories by Edwin Lefèvre and other writers—in particular, *Reminiscences of a Stock Operator*, the semifictionalized autobiography of the legendary Wall Street trader Jesse Livermore, ghostwritten by Lefèvre.[63] First published as a series of articles in the *Saturday Evening Post*, this book is still in print and continues to be regarded as an inspirational and even a practical guide by the army of amateur online day traders and modern-day tape readers. Lefèvre's story of Larry Livingston (the name he gives to Livermore) is an instructional tale of the self-taught, rags-to-riches success of a stock market legend. Livingston, the son of a New England farmer, left home at age fourteen to make his way in the world, with his first job, in 1890, being to chalk up the prices on the quotations board as they came over the wire in a broker's office in Boston. He began to speculate in bucket shops, and then in regular brokerages, earning his reputation as the "Boy Plunger." He went on to make and lose several fortunes over the course of his career.[64] *Reminiscences of a Stock Operator* is a fascinating but oddly repetitious mixture of self-serving accounts of Livingston's success (attributed not to luck, but skill), liberally sprinkled with advice, axioms, and lessons learned.[65] His basic philosophy is that "the market never lies," and in some respects, *Reminiscences* is the classic instructional manual for the ordinary American on how to train oneself in the discipline required for reading and decoding the endless stream of anonymous and abstract price fluctuations that make up the market.

At first Livingston, as a young boy chalking up the quotations on the board, does not think of stock prices as reflecting the underlying value of an individual company, or even referring to any actual productive industry. Instead, he sees them merely as numbers, which move up and down in repeatable patterns that have no reference to outside causes. The numbers Livingston chalks up are, for him at this stage, entirely abstract, the prices in his mind representing not so much traditional measures of fundamental corporate value as entirely free-floating and self-referential signifiers in the endless chain of differences the ticker churns out. "Those quotations did not represent prices of stocks to me, so many dollars per share," he admits. "They were numbers. Of course, they meant something. They were always changing. It was all I had to be interested in—the changes. Why did they change? I didn't know. I didn't care."[66] Unlike the emerging cadre of technical analysts, producing charts in the back office of some of the brokers that Livingston knows, his knowledge of price patterns is not achieved by plotting meticulous diagrams. Instead, he carries in his head a rough-and-ready sense of the typical movements of individual stocks, based solely on his observation of previous patterns. Even when faced with potential ruin later in his career, Livingston continues to insist that his campaigns against rival factions in the market are abstracted from the level of petty human concerns (although, by this stage, he has amplified his reading of the stock ticker from pure price fluctuations to broader "basic conditions" of the economy, as revealed on the tape): "Fiction writers, clergymen, and women are fond of alluding to the floor of the Stock Exchange as a boodlers' battlefield and to Wall Street's daily business as a fight. It is quite dramatic but utterly misleading. I do not think that my business is strife and contest. I never fight either individuals or speculative cliques. I merely differ in opinion—that is, my reading of basic conditions. What playwrights call battles of business are not fights between human beings. They are merely tests of business vision" (189). At least for part of Livingston's life story, as told by Lefèvre, market activity is viewed not as the human-scale drama that some other writers in the period perceive (Lefèvre himself is the obvious example), but a contest between rival interpretations of the symbols on the tape, the objective numbers seemingly far removed from individual passions.

Like *Reminiscences of a Stock Operator,* many of the guides to tape reading from this period emphasize the impersonal, objective side of speculation, which requires no knowledge of the secret combinations and pools of Wall Street. At the same time, however, they also betray a residual conviction that the stream of prices printed on the tape indeed reveals a fundamentally human drama. *The Art of Wise Investing,* for example, declares that "the stories of its magnificent triumphs, and of its equally magnificent wrecks, read like tales from 'The Arabian Nights'; some of them like passages from Dante's 'Inferno.'"[67] Moreover, many writers of Wall Street stories during this period ruefully acknowledge that, for those equipped to translate them, the dramas hammered out on the tape can outdo anything a mere hack can produce. For these writers, the tape is both an encoding of the theatre unfolding on the stock exchange floor and a powerful kind of writing in its own right, which produces dramatic effects—not just in Manhattan's financial district, but throughout the United States, and the world.[68] The tape, in turn, demands a form of reading that is alert to its hidden dramas and to the speculative, fictitious castles-in-the-air—the paper profits and losses— that it records. Although it comes as little surprise that fiction writers such as Lefèvre explored the possibility of reading, through the abstract symbols on the tape, the human tragedy and comedy beneath, the same rhetoric of the unmediated transparency of the ticker was also present in the nonfictional genres of investment guides and biographies. For example, Wyckoff's *Studies in Tape Reading* insists that, despite being physically removed from the action on the floor of the NYSE in order to focus more clearly on the numbers, the tape reader "should recognize the turning points of the market; see in his mind's eye what is happening on the floor."[69]

Livingston starts off regarding the tape as simply a stream of meaningless numbers, but even he soon begins looking for patterns that are not mere statistical abstractions, but seem to have a *personality* to them. At the beginning of his career, he is "always looking for the repetitions and parallelisms of behavior— learning to read the tape" (11). Reading the tape thus becomes a matter of finding, in the endless stream of fluctuating prices, not merely numerical repetitions, but familiar quirks and tics. Livingston describes how he "came to be interested in the *behavior* of prices" (9; emphasis added), as if they were an organism, an animal, with recognizable intentions: "Stock prices were apt to show certain habits, so to speak" (10). (This is still a far cry from behavioral economics: here, it is the market and its prices, rather than the herd-like speculators, that exhibit the behavior.) Like others during this period, Livingston compares stock market interpretation with relying on past precedence in horserace gambling. His point, however, is not that speculation is akin to gambling, but that individual stocks behave like actual horses, with their own recognizable form: "I carried the 'dope sheets' in my mind. I looked for stock prices to run on form" (10).[70]

Livingston moves beyond simple animism to seeing in the ticker's symbols the human battle taking place on the exchange floor, with the trader as a general surveying his troops, a familiar image in many of the business hagiographies and novels of the period: "A battle goes on in the stock market and the tape is your telescope" (10). He also, however, comes to see the quotations not through the objective and distancing lens of a telescope, but with a sixth sense. (Likewise, Wyckoff's list of the "proper mental equipment" for the ideal speculator, quoted above, concludes that "these qualities are as vital as natural ability, or what is called the sixth sense of trading.")[71] For Livingston, it is as if the price variations are alive, and their movements are governed by subliminal patterns of behavior that only a sensitive trader can uncover:

> I used to sit by the ticker and call out the quotations for the board boy. The price behaved as I thought it would. It promptly went down a couple of points and paused a little to get its breath before taking another dip. . . . Then all of a sudden I didn't like the way Sugar was doing its hesitating. I began to feel uncomfortable. . . . I knew something was wrong somewhere, but I couldn't spot it exactly. . . . According to my dope Sugar should have broken by now. The engine wasn't hitting right. I had a feeling there was a trap in the neighborhood. At all events, the telegraph instrument was now going like mad. (17–18)

For Livingston, then, the tape reveals a deeper, abstract structure that transcends individual human intention and is governed by its own internal, causal logic, which is machinelike. At the same time, however, the expert tape reader also sees the market as a skittish creature, whose infinitesimal behavioral quirks and intentions can only be discerned in forms of reading that stretch to the limit the pragmatic, quasi-scientific advice in the manuals. In the way that Livingston presents it, it is not the behavior of investors that makes the price of sugar hesitate;

the abstract price itself seems to have a personality all its own, just as the legal doctrine of corporate personhood granted to vast, inhuman corporations some of the same rights as individuals. The market may be a machine, but it has a soul, and only a savvy mechanic who knows its foibles can recognize when something is amiss.

Invisible Hands

In theory, the advent of the stock ticker should have shifted the focus of popular engagement with Wall Street away from the human stories of cliques, cabals, and manipulators and toward the anonymous procession of fluctuating numbers on the tape. Yet not only did there remain an obsession with the nefarious (or heroic) schemes of Wall Street insiders in the melodramatic novels, muckraking journalism, and "kings of fortune" biographies of the period, but the numerical abstractions, and even the ticker itself, were portrayed through the rhetoric of personification.

Imbuing the market with a sense of intentionality, agency, and personality has a long history. The market has often been depicted as feminine, most obviously in the guise of the goddess Fortuna or Lady Credit, while Adam Smith's trope of the "Invisible Hand" of market coordination draws on a longer tradition of providential and theatrical metaphors.[72] There is also a long tradition of seeing the work of Wall Street in animistic or anthropomorphized terms, in particular the commonplace division of the market into bulls, bears, and the lambs of the unwitting public.[73] Around the turn of the twentieth century, the ticker, I want to suggest, functioned in financial imaginings as the literal embodiment of the invisible hand of the market, a mundane and personified incarnation of the ineffable presence of the market itself. In Slavoj Žižek's terms, the invisible hand of the market is one of many versions of the "big Other," the "mysterious spectral agency" that is called into being to provide symbolic grounding for popular understandings of why history unfolds as it does (other candidates are Providence; the Hegelian Marxist, objective logic of history; and the myth of an all-encompassing Jewish conspiracy). The image of the invisible hand arises, Žižek contends, when capitalism "engenders its own form of anonymous Destiny in the guise of market relations."[74] (The sleight of hand at work in the image of the invisible hand is even more deceitful, I might add, because, in reality, the visible hand of the state creates and maintains a particular version of the market, but then disguises its own playing with it.) The stock market, embodied in the form of the ticker machine, thus becomes the almighty and eternal opponent that can never be beaten in the game of wits played by stock market operators, as Livingston asserts: "A man may best a stock or a group at a certain time, but no man living can beat the stock market!" (131).

In both factual and fictional guides to Wall Street around the turn of the twentieth century, the stock ticker takes on a talismanic status, simultaneously impervious to human feelings and yet seemingly imbued with prophetic powers and divine authority. Some commentators recognized that the unmediated "stories" told by the supposedly objective ticker could, in fact, be deliberately manipulated as part of nefarious schemes, its power of "publicity" (praised by authority figures such as Van Antwerp) allowing its deceptive tales to spread far and wide:

> About this time there was a great spur given to stock speculation by a single invention. The discovery of America is usually regarded as a rather important historical and commercial event; but to the new estate of man that grows rich without toil, the invention of the "stock ticker" outshines the achievement of Columbus. This machine has an overmastering power for good or evil. It is the most gigantic engine that was ever created to serve the speculative purposes of man. It records the daily transactions in the city of New York alone aggregating from fifty to eighty million dollars. That it could be used to create and to lead opinion, instead of merely recording it, Walter saw before it had been in use a week. He recognized its future potency, its universality, and the volume of its voice before he had watched it a fortnight. He saw in it the one essential requisite for the rapid rise or depression of values—publicity, instantaneous and widespread. He saw in it the magician's wand, and he determined to know how to juggle with it.[75]

Sharp operators thus quickly realized the potential for making the tape "speak" the message they wanted it to, knowing the methods of interpretation that the massed ranks of the ordinary investors would use to read it.[76] Others, however, came to think of the ticker not merely as a "magician's wand" in the hand of a ruthless stock market operator, but as a potentially sinister device that had a voice and a will seemingly all its own. In *The Study and Science of Stock Speculation*, for example, the author quotes from his own potboiler novel, *By Law of Might* ("a thrilling story of finance, mystery, and forbidden love," as an advertisement in the booklet declares), to convey to his readers the uncanny properties of this new machine:

> Only symbols and signs, yet that little ticking machine, with its wonderful potentiality for evil and its scroll of cabalistic names, is the modern Ananias, the devil's mouthpiece with silent voice luring as a siren to destruction tens of thousands throughout the land. It cries "Buy" when they ought to sell, and "Sell" when they

ought to buy—nominally a true record of transactions, in effect every inch a lie, a false prediction of what is to come, the promptings of the manipulator, every yard conveying with convincing earnestness greater falsehoods than the most extravagant and facile pen could frame and make appear the truth.[77]

As we will see in chapter 3, in magazine fiction and illustrations about Wall Street around the turn of the twentieth century, the stock ticker inserts itself ever more insistently at the center of attention. For example, in the opening four chapters (some seventy pages) of Lefèvre's novel, *Sampson Rock of Wall Street*, the intrusive rhythm of the ticker repeatedly demands attention from the novel's protagonists, right from the very first lines: "The stock-ticker in Sampson Rock's private office had been whirring away half an hour when Rock's cashier entered the room to lay on the desk a bulky letter. It was marked in one corner, 'Personal—Important,' heavily underscored. For additional emphasis there was a rough drawing of a hand, the dexter finger rigidly pointing cornerward."[78] With the competing claims of personal correspondence (the hand on the envelope emphasizing the individual hand that has written the letter) and the public broadcast of the impersonal ticker (which "symbolized the democracy of the money-makers" [22] in the eyes of a deluded supplicant to Rock), this opening sentence captures, in miniature, one of the central dilemmas of the novel, namely, the role of corrupt, inside information and familial loyalties in the seemingly impersonal and unfeeling realm of business. It is as if the ticker is a central character in the novel's moral dilemma, rather than merely an informational device.[79] "In the tie-vote between friendship and duty," Rock thinks to himself as he weighs up competing loyalties to a friend versus the confidential business scheme he is developing, "the ticker usually casts the deciding ballot" (26). Yet later, worrying whether this obsession with business is driving him apart from his only son, it comes to seem as though "the Lord of the Ticker was a human being after all" (58).

The novel tells the story of Sampson Rock (apparently loosely based on the life of John D. Rockefeller) and his playboy son, Sam Jr. The latter at first rejects his father's obsession with business and his manipulative practices, but then, in an effort to make an informed decision, and partly to become something in the eyes of his childhood sweetheart and potential fiancée, he agrees to start as an apprentice in his father's firm and ends up as ruthless and corrupt as the old man. In these opening chapters, Rock Sr. is repeatedly torn between focusing on what the tape is trying to tell him and listening to a series of visitors: a newspaper reporter looking for profitable market gossip; the writer of the confidential report, who must be bribed with a generous stock tip; the widow of an old friend, who is also seeking insider investment advice; and his son, who is trying to explain his refusal to follow in his father's footsteps. Rock Sr.'s first words on entering his office are "How's the market?," and he instantly focuses on the ticker tape, for "nothing that Valentine [his clerk] could say would be as illuminative as three or four inches of the little paper ribbon. A foot was a book; a yard, a history" (1).

Rock Sr. is an expert tape reader, able to focus so intently that he can see, through the marks on the paper, not merely to the drama on the floor of the Exchange, but to the nationwide industrial activity underneath, which the figures seem to represent: "He approached the ticker and gazed intently on the printed letters and numbers of the tape—so intently that they ceased to be numerals and became living figures. . . . Rock's vision leaped from New York to Richmond, from Richmond to Biddleboro, from Biddleboro back to the glittering marble-and-gold Board Room of the Stock Exchange" (16). In a fanciful conceit, the "tape-characters" are compared with "little soldier ants, bringing precious loads to this New York office, tiny gold nuggets from a thousand stockholders . . . to the feet of Sampson Rock" (16). Although the news on the ticker might cause some investors' "shrieks and sobs," those imprecations "would not reach the ears of a man whose soul had soared so high that the entire State of Virginia was spread before him in miniature, like an outrolled map" (16). The ciphers and dashes on the tape transform themselves, in Rock's imagination, into an animated map of the expanding railroad he is trying to buy. The map, in turn, becomes a "vein," and even "a living thing, born of work, stretching tentacle-like arms everywhither . . . even unto the golden remote Far West and the blue Pacific" (17). Rock's poetic tendency to read the tape as a romance of American industrial destiny and his intuitive "habit of thinking in lightning flashes" is, however, coupled with a more pragmatic, militaristic "von Moltke–like manner in which he planned some of his market campaigns" (3). Immediately after his fanciful daydream of the reorganization of the Virginia Central, we learn that "there returned to the side of the ticker a calculating machine" (17), that is, Rock himself, who becomes as impersonal and rational as the stock ticker.[80] Rock's success comes, in part, from his ability to become as machinelike as the ticker itself: "No zeal, no fire; only intelligence, dispassionate as mathematics" (21). Forced repeatedly to deal with the claims to friendship and family loyalty that his visitors represent, he is grateful to return to the ticker in his private office: "The general, while the battle was waging, had been without a telescope. Now he could see how his lieutenants were fighting" (47).

In his meetings that morning, Rock's attention continually drifts back to the ticker, even when speaking with his son, who has just returned from a year and a half abroad. Sam finds his father irritable, rather than delighted to welcome the prodigal son, and realizes that "the madly whirring ticker was discharging psychic waves into the atmosphere of this office, filling it with something unseen but most curiously felt" (49). It is as if a spectral presence has come between father and son, in a scene closer to a séance than a homecoming, and Sam begins to realize that it is the ghostly voice of the market, projected through the ticker, that is the hidden presence both in the room and in the strained relationship with his father: "The effect [of his father's "impersonal irritation"] was of listening to a voice without seeing the speaker's face" (49), a phrase that seems to apply equally to Rock Sr., the ticker machine, and the very market itself. Sam feels the presence of the zombielike, "unblinking stare of the hungry eyes which he now remembered the ticker fiends had," yet, at the same time, he begins to sense the appeal of what the "whirring and the clicking of the little wheels" is recording: not so much the "money-monotone, the sound of clashing dollars" as "the pulse-beats of the working world," with the ticker tape revealing for "a chosen few" the drama of "great plans," such as the "exact tonnage the tireless railroads were carrying" (50). With their conversation interrupted repeatedly by Rock Sr. reading the tape and barking orders to his clerk, Sam Jr. slowly becomes entranced by the power of his father, through the ticker, "to speak to the world and have the world listen," leaving him wondering whether he, like his father, could become a financial Svengali, "the lord of the ticker, so that the ticker obediently repeated the message that the master said should go forth to the thousands of well-dressed men with hungry eyes" (52).

Nevertheless, again and again, we hear in these Wall Street stories, biographies, and advice books the *ticker itself* speaking, sometimes loudly, at other times in a seductive whisper, as if it is the machine, rather than the titanic stock operator, that is the hypnotic master that must be obeyed. To the financial reporter who receives a market tip from Sampson Rock, "the ticker began to sing, goldenly, *Haste! haste!* and then, *the cash! the cash!*" (27), while the widow finds herself unable to listen to Rock's stern financial advice, as she is too busy "intoxicating herself with counting and spending the money the marvelous and kindly ticker would surely—oh, yes, surely!—make for her" (46). It becomes a case not so much of struggling to decipher the direction of price movements through the arcane symbols on the tape, as listening to the ventriloquizing voice of the market itself speak in insistent tones. The "most expert type of tape-reader," we are told in an article in the *Ticker*, "carries no memorandums, and seldom refers to fluctuation records. The tape whispers to him, talks to him, and, as Mr. Lawson [Thomas Lawson, the notorious speculator-turned-novelist, active in the early 1900s] puts it, 'screams' at him."[81] Likewise, in one of Lefèvre's Wall Street stories, one ticker fiend "could almost hear the stock shouting, articulately: '*I'm going up, right away, right away!*'"[82] For all its seeming urgency, however, without an interpreter or a medium, "the loquacious tape" can end up merely speaking to nothing but itself, the intentions of the market left frustratingly inscrutable.[83] The repeated refrain of the ticker that demands attention in several of Lefèvre's stories is, at times, merely its own mesmerizing rhythm: "'*Ticky-ticky-ticky-tick,*' said the ticker."[84] Despite the insistence of some market apologists that the market is manly, rational, and mechanical, Wall Street fiction by Lefèvre and other writers of the period makes it clear that the market is "impulsive and impressionable."[85]

If the stock ticker is an inhuman mechanical device that, at times, seems to ventriloquize the market in a general way, it is also itself repeatedly personified, endowed with human characteristics and foibles. Despite his talk of the speculator needing to develop an attitude of scientific detachment, Livingston, for example, comes to see the ticker machine as a fickle tipster, at times friendly and at others treacherous: "The ticker beat me by lagging so far behind the market. I was accustomed to regarding the tape as the best little friend I had because I bet according to what it told me. But this time the tape double-crossed me. The divergence between the printed and the actual prices undid me" (42). In Lefèvre's Wall Street stories, the speculators internalize the abstractions of price variations arriving over the tape, becoming, in the process, hypnotized mouthpieces for the anonymous market. But they, in turn, then project onto the ticker their own desires and fears:

> The very ticker sounded mirthful; its clicking told of golden jokes. . . . At times their fingers clutched the air happily, as if they actually felt the good money the ticker was presenting to them. . . . Their dreams were rudely shattered; the fast horses some had all but bought joined the steam-yachts others had almost chartered. . . . And the demolisher of dreams and dwellings was the ticker, that instead of golden jokes, was now clicking financial death. They could not take their eyes from the board before them. Their own ruin, told in mournful numbers by the little machine, fascinated them. . . . Wilson, the dry goods man . . . was now watching, as if under a hypnotic spell, the lips of the man who sat on the high stool beside the ticker and called out the prices to the quotation boy. Now and again Wilson's own lips made curious grimaces, as if speaking to himself.[86]

When the mesmerized speculator Wilson mutters to himself, it begins to seem as if his lips are not under his conscious control. The self becomes inhabited by the phantasmagoric spirit of the market, while, at the same time, the ticker itself becomes the symbol of the invisible hand incarnate, producing the uncanny spectacle of ventriloquism.[87]

In the vernacular economic writings of the period, as much as the tape is reckoned to offer a reflection of the sublime vastness of the market itself, it also functions as a projection of self, blurring the boundary between representation and interpretation. With the tape's ability to register every passing whim of traders, the market frequently figures in these writings as a barometer of people's feelings, a financial version of the meteorological pathetic fallacy (but it is also simultaneously the *cause* of those feelings). In Lefèvre's story "The Tipster," for example, the question "How's the market?" comes to replace the greeting "How are you doing?," with the speculation-crazed denizens of Wall Street feeling a complete identification with the market.[88] In Lefèvre's stories, there is thus a convergence between the self and the ticker, as people's hearts beat with the "pulse of the stock market":[89] "He had imagined he knew the market. . . . And as time passed the grip of Wall Street on his soul grew stronger until it strangled all other aspirations. He could talk, think, dream of nothing but stocks. He could not read the newspapers without thinking how the market would 'take' the news contained therein."[90] One man, suffering from "ticker-fever," becomes like a telegraphic spiritualist medium, inhabited by the electrical impulses of the tape: "He shook his right forefinger with a hammering motion," and "little by little Gilmartin's whisper set in motion within him the wheels of a ticker that printed on his day-dreams the mark of a dollar."[91] Unlike the telegraph—with the all-too-human hand of its operator—at the receiving end the automatic printing wheels of the stock ticker conjured up, for Wall Street commentators, the idea of the ticking machine in the corner of the office as a disembodied writer, an automaton tapping out the story of the market.

For numerous commentators during this period, the trader's trader is James R. Keene, the epitome of ruthless market manipulation who became the hired henchman for Standard Oil. For all his detached, masterly control of the market, at times he is described as being merely its mouthpiece. He is thus characterized partly as the "high priest of the ticker," who has the uncanny ability to become completely attuned to the rhythm of the market, his scrutiny of the tape being "so intense that he appeared to be in a trance while mental processes were being worked out."[92] We learn that "his most characteristic attitude is standing by the ticker, one elbow leaning on a corner of the high ticker stand, his cheek resting against his closed fist, his eyes fastened on the narrow paper ribbon that tells the story of a 'Keene market.'"[93] Like Sampson Rock, he is totally in control of himself and the market, yet he is also subsumed into the market's rhythms as he

"stands there immobile, his heart-beats attuned to the clicks of the ticker, paus-
ing in his scrutiny of the tape only long enough to send an order to a lieutenant,
buying here, selling there, playing a scientific game of chess with his invariable
opponent—human greed."[94]

Scholars of late nineteenth-century Anglo-American culture have shown how
the period's fascination with psychic phenomena encompassed both archaic and
scientific elements. Spiritualism, mesmerism, and telepathy, for example, promised intimacy with distant, otherworldly interlocutors, with these mystical practices
viewed as fully compatible with modern technologies of communication, such as
the wireless telegraph, and invisible forces, such as radiation.[95] Likewise, cultural historians have shown the confusions that arose not only from machines
beginning to seem more like humans, but from people coming to act more like
machines.[96] The financial rationality that the ticker tape both embodied and encouraged forms part of the disenchanted rejection of superstition, myth, and
religious faith that Max Weber famously identified as one of the key attributes
of modernity; yet, at the same time, the ticker is identified in the vernacular
economic writing of the period as the very instrument of a magical communion
with occult forces. Thus, on the one hand, traders such as Livingston, Keene,
and Sampson Rock are presented as epitomizing scientific and economic rationality, able to make dispassionate calculations and to become machinelike in their
reading of the tape. On the other hand, they are described as being hypnotized
by the tape, entering into a divine communion with Žižek's "mysterious spectral
agency" of the market, or what Fredric Jameson, in his account of "Culture and
Finance Capital," identifies as the financescape of "free-floating capital," with
"specters of value, as Derrida might put it, vying against each other in a vast,
worldwide, disembodied phantasmagoria."[97] The trancelike reading of the ticker
tape by these lords of finance allows them to possess the secrets of the market,
but they, in turn, are possessed by its unfathomable forces. Likewise, the stock
ticker itself becomes a mouthpiece for the sublime and inscrutable divinity of the
market in its entirety: "There was no god but the ticker, and the brokers were its
prophets!"[98]

Prophets of Profit

If tape reading and the speculation it enables are presented as modern, technical,
and objective, they are also described by Lefèvre, Wyckoff, and other writers of
popular market tracts in terms of intuition, supernatural possession, and something approaching mystical divination or prophecy. Like a clairvoyant, the ticker
itself mysteriously seems to detect anticipations of the future through seismic

tremors felt in the prices themselves. Far from being a mere unfeeling machine, however, it is presented in the rhetoric of technologically infused spiritualism as a sensitive medium, picking up, in advance, the movements of human history that elude conscious apprehension:

> The tape tells the news minutes, hours, and days before the news tickers, or news-papers, and before it can become current gossip. Everything from a foreign war to the passing of a dividend; from a Supreme Court decision to the ravages of the boll-weevil is reflected primarily on the tape.
>
> The tape tells the present and future of the market. On the other hand, the news ticker records what *has* happened. It announces causes for the effect which has already been more or less felt in the market. Money is made in the Tape Reading by anticipating what is coming—not by waiting till it happens and going with the crowd.[99]

As we have seen, the adept reader of the tape is supposed to merge himself with the ticker, which, in turn, becomes fused with the market itself, which then in-corporates not only the entirety of history, but all the future.

Livingston, for example, insists that his analysis of the direction of the market as a whole is merely the application of an astute appraisal, not of the underlying herd psychology of investors, but of the behavioral oddities of the price quota-tions themselves. Based on his observation that "there is nothing new in Wall Street" (10), Livingston's trading strategy is to identify, in the jargon of financial economics, endogenous rather than exogenous factors in market movements. Yet his approach is not merely to ignore insider tips or pronouncements on eco-nomic fundamentals in favor of an autodidactic version of technical analysis; nor is it to second-guess the irrational behavior of fellow investors. For Livingston and other vernacular financial analysts, the market is a sensitive barometer of all of these external and internal influences, and the trick is to turn oneself into a finely calibrated register that can pick up on its mysterious signals.

Many of the pivotal moments in Livingston's route to riches are the result not of an objective analysis of economic indicators or price patterns, but of hunches and a "curious feeling" of intuition (72) that he finds hard to explain. The public, not surprisingly, latches onto these supposed market coups as evidence of his genius, in which the credentialed expertise of financial elites is outclassed by the supernatural powers of the self-taught "Boy Plunger." Livingston recounts the following story. It is 1906, and he has gone on a short vacation in Atlantic City, having sold out all his market positions for a while. Bored from taking the sea air, out of curiosity he goes to a branch of his brokers in the town, without any intention of getting back into the market. The market is generally bullish, but Livingston's attention is suddenly grabbed by Union Pacific: "I got a feeling that I ought to sell it. I can't tell you more. I just felt like selling it. I asked myself why I should feel like that, and I couldn't find any reason whatever for going short of UP" (73). The friend who is with him is alarmed to see that Livingston starts short selling Union Pacific, an illogical act in a market that is rising. Livingston can only explain that "the urge was so strong I sold another thousand [shares]" (77). The next day news arrives of the San Francisco earthquake. Ironically, Livingston's inexplicable hunch about Union Pacific shares going to fall would, in theory, have been right, but he is annoyed to find that Wall Street does not send the prices tumbling in the way that they should: "I was short five thousand shares. The blow had fallen, but my stock hadn't. My hunch was of the first water, but my bank account wasn't growing; not even on paper" (77).

There are two inexplicable things in play here. As far as Livingston is concerned, the conundrum is that the market does not react to the news in the way he thinks it should. But the other, more profound mystery is that he has a market hunch that anticipates a completely unexpected and unpredictable event. In the book, Livingston tries to give some explanations along the way, mentioning, for example, how some friends try to tell him that "it isn't a hunch but the subconscious mind, which is the creative mind, at work. That is the mind which makes artists do things without their knowing how they came to do them. Perhaps with me it was the cumulative effect of a lot of little things individually insignificant but collectively powerful. . . . I can't tell you what the cause or motive for my hunches may be" (76). The idea of prediction as a form of subconscious sensitivity to the subtle cues of the market as a whole fits in with Livingston's presentation of stock operating as an art, rather than a strictly positivist science, but it still does not explain in any coherent, rational way how he could have possibly picked up in advance on subliminal signals, *through his reading of the tape,* that there was going to be an earthquake in San Francisco. Livingston seems to suggest that unexpected events external to the inner dynamic of the market are anticipated in some unfathomable manner by price fluctuations that only a true adept can detect. Livingston thus argues that his method of prediction allows him to take account of unexpected events through his uncanny sensitivity to the seismological fluctuation of market prices: "And right here I will say that, though I do not give it as a mathematical certainty or as an axiom of speculation, my experience has been that accidents—that is, the unexpected or unforeseen—have always helped me in my market position whenever the latter has been based upon my determination of the line of least resistance. . . . You will find in actual practice that if you trade as I have indicated any important piece of news . . . is usually in harmony with the line of least resistance. The trend has been established before the news is published" (124). Here Livingston seems to anticipate the strong version of the efficient market hypothesis (EMH), the idea that all known information—including future possibilities—has already been discounted in the price of securities, with only truly random events able to create significant shifts in prices. Yet the example of the San Francisco earthquake takes this idea to its metaphysical extreme, with the possibility that somehow the prices recorded on the ticker can even offer ghostly foretellings of the inherently unpredictable future.

The stock market is thus no longer the plaything of individual master manipulators, or a machine that ticks along under its own steam, or even the aggregation of the irrational and imitative behavior of the herd. Instead, for Livingston the market figures partly as an extension of his own mind, which is in tune with the cosmic "harmonies"; partly as an all-encompassing organism; and partly as a mystical text in which the future is already written. Prediction thus becomes more akin to spiritualist attunement to the otherworldly whispers of the deceased than the rationalized projection of future price movements proposed by either the chartists or the fundamentalists. For all that Livingston insists on working alone and never listening to the crowd (the only time he suffers a major reverse of fortunes is when he takes on a partner), his success is based on the ability of his mind to be so receptive to the vibrations of the market, and so in tune with the desires of the crowd recorded on the tape, that his very identity as the sovereign self of neoclassical economics is undermined.[100]

Livingston was not the only stock market operator in fin-de-siècle America to have been tempted by mystical forms of financial prediction. Cornelius Vanderbilt famously developed a scandalously close relationship with Victoria Woodhull and her sister Tennessee Claflin, who promoted themselves as "Professors of Magnetic, Mental, and Spiritual Science."[101] In 1870, asked how readers might go about amassing fortunes of their own, Vanderbilt told a newspaper reporter that the best way to get rich was to "do as I do. Consult the Spirits!" He added that, as for the stock of the Central Pacific Railroad, "it's bound to go up . . . Mrs. Woodhull said so in a trance."[102] Vanderbilt helped set up Woodhull and Claflin as the first female brokers on Wall Street. It is unclear, however, how much actual business the "Bewitching Brokers" conducted, with their much exaggerated claims for accurate financial prediction.[103] In a similar fashion, the Wall Street financier J. P. Morgan reputedly received financial advice through his frequent consultations with the astrologer Evangeline Adams.[104] According to the apocryphal quote attributed to Morgan: "Millionaires don't hire astrologers. Billionaires do."

In spite of Morgan's insistence that only billionaires could afford to be so reckless as to get their financial advice from such unorthodox sources, many ordinary Americans in the late nineteenth and early twentieth centuries were attracted to seemingly superstitious forms of vernacular financial knowledge, part of a more general cultural fascination with spiritualist predictions and fortune telling.[105] Ann Fabian, for example, has documented how African Americans used "dream books"—compendia of dream interpretations that linked the visions to particular numbers—to guide their play in the policy numbers game. Drawing on the writings of Marcel Mauss and Georges Bataille on alternative economies that are based not on accumulation but on wasteful expenditure, Fabian argues that these dream books in particular, and numerology in general, were part of an antirationalist revolt against the trait of calculability in capitalist society, and hence were felt to be dangerous by the moral guardians of the middle class: "The players who turned dreams into cash carried on a logical revolt against the rampant rationality of nineteenth-century business civilization. Policy preserved a place to exercise the powers of superstition and interpretation; it offered the lure of idleness. Policy players exercised forms of power that openly challenged the rational assumptions of a market economy."[106] For Fabian, dream books constituted a vernacular protest against the encroaching obsession with the bottom line: they "applied numbers to entities that could not be quantified and in so doing violated the very logic on which quantification and calculation were based."[107] Fabian's analysis of policy players' use of superstitious forms of prediction is persuasive, but it suggests that these residual forms of vernacular financial knowledge operated in an alternative, contestatory economic realm for those excluded from the mainstream. As we have seen in this chapter, however, far more mainstream and respectable forms of financial prediction relied equally on what we might now call voodoo economics, while, conversely, vernacular guides to reading the market's future were drawn to the rhetoric of statistical quantification. We therefore need to conceive of the relationship between superstitious and scientific forms of financial prediction neither as operating in worlds apart, nor in opposition to the latter, striving to replace the former in the name of progress, but as being mutually constitutive and frequently merged at the level of practice, as well as in rhetoric.[108]

The history of the emergence of financial forecasting has yet to be fully told, but most commentators agree on the basic contours: folk methods of foretelling the future in a world governed by Providence give way to modern practices of observation, recording, and prediction, based on statistical analysis.[109] In the late nineteenth century, the development of weather forecasting and economic forecasting thus share a similar trajectory, from vernacular wisdom to more scientific approaches. The invention of the telegraph, in particular, enabled meteorological observations and data about the condition of agricultural crops to be collected, systematized, and disseminated, as well as information about the distribution of standardized market prices via the stock ticker. Cleveland Abbe (known, in a telling mixture of folk and scientific rhetoric, as "Ol' Probabilities") is credited with the first attempt in the United States to establish a meteorological reporting and forecasting bureau, in 1868 and the story of the development of weather forecasting is a mixture of individual entrepreneurial activity underpinned by state support.[110] Although federal and state agencies led the way in establishing an agricultural-crop information service and a weather forecasting service in the 1870s, the development of financial information bureaus and technical-analysis services relied more on individual entrepreneurs like Charles Dow and Roger Babson, with macroeconomic forecasting emerging later, in major private and state institutions such as the Harvard Economic Service and the Cowles Commission.[111]

As we have already begun to see, however, the story of the inexorable replacement of traditional superstition with scientific objectivity in financial forecasting is not as straightforward as it might at first seem. The broad historical trajectory of the nineteenth century's slow substitution of a trust in personal authority and experience for a trust in numbers and scientific objectivity is fundamentally sound (as Theodore Porter, Mary Poovey, and Lorraine Daston and Peter Galison have influentially argued), yet the transition from a traditional to a modern epistemological regime was neither smooth nor uncontested.[112] As Preda has documented, persuading Americans that financial forecasting was a science required the development of technological, institutional, and intellectual structures of authority, yet at each stage, modern methods of prediction did not so much replace traditional, superstitious ones as become fused with them, applying a veneer of scientific glamour to folk practices. In the same way that fin-de-siècle spiritualism was less a challenge to technological modernity than an incorporation of its new possibilities of ethereal communication, so, too, did vernacular methods of financial prognostication take on the language of economic determinism. For example, the first real attempt in the United States to provide a quasi-scientific approach to business-cycle forecasting was Samuel Benner's *Prophecies of the Future Ups and Downs in Prices*, which asserted—fueled only by a faith that science would eventually provide the explanation for this "prophecy" from an "Ohio farmer"—that there were "cycles of 11 years in the prices of corn and hogs, 27 years in the price of pig-iron, and 54 years in general business."[113]

Despite Benner's identification of statistical patterns that operated at a level far removed from individual human intention, he nevertheless insisted that the business cycles he seemed to be uncovering were governed not by economic law, but providential destiny: "The author firmly believes that God is in prices, and that the over and under production of every commodity is in accordance with his [sic] will, with strict reference to the wants of mankind, and governed by the laws of nature, which are God's laws; and that the production, advance, and decline of average prices should be systematic, and occur in an established providential succession, as certain and regular as the magnetic needle points unerringly to the pole."[114] For all its talk of observable business cycles, Benner's book has more in common with the tradition of farmers' almanacs for predicting the weather, and with astrology, than with the development, for example, of actuarial science. Even Charles Dow, regarded as the "father of modern technical analysis," was deeply attracted to a pet theory of William Stanley Jevons, the British economist who led the marginalist revolution in economics. From the 1870s onward, Jevons, in a direct merging of meteorological and financial forecasting, repeatedly expounded the hypothesis that periodic stock market crises were an effect of changing agricultural fortunes that were, in turn, directly influenced by sunspots.[115] As we will see in chapter 3, the patterns that technical analysts claimed to discover in their charts often merely gave a scientific gloss to an activity that was statistically no better than finding faces in the clouds.

Conclusion: The Ghost in the Financial Machine

In their revisionist account of the historical evolution of technical analysis, Andrew Lo and Jasmina Hasanhodzic (drawing on the work of Alex Preda) describe how technical analysis in late nineteenth- and early twentieth-century America "evolved into a scientific Endeavour—complete with data gathering, hypothesis testing, and mathematical rigor," turning market analysis into a "full-time, skill-based occupation." The authors are faced with the potential embarrassment that "inevitably, an esoteric form of market analysis based on astrology quickly sprang up in the shadow of the new economic science." Yet for Lo and Hasanhodzic, this "pseudo-science" should not be regarded as part of legitimate technical analysis. "Such odd hybrids of rationalism and mysticism will always be with us," they insist, "so it is important to keep the crackpot theories separate from the legitimate ones."[116] In contrast, Burton Malkiel's *A Random Walk Down Wall Street*, a guide to investment that has gone through numerous editions since it was first published in 1973, summarizes the academic financial-economics literature that has demonstrated the statistical inadequacy of the whole spectrum of technical analysis.[117] From the viewpoint of the EMH, which, in its strong version, claims that—by definition—stock prices are unpredictable (because only unanticipated, exogenous events move prices), *all* technical analysis is a pseudoscience, because past prices, whether in the long or the short term, can never provide a guide to future ones.[118] In this chapter I have been arguing, however, that these "odd hybrids of rationalism and mysticism" are not occasional, regrettable lapses from the path of inexorable scientific progress, but are ever present in popular investment-advice literature, in emergent forms of technical analysis, and in Wall Street fiction in the decades around the turn of the twentieth century.

Drawing on Max Weber, Arjun Appadurai argues that "magical thinking"—an irrational reliance on all kinds of technical procedures for divinatory purposes—has been at the very heart of global finance since the late nineteenth century and continues to exert its influence in the present, most notably in the faith that uncertainty can be quantified and turned into manageable and exploitable risk: "These detailed charts [produced by technical analysts], which are regarded by others as entirely unscientific, have very good standing in financial markets and are in reality no different from the charts of astrologers, psychics, or tarot card operators or other diagrammatic formats for prognostication. In short, they are mechanical techniques of prediction with no interest in causal or explanatory principles." For Appadurai, the adoption in finance of "highly technicalized models of prediction, forecasting, and risk management" has not so much replaced the realms of luck and grace as become hybridized with them, "thus confusing the spheres of chance and risk as technical features of human life."[119] On the one hand, in the late nineteenth and early twentieth centuries, even before the democratization of share ownership that began in World War I, the mechanical regularity of the stock ticker and the growth of technical analysis introduced a "cognitive standardization." In so doing, the ticker and the chart helped popularize the idea of the market as an impersonal aggregation of countless transactions whose patterns could be uncovered and—if not actually predicted—then detected after the fact. Guides to technical analysis for the autodidact, as well as public relations campaigns on behalf on the New York Stock Exchange, emphasized the increased legibility and transparency of financial information that resulted from the introduction of the stock ticker, even if the NYSE continued to fight a legal battle to restrict access to this information in real time. These emerging discourses, technologies, and practices helped undermine an older critique of speculation as a rigged game of Wall Street cliques and insiders and contributed to public acceptance of the goal of a shareholders' democracy, coupled with the promotion of rational calculability as the proper attitude for market observation.

On the other hand, the influence of vernacular genres of financial knowledge, such as investment-advice manuals, biographies of traders, and the popular fiction I have been examining in this chapter, also served to make the abstractions of finance more tangible and personal, with the personification of market devices such as the stock ticker, and the depiction of the market as having a mind of its own. In these accounts, which seem to offer a view of the market from the bird's-eye perspective of statistical aggregation, the market nevertheless appears as a haunted landscape, an uncanny amalgam of natural laws and supernatural forces.

Coda

What became of Jesse Livermore? Lefèvre's book on him was published in 1923, and it should come as no surprise to learn that Livermore managed to predict the Wall Street crash of 1929, ending up with a fortune of $100 million, nor to learn that he is believed to have lost nearly all of that fortune through speculation during the 1930s. Down on his luck, he finally took his own life in 1940. His suicide note was written to his third wife, Harriet Noble. She had been married several times before, and her previous husband had committed suicide.[120] There are some things, it seems, that even Livermore did not manage to see coming.

CHAPTER THREE

Picturing the Market

The adoption of the stock ticker by the New York Stock Exchange in the late 1860s created both an impediment to and an opportunity for would-be observers of the stock market. Because the members of the Regular Board were keen to maintain their monopoly on the prices that they claimed to actively produce, they now closed the floor to nonmembers, meaning that the only way to access those prices was via a licensed stock ticker service.[1] In theory, it was still possible for nonmembers to follow the activity of the stock market from the visitors' gallery (and this indeed became an increasingly popular pastime for tourists), but from that vantage point, the lay observer was only able to gain a general impression of market movements, rather than any detailed knowledge of individual transactions. The floor of the stock exchanges and the pits of the commodity exchanges seemed to offer a graphic materialization of the abstract and impersonal forces at play in the sublime vastness of the national and global economy. More often than not, however, casual visitors to the NYSE were struck by the illegibility of the spectacle of turmoil on the floor, most obviously in times of panic: "Chairs are abandoned, men rush pell-mell into the cock-pit, and crowd, jostle, push, and trample on one another. . . . They speak all at once, yelling and screaming like hyenas. . . . Several hundred men . . . stamping, yelling, screaming, jumping, sweating, gesticulating, violently shaking their fists in each other's faces, talking in a tongue not spoken at Pentecost."[2]

As we saw in chapter 2, the stock ticker also created a new vantage point on the market, a bird's-eye view (in Richard Wyckoff's opinion) of all the transactions taking place on the floor of the New York Stock Exchange, even for those nonmembers at a remove from the heat of the action. The ticker tape afforded not merely a better way of observing the stock market; it changed what counted as the market. Yet in doing so, it presented a new dilemma: if the stock ticker now provided the best view of the market, what did that market look like? Was it possible to provide a visual analogue for the increasingly placeless interactions of the global financescape that dealt not in actual material products, but in immaterial derivatives?[3] And if the stock market itself was a sensitive register, what, exactly, did its prices represent? Financial markets have often been perceived as elusive and mysterious, since they deal primarily in abstractions that complicate and resist figurative representation. As we saw in the introduction, financial capitalism itself creates recurrent crises of representation, when the faith that is necessary to maintain belief in the value of the numerous fictive substitutes and abstractions of "real" value (paper money, credit instruments, futures contracts, and so on) periodically begins to crumble. This process unsurprisingly quickened pace when the market became abstracted from the particular locations and people of actual open-cry exchanges, as, quite simply, there is less to see. Finding representational analogues for financial capitalism became more difficult in the last decades of the nineteenth century, as the market shifted from the physical location, personalities, and embodied dramas on the floor of the New York Stock Exchange or the Chicago Board of Trade to the vast, globally interconnected circuits of supply and demand depicted in the fluctuating stock prices printed on the stock ticker.

This chapter examines the ways in which the market was visualized in different media in the late nineteenth and early twentieth centuries, during the crucial moment of the emergence of the deterritorialized and disembodied financial marketplace, enabled by the proliferation of ticker services in brokerages throughout New York, the nation, and, with the advent of transatlantic cables, the world. It will begin by sketching out the broad history of genres that attempted to picture and embody the market (such as paintings, cartoons, guidebooks, photographs, and architecture) before going on to consider the way illustrations in popular magazines during the Gilded Age and the Progressive Era grappled with the conundrum of portraying a market that was becoming increasingly unrepresentable. The solution, in many cases, was to personify the abstractions. The final part of this chapter will discuss new technologies of visualization, such as the charts produced by technical analysts, and the hydraulic machines built by economists to model the national system of supply and demand. Chapter 5 continues the discussion with an analysis of a diagram of interlocking corporate directorships produced for the U.S. House of Representatives in the Pujo Committee's investigation, an illustration that combines elements of both the anthropomorphizations that were the mainstay of muckraking cartoons and the abstractions of the market that were elaborated by the early chartists. The argument of this chapter is twofold. First, emerging technologies did not merely create new ways of visualizing the stock market, but also helped reconfigure and rationalize the very idea of the market as a coherent, predictable, self-sustaining entity. Second, many of these representations worked by simultaneously abstracting *and* personalizing the problems of finance.

Allegories of Finance

The full history of how finance has been represented in the visual arts has yet to be written, but the basic trajectory is from figurative or allegorical depictions in Britain in the eighteenth century to today's high-art engagements with the thoroughgoing dematerialization of financial capitalism.[4] In brief, the modes of representation of finance move from allegory through satire, realism, naturalism, modernism, and on to postmodernism, shadowing the changing nature of financial capitalism itself. Within this longer trajectory, the period of the late nineteenth and early twentieth centuries in the United States looks back to earlier iconographic traditions, while also anticipating new concerns with the idea of the financial sublime.

Despite these changing modes of representation, it is worth emphasizing that a number of themes and images tend to recur. Visual portrayals of the financial marketplace frequently utilize a register that is either natural (storms, floods, bulls, and bears) or providential (gambling wheels, Lady Luck, and other feminizations of finance). Many of these images both endorse and critique the overwhelming power of the market, while making evident its ineluctable dynamism and the importance of circulation and movement. This alternating impulse to either conquer or be conquered by the market is also apparent in the desire to interpret or construct its size, density, and complexity. Many visual images of the market are thus girded by different kinds of geometrical arrangements, and their structures—sometimes hierarchical and sometimes rhizomatic—are suggestive of particular interpretations of the possibility that individuals can influentially act within the market. Likewise, as the present chapter demonstrates, even images that have attempted to make sense of the processes of the market by personalizing them have given in to its abstractions, reinforcing the overwhelming power of the market by anthropomorphically depicting it as a kind of sentient being, one quite beyond the comprehension of individual human actors.

In the eighteenth century, allegorical cartoons that appealed to both literate and nonliterate readers attacked the emerging realm of finance as no better than gambling.[5] The satirical focus of their allegories was quite specific. *The Bubblers Medley; or, A Sketch of the Times; Being Europes Memorial for the Year 1720*, for example, locates the disordered crush of bodies precisely in 'Change Alley in London and in rue Quinquempoix in Paris, both streets where stocks and shares were openly sold. In these images, the libidinous irrationality of the unregulated crowd is frequently symbolized by a gambling motif, indicated by the playing cards in the *Bubblers Medley* and by the coin game and the demonic wheel of fortune in Hogarth's *An Emblematic Print on the South Sea*. The presence of a carousel, familiar in other representations from that period, such as the Dutch *Het Groote Tafereel der Dwaasheid* ("The Great Mirror of Folly"), emphasizes the visceral pleasures of gambling while still condemning the folly of betting on risky ventures.

Yet these images also suggest an analysis that is more complex than a critique of the moral dangers of a gambling mania. The South Sea Company at the center of the speculative boom of 1720 was a trading company that had assumed responsibility for managing the debt that the British government had accrued during its war with Spain. The company was formed as a Tory alternative to the Whig-controlled Bank of England, and both its rise and fall reveal the social and political implications of that nation's financial revolution in the eighteenth century, which involved not only the introduction of paper money and the emergence of the concept of national debt, but a set of new—and often largely anonymous—financial relationships, opportunities, and threats made possible by a secondary market in shares and credit.[6] It is hardly surprising, then, that at the time of the South Sea bubble, an allegorical, typological, or emblematic mode predominated, reflecting a sense that financial exchange substituted strange, imaginary, fantastical entities for "real," tangible things.

This figurative mode also anticipates concerns about the possibilities of representation itself. The trompe l'oeil form of the *Bubblers Medley* points toward an awareness of the implicit duplicity of representation itself, to the widespread anxiety about "trickery, artifice, and the kind of fictions that lay at the heart of stockjobbing" that the crash laid open.[7] The implications of the *Bubblers Medley*'s ability to so artlessly reproduce the texts that it apparently mocks have become central and recurring concerns of "money artists" from the eighteenth century to the present. Much financial imagery in nineteenth-century America responded to a similar problem of representation as that which the emergence of paper money and a credit-based economy created in eighteenth-century Britain. With over 3,000 banks issuing paper notes, it became virtually impossible to distinguish real from illegitimate money, to the extent that even the counterfeit detectors published by banks to aid the public in recognizing false notes were themselves sometimes counterfeited. The banks were confronted with both the logistical problem of how to integrate anticounterfeiting measures into their banknote design, and the iconographic question of what adornments were suitable to enact performatively a sense of dignity, reliability, and solidity to these representational proxies for value—a proxy that in some cases was a fraud, since the issuing banks were not always able to make good on their promise to exchange the paper bills for specie. Many Americans therefore became accustomed to the practice of discounting bills from distant, unknown banks, in effect learning to adopt a hermeneutic of suspicion in their reading of these publically circulating symbols.[8]

In addition to the daily, practical problems of an unreliable paper currency, the larger philosophical question about the nature of money was a recurrent flashpoint in the power struggles between farmers, industrial workers, and capitalists in the nineteenth century. The troubling chronic crises, caused in part by the lack of specie in a monetary system officially underwritten by the gold standard, led to a political climax in the presidential election of 1896. Agrarian Populists, representing the interests of debtors, favored the expansionist and inflationary possibilities of a bimetallic standard; sound-money conservatives continued to insist that only gold could provide the proper foundation for an economy; and the greenbackers represented a minority view, where only a paper currency, backed by government fiat and a faith in the nation's future, could provide a democratic form of money that could expand to match economic growth.[9] Against a background of the practical problem of counterfeiting, coupled with a metaphysical anxiety about the nature of value, satirical cartoonists, such as Thomas Nash, and trompe l'oeil painters, such as William Harnett, returned repeatedly to the representation of money itself, both as a symbol of larger anxieties about a speculative economy and as an immediate, pragmatic, representational problem in its own right.[10]

The allegorical approach to depicting finance in satirical cartoons that accompanied the financial revolution in eighteenth-century Britain continued into the nineteenth century and was adopted in a transformed mode in the United States, not least in response to the recurrent and increasingly globally interconnected panics that punctuated economic life on both sides of the Atlantic. Crashes were explained in cartoons partly through references to familiar visual tropes of natural catastrophes, drawing on biblical images of floods and plagues. But many cartoons in antebellum America also drew on traditional explanations of individual moral responsibility for financial ruin, in the absence of larger, systemic explanations: bankrupts were not victims of an impersonal economic system, but were foolhardy profligates who had brought misfortune on themselves. If the drawings did seek wider explanations, they did so through the moralized lens of political economy, in which the trials and tribulations of finance were portrayed as the result of specific policies or manipulation.[11]

Market Types

In the Gilded Age and the Progressive Era, an individual—sometimes heroic, at other times villainous—was often made to stand in visually for the vast confusion of the entire market, representing the animating spirit that operates the economic machinery and makes it tick. As we will see below, in some cases the depictions focused on a particular, identifiable, charismatic individual, but in others the desire was to portray a generic social type or to personify a particular characteristic of market society. There is a long tradition of embodying the complexity of the market in an individual, from satirical prints of the archetype of the deceptive stockjobber in the eighteenth century, to lionizing portraits of the Napoleons of Wall Street in the late nineteenth century, to the current return of representations of evil and greedy "banksters" in works such as Molly Crabapple's 2011 series of cartoonish paintings that were a response to the Occupy Movement.[12] For example, *Het groote Tafereel der Dwaasheid* ("The Great Mirror of Folly"), a Dutch collection of satirical prints and writings published as an immediate response to the financial crises that spread across Europe in 1720 as a result of the collapse of the South Sea bubble, included cartoons such as *Wind-Kraamer en Grossier* ("The Wholesale Wind-Peddler's Fair"). A speculator, seated on a cloud, with a heavenly head blowing hot air that emerges as if out of his posterior, is accompanied by a man using a pair of bellows to send aloft a cat floating from four balloons. In contrast, a French cartoon from 1784 instead depicts the type of the "Spéculateur" as a wretched specimen who has fallen on hard times, presumably as a result of being seduced into unwise financial dealings. When not a buffoon or a degenerate, the figure of the speculator in the eighteenth century—as a stand-in for the market as a whole—was seen as a dangerous threat to the social order. The possibility of a sudden reversal of the natural hierarchy through the sudden creation or panicked loss of great fortunes was equated with the immoral risks of gambling, and, more often than not, the speculator was simply depicted as an outsider (as Dutch or French in British illustrations in the eighteenth century, for example).[13] In the American painter Francis Edmonds's *The Speculator* (1852), a simple country couple are distracted from their humble productive labor of shucking corn into a handwoven basket by a foppish city slicker, who had entered this sentimental space to tempt them with real-estate speculation (the paper he unfurls before the couple and the viewer of the painting offers "1000 Valuable Lots on Rail Road Ave.").[14] During the course of the nineteenth century, the image of the stockbroker slowly became more respectable, as speculation in the market was rhetorically distinguished from gambling. The idea of the stock market as a legitimate space of economic endeavor was, in part, created by those who wanted to think of themselves as financial professionals, able to perceive opportunities and shoulder risk, and who were to be distinguished from reckless amateurs taking a flyer. The image these stock market insiders wanted to present to the public was one of prudence, efficiency, and moral rectitude, downplaying the traditional archetype of the stockjobbing villain.

Although many cartoons in the Gilded Age and the Progressive Era fixated on a particular, identifiable market manipulator of enormous reach, others featured generic types or specific traits as monstrous personifications of financial corruption. One well-known Joseph Keppler cartoon in *Puck* magazine in 1889, for example, depicted the monopoly power of corporate trusts as monstrously bloated capitalists looming over the diminished and unaware representatives of the people in the U.S. Senate. In this kind of imagery, the corpulent captains of industry appear not so much as specific individuals as generic types, abstractions endowed with human characteristics. Impersonal entities take on the mantle of people, while, conversely, persons become things. Another illustration depicted the figure of Standard Oil—already a personification of the corporate entity in the body of John D. Rockefeller—morphing into an oil barrel. Often the cartoons featured literalizations of figurative understandings, in addition to the personifications of abstractions.[15]

The Financial Bestiary

One of the most common modes of allegorizing the market in the Gilded Age and the Progressive Era was through anthropomorphization: individuals, generic types, or even abstract traits appearing in the guise of animals. Many nineteenth-century depictions of financial panics, for example, focus on the animalistic, herdlike behavior of market crowds, in which the violence of the struggle for financial survival on the floor of the exchange resembles the Darwinian jungle. These muckraking attacks on high finance referenced a long tradition of characterizing the market in bestial terms; indeed, the *Oxford English Dictionary* dates the first emergence of the term "bear" in relation to stock markets to the 1710s (the association of the term with short selling was apparently based on the proverb "to sell the bear's skin before one has caught the bear"). More generally, in eighteenth- and nineteenth-century political cartoons, animal imagery featured regularly as a visual shorthand, harking back to the classical tradition of animal fables, with political and financial actors taking on the roles and appearance of foxes, wolves, lambs, and other emblematic creatures, such as the English bulldog, the American eagle, or the Republican Party elephant.[16]

The most notable portrayal of bestial finance is undoubtedly William Holbrook Beard's painting, *The Bulls and Bears in the Market* (1879). Beard's painting also marked a new departure, however, not least because it weds the visual allegory of political cartoons to the dramatic narrative and realism of late nineteenth-century high art. Beard had already made a name for himself as an accomplished painter of humorous, anthropomorphic scenes, including several involving gatherings of rapacious and Bacchanalian bears in the woods.[17] Although the bears in those earlier images referred obliquely to professional speculators, in *The Bulls and Bears in the Market* there is no doubting that the subject is Wall Street: the stampeding herd of bulls and bears, tearing the flesh from one another, rush past the clearly designated classical portico of (an imagined version of) the New York Stock Exchange, threatening to overwhelm the viewer (fig. 3.1). If the cause of the devastating panic of 1873 is to be found anywhere, this painting suggests, it is not in the moral failings of ordinary citizens, or even in the political machinations of those in the nation's capital, but in the heart of Manhattan's financial district. The canvas combines a melodramatic panorama of the chaotic struggle between the bulls and bears, with realistic attention to the details of horns, fangs, and hooves. It also couples animal brutality with recognizably human expressions, poses, and actions, such as the bear trying to lasso a bull (in the background on the right-hand side). Beard thus reliteralizes the metaphor of social Darwinism: here in lower Manhattan, the law of the jungle reigns, with the bulls and bears personifying those "animal spirits" of greed, fear, panic, and exuberance deemed to be ruling the market, and familiar from the era's other exposés into the "men and mysteries of Wall Street."[18]

By the turn of the twentieth century, many of the depictions of a financial bestiary had become ritualized. For example, W. A. Rogers's cartoon, *Great Activity in Wall Street*, features anthropomorphized bulls, bears, and lambs (i.e., naive investors, ready to be "fleeced"), dressed up in the latest fashions and all following one another in a merry dance. The suggestion is that what looks to the outsider like "great activity in Wall Street" is merely an endless and highly regimented circle of buying and selling, governed by the fixed behavior of the different market "beasts."[19] In a neat double metaphor, a *Puck* cover from 1903 has market bulls and bears dressed as Roman gladiators (fig. 3.2).

Although bull and bear imagery was the most common, as ordinary Americans tried to make sense of the profound economic changes in the last decades of the nineteenth century, other animal metaphors were deployed, the most prom-

Figure 3.1 William Holbrook Beard, *The Bulls and Bears in the Market* (1879). Beard painted a series of humorous scenes involving animals in human guise. In this painting, the bulls and the bears of Wall Street are involved in a panicked stampede, with the innocent lambs—the gullible public—trampled underfoot. Collection of the New-York Historical Society, oil on linen, 39 × 61 × 2 in. (99.1 × 154.9 × 5.1 cm), object #1971.104.

inent of which was the octopus.[20] With the role of Wall Street, and the vast corporate conglomerations its syndicates organized, becoming more central to the life of the nation around the turn of the twentieth century, a range of cartoons proliferated that rendered corporations and financial combinations as a malevolent octopus. As chapter 5 explains in more detail, the image of the octopus conjoined a notion of evil, individual intentionality with a suggestion that corporate malfeasance was part of a complex, many-armed system. These images of corporations as a monstrous cephalopod also captured antimonopolist fears that the new industrial combinations, and the financial apparatus that created them, threatened republican virtues of individual enterprise and self-sufficiency because of their unprecedented size and reach. The octopus is scary because it can insert its tentacles into the entire business sphere and politics of the nation, and even the globe (fig. 3.3).[21]

While some of these octopus cartoons presented either a particular corporation or the entire corporate system as a beast with a will and a mind of its own

Figure 3.2 Udo J. Keppler, "The Triumph of the Bear in the Wall Street Arena," *Puck* 53, no. 1373 (24 June 1903), cover. Udo Keppler, son of the cartoonist Joseph Keppler, produced many satirical images for *Puck* magazine. This image shows the bearish tendency in Wall Street as a Roman gladiator, vanquishing the bullish spirit, with the lambs of the general public seeming to give their approval. Prints & Photographs Division, Library of Congress, LC-DIG-ppmsca-25752.

(in effect literalizing the legal fiction of corporate personality), others identified the octopus with particular robber barons, giving a name and a face to this anthropomorphic rendition of corporate will.[22] This way of thinking about massive corporations and market manipulations as simultaneously the result of animal passions and the will of a single individual was reflected in many of the satirical

Figure 3.3 Udo Keppler, "Next!," *Puck* 56, no. 1436 (7 September 1904), centerfold. In this cartoon, Keppler draws on a familiar characterization of large corporations, such as Standard Oil, as a malevolent octopus controlling the nation. Library of Congress, LC-DIG-ppmsca-25884.

cartoons of the period, which portrayed robber barons as beasts with identifiable human features. For example, a *Puck* cartoon from 1901 depicted J. P. Morgan as a bullish figure, blowing worthless soap bubbles of "inflated value" that were eagerly chased by the diverse crowd.[23] Another *Puck* cover, from 1913, featured Morgan (complete with a bulbous, purple nose) as a monstrous spider, representing "flim flam finance" at the center of the web of Wall Street (fig. 3.4). In this case, however, the caption informs us that "the flies got wise," with the public keeping clear of the web.

Personifying Finance

These anthropomorphic renditions of recognizable captains of industry were in keeping with other popular depictions of the period, which also identified the market, as a whole, with particular individuals. Despite efforts by Wall Street practitioners in the late nineteenth and early twentieth centuries to redefine the popular image of finance as professional and impersonal, the American public continued to focus on prominent individuals as embodying the stock market.

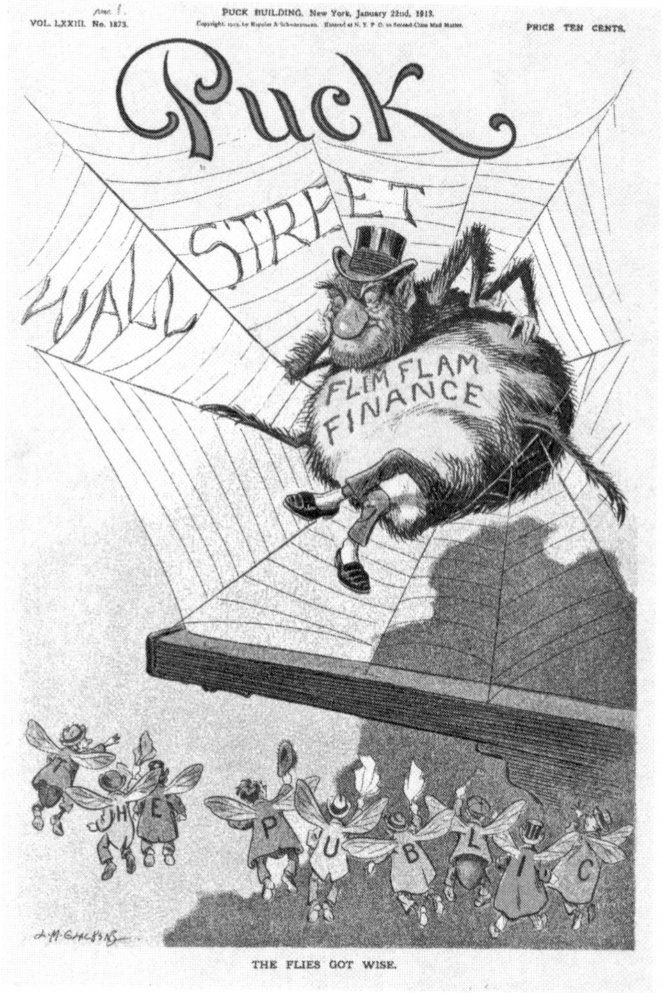
VOL. LXXIII. No. 1873.
PUCK BUILDING. New York, January 22nd, 1913.
PRICE TEN CENTS.
Puck
WALL STREET
FLIM FLAM FINANCE
THE FLIES GOT WISE.

Figure 3.4 L. M. Glackens, "The Flies Got Wise," *Puck* 73, no. 1873 (22 January 1913), cover. Although regarded as a public hero for helping to avert the financial panic of 1907, by 1913 J. P. Morgan's reputation had fallen under public suspicion. In this *Puck* cartoon, the public have "got wise" to the trickery of the spider at the center of the financial web. Prints & Photographs Division, Library of Congress, LC-DIG-ppmsca-27912.

Visual and verbal portraits of robber barons, such as Daniel Drew, Jim Fisk, Cornelius Vanderbilt, and Jay Gould in the 1870s and 1880s and John D. Rockefeller and J. P. Morgan in the 1890s and 1900s, dominated the public imagination of the market as giants that loomed over Wall Street, in the view of a satirical cartoon from 1903, for example. In the same way that many newspaper accounts of corporate corruption focused on the scandalous antics of individual Wall Street speculators, so, too, did visual representations of the brave new world of financial capitalism latch onto corporate leaders as larger-than-life embodiments of economic processes, even after the original founders of the great combinations had supposedly become obsolete as they were overtaken by the bureaucratic procedures of the very corporations they had created.[24]

The cartoons repeatedly concentrated on the personal power of particular Wall Street titans, sometimes as an all-powerful colossus, but at other times as sinister monsters or puppet masters, controlling the fate of mere mortals. In a *Puck* cartoon from 1902, for example, Morgan is a goliath, single-handedly carrying the cornucopia of the nation's industrial bounty, as "commercial might" dwarfs the now-insignificant "divine right" of old European monarchies.[25] In another *Puck* cartoon from 1910 (after Morgan had fallen out of favor in the aftermath of the panic of 1907), a huge figure of Morgan jealously gathers in a number of banking institutions in a "billion dollar bank merger," providing an answer to the question, posed by the cartoon, of why the United States had no need for a central bank.[26] In a less-reverential earlier image, Cornelius Vanderbilt is shown as "The Modern Colossus of (Rail) Roads," a giant astride different rail lines, holding onto the reins not only of two toy-sized locomotives, but also the diminutive figures of Cyrus Field and Jay Gould, whose puppet strings Vanderbilt is seen to manipulate (fig. 3.5). Or, in "A Design for Union Station," the cars of the "United States Harriman Railroads" disappear ominously into the cavernous mouth of a monumental depiction of Harriman's head, emphasizing the literal figurehead of this railroad empire, but also creating a macabre image of Harriman as a monstrous entity that swallows railroads whole.[27] Another Keppler cartoon from *Puck* features J. P. Morgan, James J. Hill, John D. Rockefeller, Henry T. Oxnard, and Jay Gould as thuggish giants who loom over Wall Street (Morgan, for instance, wields the club of "high finance"). They are ganging up on the tiny figure of Teddy Roosevelt, who rests on the sword of "public service," making the reader wonder whether this humble Jack will indeed be able to slay the assembled giants.[28]

The Visible Hand

From the 1870s into the first decades of the twentieth century, large-scale corporations continued to be viewed in the popular imagination as extensions of the sinister will of individual owners, even after that was no longer entirely accurate. These ways of representing corporations through anthropomorphization or personification were appealing, because they made sense of the complex new forms

Figure 3.5 Joseph Keppler, "The Modern Colossus of (Rail) Roads," *Puck* 6, no. 144 (10 December 1879): 650–651. Keppler Sr. mocks the divine pretensions of the robber baron Cornelius Vanderbilt, who is shown manipulating the reins of the various railroads he controlled, with Jay Gould and Cyrus Field as mere puppets. Prints & Photographs Division, Library of Congress, LC-DIG-ds-05068.

of capitalist organization through more-familiar modes of understanding, many of which (as chapter 5 will document) verged on the melodramatic or conspiratorial. The personification of abstractions was one thing, but equally important to many critical commentators was the problem of identifying who was really behind some of the new industrial combinations. This vexed Henry Adams, for instance, who remarked of the "new man" behind the great trusts: "The longer one watched, the less could be seen of him."[29] The difficulty of ascribing individual agency to collective entities continued to trouble writers at the turn of the twentieth century. For example, the novelist Harold Frederic, preparing to write *The Market-Place* (1899), his foray into financial fiction, encountered the problem of the inscrutability of business, compared with the more easily intelligible realm of politics. "Business! Business!" Frederic notes in exasperation. "You can read in histories, memoirs, state papers, every conceivable detail of how such a war was waged, such a revolution created; everything in political and social history can be investigated. But in financial history, the great capitalists who [are the] true rulers of the world work in impenetrable mystery."[30] Critics continued to insist on holding individuals to account, even if, legally, no individual per se could be held responsible in cases of corporate malfeasance or negligence.[31] If corporations endeavored to hide behind the legal protection of limited liability and collective identity, muckrakers, in the legal terminology of the age, wanted to "pierce the corporate veil" and expose to the harsh light of criticism the individuals they felt were to blame for corporate wrongdoing, who, they suspected, were hiding behind the legal fiction of corporate personality.[32] Thus in 1910, a cartoon in *Puck* tellingly insisted that antitrust campaigners should "get after the substance and not the shadow" by identifying the powerful individuals hiding behind the legal protection that the laws of incorporation permitted.[33] At the same time, however, an obsessive focus on the might of particular individual corporate titans ended up fetishizing their power, turning them into bogeymen that haunted the popular imagination and made it hard to think of the complexities of financial capitalism in any other way.

When the public were not evoking the inscrutable mysteries of Providence, popular explanations for sudden market movements that created or wiped out fortunes tended, from the eighteenth century onward, to rely on the idea of plotting and scheming behind the scenes by powerful insiders, seeing the conspiring agency of a hidden hand in place of the abstract convergence of aggregate supply and demand that constituted the invisible hand of more orthodox economic theory. It comes as little surprise, therefore, that images of finance focus—as the very word suggests—on the controlling hand of the manipulator. For example, there is a fixation on the hand in a famous Edward Steichen photograph of the notoriously camera-shy J. P. Morgan. In 1903, the painter Fedor Encke commissioned Steichen to taken some photographs of Morgan as an aid to Encke's portrait, as Morgan was always too busy to sit for the painter. The atmospheric lighting carefully orchestrated by Steichen, in a sitting lasting just three minutes, resulted in a photo that shaped the public's view of Morgan for generations to come. Not only do Morgan's eyes stare fiercely out of the gloom, but the light falling on the arm of the chair, gripped by the subject's hand, looks uncannily as if Morgan is brandishing a dagger at the viewer.[34]

When the nation's industrial and financial leaders were not, like Morgan, trying to hide from public display or sink into anonymity behind the façade of their corporate identity, they sought to portray themselves as dignified and professional. Jay Gould, for example, had himself painted as a respectable and kindly bourgeois businessmen by the German-British royal academician Sir Hubert von Herkomer (ironically best known now as the painter of *Hard Times*, a searing portrayal of rural poverty). The public, however, thought of the notorious stock market operator as the "Mephistopheles of Wall Street," a cold and calculating devil manipulating the market with sublime ease. A satirical illustration from *Judge* magazine in 1886, for example, calls to account the outrageous claim made by Gould that he never speculated.[35] The cartoon shows a caricatured version of Gould seated in the bell jar of a gigantic ticker machine, where, unseen by the frenzied stock market players beneath, he dictates market prices directly onto the ticker tape itself. Gould is thus rendered as both himself and the very personification of market manipulation. The cartoon suggests that stock prices are moved not by the invisible hand of supply and demand, but by the visible hand of the Mephistopheles of Wall Street. (The cartoon thus ironically confirms Gould's scandalous denial: he would have no need to engage in risky speculations if he were able to accurately predict price movements by creating them himself.)

The View from the Visitors' Gallery

The cartoon of a larger-than-life Gould literally writing the prices on the ticker tape provides an imaginary portrait of what critics feared was really taking place in the stock market. It resembled the view from the visitors' gallery of the Stock Exchange, but it promised to reveal what could not be seen with the naked eye from that privileged vantage point. The view from the visitors' gallery—whether real or imagined—was a crucial trope for representing the market in the later nineteenth century. As we saw in chapter 2, from the 1870s on, a number of quasi-anthropological exposés and tourist guidebooks provided an introduction to the Wall Street scene. A Baedeker travel guide for 1893, for example, recommended that "strangers, who are admitted to a gallery overlooking the hall (entr., 13 Wall St.), should not omit a visit to this strange scene of business, tumult, and excitement, a wilder scene probably than that presented in any European exchange."[36] Like a Baedeker guidebook, James K. Medbery's *Men and Mysteries of Wall Street* provides an early example of practical advice on how to visit the New York Stock Exchange: "You can reach the Long Room from the antechamber on Broad Street," while the New Street entrance presents "a better opportunity for the spectator."[37] Before explaining the history and operational mechanisms of the stock market, Medbery walks readers through the spectacle that confronted visitors to the gallery:

> The first impression on entering the Stock Exchange is upon the tympanum. A genuine tourist almost inevitably has a dreamy reminiscence of Niagara. The visitor finds himself in the vestibule of a vast chamber, which stretches a furlong deep from Broad to New Street. At the farther end, shut off by successive iron barriers with narrow gateways under watch and ward, is a huge basin-like enclosure, filled with wild human tumult. Peering down through the high-vaulted, dim-lighted space, the eye sees nothing but excited faces, arms flung wildly in air, heads appearing and disappearing—a billowy mob, from which surges up an incessant and confused clamor. The straining ear distinguishes ever and anon an individual voice rising in shriller pitch or heavier volume, only to be drowned out from the abyss.[38]

The view of the trading floor, one of the indispensable sights for any tourist in the city, is chaotic to both the ears and the eyes of the novice visitor: "New York has no more entertaining place than its Stock Exchange. It is one of the show places of the city. The visitor who for the first time looks down from a gallery upon its members in the act of transacting business, is astonished at the apparent confusion he witnesses. He seems to have entered a madhouse. The idea that the market values of our leading securities should be determined by what appears to him to be a howling mob of incurable lunatics, is incomprehensible."[39] "Intense, blinding, deafening," the Long Room at first threatens to overwhelm visitors' senses, unless they are schooled by an expert.[40] If the writers of these guidebooks adopted an ethnographic stance toward the seemingly barbaric battles and exotic rituals enacted on the exchange floor, they also characterized the stock market as a sporting contest, or a theatrical spectacle, with the plush, red velvet chairs in the visitors' gallery completing the latter effect. They note how the audience, at times, becomes caught up in the drama unfolding on the floor of the exchange as panic spreads from speculators to spectators and back again.[41]

For Medbery's and other guides to Wall Street, part of the spectacle is the quotation board itself, which records, in abstracted form, the ebb and flow of prices: "The phenomena of the boards depend upon a great number of distinct forces, all acting from without and only disclosing themselves vaguely in the prices of the daily share list. Here on the upper floor the official record has notched the last wave line of each billowing security, but below fresh elements are working, and in the heaving cauldron of the Long Room is a changeful ebb and flow that has neither rule nor limit nor certainty. There least of all should one resort for a key to the mystery of the street."[42] For visitors to Wall Street, the attraction is not merely the manic spectacle of the "heaving cauldron" or the "phenomena of the boards" in themselves, but the fact that the stock exchange in New York is the symbolic epicenter of the seismic financial movements of supply and demand that are felt across the globe. According to Medbery, "if the visitor wishes to master one problem at a time, therefore, he will keep his seat in the chamber and will find abundant room for reflection in the thought that here around him are the men who daily gauge the value of a billion and a half of national debt, whose shouts are the annihilations of millions or a crest-wave of momentary fresh wealth, rippling through bank vaults and the iron chests of the thrifty, east and west along the tremulous wire, to San Francisco at one end and Frankfort at the other."[43] If the wider economy that both reacts to and sends signals back to the Stock Exchange cannot be seen in itself, then the view from the visitors' gallery promises to provide a concrete embodiment of the panoramic reaches of trade and industry on a global scale. At the same time, however, the vista of the economic sublime that the visitors' gallery affords is, to the untrained eye, a confusing, overwhelming experience that needs a good deal of interpretation if it is to be seen as the scientific setting of prices, rather than a hellish gambling den.

The Architecture of Finance

Although outsiders to the nation's stock and commodity exchanges found them a bewildering and bestial spectacle, the image that financial insiders projected of their business was markedly different. In their promotional materials, the architectural style of their buildings, and even the iconography of their paper currency, banks and other financial institutions sought to convey a symbolic sense of solidity, prosperity, and confidence as a counterweight to the insubstantiality and incoherence of an economy floated on speculation. Although, like the guidebooks and sensational exposés, pictorial representations of New York's Wall Street and Chicago's La Salle Street in the second half of the nineteenth century increasingly focused on the exhilarating show put on by the "animal spirits" of speculation, other depictions of finance that were more sympathetic to the insiders' point of view presented it as a calm and rational endeavor. For example, even though James Cafferty and Charles Rosenberg's *Wall Street, Half Past Two O'Clock, October 13, 1857,* is meant to depict the epicenter of that year's panic, it is an oddly static painting, whose only clue to the extraordinary events taking place is in its title.

Despite supposedly encapsulating the dramatic financial events taking place within Wall Street and across the nation, Cafferty and Rosenberg's picture is not so different in its composition from Hughson Hawley's, in 1882 (fig. 3.6). The scene in Hawley's architectural rendering is similarly static and idealized, with groups of top-hatted gentleman idly talking or reading a newspaper, genteel couples strolling by, two black men standing around, and the driver of a horse-drawn omnibus holding a pink parasol. It does not show the usual armies of messenger boys running hither and thither (a lone messenger or newspaper boy is crossing the road, without obvious signs of haste); even the tall telegraph pole outside the exchange itself is shorn of the confusing web of wires that struck actual visitors to that site and show up in more-candid photos from the period. Early and more formal daguerreotypes featuring vistas of Wall Street likewise tend to portray it as a tranquil and sparsely populated thoroughfare, with the photographers technologically unable or ideologically unwilling to include what makes the street of interest in the first place.

Manuals on investment, such as Nelson's *ABC of Wall Street,* preferred to show Wall Street as a calm zone, with leisurely vistas of Wall Street, Broad Street, and the exterior of the New York Stock Exchange building. In addition, Nelson includes depopulated views of the interior of the Exchange, with its architectural harmony and dignified decoration giving no hint of the frenzied activity that takes place there. Picture books, such as *King's Views of the New York Stock Exchange,* by Moses King, a publisher of travel guidebooks, likewise contains vistas of Wall Street and its most important buildings that are either devoid of people or have merely a smattering of bourgeois city folk (both men and women) promenading in the vicinity or driving by in carriages. King's book also contains depictions of the interior of the Stock Exchange, with, for example, austere photographs of the Bond Room and Main Room, cleared of the typical signs of chaotic business that struck most actual visitors to the Exchange.

The only depiction of the trading floor in action that King's volume does include is not a photograph, but an artist's rendering, used as the illustration for the lead article, on "The Magnitude and the Necessity of the Institution" (fig. 3.7). Unlike the descriptions of the view from the visitors' gallery, this fantasy

Figure 3.6 Hughson Hawley, "The New York Stock Exchange" (1882). Hawley was a well-known architectural illustrator who depicted many of New York's buildings from the 1870s to the Depression. This lithographic rendering features the NYSE. Prints & Photographs Division, Library of Congress, LC-DIG-pga-01478.

representation shows an orderly scene, with a cluster of men calmly reading the stock ticker in the foreground and two brokers chatting alone at one of the posts (one of them is even sitting down); only in the distant background are a couple of men hazily shown raising their arms to bid on stocks, but without the sense of frenzy that usually characterizes such happenings. This is unsurprising, because King's volume was less a guidebook than a promotional tome, designed to be presented to clients as a gift. Although the lead article begins by announcing that "this simple account of 'Wall Street' and the Stock Exchange, with its accompanying illustrations, is intended for the millions of people throughout the country who are deeply interested in the 'Street,' and who hardly know what it looks like, what it really is, or who its leaders are at this time," the frontispiece tellingly includes a panel announcing that it is "Presented with the compliments of . . ."[44]

Although King's book is not quite as sycophantic as Colonel D'Alton Mann's projected vanity publication of leading New York figures (discussed in chapter 1), the vast majority of the "1,050 illustrations" proclaimed on the cover are not of Wall Street in general, but are uniform, oval photographic portraits of past presidents, officers, and current members of the New York Stock Exchange, flattering images that, in reality, tell readers more about the mustache fashions of the Gilded Age New York haute bourgeoisie than about the workings of the Exchange and "what it really is."

Figure 3.7 King's Views of the New York Stock Exchange (New York: Moses King, 1898), 1. Moses King was a publisher of travel guidebooks. This frontispiece is from his guide to the NYSE, which was a promotional volume featuring views of the building, as well as photographic portraits of all its members.

Although King's guidebook dedicates most of its space to meticulously repro-
ducing portraits of all the Exchange's membership, like other partisan depictions
of Wall Street its main way of illustrating the different operations of finance
is to focus on the solidity of the building's external and interior architecture.
For the most part, it is devoid of people, whether the public or professionals.
The neat, unpopulated images suggest that the Stock Exchange is a rational and
self-regulating machine for allocating money, with its members and officers
at a lofty, honorific remove from the thick of the action, which indeed is the
view that the Exchange wanted to present of itself. In a similar fashion, in an
effort to convey to its readers the modernity and reliability of legitimate brokerage operations, *Ticker* magazine included photos of the various departments of
J. S. Bache & Company (all empty of either clerks or clients), along with floor plans
and organizational charts emphasizing how each part of the "machine" contributed to the whole. Likewise, a series of articles launched by *Banker's Magazine* in
1906 aimed to show "Modern Financial Institutions and Their Equipment," with
accompanying photographic illustrations that include the principal officers of a
bank, along with the solidity of their buildings, the sobriety of their premises,
and even the gleam and heft of the firm's vault.[45] An advertisement for American
National Bank included in its otherwise very dry and factual prospectus a picture
of its impressive "nineteen ton vault door," a visual synecdoche for the institution's financial security.[46] Unlike nineteenth-century industry, with its potential
for publicizing itself by showing scenes of factory work and the manufactured
goods themselves, representing the productive work of finance was necessarily
less direct and more abstract. The emphasis in these kinds of images is less on
the personal probity of the bank or the brokerage officers with whom a customer
might build up a relationship (as the text of some of the guidebooks and brochures on speculation tended to stress) than on the orderly relationship between
the different parts of the financial machinery itself, as if it were a self-regulating
engine.

The image of "modern" finance in these kinds of promotional illustrations
is one in which the objective and impersonal aspects of the business figure far
more prominently than the personal ones. The view of Wall Street as a well-run
engine room, rather than a gentlemen's club, was championed not only by the
Stock Exchange itself, but also by the emerging fraternity of technical analysts
who likewise wanted to portray finance as a rational and predictable endeavor:

A passenger standing on the observation platform in the engine-room of a modern
ocean liner will observe great masses of steel, some stationary, some whirling at

terrific speed; he may go down into the boiler-room where is generated the power with which the great ship is driven, but all this will only give him a crude idea of the machinery of propulsion. He must know and be able to grasp all the component parts of that machinery, and their relation to each other, in order to appreciate what a tremendous undertaking it is to move this gigantic mass of men and materials over the watery miles separating two continents. So it is with the machinery of a large banking and brokerage house. . . . Everything is run with clock-like precision. No matter how large a business is being done, there is no confusion, the plant being designed to handle the maximum volume of orders.[47]

Even Haight & Freese's friendly guidebook to speculation, intended for the investor of small means, seeks to reassure those potential clients that its brokerage premises are not sleazy gambling dens (as adverse publicity had it), but a modern establishment, with all the accouterments that a would-be speculator would expect. "It is not from any feeling of egotism," the brochure explains, "that in addition to the above [the beginner's guide to speculation] we include authentic illustrations of the interior of our various offices, and maps showing the location of the different roads."[48] Unlike the more restrained promotional efforts of their more white-shoe counterparts who belonged to the august New York Stock Exchange, Haight & Freese's brochure does show actual people in its illustrations of its premises. Even then, the suggestion is that this is no mere bucket shop, but a thoroughly respectable brokerage, with all the same upscale furniture and sophisticated technology of legitimate, upmarket firms; the crucial difference is that the Everyman speculator could identify with the figures populating Haight & Freese's images, with their derby and bowler hats instead of the top hats associated with traditional Wall Street offices.

With its appeal to a more democratic audience, Haight & Freese's brochure does not edit out aspects of the mundane reality of speculation (such as the waste paper from the ticker strewn on the floor), even though it also tries to draw the attention of its aspirational audience of clerks and shopkeepers to the solidity of its architecture and fittings. Banks, insurance firms, and stockbrokers often included images of their own buildings in their promotional literature and (in some cases) on their letterheads. The building thus functioned as not merely the location of the firm's premises, but the embodiment of its values.[49] The architecture of financial institutions in the last quarter of the nineteenth century favored a neoclassical style, with columns, porticos, and friezes calling up notions of both republican honesty and monumental grandeur, although the interiors tended toward neogothic, combining the soaring spaces of a cathedral or a theater in the trading floor with the sumptuousness of a gentlemen's club in the smaller public rooms.[50]

Perhaps the most famous architect of nineteenth-century finance was Chicago-born Louis Sullivan, whose career uncannily paralleled that of the speculative economy itself.[51] Sullivan's first job, as a draftsman in an architectural practice in Philadelphia, ended when the firm downsized in the wake of the economic depression of 1873. He then moved to Chicago to work on the building boom, which was starting to replace structures destroyed in the fire of 1871 (a conflagration that had played a major part in the panic of 1873). Together with his partner Dankmar Adler, Sullivan designed many prominent theater and office buildings in Chicago in the 1880s and 1890s, with the Stock Exchange Building (completed 1894) combining in its vast first-floor trading room those twin elements of theatrical spectacle and commercial pragmatism.[52] Together with the Guaranty Building (which opened in 1895), the Chicago Stock Exchange marked the high point of Sullivan's career. As commissions dried up in the wake of the panic of 1893, his partnership was dissolved, and his work and private life went into terminal decline.[53] Sullivan was one of the pioneers of steel-framed high-rise buildings, whose technical innovation relied on a grammar of ornament to articulate their function to an audience that needed instruction in how to read these monumental new urban texts. (Sullivan is credited with the dictum "form ever follows function," which later became the mantra of modernism in architecture).[54] In structures such as the Chicago Stock Exchange and the Guaranty building, Sullivan exaggerated the separate functional components of the buildings by including, for example, a distinct ground-level section, to suggest a solid base; rising vertical ornamentation, to highlight the upward thrust of the main shaft; and heavy cornicing at the roof level, which spoke of commercial pragmatism rather than spiritual aspiration. In his architectural design for these financial institutions, Sullivan thus provided a visual resolution to the potentially dangerous paradoxes of a credit economy that seemed increasingly to lack a solid foundation: in effect, by means of ornamental sleight of hand, the public had to be reassured that, like the credit it symbolized, so tall a structure could rest securely on so slight a footprint, unlike traditional buildings, whose structural integrity was clearly manifest in the weight of the stone walls required to support them.[55]

Just as Sullivan's protomodernist commercial architecture did not reject ornamentation, other financial architecture in the late nineteenth and early twentieth centuries relied on decorative elements to provide a fitting interpretation of the work carried out in the building. Murals, stained glass, and statuary in the beaux art style turned to the classical rhetoric of personification to provide a concrete embodiment of the otherwise abstract work of banking, insurance, real estate, and stockbrokering.[56] The second Chicago Board of Trade building (opened in 1885), for example, was adorned with stained glass windows by John La Farge. Although the building was demolished, similar La Farge windows survive, including one, titled *Fortune and Her Wheel* (1902), in the Frick Building in Pittsburgh.[57] Likewise, Edwin Blashfield's murals, such as *The Uses of Wealth*, offered an idealized rendition of capitalism. A contemporary critic waxed lyrical about *The Uses of Wealth*, the full title of which is *Capital, Supported by Labor, Offering the Gold Key of Opportunity to Science, Literature, and Art*: "Capital—the sordid and unlovely 'Capital' of the demagogues and the statisticians—here appearing as a beautiful feminine vision, gleaming like a new sunshine in the yellows of her own gold coin and hair and robe, key and sword hilt and chased helmet, hundreds of yellow, varying, delicate, complementary colors, setting off, reflecting, and burnishing up each other in a very blaze of affluence."[58] The abstractions of capitalism are thus presented in the guise of personifications, rather than actual people, and ironically depicted in the shape of sentimental femininity, rather than the hard-nosed reality of the world of masculine business. In a similar fashion, advertisers in the first decades of the twentieth century attempted to humanize the "soulless corporation" by representing it as an idealized woman. In one example, the Bell telephone system endeavored to redescribe the potential sinister reach of its monopoly by representing the company and its networks as a helpful, nation-spanning female telephone operator.[59]

Pictures of Panic

The decoration for the palaces of finance often evoked the abstract grammar of classical and religious architecture, or it relied on idealized personifications of capital, industry, and nature. In contrast, illustrations accompanying Wall Street–based fiction in popular magazines tended to focus on the frantically waving arms and panicked faces of actual people on the floor of the stock and produce exchanges.[60] The images were less concerned with depicting specific, recognizable, Wall Street luminaries, however, than representing either generic types of speculators or, more commonly, individuals as merely part of a crowd. These illustrations often highlighted moments of high drama in the accompanying text, turning points when fortunes are won or lost, corners achieved or overthrown. In terms of genre, they have much in common with dime-novel adventure stories, although they take place not on the frontier, but in the heart of New York.[61] They also gave visible form to psychological theories about the mass hysteria of crowds that began to gain currency in the late nineteenth century, thereby extending

Figure 3.8 "The Recent Panic—Scene in the New York Stock Exchange on the Morning of Friday, May 5th," *Frank Leslie's Illustrated Newspaper* (18 May 1893), 322. The phenomenon of financial panic fascinated observers in the late nineteenth century as they struggled to make sense of how the orderly workings of the stock market could be overtaken by animal passions and mass hysteria. This illustration was drawn by Charles Broughton "from sketches on the spot." Prints & Photographs Division, Library of Congress.

the earlier understandings of animalistic passions encapsulated, for example, in Beard's painting. The image of hysterical speculators on the floor of the Exchange became a familiar visual and narrative shorthand during this period for the transformative nature—for better or worse—of financial capitalism as a whole.

As David Zimmerman has argued, writers and artists in the Gilded Age and the Progressive Era frequently invoked financial panics, not only because they were compelling events in their own right that demanded explanation, but also because they pushed to the very limits the capability of the familiar representational genres of realism or melodrama to account for them. With their descent into chaos and fear, panics embodied all that was confounding about speculation in the eyes of this period's Populist and Progressive critics (fig. 3.8). Like other accounts and illustrations of the Exchange floor, the image in *Frank Leslie's Illustrated Newspaper* combines, in the foreground, studies of the physiognomic reactions of individuals to the extreme emotions that possess them with an impressionistic swirl of deindividualized body parts seething together in a mass in the background, recalling descriptions from the guidebooks to Wall Street: "Notebooks, arms, fists, dexter fingers, hats, heads, tossing, swaying, darting hither and thither with nervous eagerness, and suggesting a perpetual explosion of bombshells from below. Now concentrating on a single stock; again breaking out into twenty different markets."[62] In the *Frank Leslie's* scene, the waving arms in particular, and the maelstromlike movement in general, evoke—as in the Niagara references in Medbery's account quoted above—the recurrent nineteenth-century image of financial panic as a form of individual and collective drowning.[63]

Scenes of Reading, Scenes of Writing

Although theatrical scenes from the floor of the stock and commodity exchanges continued to feature regularly in popular representations of the market well past the turn of the twentieth century, it is striking how often the dramas of Wall Street in the Gilded Age and the Progressive Era are illustrated, both visually and verbally, not with noisy scenes of crowds and mass hysteria, but with vignettes of concentrated reading of the ticker machine, which is writing its message on the tape. Again and again, these tales of fortunes won and lost are depicted in their most dramatic moments by scenes of men (and it is nearly always men) poring over the ticker tape that cascades into the wastepaper basket (fig. 3.9).

The ticker machine itself is often at the heart of the action. In some cases, the picture of tape reading captures the moment when an arch-speculator realizes that his villainous scheme to corner the market has been foiled; in others, we

" ' *Bring your friends here this afternoon.* ' "

Figure 3.9 W. R. Leigh, illustration for Edwin Lefèvre, "The Break in Turpentine," *McClure's Magazine* (April 1901), 543. Lefèvre's short stories gave a broadly sympathetic, insider's view of Wall Street, albeit with a gentle criticism of amateurs and outsiders who got caught up in "ticker fever." The stock ticker is a constant presence in both the stories and the accompanying illustrations. Harvard College Library.

are meant to see the calm concentration of a heroic Napoleon of finance, who is able to apprehend the entire direction of the market from a trancelike study of the tape itself (fig. 3.10). In both cases, however, the depiction of someone reading the tape acts as a representational proxy for the whole of the disembodied and placeless market of similar readers. Thus the trading room of the New York Stock Exchange no longer served as an unambiguous symbol of the origin and end point of all the financial energy circulating through the nation's economy. At the same time, however, the placeless and impersonal market that was beginning to replace this actual marketplace could not be represented directly and realistically.

"'GREENER,' PANTED THE PORTLY MAN, 'WHAT'S THE MATTER WITH IOWA MIDLAND?'"

Figure 3.10 W. R. Leigh, illustration for Edwin Lefèvre, "The Man Who Won," *McClure's Magazine* (August 1901), 363. The scene of intense tape reading was a repeated trope in Lefèvre's stories. Harvard College Library.

In this way, the stock ticker and the ticker tape became a visual fetish in all kinds of illustrations. If *King's Views of the New York Stock Exchange* presented potential investors with an idealized view of the work of Wall Street through the medium of dignified portraits of its elder statesmen, a privately printed and distributed collection of caricatures of leading Exchange figures in 1904 showed instead how the nation's financiers pictured themselves when they were not having to appeal to ordinary mortals. The images show the members of the Exchange as hearty fellows, referencing their individual passions for, say, carriage driving, hunting, or yachting, but always with the ticker, the tape, or other symbols of their occupation woven into the image. The caricature of Alfred M. Judson, for example, shows him riding the stock ticker as if it were a horse (which also resembles a phallus). Likewise, the portrait of Charles E. Knoblauch in the same volume shows him as a cowboy, riding a submissive bull, bear, and lamb simultaneously, with a ticker strapped to his back like a rifle (fig. 3.11).

Although these flattering caricatures portray the NYSE members as using the ticker tape to rein in the market, other illustrations show speculators bound—almost erotically—by the tape. For example, the cover of David Graham Phillips's novel, *The Deluge*, features an impish Cupid caught up in the tape flowing out of a ticker machine, whereas in Phillips's novel *The Cost*, the ticker is the melodramatic instrument of death: "In his struggles the tape had wound round and round his legs, his arms, his neck. It lay in a curling, coiling mat, like a serpent's head, upon his throat, where his hands clutched."[64] In contrast, the illustration accompanying a story in *Ticker*, entitled "Your Own Brains, versus Brains Bought, Begged or Borrowed," depicts a decadent, dandyish figure louchely smoking a cigarette in a frilled armchair while nonchalantly holding a pet bull and a bear by the reins of the tape, which is flowing in art nouveau coils out of the ticker machine beside the chair.[65] The image represents an ambiguous, sexualized fantasy of gaining dominance over the market, rather than being seduced by it. In comparison with the Rough Rider version of masculinity presented in the caricatures of Judson and Knoblauch, the mesmerizing power to control the market makes the speculator a passive, languid, androgynous figure, whose knowing gaze flirts with the imagined reader of *Ticker*.

The tape provides the connective ribbon that unites all the players, creating a visual representation of the abstract information that constitutes the market. It is ubiquitous, fetishized, and yet strangely invisible, not least because so much was produced every day, only to be outdated instantly. With their continual printing of prices, ticker-tape machines produced vast quantities of waste paper. The advent of the ticker-tape parade thus coincided with the proliferation of ticker machines, and it provided a convenient solution to the problem of all the instantly worthless paper produced by the tickers. The first such parade was held in lower Manhattan on 28 October 1886, for the dedication of the Statue of Liberty. Illustrations of ticker-tape parades in the late nineteenth century show how they constituted a carnival of (literal) waste in which paper profits and losses returned to mere paper, more in keeping with Georges Bataille's notion of the economy of expenditure than with the image of modern, technologically mediated, rational investment depicted in many investment-advice manuals and promotional works for the NYSE. Unlike the images of solitary tape reading, the ticker-tape parades

Figure 3.11 Portrait of Charles E. Knoblauch, in George E. Croscup, ed., *Stock Exchange in Caricature: A Private Collection of Cartoons, Caricatures, and Character Sketches* (New York: A. Stone, 1904), n.p. In contrast to the satirical cartoons of robber barons in the popular press, George Croscup's privately printed collection of caricatures of leading NYSE personalities portrayed them as dashing and energetic men-about-town. Harvard College Library.

were collective outpourings of emotion: the account of the first parade suggests that it was a spontaneous prank, rather than a planned and dignified act of commemoration. These events were, in effect, belated reactions to political events, the aggregate responses to which had already been registered and discounted on the very tape that was floating down on the parade.[66]

As we saw in chapter 2, the ticker enabled readers to follow all the action in the market from a privileged, bird's-eye viewpoint. Thus they began to see the market in a different way: not as the record of personal struggles between identifiable traders, but as the abstract geography of a global financescape. The view from the visitors' gallery of the bulls and bears battling it out on the floor of the Exchange is replaced by the vantage point of a lone individual absorbed in reading the abstract procession of numbers coming over the ticker. It was not merely because the trading floor was now closed to the would-be market watcher, but because the tape offered a better lens through which to view the market's transactions—better even than participant-observer accounts of action on the floor in the newspapers' market reports and market circulars, which claimed to provide the inside scoop on secret deals and manipulations. For many of the advice manuals promoting tape reading, the ideal market observer would be far removed from the scene of action, precisely in order not to be distracted by the commotion on the floor of the exchange. For example, Richard Wyckoff's *Studies in Tape Reading* (a digest of advice compiled from *Ticker*) offers a recommendation for the would-be tape reader: "For perfect concentration as a protection from the tips, gossip, and other influences which abound in a broker's office, he should, if possible, seclude himself. A small room with a ticker, a desk, and private telephone connection with his broker's office are all the facilities required."[67] Likewise, Edwin Lefèvre's novel, *Sampson Rock of Wall Street*, contrasts the tumult that Rock knows must be taking place on the floor of the Exchange with the calm overview of the market he is able to achieve in the inner sanctum of his private office:

> In the big marble Board Room the air was filled with the exultant whoops of the bears who were winning, the maddened shrieks of the bulls who were losing and would not lose more—the primal passions made audible in the discordant chorus of the dollar-hunters, made visible about the various "posts" in a sea of heads that broke into a foam of fists clinched and defiant—with, here and there, the quivering, outstretched fingers of a drowning man. And beside the man who had said, "Let there be storm," out of sight and out of hearing of the money-mad mob, under its protecting glass dome, as though it were a fragile plant, the little ticker in this office was impassively ticking, ticking, ticking!—singing its marvelous song of triumph and defeat in one.[68]

Reading the tape in the quiet of his office, Rock can "see" not only the drama taking place on the trading floor, without actually becoming caught up in it, but even (as we saw in chapter 2) a heroic vision of the unfurling landscape of his transportation empire and the products of industry that it is carrying. Rock must engage in an intense and imaginative act of reading, however, to make these economic abstractions come to life, but, unlike the spectacle of the trading floor, with its "sea of heads" and "foam of fists," there is nothing much for an observer to see, other than a man reading the inscrutable symbols mechanically printed on the tape. For all that the ticker represents a technologically modern form of finance, the images of stock market operators engaged in trancelike reading conjure up all the worst fears of the period about the occult nature of speculation, in which fantastical profits and even entire towns are magicked out of thin air, and speculators are mesmerized by sinister market forces.

Since the intangible, placeless market cannot be represented directly (or, rather, since the view of the marketplace from the visitors' gallery no longer provides a privileged vantage), scenes of solitary tape reading thus become a representational proxy for what is not visible directly. As Zimmerman notes in his study of panic fiction, "the stock market offered a thrilling read—literally," with crowds of investors across the nation poring over market reports and the stock ticker. The market itself, Zimmerman continues, is "constituted and sustained by these acts of reading"; it is "composed of readers who are intensely aware that other investors are reading the same material at the same time and that their collective interpretations and predictions will have an effect on the market."[69] Speculators try to second-guess not only how the market looks to those other readers, but how they, in turn, picture other speculators' second-guesses, sudden elations, and panicked reactions, and so on, into the potentially infinite hall of mirrors. In a market in which participants obsessively watch each other, stock prices are not a realistic representation of fundamental corporate value, or even investor sentiment, cashed out via the utilitarian calculus of marginalist economics into hard numbers, but, as John Maynard Keynes famously put it, are a beauty contest in which investors have to guess what average opinion will conclude the average view of the winning photo will be, potentially creating an infinite regress of second-guessing.[70] In the decades around the turn of the twentieth century, explanations for market panics began to draw on psychological theories of crowds, in particular the notion that herd behavior works through a process of hypnotic emulation, in which (as Zimmerman puts it) "the self finds itself given over to mimesis, not only of an other but also the countless others whom this other mimes."[71] The scenes of tape reading thus provide a visual simulation of a heroic individual's supposed control of the market, yet the prices on the tape are created not by reason, but are the result of the contagious mimicry of other acts of reading, such that the boundaries of the self succumb to the fluid circulation of desire and fear in a hysterical crowd.

The visual shorthand of a stock operator intensely reading the ticker tape thus left viewers imagining how he saw the drama unfold in his mind's eye, not just on the exchange floor, but in the vast network of other speculators connected by wires and tape across the nation. Illustrations of tape reading also conjured up a technological and demotic updating of the Habermasian public sphere in the eighteenth century, an imagined community joined, in this case, not by the tape readers' participation in the virtual "republic of letters," but by their shared fixation on the printed characters of the ticker tape in brokers' offices across the city, the nation, and the globe. In a similar fashion to the "consensual hallucination" that brings the Internet into being, the immersive experience of tape reading afforded by the imaginative projection of a sometimes virtuous, sometimes crazed republic of speculators helped concretize the idea of the market as a vast, animated landscape that was not coterminous with the actual marketplaces of the nation's exchanges and could only be "seen" via the tiny marks on the ticker tape.[72]

Despite fin-de-siècle manuals and magazine illustrations shifting their focus from panicked crowds to the intensity of a solitary study of the ticker tape, however, speculation was often a communal activity in the Gilded Age and the Progressive Era. "Dealers hover over, and intently watch the 'ticker' as it rapidly unwinds the tangled web of financial fate," George Rutledge Gibson observed in his guide to stock exchanges.[73] Although the New York Stock Exchange endeavored to restrict access to its price information, stock tickers were increasingly to be found in semipublic places (there are many accounts, for instance, of speculators gathering around the ticker machine at Delmonico's restaurant in Manhattan). The promotional booklet put out by the bucket shop operators Haight & Freese, for example, contains photographic illustrations of some of their brokerages, showing off their well-appointed spaces for clients. In the photos, would-be speculators huddle round the ticker machines or sit and watch the fluctuating prices posted on the quotation board (fig. 3.12).

Drawing on the work of Jonathan Crary on the emergence of a distinctly modern form of visual observation in the nineteenth century, Alex Preda explains how viewing the market by reading the tape required new modes of concentration that, in turn, involved submitting oneself to the rhythms and timetable of the stock ticker.[74] As the photo of Haight & Freese's patrons suggests, viewing the market thus holds similarities with another new, communal viewing technology of the later nineteenth century: moving pictures. As with movie audiences, the experience of watching the market by watching the quotation board meant clients were not merely emotionally invested in the highs and lows of particular

Figure 3.12 Haight & Freese's Guide to Investors (Philadelphia: Haight & Freese, 1899), frontispiece. In the decades around the turn of the twentieth century, Haight & Freese ran a large number of brokerage offices. They were bucket shops, in which the customers, in effect, bet on the rise and fall of stock prices without actually purchasing any securities. This photo from their promotional guidebook shows the orderly ranks of attentive customers following the fluctuation of commodity prices.

stocks, but were also gripped by the sheer movement of the unfolding spectacle. Like the cinema, it was an experience of isolated, immersive identification with what was represented on the tape, which nevertheless took place within a collective setting. The brokerage was a place in which insider knowledge and camaraderie (but also, perhaps, hysteria) could be shared with fellow viewers—precisely the distractions that tape-reading manuals warned against.[75] Unlike illustrations of the floor of the New York Stock Exchange, which focused on the spectacle of manic activity (even if they also showed the traders not in control of themselves, but in thrall to bestial impulses or hypnotic mimicry), the pictures of the cinematic audiences in bucket shops captured the passivity of the experience—not least because the bucket shop bettors only had the illusion of active participation, since, unlike their counterparts in the legitimate exchanges, their purchases had no power to move the market itself.

Plotting the Market

Some advocates of tape reading claimed that it offered an objective and lofty overview of the market as a whole, safely removed from the corrupting passions or partial vision of floor traders: "A floor trader who stands in one crowd all day is like the buyer for one department—he sees more quickly than anyone else the demand for that class of goods, but has no way of comparing it to that prevailing in other parts of the store. . . . The Tape Reader, on the other hand, from his perch at the ticker, enjoys a bird's-eye view of the whole field. When serious weakness develops in any quarter, he is quick to note, weigh, and act."[76] Other commentators, however, warned that the optic provided by the stock ticker was in danger of giving a distorted picture of the market by the way that it created (as Preda puts it) a view from a microscope, rather than a telescope. "The greatest difficulty of the tape-reader," an article in *Ticker* warned, "is that he becomes so sensitive from working close to the tape, that his judgment is rendered narrow. He endeavors to catch every small fluctuation in the market."[77] From the 1890s onward, the vanguard of technical analysis began instead to recommend the chart as providing the best perspective on the market. "Charts are simply a bird's-eye view of market movements," H. M. Williams declared in *The Key to Wall Street Mysteries*, while the bucket shop operator Lewis Van Riper averred that "in this way one is able to comprehend at a glance every stock movement of importance in the same way that a picture describes to the mind the events which could only be told imperfectly, though requiring hours to relate."[78] The story that the charts promised to reveal, however, was not simply a record of the trading on a particular day, month, or year, or even the truth about hidden manipulation by market insiders. Read in the right way, their patterns instead promised to reveal trends and forces that operated according to their own logic, far removed from individual intentions, in the same way that Darwin's theory of evolution, Marx's theory of history, and Freud's theory of psychology developed accounts of the deeper processes at work beneath the surface noise of human agency.

The early chartists were keen to promote their special expertise (which could therefore be commodified in the form of investment-analysis services), emphasizing what they believed was their objectivity and statistical rigor. Trained as a statistician at the Massachusetts Institute of Technology, Roger Babson, in particular, adopted the language of Newtonian physics in his production of charts that plotted the cyclical motion of the action and reaction in stock prices, along with indices of various "business conditions." By dealing with abstract patterns, Babson's charts were promoted as capturing, with scientific accuracy, the underlying statistical regularities that were not otherwise visible to even the most-experienced of tape readers (fig. 3.13). Babson argued that the aim of drawing the "Normal Line" (now more commonly known as a trend line) was to make immediately manifest the equal and opposite shaded areas above and below

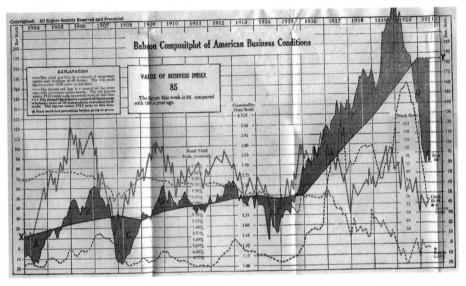

Figure 3.13 From the "Babson Compositplot of American Business Conditions," Roger
W. Babson, *Business Barometers Used in the Accumulation of Money* (Wellesley Hills, MA:
Babson Institute, 1921), inset after p. 106. The business statistician and forecaster Roger
Babson began to produce his charts of American business conditions in the early 1900s.
His fundamental assumption was that stock prices were governed by a force akin to
gravity, and that a period of boom would be matched by a corresponding period of bust.
Harvard College Library.

the line, since, according to his theory, the area of a boom matched the area of
the subsequent bust. Yet deciding where to draw this line was presented not as a
matter of mechanically applying statistical laws, but an act of interpretation based
on experience, an art rather than a science. Moreover, if the line could only be
inked in once a cycle had completed, it meant that using such charts to predict
future stock-price movements was impossible, as academic studies of the predic-
tive accuracy of chartism have since demonstrated.[79]

Other chartists around the turn of the twentieth century, however, claimed to
have discovered more immediately useful, recurrent patterns in the charts. As we
saw in chapter 2, in the same way that securities prices and the stock ticker itself
were repeatedly personified, so, too, in the popular guides to chartism, technical
charts were described in often decidedly human terms, such as the "head and
shoulders" formation. Even when the patterns of abstract data were not read in
directly anthropomorphic ways, the shorthand names and instantly recognizable
shapes lent a homely familiarity to a statistical knowledge that had promised
to reveal the uncanny, inhuman patterns inherent in the aggregated data. Bab-

son's charts turn the data into now-familiar patterns of mountains and valleys, a sublime landscape of economic highs and lows that simultaneously invites and rejects human identification.[80] As Audrey Jaffe observes in her study of the idea of the statistically "average man" in Victorian culture, the trajectory of the impersonal stock market graph is often "assimilated to a narrative of feeling. . . . Universally apprehended as a picture of emotions—a snapshot of the national (or global) mood—it is understood to swing (for example) between elation and depression, optimism and alarm. Looking to the numbers to see how we feel, we both personalize them—render them a projection of our individual and collective narratives—and depersonalize them, conceding our authority to know ourselves to an abstract system that seems to have captured this knowledge. . . . Is the market a projection of the man, or is the man a projection of the market?"[81] Even in their most abstract, depersonalizing form, then, the graphs of stock market prices tempt readers into an affective identification that is often registered by the insistent personification of financial data.

Although the work of the early chartists might have been based on mistaken statistical reasoning, it nevertheless contributed to an important reconfiguration of the vernacular epistemology of the market. In addition to their simultaneous appeal to both projection and identification, the charts helped rationalize the market, making speculation seem sensible, because price movements were at least intelligible, if not always entirely predictable. In the eyes of their proponents, the charts seemed to provide instant visual evidence of a profound order to the financial universe, a regularity that could not be seen by those immersed in either the tumult of the trading floor or the ebb and flow of prices on the ticker tape. In effect, chart reading developed a theory about the representational capacity of securities' prices themselves. The price fluctuations shown on the charts were not the reflection and the result of important political events taking place outside the realm of the market, nor were they representations of the fundamental underlying value of particular corporations or the economy as a whole. Instead, they registered movements that were intrinsic to the market itself. In short, these abstract diagrams of endogenous market events worked not through the genre of realism but instead were, in an important sense, *self-referential* artifacts, akin to forms of modernist art that were beginning to emerge at the same time.[82]

If the charts did represent something beyond their immediate selves, it was the market in its totality, as an omniscient being with a life and a mind of its own. Indeed, the charts did not so much reflect a preexisting financial universe as help to call the very idea of the market as a coherent entity into being, one that could be grasped "at a glance." As Preda notes in a discussion of why chartism has persisted, despite its theories having been disproven by academic economists, the power of technical analysis lies not in its ability to accurately represent financial reality, but in its role as a coping mechanism for would-be investors in the face of market uncertainties. The result of the increasing popularity—but not necessarily the accuracy—of chart theory, Preda argues, is that the market is created in its image: "In the process of using the theory as an uncertainty-processing instrument, new entities are created, corresponding to the theory's representations."[83] It is therefore worth remembering that the chartists drew their inspiration from the work of Charles Dow, whose creation of the Dow Jones Industrial Average (DJIA) likewise contributed to the performative construction of the market during this period. As we saw in chapter 1, in his editorial in the first edition of the *Wall Street Journal*, Dow declared that the newspaper would "present in its market article, its tables, and its advertisements a faithful picture of the rapidly shifting panorama of the Street."[84] Although his paper did contain hands-on reporting of the personalities and events of the New York Stock Exchange, its inclusion, from the first edition on, of the Dow average meant that it also attempted to present, through the language of statistical averages, a panoramic overview of "the Street." Wall Street was now conceived less as a geographically specific place, prone to fraud and the manipulation of insiders, than as an synecdochic shorthand for the entirety of the market, which, crucially, operated through its own impersonal laws that could be discovered by plotting them in tables and charts. The shares picked by Dow (twelve originally, increased to thirty in 1928) were deemed by him to be leaders in their respective fields and were chosen to be representative of the market as a whole, although the relationship between this average and what it represented remained opaque, as Dow did not reveal which stocks the average contained and expressed it in terms of index points, rather than actual prices. For Dow, the average functioned as an impersonal thermometer, taking the temperature of the market as a whole, and it was part of his concerted effort to portray finance as a rational endeavor. Leaving aside the issue of the accuracy of Dow's average as a recording and representational technology (it has been recalibrated on several occasions, and other indices have joined in the competition to provide the best tracking device), the significance of the DJIA is that it helped consolidate the idea of the market as a vast, self-contained, self-regulating system. It was a performative device that helped create the very object it claimed to represent. As Marieke De Goede has argued, the DJIA "has to be understood as a technology that did not simply represent financial reality but fundamentally transformed the operation of modern credit practices, making it possible to image the financial market as a coherent entity."[85]

In their plotting of the market's fortunes, the Dow average and the charts produced by technical analysts around the turn of the twentieth century also need to be seen in the context of the larger history of efforts to identify and represent the market in particular, and the economy in general, as a whole—as a vast, impersonal machine of intricately interrelated parts that could be analyzed mathematically. Here the marginalist revolution in economics is crucial. The central insight of the marginalists was that the value of an object resulted not from its inherent qualities, or even the labor that had gone into making it, but from its desirability or utility to consumers. If utility could be quantified, then, in theory, the morally and philosophically complex issues of political economy could be boiled down to plotting on a graph the relationship between supply and demand. Marginalism presupposed that there are economic laws that, like natural laws, can be discovered through the accumulation of data. Although explanations for the causal origins of these statistical regularities varied (including Stanley Jevons's theory, adopted by Charles Dow, that a ten-year business cycle was the result of a recurrent pattern of sun spots), the professionalization of economics in the late nineteenth and early twentieth centuries was predicated on studying economic activity in an apparently scientific fashion.[86]

In addition to applying mathematical techniques to the mysteries of economic life, economists in the late nineteenth and early twentieth centuries also began to consider this accumulated, abstracted data as part of a larger, integrated, universal system. Where political economy had been concerned, from a moral point of view, with weighing up the competing claims to resources among social classes, the new mathematical economists were eager to discover the underlying economic relations between production and exchange, removed from their immediate social, class, and geographic particulars and put into the purer graphical language of supply-and-demand curves. Indeed, many of these pioneering econometricians were keen to display their data in graphical form, to make immediately apparent the underlying patterns and immutable laws that they believed themselves to be discovering.[87] For example, the British economist Alfred Marshall (whose textbook on economics became the standard work on both sides of the Atlantic) noted that "the graphical method of statistics, though inferior to the numerical in accuracy of representation, has the advantage of enabling the eye to take in at once a long series of facts."[88] What the eye was meant to grasp in a single glance was a picture of a complete and coherent system of interrelated parts, with economists increasingly turning to theories where movements in the market could be explained entirely by reference to the internal structure of the economic machine itself.[89]

Economic Plumbing

As Philip Mirowski has pointed out, neoclassical economists in the nineteenth century borrowed many of their terms and concepts from physics and engineering, not least the idea that all the individual economic impulses were, in fact, part of a unified force within a larger, coherent, interconnected system. (In the case of the marginalists, "utility" served as the unifying force, which therefore permitted a uniform measurement across varied economic phenomena.)[90] For some economists, the physics metaphors were understood literally, with, for example, Irving Fisher, in his pioneering PhD dissertation in 1892 (Yale's first in economics) setting out detailed plans for a hydraulic model of price fluctuation (fig. 3.14). He built this model for use in his teaching at Yale and had another one made in 1926, when the original prototype wore out. Whatever else it purported to demonstrate, Fisher's contraption served to make visible and tangible the idea of the economy as a complex but well-ordered system in which prices would find their equilibrium level as naturally as water under the influence of gravity.[91] As much as Fisher's model brought a mathematical objectivity to the representation of economics, it also portrayed the interaction of supply and demand as a quasi-autonomous machine-beast.

Like the other representational technologies examined in this chapter, Fisher's all-too-solid machine allowed economic activity to be conceived as both an *abstraction* and a *totality*. This conceptual revolution involved, first, reframing the myriad data of economic life as abstracted from local particulars, and second, portraying those diverse factors as part of a coordinated system, whose patterns might not necessarily be observable at ground level.[92] As with the rhetorical transition from accounts of marketplaces to talk of the market itself, it is important to remember that "the economy" is not a timeless and neutral category. Although it now seems obvious—the economy being the proper object of knowledge in economics—before the twentieth century, "economy," in the writings of political economists, referred simply to the idea of frugality or economizing, the proper and efficient use of resources. The use of the phrase "*the* economy"—in the sense of the whole aggregate of statistics regarding production, consumption, inflation, and employment that make up a bounded *national* entity—only emerged in interwar economic discourse as part of institutional efforts (such as the foundation of the National Bureau of Economic Research in 1920 and the Cowles Commission in 1932) designed to gather statistical information to aid the state's inter-

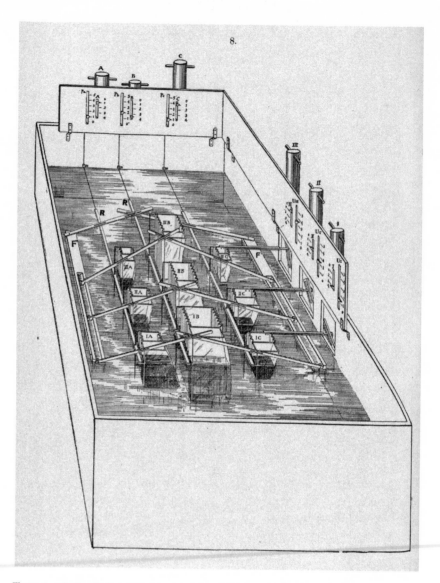

Figure 3.14 Irving Fisher, "Mathematical Investigations in the Theory of Value and Prices," *Transactions of the Connecticut Academy* 9 (July 1892): 38. Irving Fisher pioneered the introduction of mathematical techniques in economics around the turn of the twentieth century. He was also influenced by approaches developed in physics and engineering. Despite pushing economics in a more abstract direction, he also designed and built hydraulic models for use in teaching, to demonstrate the workings of price fluctuation. Harvard College Library.

vention in and manipulation of national economic life.[93] Progressive Era critics originally promoted such fact-gathering institutions as the National Bureau of Economic Research with the hope that they would produce intelligible, graphical representations and statistical overviews of the complex corporate behemoths that emerged rapidly in the years around the turn of the twentieth century, so the U.S. Congress might regulate and tax them based on objective evidence, rather than the patchy and partial information offered up by the corporations themselves. The historical irony, as Mary Poovey points out, is that the information on the valuation of corporations gathered for the National Bureau ended up helping the corporations make better accounting sense of their business and, in the process, improved their profitability.[94]

Although these early twentieth-century actual and virtual models produced by professional economists were born from very different needs and institutional contexts than those of the early chartists, they, along with the various attempts to picture the market explored in this chapter, share the performative capacity to make the object of their inquiry (at first the market, and then the economy) come alive. At the same time as they produce an abstracting and totalizing view, however, the modes of financial representation we have seen in this chapter also rely on older visual tropes that make the impersonal data more concrete and more familiar, even if it increasingly comes to seem as though it represents nothing other than itself. Chapter 5 explores a diagram produced by the Pujo Committee's investigation into the so-called money trust, one that presents the totality of financial capitalism as both an abstract network and a quasi-conspiratorial picture of hidden intentions. This diagram marks a startlingly original attempt to create a panorama of high finance, but it also pushes to the limit the representational technologies of the era in combined concrete and abstract visual forms.

CHAPTER FOUR

Confidence Games and Inside Information

Those palazzos, with all their costly furniture, and all their splendid equipages, have been the product of the same genius in their proprietors, which has made the "Confidence Man" immortal and a prisoner at "the Tombs." His genius has been employed on a small scale in Broadway. Theirs has been employed in Wall Street. That's all the difference. He has obtained half a dozen watches. They have pocketed millions of dollars. He is a swindler. They are exemplars of honesty. He is a rogue. They are financiers.

"'The Confidence Man' on a Large Scale," New York Herald *(1849)*

We are now forming new combinations of the $25, $50, $100, and $500 classes for this purpose, which we confidently recommend to our old customers and friends. While all of these combinations afford equal privileges and prospects, we would remind our friends that experience has proved that the larger amounts, having the greatest power, usually yield the greatest profits.

Lawrence & Company, Special Announcement (1879)

This vast mysterious Wall Street world of "tips" and "deals"—might she not find in it the means of escape from her dreary predicament?

Edith Wharton, The House of Mirth *(1905)*

An issue that repeatedly vexed Americans in the Gilded Age and the Progressive Era was the role that personal connections should play in market exchanges in general, and in the workings of the stock market in particular, that supposedly purest expression of the free market. Were those personal connections, in fact, the systematic operation of social capital? Were the fluctuations in prices in the stock market a result of the vast, impersonal, uncontrollable aggregation of individual desires, or were they being manipulated through inside information by the elite? On the other hand, in a modern economy, was there still room for friendship in business transactions? What role did seemingly noneconomic emotions, such as trust, play in the age of Trusts? This chapter will argue that the continuing importance of the rhetoric and the reality of personal connections in a seemingly impersonal market complicates the standard story of the great transformation—from an economic order governed by traditional relationships of status to one ruled by the law of a free-market contract—as far from straightforward.

The chapter explores a number of different accounts and episodes that highlighted the problematic relationship between a sentimental and an exchange economy, focusing on the idea of inside information, not only as a business practice and a legal category, but also as a form of understanding and a narrative structuring device. It begins by considering the confidence trick and other forms of fraud that worked by appealing to personal connections. I first discuss Herman Melville's tricksy novel, *The Confidence-Man* (1857), because, in a prescient fashion, it worries away at the question of just how much trust and suspicion were appropriate in the rapidly expanding marketplace of midcentury America. Melville's novel, I argue, shows how the confidence game worked, not merely by gulling innocent greenhorns new to the city, or even by using clever psychology to speak to the unspoken greed of the not-so-blameless victims. It shows instead how the con trick functioned: by mimicking the rhetoric and reassurance of a contract infused with the "Wall Street spirit," while, at the same time, appealing to an older tradition of personal connections.[1] The chapter next examines what we might term the industrialization of the confidence trick around the turn of the twentieth century, with the mass production of fraud raising to a new level the fundamental sleight-of-hand between gift and grift that is at the heart of Melville's novel. It was not just the conceptual slipperiness of the confidence trick that made it so appealing and persistent; the legal definitions of "larceny by false pretenses," "inside dealing," and other forms of fraud remained fraught and fluid throughout the period. In many respects, the modern prohibition against the use of inside information in business transactions in general, and in the stock market in particular, did not come into effect until the New Deal reforms of the 1930s. This chapter argues that inside dealing, in the broadest meaning of this term, was not merely an occasional lapse, but was absolutely vital to both the way Americans thought about the market and the way they interacted with it.

The second half of the chapter explores the role of inside information in the novel, focusing in detail on William Dean Howells's *The Rise of Silas Lapham* (1885) and the three major novels of Edith Wharton. The reason for looking closely at these novels is that writers in this period returned repeatedly to the question of the possibility or impossibility of a moral economy in a world that seemed increasingly governed by the blind forces of economic and biological determinism—a preoccupation that, in turn, was part of the larger aesthetic and ideological debate between the older conventions of sentimentalism and the newer logic of realism and naturalism. This thematic dilemma, I contend, also underpins the formal difficulties many writers in this period encountered as they struggled to bring together (or, in some cases, to keep apart) the love plot and the business plot in their novels.

The Con Trick in the Age of Contract

Melville began work on *The Confidence-Man* during 1855 and 1856, a moment of economic boom before the panic of 1857, which once again plunged the American economy into crisis. Even before the crash, Melville's own finances were in a perilous state, in part because he had received a hazily phrased loan to buy a house in the Berkshires in Massachusetts from his father-in-law, Lemuel Shaw, chief justice of the Massachusetts Supreme Court, whose legal work, ironically, significantly contributed to a rethinking of the traditional nature of obligations in an emerging corporate economy. Making matters worse, *The Confidence-Man* was the nail in the coffin of Melville's career as a commercially successful novelist, and, to cap it all off, even Dix & Edwards, the publishers of this novel, went bankrupt in the panic of 1857, a nationwide financial meltdown widely blamed on a "want of confidence" (*CM*, 71). The circumstances in which Melville composed *The Confidence-Man* encapsulate the dilemmas with which the novel grapples. *The Confidence-Man* provides a series of meditations on how much trust and how much suspicion were appropriate in the global marketplace emerging in the 1840s and 1850s, an economy animated by the wild confidence of boosterism, but also racked by the endless suspicion of having to deal with strangers. Was confidence vital to the promotion of a credit-based, expansionary economy, or was the human bond of trust damaged by the emergence of that economy? As the protagonist of *The Confidence-Man* piously explains as he fleeces another victim: "Confidence is the indispensable basis of all sorts of business transactions. Without it, commerce between man and man, as between country and country, would, like a watch, run down and stop" (155). *The Confidence-Man* is less a transcendent critique of capitalism as such than an embodiment of the emotional and conceptual problems caused by the intrusion of the placeless financial market into every corner of American life.[2] In the world of Melville's novel, there are few, if any, guarantees of knowing the true worth of the person or the banknotes the hapless characters are doing business with. The society depicted in this book is one in which the traditional bonds and obligations of kinship, neighborhood, and shared political, religious, and cultural commitment have been unmoored. This situation creates an alienated and individualist society in which freedom of contract is seemingly the only rule governing relationships between people. In this world of chance encounters with strangers, a mastery of the everyday semiotics of commercial culture is crucial. The novel offers a self-reflexive meditation on the problem of reading in a market society. The potentially infinite regress of a literary interpretation of an author's meaning is equated with the difficulty of "reading" a person or a banknote in conditions of radical uncertainty, which are exacerbated by the permanent possibility for fraud.[3]

Through its focus on the confidence game and a series of staged dialogues debating the role of friendship in business, *The Confidence-Man* provides conflicting answers to the question of the role of personal trust. The plot of the novel, such as it is, involves a con artist who appears in different disguises aboard the appropriately named *Fidèle*, a Mississippi paddleboat. The novel plays on the genre of western tall tales of frontier rogues, such as Simon Suggs; popular exposés of urban crime and fraud; and a popular fascination with the life and work of P. T. Barnum. It riffs in particular, however, on the primal scene of modern confidence trickery, the arrest in 1849 (and again in 1855) of a scam artist the newspapers dubbed the "Original Confidence Man."[4] The novel offers seemingly endless variations on this basic story, in which the different incarnations of the con man function as copies of his initial fake, joined in a futile quest for what Michael Rogin terms "the single, authentic confidence man."[5] He appears as a new social type, yet also as a personification of the abstract possibility of endemic deception that is at the heart of a market economy. Moreover, each avatar of the novel's central figure can be substituted for any of the others, a form of repeated circulation and depersonalization of literary character that works in a similar fashion to the fungibility of both money and language. The novel thus provides both a focus on the individualism that is produced by contractarian capitalism, and a peculiarly impersonal form of narrative in which the individuals are interchangeable. Not merely do the numerous guises of the confidence man begin to collapse into one another, but the separation between con man and dupe also becomes blurred, as does the division between the con man and the narrator, who becomes, in modern terminology, increasingly unreliable.[6]

Why did the figure of the confidence man (and it usually was a man) haunt the American imagination from the mid-nineteenth century onward?[7] Karen Halttunen argues that fears about con men, not just in fiction, but also in middle-class conduct books and advice literature, result from a republican ideology of trusting in appearances and in plain speaking when confronting the prospect of dealing with strangers—confidence men, *avant la lettre*—in the emerging national marketplace from the 1830s on. Halttunen goes on to argue that the middle class developed a sentimental "cult of sincerity" as a defense mechanism in the face of social mobility and its attendant potential for duplicity, but, she concludes, by the 1870s, the idea of sincerity had itself become a self-conscious posture, a ritualized and melodramatic performance that was the forerunner of the Dale Carnegie "how to win friends and influence people" model of the self-as-salesman. Halttunen's analysis of the cultural function of fears in the advice literature of mid-nineteenth-century America about "confidence men and painted ladies" is compelling, but it focuses primarily on the social interactions in the parlor. Melville's novel, I want to suggest, points to a different understanding of the cultural logic of the con man, one in which the sentiment of confidence is essential to economic development, although the confidence trick was permanently in danger of undermining it.[8]

The newspaper reports of the 1849 arrest in New York of the Original Confidence Man explained his modus operandi, with most recounting a scam reduced so close to its bare bones that its audacious simplicity is as staggering as the gullibility of the victims is laughable. The well-dressed and affable William Thompson (one of his many aliases) would approach a likely looking gentlemen on the streets of New York and engage him in conversation. Thompson would first inquire whether the mark had confidence in him and then ask him to lend Thompson his watch as proof of that sentiment—"Have you confidence in me to trust me with your watch until tomorrow?"—only for Thompson to walk off and never be seen again.[9] Over the course of a few days, Thompson made off with three watches, worth over $300, but was arrested when one of his victims spotted him on the street. It was this simplified version of the Original Confidence Man that occasioned much newspaper commentary, most of its lamenting the abuse of trust in the changing commercial landscape of American society. This rendition chimes in most clearly with Halttunen's analysis of the con man's affront to the prevailing republican ideology of simplicity and sincerity, but it seems to have very little to do with later commercial fraud. From the point of view of the supposedly innocent mark, he is merely asked to offer up a token of an almost metaphysical faith in human goodness, one that is more a gift than a form of security for a loan. On this account, the moral crime of the con man is that he betrays the sentimental generosity of the victim. Indeed, in this iteration it is hard to explain why the con trick should be considered illegal, rather than merely immoral, because the "friendly loan" could, in theory, be repaid at some future stage, with the debt cancelled out by the return of the watch, turning what might look like a loan back into a gift.

In all likelihood, however, the actual scam was a little more elaborate, even if many at that time chose to read it as a simple parable of the corruption of worthy sincerity. Thompson, it turns out, would show the victim a roll of cash that he was planning to invest in a secret get-rich-quick business proposal. He would promise to let the mark share in the scheme if the latter would provide a token of his trust, in the form of a gold watch, that, in effect, was to serve as collateral.[10] Even this first incarnation of the confidence man thus relied on the victims being less than innocent, already corrupted by market desires; the trick plays on their hopes of getting something for nothing. As with later elaborations of the confidence trick, Thompson's marks presumably thought they were getting privileged information, an inside tip, a sure-fire way to get rich quick that beats regular dealings in the market and defies the Protestant work ethic of slow, steady accumulation.[11] Melville's novel, I want to suggest, captures the slippage between these two differing accounts of the Original Confidence Man, suggesting that there was less a slow fall from grace from the republican-spirited greenhorn to the greedy mark than a permanent, dialectical intertwining of the two modes of economic being they respectively represent.

In Melville's story, a man posing as an agent for the Seminole Widows and Orphans Asylum strikes up a conversation with a widow by pretending to piety. He then says, in a direct echo of the phrase used by the Original Confidence Man, albeit in a variation that suggests an interest that is less economic than metaphysical: "By the way, madam, may I ask if you have confidence?" Responding to the widow's confused, stuttering reply, he makes his meaning more clear: "Could you put confidence in *me*, for instance?" And then comes the sting: "Prove it. Let me have twenty dollars" (56–57). Only when the widow fumbles for a polite way of asking why, exactly, he wants the money, does the confidence man reveal that it is not for himself but for charity, the spurious Seminole Widows and Orphans Asylum. Even this version of William Thompson's routine—which seems to operate more in the realm of charity than commerce—blurs the line between a financial and a sentimental economy by having the con man force the widow to give him twenty dollars as tangible proof of her confidence in him, or, to put it another way, she is ironically forced to put a monetary value on a noneconomic emotion, creating a dangerous fusion between the two ways of valuing that are seemingly incommensurate.[12]

The same logic is repeated in the scene between the confidence man and a distrustful and ill miser below decks. The confidence man (in the guise of the ironically named Mr. Truman, an agent of the fraudulent Black Rapids Coal Company) gives the miser a glass of water, an act of kindness that seems to have no strings attached. The miser then asks, "How can I repay you?" and the scene continues:

> "By giving me your confidence."
>
> "Confidence!" he squeaked, with changed manner, while the pallet swung. "Little left at my age, but take the stale remains, and welcome."
>
> "Such as it is though, you give it. Very good. Now give me a hundred dollars." (90)

These attacks on hypocrisy—of not putting your money where your mouth is, especially when it comes to Christian charity—perform a repeated sleight-of-hand in which a gift is turned into a monetary transaction, with the confidence man getting people to put a price on something that is, in theory, priceless. The double irony is that this exchange is, in reality, a form of theft. In a similar vein, there is the satirical episode of the businessman with gold sleeve buttons who has a plan for injecting the "Wall Street spirit" into the realm of philanthropy, organizing charity on an industrial scale and level of efficiency, undermining the very idea of charity as selfless giving. The novel repeatedly suggests that a moral economy is inseparable from economic calculations, and, vice versa, that market transactions are conducted through sentimental forms.

The Original Confidence Man was arrested again in Albany, New York, in 1855, just as Melville was writing his novel in nearby Pittsfield, Massachusetts. Now going under the alias of Samuel Willis, the confidence man went into a jewelry store and asked the owner to step aside for a private matter. He then asked whether the jeweler was a Freemason. (It is not clear from the historical record if this was a lucky—albeit reasonable—guess, or whether Thomson had inside information in advance.) Having made an appeal to this secret, personal connection, Thomson then told the jeweler how he had fallen on hard times before asking him, as the newspaper account puts it, "if he would not give a brother a shilling if he needed it?" The proprietor of the jewelry store, the report concludes, "was induced to give him six or seven dollars."[13] In the version of this story in Melville's novel, John Ringman, another of the many incarnations of the confidence man, strikes up a conversation on board ship with a well-to-do businessman called Mr. Roberts. (A previous avatar of the confidence man has been seen picking up a business card dropped by Roberts.) Ringman tries to persuade Mr. Roberts that they have met before, calling up details of how they had both done business in an office in Philadelphia, how they had hit it off, how Roberts had invited Ringman back to his house for tea, and so on. This encounter is fascinating, because it blends together elements of both a traditional gift economy and a newer, contract-based exchange. The appeal to a Masonic connection is obviously designed to make the mark respond not as a stranger, but as a "brother."[14] In part, this appeal to a Masonic connection has the effect of making Ringman seem more respectable by presenting himself as a business equal with Mr. Roberts, but it also makes him more suspect, because it conjures up a form of business orchestrated by hidden connections rather than by pure freedom of contract. The encounter also evinces a tacit appeal to intimacy, a form of knowing confidence between men who share a recognition of sameness that exceeds the bounds of strict business. The name Ringman evokes marital respectability, but it also suggests anal sex. It is thus perhaps not without reason that the confidence man is called a "queer sort of chap," a "queer man—a very queer and dubious man," a "queer customer," and a "man-charmer" (131, 136, 280).[15]

Ringman's subsequent extended story about how he has fallen on hard times is equally significant in terms of the shifting debates about debt, bankruptcy, and moral culpability in the middle of the nineteenth century. Ringman is appealing to an older notion of economic misfortune and debt, not as the result of personal liability, but as the effects of an impersonal Providence. "Judging from his auditor's expression," the narrator comments, "it seemed to be a tale of singular interest, involving calamities against which no integrity, no forethought, no energy, no genius, no piety could guard" (29). If Ringman's approach to Roberts conjures up the specter of a risky—and potentially unmanning—financial exchange with a stranger, it is a very odd kind of impersonal contractarianism, because it is framed almost entirely in the language of a personal connection achieved through telling a story. There is no explanation, for example, of what the terms of the loan might be; it is as if, between gentlemen and fellow Masons, the embarrassing financial details are best left unspoken. Unlike the earlier scene in Melville's novel, in which it seems that the con man is pretending to be a crippled black beggar (the Black Guinea) appealing directly for alms, Ringman does not ask for charity as such, but instead asks for a loan, framing a charitable encounter as a contractual transaction, using virtually the same words as those in the newspaper article about the reappearance of William Thompson/Samuel

Willis: "And would you not loan a brother a shilling if he needed it?" (28). It is therefore worth noting that in the original newspaper report, the confidence man asks the victim to "give" him a shilling, but in Melville's version, Ringman asks for a "loan," albeit still in the euphemistic amount of a "shilling." What this scene suggests is that it is not doing business with a stranger that, in itself, is the problem, as the antebellum advice literature studied by Halttunen suggests. Instead, the confusion comes from mistaking a contractual relationship for one based on friendship, status, charity, and gift.

The mistake Mr. Roberts makes is to place trust in personal character, rather than the impersonal guarantee of freedom of contract. Ringman the con man dresses up an impersonal economic relationship in the language of sentimental intimacy that both sides try to pretend is otherwise, conveniently passing off as a gift what is, in fact, a loan. The con man flatters the mark by implying that they are both men of business, even as he silently pockets a charitable donation, which is a form of theft.[16] As soon as Ringman has extracted a donation from Mr. Roberts, he turns cold and impersonal, breaking the spell of their supposedly friendly encounter and indicating that his bonhomie was purely instrumental. Ringman does, however, leave Roberts with a parting gift: a piece of information. It is a gift that serves as partial repayment for Mr. Robert's charitable donation, which had been dressed up as a loan; a gift that, in turn, was actually a form of payment for the sob story that Ringman had told. Ringman gives Mr. Roberts an inside stock tip for the Black Rapids Coal Company, whose transfer agent— another guise of the con man—happens to be on board: "My object, sir, in calling your attention to this stock, is by way of acknowledgement of your goodness" (31). But this free gift, given supposedly with no strings attached, is yet another ploy to con Roberts by making the seemingly impersonal world of financial capitalism appear to operate through inside information.

Melville's novel thus shows how the confidence trick worked: contractarian forms of exchange masquerading as gifts, and vice versa. The emerging market for industrial securities in mid-nineteenth-century America was not simply fuelled by a new and unwelcome spirit of speculative risk taking and calculability, although this was the interpretation that many at the time made after the appearance of the Original Confidence Man. Instead, as Melville's anatomy of the confidence trick suggests, many speculators were looking to *avoid* risk by receiving surefire tips as gifts, grafting a newer economic epistemology onto a traditional system of favors and reciprocities.

Melville captures the persistence of status in the age of contract with savage irony in a twinned pair of stories toward the end of the novel, which speak poignantly to Melville's frustration at both the vagaries of a brave new world of fluctuating market values and the claustrophobic chains of familial obligation in which his economic affairs had become entwined. The first story emerges out of an encounter between the "cosmopolitan" Francis Goodman and Egbert (who, most commentators on the novel agree, is a thinly disguised parody of Thoreau). The conversation goes round in circles as Egbert intransigently refuses to budge from his clear separation of a moral economy from a financial economy. In order to defend his position that a "friendly loan" always ends in disaster, Egbert recounts the fairy-tale story of China Aster, the moral of which is presumably that business motives should not interfere between friends, and that a loan should be regarded as a gift, rather than a humiliating act of charity or a hard-nosed contractual agreement.

The story immediately following the tale of China Aster, however, has the opposite moral. The con man, in the guise of the cosmopolitan, tries to convince the ship's barber to remove the sign that he has placed outside his shop, announcing "No Trust" (10)—literally meaning that no credit will be given, but also suggesting that all business in a modern market society is conducted under the sign of suspicion. Most firms at the time, however, were forced to do business on credit, in part because there was very little hard currency in circulation; what little there was came in the form of paper money, which was prone to counterfeit. One reason financial panics were so frequent and so widespread is that the whole nation was caught up in an interconnected web of credit and obligation. Yet the barber's sign, proclaiming a refusal of trust, can also be read as an affirmation of trust—in hard cash, rather than in insubstantial credit. The con man eventually manages to dupe the distrusting barber into shaving him for free by drawing up a contract in which he agrees to indemnify the barber for any loss occurred by the latter agreeing to "trust" his customers. The contract is thus used to guarantee trust, but the promise of a contract is predicated precisely on a *lack* of trust—or, more accurately, a rational, calculating trust in the abstract and impersonal guarantee of the law, rather than on incalculable trust in a person, which involves a measurement of character as collateral (as J. P. Morgan continued to assert in the Pujo Committee hearings). The con man's contract turns out not to be worth the paper it is written on, because the con man leaves, having neither paid for his shave nor left any collateral to back up his offer of insurance.

The moral of the story, we are led to believe, is that there is no place for personal connections in the impersonal transactions of the market: trust no one. Yet Melville's novel helps us see that the con artist's routine blurs the boundary between an older, gift-based system of exchange and a newer, contractarian, market-based economy, suggesting that the two are permanently intertwined. The confidence trick works by promising to transform a risky encounter with an anonymous stranger on the shifting sands of the placeless market into an intimate engagement with a friend that is governed not by the harsh doctrine of caveat emptor, but by a more-sentimental appeal to friendship and a gift economy, the latter through the hope of access to inside information. As Melville shows, the con trick was thus not so much an unwelcome assault on more innocent modes of social exchange as a clever and confounding incorporation of those traditional ways of being into the newer forms of market activity. Although accounts of the development of the confidence trick in the latter half of the nineteenth century emphasize how the mark was no longer the innocent greenhorn of midcentury conduct books, but instead a deceitful person, Melville's novel suggests that the confusion between gullibility and greed was present from the outset—and that the con trick plays on that confusion. What is significant about the confidence trick, as it developed in the second half of the nineteenth century in the United States, is that its ambiguous, two-faced appeal also provided the structuring principle for other economic activities, from credit reporting to inside dealing in the stock market. In its confounding of gift and exchange economies, the confidence trick was not merely a quaint frontier tale or an affront to the middle-class sincerity of the parlor, but instead was central to the development of American capitalism in the Gilded Age and the Progressive Era. As Stephen Mihm notes in his study of counterfeiting in the nineteenth century, "confidence was the engine of economic growth, the mysterious sentiment that permitted a country poor in specie but rich in promises to create something from nothing."[17]

"The Confidence Man on a Large Scale"

Most commentators at the time were initially merely amused or mildly intrigued by the appearance of the Original Confidence Man, although, as Halttunen notes, the reaction to the con man's assault on middle-class sensibilities became increasingly pious. Some writers were sanctimoniously proud of the honest, trusting character of Americans revealed by the easy success of the con man's schemes. For instance, Evert Duyckink, writing in the *Literary World* and quoting an article in the *Merchant's Ledger*, insisted that "it is not the worst thing that may be said of a country that it gives birth to a confidence man. . . . 'It is a good thing, and speaks well for human nature, that, at this late day, in spite of all the hardening of civilization and all the warnings of newspapers, men can be swindled.'"[18] A few writers, however, voiced a more astute interpretation of the episode, most notably an acerbic editorial in the *New York Herald*, three days after its initial news report, that ironically compared William Thompson with the "real confidence men" of Wall Street who were beginning to fleece the gullible public on an epic scale:

> As you saunter through some of those fashionable streets and squares which or-
> nament the upper part of this magnificent city, you cannot fail to be struck by the
> splendor of some of the palazzos which meet the eye in all directions. . . . Over the
> whole scene there is an air of that ostentatious expenditure, and that vulgar display
> in which the possessors of suddenly acquired wealth are so prone to gratify their low
> and selfish feeling. . . . Those palazzos, with all their costly furniture, and all their
> splendid equipages, have been the product of the same genius in their proprietors,
> which has made the "Confidence Man" immortal and a prisoner at "the Tombs."

The difference between the two is one of scale: "His genius has been employed on a small scale in Broadway. Theirs has been employed in Wall Street. That's all the difference. He has obtained half a dozen watches. They have pocketed millions of dollars. He is a swindler. They are exemplars of honesty. He is a rogue. They are financiers." The article sarcastically notes that the Original Confidence Man's fault was his lack of ambition. His methods would have been lionized if he had engaged in fraud on an industrial scale, a way that would soon become the norm with the antics of the robber barons:

> He struck too low! Miserable wretch! He should have gone to Albany and obtained
> a charter for a new railroad company. He should have issued a flaming prospectus
> of another grand scheme of international improvement. He should have entered
> his own name as a stockholder, to the amount of one hundred thousand dollars. He
> should have called to his aid a few chosen associates. He should have quietly got
> rid of his stock; but on the faith of it got a controlling share in the management of
> the concern. He should have got all the contracts on his own terms. He should have
> involved the company in debt, by a corrupt and profligate expenditure of the capital
> subscribed in good faith by poor men and men of moderate means. . . . He should
> have run the company into all sorts of difficulty. He should have depreciated the
> stock by every means in his power. He should have brought the stockholders into
> bankruptcy. . . . Long life to the real "Confidence Man!"—the "Confidence Man" of
> Wall Street—the "Confidence Man" of the palace uptown—the "Confidence Man"
> who battens and fattens on the plunder coming from the poor man and the man
> of moderate means! As for the "Confidence Man" of "the Tombs," he is a cheat, a
> humbug, a delusion, a sham, a mockery! Let him rot![19]

The *Herald*'s witty conclusion is that the "original" confidence man is a fake, because the stock market is the real con game, with its abuse of trust on an industrial scale.

Like Melville's novel, what this editorial suggests is that the confidence trick was not a curiosity or an aberration, but was central to the American way of understanding and doing business in the increasingly corporate and finance-driven society of the nineteenth century. The con man is not merely an outlaw, but is fully part of the structure of the expanding, deterritorialized market, an inevitable consequence of the nation's faith in social and economic mobility and the seeming absence of inherited structures of tradition and authority. As Amy Reading notes in her study of Frank Norfleet, a victim of a swindle in the 1910s: "Con men work firmly within the structures of American democratic capitalism, exploiting uncharted territory inside the system itself. . . . The new nation would never have prospered without imposture, speculation, and counterfeiting, because America was, from its inception, a confidence trick."[20] Indeed, it is arguable that market capitalism does not rely on the Weberian spirit of plodding, Puritan accumulation predicated on rational calculability, but on fictional expectations of an unknowable, speculative future, for which confidence is more important than knowledge.[21] The confidence man's habit of making the future seem tangible is thus also deeply connected to other national archetypes, such as the self-made man, the trickster, the gambler, the Barnumesque hoaxer, the frontier booster, and the traveling salesman.[22] Confidence tricks (along with other forms of swindling, such as bigamy) should therefore be considered "crimes of mobility."[23] Yet, as the *Herald*'s editorial makes clear, the confidence trick did not work outside the rules of financial capitalism, but it was central to the expanding influence of corporate capitalism. Confidence men provided a "negative analogue" that made regular Wall Street business seem respectable by contrast.[24]

Far from a mere historical curiosity, the confidence trick remained a compelling and increasingly common scenario well into the first decades of the twentieth century, a mainstay of lurid criminal confessions and exposés written by those trying to educate the public in the ways of the con man. What these books document is that by the 1880s, the small-scale, opportunistic confidence trick employed by William Thompson had developed into a very elaborate and often highly routinized scam. The short con mutated into the long con, as these more elaborate scams came to be known. "If the short con is an anecdote," Luc Sante notes, "the long con is a novel."[25] A regimented script began to emerge that played almost scientifically on the psychological weaknesses of potential marks, and it began to make the crucial assumption that you could only con a dishonest person, who, in many cases, became complicit in the illegal activity proposed in the con (and hence was less likely to complain to the authorities).[26] In each of these scams, there was what the historian of the con, David Maurer, identifies as a ten-stage process that resembles the formulaic conventions and variations of a dramatic genre:

1. Putting the mark up (locating and investigating a well-to-do victim)
2. Playing the con for him (gaining the victim's confidence)
3. Roping the mark (steering him to meet the insideman)
4. Telling him the tale (permitting the insideman to show him how he can make a lot of money dishonestly)
5. Giving him the convincer (allowing the victim to make a substantial profit)
6. Giving him the breakdown (determining exactly how much he will invest)
7. Putting him on the send (sending him home for this amount of money)
8. Taking off the touch (playing him against the big store and fleecing him)
9. Blowing him off (getting him out of the way as quietly as possible)
10. Putting in the fix (forestalling action by the law)[27]

Three scenarios in particular came to dominate the world of the confidence game: gold bricks, green goods, and the wiretap (the big store). The simplest of these was the gold-brick routine, in which a seemingly naive or desperate miner would look to sell a solid brick of gold below market value. The brick would appear to the mark as genuine. In some cases it was, and would be swapped for a fake one by sleight-of-hand at the moment of trade, or a gold plug was inserted in a lead brick, so that a sample dug out for the mark to take for assaying would come back positive. The green-goods game involved advertising counterfeit money that could be sold to a willing mark. The money shown to the victim would be genuine, but it would either be substituted at the vital moment for a wad of worthless paper or sawdust, or the transaction would be interrupted by accomplices of the con man posing as police (stage nine in the outline above).

In the wiretapping game, the mark would be introduced—often with the seemingly fortuitous discovery of a dropped wallet—to an apparently high-rolling businessman who made his money from betting on a rigged horseracing game or from a stock market ploy. The scheme would involve illegally tapping into the official race results or stock prices over the telegraph and delaying them long enough to allow surefire bets to be placed in a betting parlor or a bucket shop. At first, the grift gang would painstakingly carry out the wiretapping, but by 1900 a more devious version was developed, in which the mark would be shown the scheme apparently working in a elaborate mock-up of a poolroom or bucket shop that was peopled entirely by accomplices of the con man running the game. The victims would be enticed into getting more money to invest in the supposedly risk-free deal, only for them to end up losing it all as any number of carefully scripted, smoke-and-mirrors impediments frustrated their ambitions to get rich quick.

These scams became routinized around the turn of the twentieth century and, at first sight, are far removed in both practice and spirit from the simple charms of William Thompson—at least in the way the ploy of the Original Confidence Man was usually reported. No longer was the confidence man a lone artisan, plying his trade one mark at a time; the scam had become a corporate affair. The wiretapping game, in its most elaborate forms, needed a large organization of bunco men, and marks were fed into the assembly line by the dozen by a team of expert ropers. Even the green-goods game became scaled up into an industrial operation. It was an increasingly hierarchically organized and highly capitalized affair, usually with one mastermind behind the scenes, bankrolling the operation, and, like more-legitimate businesses during the "managerial revolution," with a hired general manager, who would be put in charge of administering the complex details of the operation. Paddy O'Brien, for example, employed between thirty and forty green-goods men in Chicago, while James McNally's agents, between them, had 800 aliases, issuing 750,000 circulars and spending $5 million on printing.[28] Many commentators—both at the time and since—have romanticized what they consider the consummate artistry of the golden age of the confidence trick (c. 1880–1920), highlighting the way the scam merchant played out the drama like a master playwright. For example, even the hard-headed private detective George McWatters, in his exposé published in the Pinkerton Detective Series, writes with grudging admiration of "Colonel Novena, the Prince of Confidence Men," who was a "true artist."[29] Con artists characterized themselves—and were viewed in popular commentary—as ruggedly independent artisans who rejected the soul-destroying strictures of emerging corporate capitalism. Nonetheless, they perfected the long con through what might be viewed as the same techniques of Taylorized management that were beginning to reshape industrial labor. "Wiretapping," noted the lawyer and thriller writer Arthur Train in 1906, had become "an industry, a legalized industry with which the authorities might interfere at their peril."[30]

Despite the industrialization and financialization of the confidence game at the tail end of the nineteenth century, it nevertheless continued to operate through the same basic logic employed by the Original Confidence Man. The proposition

that hooked the sucker remained the idea of inside information: the hope of getting ahead in the harsh, impersonal marketplace by befriending someone who
knew the ropes, in order to even up the informational asymmetry and provide
a shortcut to the social capital that was vital to the workings of a market society.
The victim of the con wanted to get rich, not merely quickly and without effort, but also without risk, using inside information and personal connections to
turn a hazardous speculation into a guaranteed deal. The marks—usually from
a second-rate city or the countryside—were made to feel that by using their old-
fashioned native savvy, they could play in the brave new world of the stock market
on a par with the big-city manipulators. The rubes might not be skilled in reading
the market, but they prided themselves on being able to read people; the irony
was that it was the con man who was the one genuinely skilled in decoding the
semiotics of psychology. The operation worked by deliberately confusing what
seemed to be a legitimate, if somewhat irregular, business deal with a personal
favor—the inside tip that was given (or should that be "gifted"? or "traded"?) in
recognition of the return of the dropped wallet, an event that would usually set
the game in motion in the first place.

Gold bricks, green goods, and the wiretap, however, were just the tip of the
iceberg of an entire industry of fraud, which often mimicked legitimate forms of
stock market and other financial transactions. Instead of coming up to one prospective mark at a time on the streets of New York or Chicago or Denver through
a wallet drop, the "modern" con man approached a vast regional, and even national, audience through mass mailings and newspaper advertisements. "All the
more important swindling schemes of the time which are intended to reach the
mass of the people," the New York postal inspector and prominent antivice cam-
paigner Anthony Comstock observed, "depend upon two mighty agencies of our
present civilization, the Newspaper and the United States Mail. By means of
these two instruments for good or evil, it is possible to reach every household
in the land."[31] The advertisements and circulars enticed ordinary Americans to
take part in schemes that would supposedly guarantee advantageous results in
stock market speculation. Comstock, for example, tells the story of Lawrence
& Company, a fraudulent brokerage office set up by Benjamin Buckwalter,
a former snake-oil salesman who had advertised under the operatic moniker
"Dr. Gounod." A newspaper advertisement would declare that it was "just your
time" to "make money safely, easily, and rapidly" in the stock market through
the "combination method" of speculation.[32] Those who replied to the advertisement would be sent a lengthy circular that conjoined a bamboozling explanation
of how the combination system worked with a direct, friendly approach to the

reader. The scheme supposedly allowed small investors to pool their capital, so they could collectively engage in a large-scale speculation that would put them on an equal footing with noted Wall Street figures such as Jay Gould. Suckers who accepted the bait would send in their money to Lawrence & Company, along with a signed form that would give the broker complete legal freedom to make investment decisions on the client's behalf. Discretionary brokerages (as they were termed) proliferated rapidly in this period and were, in the eyes of their more-legitimate counterparts, a scourge on the profession. What made fraudulent discretionary brokerage firms like Lawrence & Company even more treacherous was the fact that they did not actually invest the pooled money in the stock market on behalf of their gullible clients. Despite an elaborate show of keeping records of his alleged stock market transactions, in the hope that he could legally defend his practice if the books were examined, Buckwalter would merely pocket the money sent in by the public. Investors were strung along by a series of seemingly personal form letters, with detailed statements of account, showing that their initial speculations had made tremendous profits, which were now being reinvested as a deposit in the next combination, but that a further contribution would be needed to secure the deal. In reality, all of this was a fiction. Once a sucker had been bled for as much as Buckwalter thought he could stand, the "Royal Bounce" letter (as Comstock terms it) was sent, explaining that, sadly, the latest combination had failed and the victim's account was therefore wiped out.

At the height of the operation, Buckwalter was raking in more than $20,000 per month, with only a small proportion going toward the expense of hiring clerical staff and an office.[33] When Comstock raided the firm's office (not the grand Wall Street premises that the vignette on the letterhead notepaper seemed to promise, but a shady cubbyhole in an unprepossessing building around the corner), he discovered a "sucker list" of more than half a million names and seized some 40,000 letters from victims, the most tear jerking of which Comstock reprinted. Other, similar scams included "1% margin syndicates" (in which participants would be asked to stake a risibly small margin that would inevitably get wiped out); "stock promoters" (who would mail out elaborate prospectuses for firms whose prospects were grossly exaggerated, or even for firms that did not exist); "guarantee brokers" (who would faithfully return all the money from failed investments, less an eye-watering 12.5 percent "insurance charge" each month); "investment syndicates" (such as E. S. Dean & Company and the Franklin Syndicate, which operated a Ponzi scheme long before Ponzi himself, paying out up to 10 percent in weekly returns to early investors, simply by handing over the money received from subsequent ones); and the "advance-information brokers" (who promised, for a fee, "inside and advance information" on the future course of grain and stock markets, but who would instead use the clients' money to bet on both sides of the market, take a cut from the winners, and offer commiseration to the losers, all the while happily pocketing the regular subscription fee from both).[34] Most prominent of all was the development of the bucket shop, which mimicked regular brokerages, but with the crucial difference that bettors were not buying actual agricultural produce, or even their derivatives, such as commodity futures, but were instead, at best, betting against the house on the rise and fall of actual stock exchange prices, and, in the more-fraudulent versions, betting against manipulated or entirely fictitious quotations coming in over the ticker.

In comparison with the work of the Original Confidence Man in 1849, and even the more elaborate "big store" variations that began to emerge in the 1880s and 1890s, the scale of these late-century frauds operating through mass mailings and advertising was astounding. Writing in 1904, John Hill, a director of the Chicago Board of Trade tasked with combatting bucket shops, estimated that $100 million was invested in fraudulent stock promotions in 1902, while another $100 million annually was lost by the public in other get-rich-quick schemes, not including the rapid proliferation of bucket shops themselves, whose organization was increasingly complex. William Rodman Hennig, for example, started out in the tape game but then moved up to running a full bucket shop, with a central staff of twenty clerks, bookkeepers, and telegraph operators and more than thirty branch offices. In response to the legal challenges championed by Hill, Hennig created a quasi-trade organization for bucket shops that was designed to ape the respectability of the more legitimate exchanges. When that failed to achieve the desired results, he announced that he was establishing an entire parallel exchange to generate proprietary stock prices that the bucket shops could then use without fear of legal challenges.[35]

Despite the seemingly industrial and impersonal scale of these operations, however, they continued to make a pseudopersonal appeal to their victims, just like the trick played by the Original Confidence Man. The letters sent out by firms such as Lawrence & Company were lithographically printed to make them look handwritten, a technique that many anxious commentators feared would dupe the gullible public. "Many of this class," Comstock advised, "seek to overcome the growing prejudice against all this kind of advertising by sending personal letters: and these communications, which come unsolicited, are always to be regarded as very suspicious, the same as a printed circular."[36] Likewise, McWatters warns "youthful readers" that these mass-produced copies are designed to fool the recipients into believing that they are handwritten for their benefit: "Probably one-third of those who receive these letters do not know that they are in fact 'printed,' and each ignorant receiver feels flattered as he reads the letter that the 'speculator' has taken pains to write to him so extendedly."[37] With the modernization of the con trick, the mimicry of intimacy is now doubly false, providing a fake appeal to a personal connection that is itself cast deceitfully in pseudoauthentic lithographic "handwriting." Even large bucket shop chains, like Christie Stock & Grain, relied on an oddly personal tone in letters that gave their postal clients the brush off. "Well, old friend," one missive began, "we got in wrong this time, even though your corn was sold at what seemed to me an outrageous high price last evening. We had an old-fashioned runaway market to-day and there is no doubt that the December option is controlled by parties strong enough to do as they please with it, and it would be folly for any one to mix up with them."[38]

Comstock also documents how the newspaper advertisements placed by fraudulent brokerages, such as Lawrence & Company, also worked through a sleight-of-hand that was designed to evoke personal trust. Not only did the advertisements address their audience directly, in the second person, as if speaking to a business equal, but they were to be typeset, to appear supposedly in the editorial voice of the newspaper, rather than as a separate advertising column. The advertisements treacherously called upon the trust readers have in their newspaper's friendly voice of authority. As Comstock explained, the editor thus "appears as voucher for the fraudulent banking establishment advertised in his paper; and straightaway these readers invest their capital and savings. This trust is reposed especially in the word of the editor of a religious journal or of a reputable secular paper, which has for years been a companion in the household."[39] The advertisements and circulars also included testimonials from allegedly satisfied customers (in the case of pyramid schemes, such as the Franklin Syndicate, early investors would genuinely promote their success in person to eager denizens living in their neighborhood), along with worthless but rhetorically persuasive personal "guarantees" from the head of the firm. The scams thus combined what looked like impartial details of the success of the investment scheme, as if the numbers spoke for themselves, with an appeal that rested on placing trust both in the people that ran it and in the opinion of those who supposedly had profited by it. One correspondent of Lawrence & Company, for example, confessed that "I have read your circular carefully; and though I do not fully understand some of the terms, and methods, yet *I* BELIEVE *you*; and this doubtless is better than if I believed myself and doubted you."[40]

Most of the schemes relied on a populist appeal, both by offering the semblance of participation in the stock market for would-be investors of very humble means, and by evoking the democratic sentiment of average Americans being able to enjoy a share of the same successes as the elite. Many circulars for the "combination method" routinely evoked the idea that by pooling their resources, ordinary investors could be the equal of Jay Gould. Lawrence & Company, for example, noted that even for Gould, combinations were "the sole secret of his success," but whereas he was said to admit only a favored few into his syndicate, with Lawrence & Company, "*any one* can participate in the business of the street at *any time*."[41] In the follow-up letters that strung the mark along, however, the emphasis instead was on the fact that the next combination was reserved for special "friends" only: "We are now forming new combinations of the $25, $50, $100, and $500 classes for this purpose, which we confidently recommend to our old customers and friends. While all of these combinations afford equal privileges and prospects, we would remind our friends that experience has proved that the larger amounts, having the greatest power, usually yield the greatest profits."[42] The interpellated investor was figured as both a generic Everyman and an "old friend." The mass-produced confidence trick thus worked by making a simultaneous appeal to the inclusivity and exclusivity of the deal. Having access to confidential information or to the secret techniques employed by the big players was key to this advertised dream of leveling the social playing field. As an advertisement for an advance-information bureau stated, its aim was "to furnish a service that will put the small investor on an equal footing with the large trader, or, to use the parlance of the 'Street,' the 'insider.'"[43] In contrast to the Progressive Era's political faith in transparency, regulation, and "system trust," the appeal of the industrialized form of the confidence swindle was that it would combat the inequalities produced by Wall Street by allowing outsiders to become insiders.

Tips Are Valueless

Many critics were adamant, however, in insisting that participation in the stock market was indeed best left to insiders, a conviction that was only strengthened by the mounting evidence of the susceptibility of the public to confidence rackets promising surefire tips and other ways of beating the market. Despite its campaign in the 1910s and 1920s to promote a "shareholding democracy," in the decades around the turn of the twentieth century, the New York Stock Exchange, in particular, warned against the democratization of finance. The Hughes Committee (which had investigated speculation in securities and commodities in the wake of the panic of 1907) likewise counseled that speculation per se should not be banned, but was best left to the professionals, who were able to adjudge and shoulder the risk. It identified, as the lowest of five categories of patrons of the exchanges, those "inexperienced persons, who act on interested advice, 'tips,' advertisements in newspapers, or circulars sent by mail, or 'take flyers' in absolute ignorance, and with blind confidence in their luck." These feckless outsiders, it concluded, "almost without exception . . . eventually lose."[44]

The obvious popularity of confidence scams that promised inside access to the stock market also worried many of the popular writers who were trying to make financial speculation seem safe, and thus suitable for ordinary Americans. Respectable investment-advice manuals—such as John Moody's 1904 reissuing of John F. Hume's 1888 *Art of Investing* as *The Art of Wise Investing*—decried a "new form of advertising for 'Lambs' [that] has become popular," in which "for a small sum, paid 'weekly' or 'monthly,' the subscriber will receive 'sure tips' on the market's movements, and that in consideration of one-quarter or one-half of the profits secured, the 'Advisory Brokers' will handle the deals for the 'Lambs' who don't know how to do it for themselves."[45] For those seeking market information, Hume instead recommended John Moody's Bureau of Corporation Statistics, whose reports "are not influenced or 'inspired' and have no bearing on Wall Street 'tips' and 'gossip.'" He counseled trusting in objective data rather than personal connections, a position that needs to be tempered by the fact that his book was published by Moody. Most stock market guides for the common man published in the decades around the turn of the twentieth century warn that the promise of surefire tips and inside information is illusory, absurd, or deceptive. Other commentators, however, such as Thomas Gibson in *Pitfalls of Speculation*, insist that the dream of beating the market by such means is also "illogical." The reason is that "any wide-spread dissemination of advance information as to a projected movement would defeat its own object"; in other words, rumors spread quickly and the market will instantly discount the anticipated event in much the same way that the efficient market hypothesis, a century later, would insist takes place. Gibson therefore concludes that "tips are valueless," and is dismayed to admit that "the public continues to use them largely as a basis for trading."[46]

Early advocates of chart and tape reading took the idea of the self-negating nature of inside information even further. Richard Wyckoff, in *Studies in Tape Reading*, notes that "the insider who knows a dividend is to be jumped from 6 per cent, to 10 per cent, shows his hand on the tape when he attempts to turn his knowledge into dollars."[47] In this line of thinking, any private information quickly becomes public knowledge (at least for those able to "read" the tape correctly), so tipsters and their clients are unable to capitalize on their access to privileged information. In fact, Wyckoff's claim is even stronger; he suggests that good tape readers are able to glean genuine inside information through an alert reading of the tape alone. He tells one story, for example, about an anticipated U.S. Supreme Court decision that would have a significant effect on stock prices, with the tape revealing the outcome even before the news wires: "That not even the insiders knew what the decision was to be is shown in the dullness of the stock all morning. Those who heard the decision in the Supreme Court chamber doubtless did the double-quick to the telephone and sold the stock short. Their sales showed on the tape before the news arrived in New York. Tape Readers were, therefore, first to be notified. They were short before the Street knew what had happened."[48] Wyckoff's argument is that equal access to stock market information via the stock ticker will ensure that finance is democratized for those who can read the tape, thereby undermining the usual dubious channels of privileged access.

A similarly prescient faith in the ability of the impersonal market itself to anticipate any significant inside information is evident in Henry Emery's academic study of speculation, albeit with a very different conclusion. At first it seems as though Emery acknowledges the potential importance of inside information when he argues that the reason the "outside public" are so easily fleeced is that they have no access to advance knowledge of market movements, unlike genuine insiders. He notes that "with scarcely an exception . . . every successful operator in the stock or grain market has been distinguished by his unusual success in securing accurate information in advance of his competitors." Emery goes on to argue, however, that in reality, access to inside information plays a comparatively insignificant role in speculation, because in the stock and produce markets, "events are anticipated and exert their influence before they arrive," such that "it is often surprising to see how absolutely without effect is the final occurrence of an event of importance, provided it has been expected."[49] In another anticipation of the efficient market hypothesis and its notion of the uncanny accuracy and efficiency of the collective wisdom of the market, Emery is suggesting that the market will always have already discounted any inside information. As chapter 5 explores in more detail, Emery was not alone in arguing that the democratization of finance—in the sense of speculation no longer being confined to a small clique of insiders, but opened up to the masses—would diminish the possibility of manipulating the market through inside information, and perhaps even make it impossible. If the robber barons had once been able to cannily use their positions as company directors to manipulate the market or engineer a corner in those securities, the argument went, then more-widespread speculation would make it much harder for any one individual to control the market and would make the information conveyed in prices more truly representative of actual conditions.

The Special Circumstances of Inside Information

Although Emery suggested that the problem of inside information was exaggerated, he remained concerned that company directors could still use their privileged position to manipulate the market in securities: "If they wish to speculate in the shares of their companies, they are in a position of extraordinary advantage. By means of one line of policy or another, combined with the use of false information to the public, they may move the price to suit their private purposes. . . . Speculations of this order constitute the worst evil and the most flagrant scandals of the stock exchange."[50] Sereno Pratt, editor of the *Wall Street Journal*, secretary of the New York Chamber of Commerce, and author of the sober guide, *The Work of Wall Street*, took similar exception to the abuse of inside information: "There is still another class of speculators who are called 'insiders.' They are directors or officials of corporations or in other positions where it is possible to obtain inside information as to the business of the companies whose stocks are traded in[,] in Wall Street. They know things in advance of the public or even the professionals. They are able to speculate on the vantage-ground of certain knowledge." Pratt takes some comfort in the fact that "even insiders sometimes slip in their operations," noting that "there have been speculative directors who, selling the stock of their own company short, have found themselves cornered." Like Emery, though, Pratt is still concerned about the power that directors hold and the dangers of insider trading: "A director of a great corporation whose securities are listed on the Stock Exchange is an influential individual, with sources of information and opportunities of manipulation denied to others. He is the true 'insider' of the stock-market."[51]

The problem of inside information thus raised a number of political, ethical, and legal questions. Should promising to provide inside information be made illegal, because so many gullible outsiders get hoodwinked by confidence artists, or should the doctrine of caveat emptor apply, meaning that victims of scams had only themselves to blame? Was there any need for governmental or even industry regulators to do anything about speculators using inside information, if the abstract market was able to regulate itself and negate any advantages of advance knowledge? If you can never beat the market, was using inside information unethical, or merely inadvisable? Or, in the absence of any legal requirements for full transparency in corporate reporting, was having access to inside information a vital function that provided the trust that oiled the machinery of finance?

As chapter 5 examines in more detail, despite J. P. Morgan's rejection of the Pujo Committee's accusation that the interlocking directorships of corporations and banks amounted to a vast, yet intimate, conspiracy in the control of a handful of insiders, he relied on the seemingly outdated rhetoric of personal connections and character in his defense of his business practices. Corporate directorships and informal social and kinship ties provided Morgan & Company not merely with specific inside information, but a level of confidence that could not be achieved in any other way. While critics argued that this privileged access was open to abuse, the coterie of investment bankers and corporate financiers insisted that the public should have confidence in them—not because of any regulatory requirements (which, they argued, could easily be corrupted), but because of their personal professionalism and patriotism. Trust the person, not the rules, they insisted.

Far from being defensive about the charge of inside information, some bankers were proud of the service they could provide to their clients, precisely because of their personal connections and privileged position. George Perkins, for example, worked simultaneously for the New York Life Insurance Company and J. P. Morgan & Company. Morgan wanted help in selling $500 million worth of shares as part of his massive consolidation of U.S. Steel. As a component in that larger campaign, Perkins was personally given $3 million worth of shares to dispose of. His preferred solution was for New York Life to buy the $3 million block, but because the terms of an agreement the insurance firm had regarding trading in Germany prevented it from owning any stock, Perkins instead sold the block to the New York Security and Trust Company, of which he was also a director. With the promise to the trust company's fellow directors that New York Life would continue to keep its sizeable cash deposits there, the trust company agreed to return 75 percent of the profits from the deal to New York Life. Perkins's cozy personal relationship with the three firms allowed him not only to circumvent laws, but to engage in a financial speculation with seemingly no risk. Like Morgan, Perkins felt that this kind of gentlemanly cooperation was preferable to the ravages of unfettered competition and was even willing to defend this position when called before the Hughes Committee's investigation of the shady conflicts of interest and cozy relationships between the "Big Three" insurance firms. The Hughes Committee revealed, for example, how Perkins had sold $4 million worth of International Mercantile Marine bonds to J. P. Morgan & Company on the last day of the year, in order to move the loss-making bonds off the books of the insurance company before it made its annual report, only to buy them back two days later. When Hughes sarcastically asked whether "you conducted that transaction with yourself," Perkins replied that he had merely acted as agent for the two firms. Although rattled both by his cross-examination at the hands of Hughes and by a public campaign led by a young Louis Brandeis, Perkins was "prepared not only to defend the insider transaction but to boast of it."[52] He was proud of the way he was able to engineer mutually profitable, risk-free deals for both the New York Life Insurance Company and J. P. Morgan & Company, and—had he not been prevented by Hughes from making a public statement—would have insisted that the transaction "was only possible because of the advantages of my connection with J. P. Morgan & Co."[53] As far as Perkins was concerned, inside information was not only legitimate, but essential to the proper workings of high finance.

The legal status of inside information was hazy, at best, during this period. Although corporations were required to submit annual reports to their state's authorities, there was no requirement for them to be independently audited. Many corporate reports functioned as thinly disguised and often quite inaccurate advertisements for the firm. Company directors thus had no incentive to share their privileged knowledge of the true state of affairs of the corporation and, in fact, could make personal fortunes on the stock market by manipulating their secret knowledge. Perkins was convinced that his transactions were morally justified, because he saw himself working ultimately for the benefit of the masses of insurance policy holders by reducing competition and thereby reducing risk, rather than being a party to the selfish abuse of public trust that had typified the era of the robber barons. Perkins assumed that he was fulfilling his fiduciary duty of trust by using inside information.

Although the Hughes Committee and the public were outraged at some of the details of the internecine connections between insurance companies, banks, and industrial corporations, the kind of insider dealing that Perkins engaged in was not technically illegal. The dubious practices that Perkins followed were not outlawed until the advent of New Deal legislation that was designed to regain public trust in the stock market after the Wall Street crash of 1929. Even then, despite a sweeping prohibition on fraudulent securities practices, insider trading as such was not singled out for particular attention.[54] Although the Securities Exchange Act of 1934 did not fully identify and prohibit insider trading, as it has since come to be theorized in legal scholarship, it nevertheless signaled a desire to overturn the presumption that such manipulative practices were part and parcel of Wall Street business. A later U.S. Supreme Court ruling summarizing the broad intent of this New Deal legislation concluded that "a significant purpose of the Exchange Act was to eliminate the idea that the use of inside information for personal advantage was a normal emolument of corporate office."[55] Before the twentieth century, as an article in a law journal (summarizing received legal wisdom) noted in 1910, "the doctrine that officers and directors [of corporations] are trustees of the stockholders . . . does not extend to their private dealings with stockholders or others, though in such dealings they take advantage of knowledge gained through their official position."[56] *Strong v. Repide* (1909), the first case on insider trading heard by the U.S. Supreme Court, began to chip away at this prevailing wisdom. The case revolved around the question of whether the director of the Philippine Sugar Estates Development Company should have revealed to a shareholder—whose shares the director secretly bought on the cheap—the negotiations he was involved in to sell the company's assets to the U.S. government. While the Supreme Court broadly affirmed the ruling that company directors were under no special obligation to disclose all material facts, it argued that in the case at hand, there were "special circumstances" that made it permissible for the law to intervene in the transaction, a compromise that neither explicitly condoned nor prohibited inside information.

In cases involving confidence tricksters and inside information, the law was even more murky, with suits brought by victims of swindling often failing to obtain a conviction. The defense would cite *People v. McCord* (1871), a case in which the victim of a fake arrest tried to bribe Henry McCord, a con man posing as a detective issuing a warrant. The Illinois Court of Appeals overturned McCord's initial conviction, arguing that the injured party was complicit in the crime proposed by the con man. *People v. McCord* was later cited in other cases involving confidence tricks, such as attempting to obtain advance information of stock-price movements by illegally tapping telegraph wires, or by trying to buy forged currency in the green-goods game. The victim was deemed to be a confederate in the intended crime and therefore not deserving of the protection of the law. In both *Strong v. Repide* and *People v. McCord*, the underlying assumption was that people engaging in the financial marketplace should do so with their eyes wide open, with their sovereign individual freedom trumping the need to protect the unwary from the dangers of inside information, whether real or fictitious.[57] The law was not particularly concerned with financial fraud; instead, it was left to individuals and businesses to provide a private solution to this public problem.[58]

In the late nineteenth and early twentieth centuries, crony capitalism—using inside information, relying on personal favors, and betraying both public and private trust—was thus a matter of routine. This was no longer the shameless political vote rigging and blatant abuse of privilege that had characterized the Tammany Hall and Erie Railroad shenanigans, however. Instead, it was a system of corruption that was championed as technocratic and professional. As Richard White argues, in this historical moment, "the corrupt explored new frontiers:

they corrupted information, particularly financial information, on a scale never before possible."[59]

Love Plots and Business Plots

The questions presciently raised by Melville in *The Confidence-Man* remained a pressing concern in the latter part of the nineteenth century. Why was the confidence trick so troubling, yet so alluring? Did it work by appealing to the moral code of friendship, or by abusing it? Should personal friendship and impersonal business mix? By the final decades of the nineteenth century, traditional ways of organizing social dealings through established hierarchies of status and chains of obligation had supposedly given way to more impersonal and abstract modes of economic interaction, governed by the developing laws of contract. In Nikolas Luhmann's terms, personal trust had seemingly been rendered redundant by system trust.[60] Yet an older gift economy was not simply replaced by an encroaching exchange economy, but was folded within it. Although the law governing insider dealing clung resolutely to the laissez-faire doctrine of caveat emptor, the persistent fascination and anxiety surrounding confidence games suggested otherwise. The scams promised a personal connection to financial success that bypassed both hard work and the laws of supply and demand.

The second part of this chapter explores in more detail the way that the relationship between economics and morality was worked through in a number of American novels of the period, focusing in particular on fiction by William Dean Howells and Edith Wharton. The first reason for looking closely at novels as a cultural form is that in their plots, writers returned repeatedly to the theme of the possibility or impossibility of a moral economy in a world that seemed increasingly governed by the blind forces of economic and biological determinism—a thematic preoccupation that, in turn, was part of the larger aesthetic and ideological debate between the older conventions of sentimentalism and the newer logics of realism and naturalism. Confronted with the increasing importance of distant financial episodes in determining everyday reality, many novelists felt obliged to explore either the "romance and adventure in Wall Street" (in the words of Lafcadio Hearn), or, for those less sanguine about the effects of finance, a sense of the floating, unsubstantial nature of reality in an era repeatedly beset by panics in which all that had been taken to be solid and dependable melted so quickly into thin air.[61] The other reason for focusing on the novel is that, during this period, it is, as Wai Chee Dimock notes, the cultural form that enacts in its structure of multiple plot lines the potentially infinite chains of causality, obligation, and personal connectedness that continue to exist between individuals in an increasingly vast and complex market society. "In the very form of the novel," Dimock observes, "in its web of causality and its need for closure, we see a universe of alternating expansion and contraction that would seem to correspond, more or less, to the alternately expanding and contracting cognitive universe that facilitates both capitalism and humanitarianism."[62] It is thus not merely in its story lines, but at the level of form, that the realist novel investigates the idea of personal entanglements in an age of impersonal financial strictures.

The relationship between morality and economics in general, and the concatenations of interpersonal causality in particular, are worked through most obviously in the intertwining of a love plot and a business plot in the Gilded Age novel. The relationship between the two plot lines in many novels from around the turn of the twentieth century is troubling. In many of the popular fictions of finance that appeared in large numbers during this period, the two plots find mutual resolution in hackneyed endings. In these Wall Street stories, the business plot is often melodramatically entwined with the love plot, with rivalries and malfeasances on the floor of the stock exchange paralleled, but also eventually resolved, by romantic entanglements outside the realm of the market. The specialty of author Will Payne, for instance, was a love subplot in which the son and daughter of warring financiers eventually marry, providing a connubial solution to the financial problem that the novel raises, albeit at the expense of plausibility and aesthetic sophistication. In other cases, though, the connection between the various plot strands is less easily resolved, and both readers at the time and more recent critics have disagreed about the logical justification and aesthetic success of the conflation of seemingly unconnected stories and genres within the same novel.[63]

The Personal Considerations of Silas Lapham

Against the backdrop of William Dean Howells's tale of the financial ruin of its self-made businessman protagonist, *The Rise of Silas Lapham* raises the question of his moral rejuvenation in the face of adversity. Having made his fortune from the fortuitous discovery of a natural mineral paint on the family farm, Lapham tries to gain entry for his two daughters into polite Boston society. While on vacation, his wife and elder daughter Irene had nursed Mrs. Corey, who is from one of the most refined Boston families. Feeling a debt of obligation to Mrs. Lapham, she arranges a visit and then a dinner party, one result of which is that her son Tom Corey becomes attracted to Penelope, the younger Lapham daughter, although everyone else is convinced that it is Irene who has caught his fancy—not least Irene herself, who is besotted with Tom. In part flattered by the attentions of

Corey Jr., Lapham offers the young dilettante a position in his paint firm, a business decision that seems entwined with sentimental considerations, despite Lapham denying to his wife that this was the case. The central drama of the novel comes when the truth of Corey's affections are made known: what is the best way out of a situation that, whichever way it is solved, will inevitably cause distress to one of the Lapham sisters? The solution to the love triangle proposed by the Reverend Sewell, whom the Laphams approach for advice, seems to belong more properly to the world of business. The utilitarian calculation of an "economy of pain" dictates that there is no point in all three young people being made to suffer needlessly for a falsely sentimental notion of sacrifice (i.e., if Penelope allows Irene to marry Tom), when common sense dictates that the pair who are truly in love should marry, and the unrequited sister should accept the reality of the situation as unfortunate and not blameworthy.

Compounding Lapham's troubles is the return of Milton K. Rogers, his feckless former partner, who fell on hard times after Lapham bought him out once he no longer needed the other's initial input of capital. In an act that is part sentimental charity and part hard-nosed business, Lapham agrees to buy some mining shares from Rogers, but it turns out that they are nearly worthless, as the regional railroad has changed its commitment to connect up with the mines (and is perhaps deliberately reneging on the deal in order to force a fire sale of the property). In order to recoup some of his losses from these shares, Lapham takes to stock market speculation, but he ends up losing even more money, something he can now ill afford, as general business conditions are falling into a slump. The paint business suffers, and things take a turn for the worse when the appearance of a new paint firm in West Virginia ultimately forces him to sell out to his younger rivals. Lapham's fall is complete when the new house he had commissioned burns to the ground, a disaster made worse by the fact that he had allowed the insurance policy on the property to lapse. Alongside the love triangle involving the tale of Irene, Penelope, and Tom on the one hand, and Lapham's descent toward bankruptcy on the other, there is another plot line that concentrates on Zerilla Dewey, who works as a secretary for Lapham. The reader eventually learns that Zerilla is the daughter of the man who, during the Civil War, took the bullet destined for Lapham, an act for which the latter feels eternally grateful. Lapham considers it a debt that can never be repaid. Unbeknownst to his wife and family, he supports the girl, her alcoholic mother, and the latter's equally hapless partner.

Many original reviewers of the novel were mystified by its title, which seemed to promise uplift rather than decline, and could not find any connection between the different stories covered in the novel. Some even flat out ignored the far-from-incidental account of Lapham's lurch toward bankruptcy, seeing the novel merely as a story of a tragic love triangle.[64] Several modern critics of *The Rise of Silas Lapham* have likewise been unconvinced by the relationship between the various parts of the novel, seeing it as aesthetically flawed.[65] In contrast, Donald Pizer insists that "the apparent conflict between the attack on self-sacrifice in the sub-plot and Lapham's self-sacrifice in the main plot" is, in fact, reconciled within a "single moral system," suggesting that the tensions between the love plot and the business plot are illusory, because they are both governed by the same sentimental code.[66] In a similar vein, but with the opposite conclusion, Wai Chee Dimock argues that Sewell's utilitarian "economy of pain" provides a cognitive frame that, at a thematic level, joins the love plot and the business plot and is matched, at a formal level, by the novel's aesthetic balancing of its different plot lines, which function, at a structural level, as an analogue for poetic justice.[67] Where Pizer views all the plot lines of *The Rise of Silas Lapham* as operating within a single moral framework, Dimock (in keeping with other New Historicist interpretations of American naturalism) reads the different elements as part an all-pervasive economic logic.

As we have seen, however, the love plot and the business plot in *The Rise of Silas Lapham* remain confused and conflicted, neither fully demarcated in separate spheres nor fully integrated. Hildegard Hoeller argues that the tensions within Howells's novel and other works of late nineteenth-century American literature result from the operation of two different economies within the novel, namely, a gift economy of personal obligations and an exchange economy derived from the world of contractual business relationships.[68] For example, Hoeller rightly points out that the conflict between these two modes of interaction actually provides the starting point for the whole narrative, with the worrying sense of limitless obligation felt by the Coreys to the Laphams for Mrs. Lapham's kind act. Hoeller's reading of the discord between the two perspectives draws on the anthropological and philosophical meditations by Lewis Hyde and Jacques Derrida on the conceptual impossibility of a true, altruistic gift.[69] The implication is that the unresolvable confusions between obligation and an exchange economy in the novel result from the timeless, contradictory nature of the gift itself.

I want to suggest instead that *The Rise of Silas Lapham* repeatedly returns to the confusion between gift and exchange, because it had become a pressing problem by the 1880s. Lapham is presented as the epitome of the modern businessman, in contrast to the obsolescence of the aristocratic world of Corey Sr. The Coreys worry that Lapham is too focused on business—"I don't think it would strike him as businesslike" (68)—with Corey Sr. struggling to find some way of understanding his counterpart.[70] He charitably suggests that for men like Lapham, money is "the romance, the poetry of our age" (64). Despite the increasing dominance of the corporate form, Lapham, early in his career, rejects even a straightforward partnership, as it would signal a dilution of his manly sense of independence. Later, after his bankruptcy, he becomes more obsolescent still, as his paint-mine firm becomes merely part of a larger corporate structure. The novel suggests that the Brahmin Coreys are outdated in comparison with Lapham the businessman, but he, in turn, is a dying breed of ruggedly individualist proprietor. In a similar contradictory fashion, Lapham makes his fortune by an obsessive and hard-hearted dedication to his business, seemingly to the exclusion of all other virtues, yet his feeling for the paint he manufactures is highly personal, the antithesis of mere exchange value. His paint firm, the narrator informs us, "was something more than a business to him" (50), and he recognizes that the mineral source of his paint is a gift, a natural boon. As Brook Thomas notes, Howells's novel—as if trying to work out the troublesome border between the separate spheres of feminine sentiment and masculine trade—repeatedly invokes the very word "business" in domestic contexts, with Silas, for instance, telling his wife Persis, "You mind your own business, Persis . . . if you've got any" (284).[71] When Lapham and his wife discuss whether he should take Tom into the firm for the sake of Irene, Lapham stumbles to the conclusion (drawn from the rhetoric of paint making) that "I don't object to him, as I know, either way, but the two things won't mix" (90). And Persis hesitatingly feels her way toward agreement: "But if you really think it won't do to mix the two things . . ." (91). From the other side of the transaction, Mrs. Corey wonders whether her son's advancement in the world of business is not the result of his objective merit: "And you don't suppose it was any sort of—personal consideration?" (101).

Despite Howells's insistence that the story is one of the moral rise of its protagonist despite his business fall, Lapham's problems stem from the inconsistent way in which he manages to "mix the two things" of business and personal affairs. Lapham blames his downfall on his dabbling in the alien and amoral new realm of stock market speculation, with Silas confessing to Irene on her return from her self-imposed exile: "I don't know as you'd call it wrong. It's what people do all the time. But I wish I'd let stocks alone" (287). Yet it turns out that his difficulties arise from other factors, some of which are mere contingencies of "this economic chance world," while others are a result of his repeated and contradictory efforts to maintain an old-fashioned moral rectitude.[72] Lapham does business with Rogers as a personal favor but presents it as a commercial transaction; yet he then refuses the possibility of conducting some business with the representatives of

wealthy English investors in a manner that, while on the surface is entirely respectable, smacks of knowing collusion: Lapham "with difficulty kept himself
from winking" (325). As far as his treatment of Rogers is concerned, Lapham is
adamant, protesting a trifle too vehemently that "it was a perfectly square thing,"
because "it was a business chance" (46). Lapham insists on keeping up the fiction
that they are engaged in a business relation rather than charity: "Rogers came to
borrow. He didn't come to beg" (131). Persis demands, however, that the loan is
never to be recalled, no matter how much Lapham might need it, a gesture that,
in effect, turns the loan into a gift. Despite Lapham's insistence on keeping his
dealings with Rogers on a purely business footing, he seals his own financial ruin
when, for reasons of moral scrupulosity, he refuses to indulge in the transaction
that Rogers proposes with the English agents, even when Rogers offers to buy
the property directly from Lapham, so that the latter's conscience (and his legal
liability) will be clear: "You will not have an iota of responsibility," and "any lawyer
would have told him the same" (329). Rogers's reading of the business ethics of
the case differs from Lapham's: "I did not think that was necessary," he informs
Lapham, "to tell the parties about the G, L & P [Railroad]" (321). At the same
time, however, he invokes the old-fashioned sanctity of a businessman keeping
his promises when he tries to persuade Lapham that the latter must meet with
the English agents.

   With the G, L & P deal, it seems that nearly everyone is "in the know" yet
willing to maintain the fiction of impartiality: Lapham knows that Rogers knows
that the English agents know that the property is worthless, and that, in any case,
the English investors are able to sustain the loss. This only leaves the question
of whether the unknown wealthy English investors are merely the fools of stock
market lore, or whether they are turning a blind eye themselves to the specifics of
a deal they must know is probably too good to be true in order to pass it on to an
even greater fool. Lapham comes to realize that the inside deal being proposed,
through euphemism, is that the Englishmen will buy the stock issues at an inflated price from Lapham but will then expect a kickback, each side benefitting
from a "personal consideration." Despite having earlier boasted to Persis that
"I've got the inside track" on the deal, Lapham insists on conducting business
with the highest level of morality, even if it means his financial ruin. He explains
to Persis: "Most likely Rogers was lyin', and there ain't any such parties; but if
there were, they couldn't have the mills from me without the whole story. Don't
you be troubled Persis. I'm going to pull through all right" (279). When presented
at the eleventh hour with the opportunity of selling his paint firm to a speculator
from New York, Lapham toys with the tantalizing possibility of rescue but then

realizes that he could not withhold information about the rival West Virginian paint company from the prospective New York buyer. Despite supposedly being the representative of a new age, in which everything is reduced to the bottom line, Lapham instead seems to represent an older order, as he finds himself unable to compartmentalize his business and his morals. Unlike Melville's sly narrator, Howells—and, indeed, the realist novel as a cultural form during this period—cannot recount his protagonist's rise and fall "without the whole story," that is, without the full disclosure to the reader of all the "material facts" (as the *Strong v. Repide* decision termed it) of the hidden consequences of each character's actions, appearing in seemingly ever-widening ripples of influence that blur the boundaries between the various love plots and business plots. Lapham finds himself caught up in a web of global business connections that are increasingly being woven by a stock market that is geographically remote. At the same time, however, he is entangled in a series of domestic moral obligations that cannot easily be repaid. There is no easy, dialectical synthesis of the two perspectives. Rather than a smoothing out of the apparent tension between a moral economy and an exchange economy, the novel provides what we might term an imaginary *irresolution* of real social contradictions.[73]

Friends

In her autobiography, Edith Wharton observed how her friend Henry James "often bewailed to me his total inability to use the 'material,' financial and industrial, of modern American life. Wall Street, and everything connected with the big business world, remained an impenetrable mystery to him."[74] In contrast to some examples of financial fiction from the turn of the twentieth century, Wharton's novels do not undertake a sustained examination of "Wall Street, and everything connected to the big business world." Yet they nevertheless engage dramatically with the tensions between the realm of morality and the realm of economics, doing so in more ways than the familiar exploration of marriage as a market in the nineteenth-century novel of manners. In Wharton's novels, the link between Wall Street and Fifth Avenue, at the level of both content and form, is a moral quagmire of inside information that blurs the boundary between older, more personal forms of interaction and seemingly more modern, impersonal ones.

In his revisionist account of the transcontinental railroads in the nineteenth century, Richard White argues that "friendship" greased the economic and political machinery of railroad corporations, whose focus was often more on making money through financial scheming than on building a robust transportation system. Despite all the contemporary popular talk of gloves-off battles between the era's robber barons, the key players in nineteenth-century financial skullduggery routinely invoked the notion of *friendship* in their creation of reciprocal chains of influence and obligation. The sentimental virtue of affection, however, was not necessarily part of what was meant by calling an amenable politician or financier a "friend." Instead, "friendship was a code: a network of social bonds that could organize political activity."[75] White insists that corruption is not always inevitably the same, but has its own history, and that what made Gilded Age and Progressive Era corruption distinctive is that a stylized performance of genteel friendship was preferred to brazen bribery. It involved manipulating information, especially corporate financial information, thus creating an informational asymmetry in the rapidly expanding and largely unregulated markets of the period, one that could be exploited for profit.[76] What passed hands between the railroad corporations and their "friends" was not, if it could be avoided, anything so vulgar as a direct money bribe (though, of course, that did happen), but information among insiders. White draws attention to the ubiquity of references to "friendship" in the public and private correspondence of Gilded Age robber barons, making clear how financial corruption was normalized, becoming part of the ordinary way of doing business.

For White, the best guide to this elite world of corrupt friendship is not a muckraking journalist, but the novelist Edith Wharton:

> Friendship was where the kind of men found in an Edith Wharton novel obtained their footing. In a Wharton novel the businessmen husbands or fathers—so necessarily present and as necessarily alien to the love affairs and friendships, to the flirtations and conversation, around which the novels revolved—only blundered and did damage. The female characters created networks too insubstantial to support the ponderous men whom they accidentally ensnared. But in the hotel rooms, clubs, and offices men spun out their webs of friendship. The material networks—the bands of steel that girded the continent—also depended on inchoate networks that mirrored the secrets, courtships, and flirtations of drawing room and dining room. The cultural connections of business and politics were the domain of friends.[77]

Wharton's three great novels about the upper class in Gilded Age New York—*The House of Mirth* (1905), *The Custom of the Country* (1913), and *The Age of Innocence* (1920)—operate, in both their thematic concerns and their narrative structure, through the control of access to inside information.[78] I want to suggest, however, that in Wharton's novels, the "inchoate networks" of the boardroom are not merely "mirrored" by the "secrets, courtships, and flirtations" of the drawing room, but are influenced and enabled by them, as well as vice versa. Where *The Rise of Silas Lapham* can be read as a nostalgic attempt to apply the uncorrupted domain of personal ethics to the corrupting world of business, Wharton's novels suggest instead that business relations in the Gilded Age take their cue in part from the already corrupt world of high society.

In her fictional as well as her autobiographical writings, Wharton provided an ambiguous lament for the passing of the world of her childhood. Although the new-money families are at times viewed as refreshingly entertaining, they are more often seen as scandalous invaders; furthermore, her novels retain a sense of nostalgia for an aristocratic ideal of noblesse oblige that is more in tune with traditional American notions of democratic classlessness than the self-conscious elitism of the nouveau riche. In the last quarter of the nineteenth century, the Anglo-Dutch patrician families of New York merchants and landowners—who, in Wharton's eyes, epitomized respectability, business probity, and a sense of aristocratic rootedness, but also restrictively clung to tradition and gentility—were increasingly overtaken by those who had made sudden fortunes in corporate or financial speculation. As Sven Beckert notes, what had held the older mercantile class together was a close-knit system of kinship, the forging and maintenance of which was dominated by women. "It was in the family parlor, not the counting house," Beckert argues, "that New York's merchant elite worked hardest to remain a community."[79] In the parochial New York of the 1870s that *The Age of Innocence* looks back on, "as through the wrong end of a telescope" (74), the matriarch Mrs. Manson Mingott insists that "everybody in New York has always known everybody" (27), or, as the arriviste Undine Spragg, in *The Custom of the Country*, observes of the esteemed but increasingly marginalized Dagonet family circle she marries into: "They were all more or less cousins" (36). The emphasis on family ties and the construction of strong social bonds was, for this earlier mercantile elite, a necessary solution to the problem of trust in dealing with trading partners who were spread out over the vast distances of national and, increasingly, global markets. Beckert argues that by the end of the nineteenth century, New York's bourgeoisie had consolidated itself as a cohesive upper class by embracing an increasingly self-conscious cultural identity of elitism, backed up Darwinian racial thinking.[80] The genteel networks of influence that held together the earlier merchant dynasties were not, however, swept by the invading hordes of new money, but, in fact, made the transition possible. Wharton's novels provide an anatomy of these circuits of information.

Tips and Deals

At first sight, there seems to be a vast gulf between Fifth Avenue and Wall Street in Wharton's novels. For example, when Lily Bart, a socialite in quest of a suitably distinguished marriage, whose story is told in *The House of Mirth*, is repaying her hostess's hospitality by helping her out with her correspondence, the narrator describes how the household bills provide an "incongruously commercial touch to the elegance of her writing table" (63). Likewise, Ralph Marvell, Undine's old-money husband in *The Custom of the Country*, snobbishly reflects that "what [the portrait painter] Popple called society was really just like the houses it lived in: a muddle of misapplied ornament over a thin steel shell of utility." Its "steel shell was built up in Wall Street, the social trimmings were hastily added in Fifth Avenue," he continues, and "the union between them was as monstrous and factitious, as that between the Blois gargoyles on Peter Van Degen's roof and the skeleton walls supporting them" (73). The source of wealth for families such as Ralph Marvell's is discreetly obscure, as they live off inheritances, with the men barely engaging in any productive work. (Newland Archer, for example, the protagonist of *The Age of Innocence*, dabbles at law and mainly spends his time in the office reading the newspaper.) Occasionally, though, the world of finance does directly intrude when, for example, in *The House of Mirth*, we hear disquieting rumors that it had been a "bad autumn in Wall Street" (194), or, in *The Age of Innocence*, that "Beaufort's fortune was substantial enough to stand the strain; yet the disquieting rumors persisted, not only in Fifth Avenue but in Wall Street" (210). Lily, once she is embroiled in a financial speculation engineered by her would-be lover, Gus Trenor, realizes, to her cost, that she does not understand "this vast mysterious Wall Street world of 'tips' and 'deals'" (*HM*, 131). Likewise, for Mrs. Spragg, the wife of a midwesterner who has made a fortune in real estate speculation, her "knowledge of what went on 'down town' was of the most elementary kind" (*CC*, 16).

Yet the worlds of business and the drawing room are shown to be intimately linked. For Undine, "it was of no consequence that the details and technicalities [of finance] escaped her. . . . Every Wall Street term had its equivalent in the language of Fifth Avenue" (*CC*, 537). In Wharton's New York novels, gossip, tips, favors, deals, and—above all—the networks of information conducted by "friends" do not merely find their "equivalent" on Fifth Avenue, but instead are part of the very same economy. In her reading of *The House of Mirth*, Wai Chee Dimock demonstrates how the logic—and language—of the market pervades the entire social world, such that the two realms can no longer be thought of as distinct or in contradiction.[81] The novel portrays Lily as a victim of a society in which women are commodities, whose value rises and falls like a corporate stock, and the relations between men and women are reduced to transactional exchanges. Although Dimock rightly draws our attention to the pervasive influence of Wall Street on Fifth Avenue in *The House of Mirth*, it is also important to understand how this and other Wharton novels chart the converse—the influence of the logic of the drawing room in the counting house—with the incorporation of a seemingly genteel economy of "friendship" in downtown's supposedly hardnosed realm of exchange. Wharton's novels suggest that Wall Street's "'tips' and 'deals'" at the core of its heartless exchange economy result from a striving to gain advantage through corrupt inside information that is dressed up in the refined language of favors and obligations, which Beckert shows was the social glue that kept the mercantile elite together.

Fraternal Intimacy

Not only does the euphemistic refusal to specify the exact terms of a deal create an uneasy parallel with the moral confusions of the intrigues of the drawing room, but a Wall Street deal is often enabled by or is used to cement a Fifth Avenue connection. In the case of the nouveau riche, Jewish real estate speculator Rosedale, for example, we learn that "already his wealth, and the masterly use he had made of it, were giving him an enviable prominence in the world of affairs, and placing Wall Street under obligations which only Fifth Avenue could repay" (*HM*, 387). The glimpses we are afforded of "big business" suggest that money is being made not from an impartial and impersonal interaction with the "vast mysterious world of Wall Street," but from personal connections and inside information. In *The House of Mirth*, for example, we learn that Mr. Bry, one of the new-money set who continues to prosper despite the economic downturn that causes the other, more established members of the elite to tighten their belts, "has promised [the Duke] a tip, and he says if we go he'll pass it on to us" (331). It turns out that Gus Trenor generates speculative windfalls for Lily not because, as he complains to Lily, "a fellow has to hustle" (129) in his exhausting work downtown, but because he has traded access to society for the social outsider Rosedale in exchange for some financial inside information—a "half-a-million tip for a dinner" (130).[82] Trenor reassures Lily that he can make a "handsome sum of money for her without endangering the small amount she possessed" (135), and readers are therefore left to presume that this deal is less the result of smartly calculated risk taking than the reaping of the rewards of the instrumental friendship between Trenor and Rosedale. Lily mistakes (or rather, deludes herself into mistaking) the arrangement between herself and Trenor as one of "fraternal intimacy," rather than the quid pro quo of money for sex, just as in Wall Street, corruption is masked as friendship: "In her innermost heart Lily knew it was not by appealing to the fraternal instinct that she was likely to move Gus Trenor; but this way of explaining the situation helped to drape its crudity" (131). Lily realizes that she needs to make Gus feel that her request was "uncalculated" (136), relying on those qualities of loyalty and benevolence that White argues were essential to making corruption palatable. "The haziness enveloping the transaction," the narrator comments, "served as a veil for her embarrassment" (136). Redescribing a bribe as a favor, and enveloping the exchange in the fuzzy language of "uncalculated" friendship, is precisely what made Gilded Age corruption so successful.

Lily wishes she "had a clearer notion of the exact nature of the transaction which seemed to have put her in his power" (186), and it is only later that she comes to realize that "what he said he had made for me he had really given me" (472). Although Lily might profess to comprehend little about the technical details of Wall Street, her seemingly willful misunderstanding of Trenor's bribe as a gift (which she later tries to redescribe as a loan that can simply be repaid) suggests that she would be no stranger to the euphemistic world of corrupt business explored by White, an elaborate game where everyone knows the rules, which must never be spoken out loud. When Lily continually rebuffs Trenor's increasingly rapacious advances, in his frustration he breaks the taboo and accuses her of "dodging the rules of the game" (234). Instead of acceding to the corrupt logic of extramarital seduction, Lily tries instead to reinterpret their "friendship" in the more traditional sense of a relationship of affection, rather than the euphemistic kind of arrangement that Trenor means. Trying to call his bluff in an effort to stave off his threatening advances, she thus asks, with a deliberate disingenuousness, "What more have you done than any friend might do, or any one accept from a friend?" (149). Trenor laughingly dismisses Lily's misguided offer to repay any money she might owe him: "'Oh, I'm not asking for payment in kind'" (235). The irony is that payment in kind—sexual favors rather than repayment of the money—is exactly what he is asking for, but the euphemistic "haziness" surrounding the whole transaction obliges him to insist on the opposite, even when the mask of social respectability has been dropped.

Lily is equally hazy about the nature of friendship in connection with her female acquaintances. As Judy Trenor becomes cooler toward Lily (when she presumably learns about Lily's arrangement with her husband), Lily tries to convince herself that she "believed in the sincerity of her friend's affection, though it sometimes showed itself in self-interested ways, and she shrank with peculiar reluctance from any risk of estranging it" (208). As if hedging her bets against a possible estrangement with Judy, Lily turns back toward her old on-off friend, Bertha Dorset, with a "renewal of friendliness," prompted by the "discovery that they could be of use to each other" (206). Bertha, it turns out, is an expert manipulator of friendship, inviting Lily on a Mediterranean cruise to keep her husband amused while she has an affair with the young would-be poet Ned Silverton. When Bertha is in danger of being exposed, she does not hesitate to cast Lily aside, leaving Lily to wonder to her friend, Gerty Farish (whom Lily uses just as shabbily, albeit without conscious malice): "Who are one's friends at such a time?" (361). Lily's friends end up believing Bertha's version of the events in Nice (that Lily was dismissed for having an affair with George Dorset), because it is more in their interests to do so. As Lily's life crumbles around her toward the end of the novel, she becomes more suspicious of the notion of friendship. When Rosedale rejects Lily's belated renewal of a marriage proposal, he asks: "Ain't we going to be good friends all the same?" Lily, suspicious of coming under another imprecisely defined obligation, asks the question that dare not speak its name: "What is your idea of being good friends?" (410). Wharton's novels thus show not so much a relentless "reduction of human experiences to abstract equivalences for exchange," as a series of uneasy tensions and ligatures between the speculators of Wall Street and the social elite of Fifth Avenue, with both operating through the code of instrumental friendship, despite the separate sphere of business supposedly animated by more-impersonal forces.[83]

Knowing People

Euphemism was vital to the operation of the system of Gilded Age corruption that White describes, and it is equally central to the social world dramatized in Wharton's New York fiction, with its focus on the "verbal generosities" that (in protagonist Newland Archer's eyes) provide merely a "humbugging disguise of the inexorable conventions that tied things together and bound people down to the old pattern" (*AI*, 41). Like expert Wall Street operators, the "knowing people" of polite society are able to decode the "faint implications" (14) of everyday exchange, and it is the sharing of nonpublic knowledge that both forges these people into an exclusive class and permits them to profit, in both Wall Street and Fifth Avenue, from their inside information. For example, when Mrs. van der Luyden is persuaded to issue a dinner invitation to May's cousin, Countess Ellen Olenska (who is separated from her husband), that evening at the opera, "some of the younger men in the club box exchanged a smile at this announcement" (55). Except for those excluded by reasons of age or class from the inner circle, everyone in this incestuous world supposedly knows what everyone else is alluding to but cannot speak out loud about it.[84] Most notably, Newland Archer prides himself on the fact that he and his new wife, May, understand the conventions of polite society so well that much that might otherwise cast a shadow on respectability can remain unspoken. In contrast, Ellen doesn't always seem to get what Newland means; he wishes she could be more "feminine" and intuitive and spare him from having to state things in plain words (140). He tries to avoid putting into words, either to Ellen or to himself, what he actually wants: "'It is your idea, then, that I should live with you as your mistress—since I can't be your wife?' she asked. The crudeness of the question startled him" (292). At the same time, he also becomes increasingly frustrated by the inability of his social world to actually name things for what they are. He wishes, for instance, that he could say out loud to the men of his club: "If you'd all of you rather she should be Beaufort's mistress than some decent fellow's wife you've certainly gone the right way about it" (144).

The rigid refusal to address certain topics openly had begun to crack by the time of *The House of Mirth* (set in the same historical moment as the novel's publication in 1905), but that social world still operates through codes of shared inside information. Even though "Evie Van Osburgh's engagement was still officially a secret," it was "one of which the innumerable intimate friends of the family were possessed" (158). Bertha Dorset, we are informed, works her devious schemes by "insinuations intelligible to every member of their little group" (177), and Lily is well aware that Bertha's speech is rarely as innocuous as it might seem to the uninitiated outsider: "For of course she always means something" (406). What distinguishes insiders from outsiders in this upper-class enclave is an understanding of the social codes of this "hieroglyphic world" (*AI*, 42), when what is left unsaid can itself be deeply meaningful—and profitable: "Lily, well versed in the language of these omissions, knew that they were equally intelligible to the other members of the party" (*HM*, 368). Lily's sanctimonious cousin Grace Stepney, who ends up inheriting Mrs. Peniston's fortune (despite the fact that "it had been, in the consecrated phrase, 'always understood' that Mrs. Peniston was to provide handsomely for her niece [Lily]" [357]), takes vindictive delight in breaching etiquette by informing the old lady about Lily's supposed indiscretions: "I didn't suppose that I should have to put it so plainly. 'People say that Gus Trenor pays her bills'" (202). Unlike many of the other characters who can afford to operate through the indirection of social niceties, the twice-divorced society fixer Carry Fisher has a streak of keen-eyed realism, in evidence when she "brutally put[s]" (365) the truth of Lily's situation to her. Rosedale, an outsider in this social world, likewise favors plain speaking: "Now we're talking let's call things by their right names" (418). Yet Lily is aware that even his proposal of a "plain business arrangement" (483), a straightforward loan of the kind that businessmen might make between themselves, might be viewed differently among her class. In this world, Lily learns that there is no such thing as a plain business arrangement. Nevertheless, she still shies away from the private exchange of information between "friends" that Rosedale proposes, namely, using the love letters that Lily had bought from the charlady to blackmail Bertha Dorset into rehabilitating Lily's reputation. The plan only seems troubling to Lily when she strips it of its "verbal generosities": "After all, half the opprobrium of such an act lies in the name attached to it. Call it blackmail and it becomes unthinkable; but just explain that it injures no one, and that the rights regained by it were unjustly forfeited, and he must be a formalist indeed who can find no plea in its defense" (485). Barefaced bribery, as White notes, is a cultural failure, when there are more sophisticated and "polite" ways of doing business between "friends" that involve information, rather than money.[85] As Dimock has documented, the rhetoric of business insinuates its way into the domestic sphere in Wharton's novels. At the same time, however, these fictive works show how the circumlocutions of polite society are central to the operations of the world of business.

The Innocence of May

The plots of Wharton's New York novels revolve around privileged access to information and gossip and focus on the question of who knows what. This is most notably so in *The Age of Innocence*, which hinges on the issue of just how innocent May Archer is and just how much she actually knows at each stage. Newland prides himself on his wife's perspicacity, the product, in his view, not of a cynical knowingness, but of her very innocence and whole-hearted immersion in the codes of polite society: "He never saw her, or exchanged a word with her, without feeling that, after all, May's ingenuousness almost amounted to a gift of divination" (119). He is convinced of her essential ignorance of any thoughts, emotions, or situations that would upset the calm surface of their genteel world.

The central irony of the novel, however, is that it is not May, but Newland, who is deluded. Despite seeming to embody the lost innocence of old New York, she is far more knowing and plays the game of "friendship" with more sophistication than Archer can imagine. When Newland tries to get May to agree to marry him sooner (presumably in order to prevent himself from becoming more emotionally entangled with Ellen, who is separated from her Polish husband), she asks him straight out if there is anyone else, showing that she understands Newland better than he understands himself. May confesses that "you mustn't think that a girl knows as little as her parents imagine. One hears and notices. . . . Every one was talking about it [Newland's affair with a married woman] two years ago at Newport" (148). Newland, blind to the fact that May might actually be euphemistically referring to his current infatuation with Ellen, expresses his relief: "My dear child—was *that* it? If you only knew the truth!" With more knowledge than a mere "gift of divination" would permit, May perceptively—yet still with the surface appearance of ingenuousness—asks, "Then there is a truth I don't know?" (148).

With all the skills of a confidence trickster, May performs the role of the ingénue to perfection. When Newland proposes a visit to Washington, DC, May realizes that he is lying yet, "looking him straight in the eyes with her cloudless smile" (269), insists that he sees Ellen Olenska while he is there, both letting her husband know that she is aware of what he really intends, while still keeping up the pretense of social decorum. Newland thinks that, as a skilled semiotician of social exchange, he can perfectly decode their restrained dialogue, which seems to him to be both the strength and the constricting weakness of their emotionally repressed social class. But he is deluded, and it is May who inhabits the logic of euphemism with a scary conviction. Even when she disingenuously calls Newland's bluff after she later catches him lying about his trip to Washington, her voice "was as clear as a bell" (285). Despite seeming not to be privy to her husband's secrets, May knows more of what is going on than Newland and uses her privileged information to bend circumstances to her will. When May reveals that she had a "really good talk" (317) with Ellen, Newland fails to pick up on its significance. Newland hopes this means that May might, after all, understand his feelings for Ellen, but to his disappointment, his wife merely seems to want to explain why the family has cut her cousin off. The irony, however, is not only that May indeed knows about Newland's affair with Ellen, but that she uses her knowledge—unbeknownst to her husband at this point—that she is probably pregnant to force Ellen to quit as her rival by returning to Europe. May then keeps to herself the knowledge that Ellen is going back to Europe and only reveals that fact—seemingly in full innocence—to Newland when it is too late for him to do anything about it.

For all that Newland thinks of himself as an astute and well-informed reader of his "hieroglyphic world," it turns out that he is kept out of the information loop as May's extended family tribe (in Wharton's anthropological terminology) rally round to protect her. He is shocked by the "discovery that he had been excluded from a share in these negotiations, and even from the knowledge that they were on foot" (254). It turns out that he, not May, is the naive one, blinded by his infatuation with Ellen and his conviction that his wife, with her "transparent eyes," is incapable of scheming. Despite the 1870s coming to seem, in retrospect, an "age of innocence," it turns out that all along, everybody had known this crucial piece of hidden information about May. Yet, as in the game of "friendship" White describes, they have all conspired to pretend otherwise and have collectively refused, in a "tissue of elaborate mutual dissimulation" (342), to name Newland's corruption out loud for what it is: "And then it came over him, in a vast flash made up of many broken gleams, that to all of them he and Madame Olenska were lovers, lovers in the extreme sense peculiar to 'foreign' vocabularies. He guessed himself to have been, for months, the center of count-less silently observing eyes and patiently listening ears. . . . The whole tribe had rallied about his wife on the tacit assumption that nobody knew anything, or had ever imagined anything, and that the occasion of the entertainment was simply May Archer's natural desire to take an affectionate leave of her friend and cousin" (338).

Newland rails against the way that people in old New York "dreaded scandal more than disease" (338), and he finds their "deathly sense of the superiority of implication and analogy over direct action" (339) oppressive. Despite his desire to break free from the rigid, hypocritical conventions that maintain the social solidarity of this elite class at the expense of truth and individual freedom, at the end of the novel, Newland nevertheless convinces himself that "after all, there was good in the old ways" (350) that had sustained "a kind of innocent family hypocrisy, in which children and father had unconsciously collaborated." On a trip with his father to Paris (during which Newland prefers not to engage in "direct action" by actually meeting Ellen), Dallas mentions that on her deathbed, his mother May had revealed to him that she indeed knew about Ellen: tellingly, as far back as the moment when, "once, when she asked you to, you'd given up the thing you most wanted" (359). Yet even Dallas, the voice of modernity and so-cial mobility (he is marrying the daughter of the ruined banker, Julius Beaufort, and Beaufort's former mistress, Fanny Ring), wonders if, after all, there was not some value in the customs that had kept his parents' restricted social class tightly knit together: "You never did ask each other anything . . . [and yet] I back your generation for knowing more about each other's private thoughts" (359–60). The collective enactment of innocence might be as hypocritical as the performance of friendship without affection White describes, but *The Age of Innocence* neverthe-less refuses to entirely condemn the social logic of circumlocution, in contrast to an unflinching and seemingly Progressive regime of transparency.

Noblesse Oblige

Wharton's novels view the lost world of old New York from an ironic as well as a sometimes nostalgic distance. The rhetorical framing of New York's mercantile elite as if it were a primitive tribe, with its own arcane codes of etiquette, styles of dress, and rituals of marriage, introduces a relativizing defamiliarization that also serves to naturalize class as an anthropological given. The stance of "looking through the wrong end of a telescope" (*AI*, 74) at the New York of Wharton's childhood comes, in part, from the conviction that business and personal ethics have changed for the worse by the turn of the twentieth century: "The idea of absolute financial probity as the first law of a gentleman's code was too deeply ingrained in [Newland] for sentimental considerations to weaken it. An adventurer like Lemuel Struthers might build up the millions of his Shoe Polish on any number of shady dealings; but unblemished honesty was the *noblesse oblige* of old financial New York" (*AI*, 276–77). Despite these allusions to a vanished ideal of conduct, Newland's mother, for example, insists that, strictly speaking, America has no aristocracy, in the sense of a titled nobility, and it is supposedly this lack of objective distinction that makes the elaborate codes of behavior in polite society so important. Likewise, in *The Custom of the Country*, readers are meant to laugh at Undine who, thanks to religiously following the society column in the newspapers, "knew all of New York's golden aristocracy by name, and the lineaments of its most distinguished scions had been made familiar by passionate poring over the daily press" (28).

Although Wharton's novels cast doubt on the idea of a literal American aristocracy, they nevertheless manifest a residual hankering for a time when the upper class was supposedly held together not by money and contract, but by a sedimented sense of kinship and a feudal understanding of the obligations to other classes that was markedly different from the social Darwinism of William Graham Sumner's popular tract, *What Social Classes Owe to Each Other* (1883).[86] For the old New York families in Wharton's novels, the barbarians at the gate are not the immigrant and racial masses, but the newly rich beneficiaries of industrial and financial capitalism. The novels suggest that the reason for clinging so anachronistically to the pseudoaristocratic trappings of status and kinship was that it was the obfuscating fig leaf that justified overturning America's faith in democratic classlessness: wealth without a sense of noblesse oblige was just vulgar materialism. As Wharton noted in a letter to a friend, "social conditions as they are just now in our new world, where the sudden possession of money has come without inherited obligations, or any traditional sense of solidarity between the classes, is a vast & absorbing field for the novelist."[87] Most notably, at the end of *The House of Mirth*, Lily feels no sense of "class distinction" (460) when she sits in the kitchen of Nettie Struther, the object of Lily's past charity. The narrator sympathetically captures Lily's unarticulated nostalgia for kinship and rootedness that, as *The Custom of the Country* also makes clear, seems to emerge more organically in European society: "In whatever form a slowly accumulated past lives in the blood—whether in the concrete image of the old house stored with visual memories, or in the conception of the house not built with hands but made up of inherited passions and loyalties—it has the same power of broadening and deepening the individual existence, of attaching it by mysterious links of kinship to all the mighty sum of human striving" (*HM*, 516).

Hildegard Hoeller reads the scene with Nettie Struther and her baby not as lapsing into sentimentalism, which most critics have viewed as quite jarring in the face of the hard-nosed, satirical realism that structures the rest of the novel, but as offering a glimpse of a female-centered gift economy. In this reading, the bonds of maternal and sisterly love present a viable alternative to the exchange economy in which Lily has become entrapped.[88] Yet I would argue that in *The House of Mirth* and Wharton's other New York novels, an older, quasi-aristocratic, woman-centered ideal of an economy structured by personal connections and obligations does not stand in utopian opposition to a newer, impersonal, manly economy of exchange and contract. Instead, there is a continuity between the two modes, with the economy of exchange wrapped up in the language of gift. The spirit and language of personal connections persisted long into the era of corporate capitalism, with the socialization of ownership enabled by limited liability and the democratization of the financial markets. As White's studies of the patterns of representation of a small number of interconnected families on the boards of railroad corporations make clear, the period of the rise of what Wharton called the "vast mysterious world of Wall Street" did not destroy an older appeal to blood, family, and noble obligation, but was made possible by the concentration of ownership through kinship networks. What these families got out of their persistent representation on corporate boards of directors was not a monopoly of control per se, but corrupt access to inside information. As one study concludes, "the emergence of bureaucratic corporations did not mean the end of insider networks based on family and kinship."[89]

Privileged Circle

Wharton's novels dramatize the problem of inside information, not only at the level of the plot, but also in their formal narrative features. In addition to May, who knows more than her self-deluding husband, the reader is also invited to collaborate in this secret knowledge through "implication and analogy." *The House of Mirth*, *The Custom of the Country*, and *The Age of Innocence* are focalized, to varying degrees, through leading characters who are not as astute as they think they are, and we therefore learn to read between the lines, to see what they cannot. In this way, the novels use irony to create a sense of complicity between narrator and reader, making us privy to the codes and cues that place us in a position of superiority. For example, we are not told directly that Undine Spragg is socially gauche, because, it is assumed, the right sort of people instinctively know the social codes without these ever having to be spoken out loud.

Readers are not told directly what to think by an omniscient narrator; instead they are invited to glean and hoard crucial pieces of information—tips, as it were—that are there to be discovered by those in the know. In *The House of Mirth*, for example, we become like Rosedale, an outsider who is hoarding information in his campaign to become an insider. Precisely because he is not "one of us," Rosedale needs to use privileged information to insinuate his way into the inner circle of the elite—which, in turn, will bring about financially meaningful personal connections. Like the observant reader, Rosedale is "a man who made it his business to know everything about every one" (23). When he meets Lily, coming out of the Benedick building after having taken tea in Lawrence Selden's apartment there, Rosedale knows that she is lying in her claim that she has been visiting her dressmaker. Lily "detected in Rosedale's eye a twinkling perception of the fact" (153), and her silence gives "special meaning" to Rosedale's seemingly harmless comment about owning the Benedick and therefore knowing that it is a residence for bachelors. This secret knowledge inserts Rosedale—and, by implication, the reader—into a "privileged circle," and permits Rosedale to smile a "knowing smile" (155). The way that Lily later glosses over her behavior ironically provides a "confirmation of his suspicions" (184), a confirmation that is now shared with the reader, putting us in Rosedale's morally compromised position of banking useful information while also having sympathy for Lily as the victim of this transaction between "friends."

In contrast, in some instances the reader becomes merely one of the social crowd, rather than being granted privileged access, learning significant plot developments accidentally, through tidbits of gossip that are dropped into the conversation, thus putting us temporarily in the position of Lily as she begins to fall out of the "privileged circle." For instance, we only learn in passing that Judy Trenor has quarreled with her husband, Gus, from the idle gossip that Grace Stepney reports to her aunt, Mrs. Peniston (*HM*, 203–4). The significance of this will not be lost on readers who share Lily's awareness of the reason for Judy's behavior (and the sense of injustice created by the mismatch between public gossip and our inside knowledge of the actual circumstances). Or, for example, in *The Custom of the Country*, after Undine's argument with her aristocratic French husband over the impossibility of selling any of the estate's heirlooms, the reader is not privy to the fact that on Undine's brief escape trip to Paris, she has contacted an art dealer to come and appraise the chateau's priceless tapestries (527–38). This lack of full disclosure serves the immediate narrative purpose of making the appearance of Elmer Moffat at the chateau all the more of a surprise, but it also enacts, at a structural level, the pleasures, frustrations, and moral complicities of being granted or denied inside information.

In both their content and their form, then, Wharton's New York novels exhibit an ambivalent attitude toward the social and economic changes of the late nineteenth century. On the one hand, they lament the passing of a tightly knit, mercantile upper class that was supposedly founded on financial probity and a quasi-feudal rootedness (which admittedly verged on claustrophobia). On the other hand, they also make it apparent that those seemingly outmoded values of kinship and friendship, and the social mechanisms of being "in the know," make possible the very scheming that, with the emergence of corporate and financial capitalism, threatens to undo those old moral certainties and manners, and upper-class identity.

Conclusion: The Confidence Trick of Finance

What Wharton's novels make clear is that the world of Fifth Avenue and the world of Wall Street were not so far apart in the Gilded Age and the Progressive Era, either conceptually or in practice. Henry James feared that the novelist was ill equipped to chart the changes taking place in both the social world of Manhattan and the national economy as a whole. What Wharton's fiction helps us understand, however, is the deep connection between the personal and financial realms during that period, an intertwining that takes place not only in the story lines, but in the formal structures of the genre. Likewise, the figure of the confidence man might, by century's end, seem to be merely an archaic and romantic outlaw, yet we have seen how the con trick—by that point enacted on an industrialized scale—continued to work the rich seam revealed by the fault line between business and friendship. Rather than merely sweeping away older modes of personal connection, however, the brave new world of financial capitalism—with its reliance on the impersonality of contracts and its confidence in abstract systems, rather than individual people—was enabled, both conceptually and practically, by the possibility obtaining of inside information.

CHAPTER FIVE

Conspiracy and the Invisible Hand of the Market

The sense of conspiracy and secret scheming which transpire is almost uncanny. "Big business," and its ruthless tentacles, have become the material for the feverish fantasy of illiterate thousands thrown out of kilter by the rack and strain of modern life.

Walter Lippmann, Drift and Mastery *(1914)*

If, however, we mean by this loose, elastic term "trust" as applied to the concentration of the "money power" that there is a close and well-defined "community of interest" and understanding among the men who dominate the financial destinies of our country and who wield fabulous power over the fortunes of others through their control of corporate funds belonging to other people, our investigators will find a situation confronting us far more serious than is popularly supposed to exist.

Samuel Untermyer, "Is There a Money Trust?" (1911)

The question of who or what controls the market became an increasingly pressing concern in the course of the nineteenth century. With alarming regularity, the United States was beset by financial panics that spread out from Wall Street—as well as State Street in Boston and La Salle Street in Chicago—and derailed the wider national and, often, global economy. These market-induced calamities created lengthy periods of deflation, anxiety, unemployment, bankruptcy, and ruin for ordinary Americans who were far removed from the goings-on of the stock and produce exchanges. Individuals found themselves caught up in inscrutable economic forces that they could neither picture in their mind's eye nor control. The cause of these cataclysmic events that seemed to come without warning evaded familiar modes of explanation, in both ordinary and elite circles. The rise and fall of prices had traditionally been explained with reference to the natural fluctuation of harvests, controlled by the unreadable hand of Providence, coupled with a moralized view of individual economic failure.[1] In the earlier part of the nineteenth century, many political economists on both sides of the Atlantic followed Adam Smith's reformulation of the notion of Providence, seeing the work of a benevolent "invisible hand" in the overall financial life of a nation, a vision of coordination that emerged as if it had been planned, but the mysterious and unattributable genius of this lay in the supposed fact that the best outcome could emerge only if there was no central planning, in the form of either governmental regulation or other interference in the market.[2]

Yet the panics of 1873, 1890, and 1907 (in particular)—and the harsh economic times they brought about—challenged both traditional religious accounts and Smithian forms of liberal neoprovidentialism. The rise of large business concentrations, along with a manifestly unjust distribution of goods, undermined a traditional faith in an invisible hand that benevolently provided order in the decentralized laissez-faire economy that privileged the rights of individual proprietors. If the market was like a self-regulating machine, many Americans wondered, why did it periodically seem to implode, causing disaster across the nation on a scale that was out of all proportion with what seemed to be the proximate causes in the intricate financial cogs and mechanisms of the stock exchanges? Many in the emerging profession of economics continued to insist that financial panics were aberrations, occasional interruptions in the otherwise intelligible operation of the economy, whose laws of supply and demand could now be explained by reference to mathematics and physics, rather than theological metaphors.[3] Others, such as Arthur Hadley and Jeremiah Jenks, developed new theories of business cycles to explain how overproduction (and the economic chaos of falling prices it brought about) was not a failure of the normal equilibrium of supply and demand, but a predictable tendency of an economy increasingly dominated by vast corporations with fixed capital costs. The conclusion was often that ruinous overproduction could be avoided by embracing cooperation, and even monopoly, rather than competition.[4] As we saw in chapters 2 and 3, the emerging genre of popular investment advice wavered between exogenous explanations of market movements that needed to be understood by studying trends of fundamental values within the wider economy and society, and endogenous accounts that began to find hidden patterns and rhythms by charting the very prices themselves. Manufacturers blamed excessive labor regulation and overproduction; workers, in turn, pointed to the unjust use of antitrust legislation against labor, and the fact that mechanization was depressing wages. At the same time, other commentators turned to the emerging social sciences to provide a better explanation of economic panics, with early studies of the psychology and sociology of crowds, for example, accounting for the dizzying rapidity with which financial contagion seemed to spread.[5] In the last quarter of the nineteenth century and the first decades of the twentieth century, however, a number of other writers and political agitators claimed to find a hidden hand, rather than an invisible hand, at work in the market. Both Brahmins and farmers alike turned to the language of conspiracy to make sense of the chaotic progress of the financial markets in particular, and the American economy in general. The wild swings of the market were not simply the byproduct of a business cycle in the era of large industrial combinations, they argued, but the direct and deliberate result of secret manipulation by powerful forces in business and government.

This chapter analyzes a range of conspiracy-minded interpretations of financial capitalism from the 1870s to the early 1900s, viewing them not as merely misguided and erroneous beliefs, but as creative—if also somewhat contradictory—attempts to provide a mapping of Wall Street's place in the American economy. The turn to what we would now label a conspiracy theory has long been derided as mistaken and delusional, if not actively paranoid.[6] In *Drift and Mastery* (1914), for example, the young Walter Lippmann warned that the excessive fervor of conspiracy-minded muckraking might lead American society into a dangerous, rudderless drift in a world that modernity was making increasingly hard to comprehend:

> The sense of conspiracy and secret scheming which transpire is almost uncanny. 'Big business,' and its ruthless tentacles, have become the material for the feverish fantasy of illiterate thousands thrown out of kilter by the rack and strain of modern life. It is possible to work yourself into a state where the world seems a conspiracy and your daily going is beset with an alert and tingling sense of labyrinthine evil. Everything askew—all the frictions of life are readily ascribed to a deliberate evil intelligence, and men like Morgan and Rockefeller take on attributes of omnipotence, that ten minutes of sanity would reduce to a barbarous myth.[7]

Although many historians have tended to follow Lippmann by viewing conspiracy-minded imaginings of the "money power" as the work of those at the intellectual or political fringes of American society, in contrast this chapter will argue that these accounts have much in common with the other emergent, vernacular forms of financial knowledge explored elsewhere in this book. In particular, conspiratorial interpretations of market activity in America's Gilded Age and Progressive Era share a combination of personal and abstract registers with other genres.

The need to personify abstractions remained, long beyond the disenchantment of modernity. While these forms of lay economic analysis may be guilty of simplifying complex economic processes by reducing them to melodramas in which individual, villainous intention is the root cause of all social effects, they serve, at the same time, as sophisticated transcoding metaphors that rethink the relationship between impersonal structure and personal agency. Often they do so by creating personifications that function as human-scale proxies for the sublime unrepresentability of vast industrial combinations. The situation was complicated by the competing legal debates about corporate personality, combined with the emerging techniques of corporate public relations, which tried to personalize the soulless corporation.[8] Many oppositional voices of different political stripes wanted—in the legal terminology of the period—to "pierce the corporate veil" in order to find out who was really behind the actions of faceless corporations, and to hold them accountable.[9]

Many feared that the rise of the large industrial combinations would mean the demise of the republican promise of individualism, as both the small businessman and the farmer, on the one hand, and the lower-middle-class clerk on the other, were swept aside by the unrivalled power of the corporations and their bureaucratic systems.[10] Others, however, worried that the corporations (and, indeed, the market itself) were the playthings of corrupt robber barons, able to pull the strings of the financial system. The question, for Populist agitators and Brahmin commentators alike, was whether the mass of entangled financial transactions that were increasingly being channeled through Wall Street and the nation's other stock exchanges constituted a coherent system, and, if so, whether anyone was in control of it. Did the interconnecting network of plutocratic relationships constitute a financial conspiracy against the interests of the nation, or was what might look like a conspiracy to the uninitiated merely the unintentional but not unexpected outcome of a social class pursuing its own vested interests? Was there a plan behind the economic upheavals that beset the United States, or were they simply the result of the blind workings of the market? Was there a hierarchical chain of command, or did financial capitalism constitute a decentered and deterritorialized system—and, if so, how did agency emerge from the interplay of structural forces? Could corporations be thought of as having intentionality and, thus, a legal liability separate from the individuals who owned and directed them? Moreover, if there was something systematic at work, then how could or should it be represented, both in visual diagramming and in dramatic narratives? The problem of a financial conspiracy in the age of the corporation thus presented an ontological, epistemological, and aesthetic problem. In the era of giant pools, trusts, and corporations, the nature of agency, causality, and responsibility came under increasing scrutiny by legal and economic theorists and novelists, as well as ordinary farmers and political radicals. Looked at in one way, the modes of conspiratorial representation explored in this chapter failed to understand the nature of class privilege in seeking to pin the blame on a few individual, malevolent robber barons. Looked at in another way, however, these popular ways of explaining finance constituted an attempt to combine an understanding of both agency and structure, long before those social scientific terms had gained intellectual purchase. Often they did so by seeing structure *as* agency, and system *as* conspiracy, by personalizing the impersonal abstractions of economic theory.

This chapter begins by looking at early Gilded Age accounts of financial skullduggery, focusing in particular on the work of Charles Frances Adams regarding the corruption scandals of the Erie Railroad. It also reexamines some of the classic works of conspiracy-minded Populism from the 1890s, such as William H. "Coin" Harvey's *Coin's Financial School* and Sarah Emery's *Seven Financial Conspiracies*. It contrasts these portrayals of conspiratorial causality with the view from probusiness apologists around the turn of the century, who argued that accounts of individual manipulation of the market were now outdated. The discussion also encompasses the changing meanings of conspiracy in legal and economic debates during that period concerning the regulation of large corporations and financial syndicates. The chapter then turns to the way in which popular and literary novels of the period explored the question of individual agency in the age of the impersonal trust, concentrating in particular on Frank Norris's *The Octopus* (1901). Finally, the chapter considers the investigation into the so-called money trust by the U.S. House of Representatives' Pujo Committee in 1912–1913, discussing, in particular, a diagram produced by the investigation as one of a number of early attempts to provide a conspiratorial "cognitive mapping" of the uncharted landscape of financial capitalism.

Chapters of Conspiracy

It comes as little surprise that financial capitalism was viewed in the popular imagination through the lens of conspiracy theory in the late nineteenth century, because the years immediately following the Civil War were a golden age of actual Wall Street conspiracy. The corrupting influence of corporate finance over the government and legislatures was widely condemned at the time as the "great barbecue," a shameful and dangerous moment in the history of the republic. A series of high-profile scandals and financial cataclysms shaped public perceptions of Wall Street for a generation: the gold conspiracy, the Crédit Mobilier, the collapse of the Northern Pacific Railroad (which led to the implosion of Jay Cooke's bank), and, the most sordid and long-running saga of them all, the Erie Railroad debacle.[11] The tales of watered stock, bribed judges, and insider dealing carried out by Daniel Drew, Cornelius Vanderbilt, Jim Fisk, and Jay Gould disgusted but also fascinated the reading public. The robber-baron directors of the Erie Railroad continually plundered its assets for their own personal gain, all with the connivance of their paid political hirelings. Drew started it off in the 1850s by using inside information gained from his position as a director to wager on the railroad's stock; indeed, his main reason for buying his way into a directorship seems to have been the profit that could be derived from insider trading, rather than any long-term business interest in the company as such. Likewise, Vanderbilt became involved in the Erie Railroad not because it was a good prospect (it was, in fact, notoriously run down), but because it would help him establish a monopoly over railroads into New York, and thus enable him to corner the market and push up the share prices without hindrance. Drew, now joined by Fisk and Gould, prevented the Vanderbilt takeover by endlessly printing worthless new stock certificates. Both sides then resorted to rampant bribery of the judges and senators in the state capital, Albany. The combatants wanted control of the company, either in order to exploit inside knowledge for their personal gain in the stock market, or to create a stranglehold on railway traffic into New York and thus skew the market.

Although the beginnings of popular involvement in the securities market began with Jay Cooke's promotion of Union bonds during the Civil War, the flood of revelations about financial corruption in newspapers and popular periodicals in the 1860s and 1870s frightened off many ordinary, would-be investors for a generation. By the 1880s, however, those stories of skullduggery and intrigue had become part of Wall Street lore, constituting the mythological origins of "the Street" that were endlessly recounted in popular compendia and memoirs, such as those published by William Fowler and Henry Clews. While critics saw the entire financial system as immoral, Wall Street insiders often used the tales of past excesses to emphasize, by way of contrast, the professionalism of the current practitioners of speculation. Indeed, as Richard R. John has demonstrated, far from being confined to later and more-radical sources, the term "robber baron" was used within the business community as early as the 1880s, to stigmatize Jay Gould as acting beyond the pale of proper business conduct.[12]

All the scandals during this period of Wild West lawlessness on Wall Street revolve around the corrupt relationship between government and business, highlighting the fact that the market was far from being the self-regulating realm described by laissez-faire economic theorists who argued for the reduction of state interference. Before New Jersey and Delaware changed their laws in the 1890s to make incorporation less restricted, corporations were creatures of the state, granted charters to raise capital for carrying out large, public infrastructure projects (and were thus considered by legal theorists, in the parlance of the day, as "artificial entities"). As the scandals made clear, governmental largesse was at the heart of much corporate activity, either legally, in the form of licensed monopolies, vast land grants, and generous federal subsidies to the railroads, for example, or, illegally, through the repeated buying of legislative and judicial favors. Most of the critical attacks on this system of corruption focused on the individual, whether literally, in the guise of a particular larger-than-life robber baron, or symbolically (as we saw in chapter 3), with the satirical anthropomorphization of corporate officers and political officials as fat cats, bears, octopuses, and so on. The potentially impenetrable activity of corporate finance was turned into a human melodrama, with the Erie Railroad itself popularly dubbed "the Scarlet Woman of Wall Street."

While many critical commentators at that time saw the wild fluctuations merely as an occasional manipulation of the market by powerful individuals, others considered conspiratorial treachery to be part of a systemic pattern of corruption. For example, in 1871, the brothers Charles Francis Adams and Henry Adams (grandsons of John Quincy Adams) published *Chapters of Erie and Other Essays*, an exhaustive and damning indictment of the Erie Railroad machinations and the gold conspiracy, among other events. As pillars of the Boston establishment, the Adams brothers were not the typical wild-eyed, socially marginal conspiracy theorists later condemned by Lippmann. (Indeed, the Adams brothers feared the erosion of what they saw as the benign, paternalist influence of the gentry class in the face of the rise of the masses from below and the vulgar greed of the new corporate leaders from above.) "The stock exchange revealed itself as a haunt of gamblers and a den of thieves," Charles Francis Adams acidly noted, and "the offices of our great corporations appeared as the secret chambers in which trustees plotted the spoliation of their wards." Furthermore, "the law became a ready engine for the furtherance of wrong, and the ermine of the judge did not conceal the eagerness of the partisan; the halls of legislation were transformed into a mart in which the price of votes was higgled over, and laws, made to order, were bought and sold while under all, and through all, the voice of public opinion was silent or was disregarded." Adams saw the episodes as part of a larger *system* of corruption, in which the virtues of republican government were in danger of being overwhelmed by the extraordinary influence that large combinations could exert: "It tends always to development—always to consolidation—it is ever grasping new powers, or insidiously exerting covert influence. Even now the system threatens the government."[13]

At the same time, however, the system of corporate power was, in their eyes, worryingly concentrated in a few powerful hands. "The belief is common in America," Adams noted, "that the day is at hand when corporations far greater than the Erie—swaying power such as has never in the world's history been trusted in the hands of mere private citizens, controlled by single men like Vanderbilt, or by combinations of men like Fisk, Gould, and Lane . . . will ultimately succeed in directing government itself." This combination of systematic corruption and enormous power in individual hands raised the specter of tyranny in American political and economic life: "As the Erie ring represents the combination of the corporation and the hired proletariat of a great city; as Vanderbilt embodies the autocratic power of Caesarism introduced into corporate life, and as neither alone can obtain complete control of the government of the State, it, perhaps, only remains for the coming man to carry the combination of elements one step in advance, and put Caesarism at once in control of the corporation and of the proletariat."[14] The pessimistic concern of these Brahmin commentators was that the only way to combat the antirepublican influence of industrial combinations was to grant equally undemocratic powers to the political executive.

For the Adams brothers, the discovery of a series of individual financial conspiracies was coupled with a tragic sense of the pervasive reach of systematic corruption. Individual acts of criminal activity were revealed to be behind the great affairs of Wall Street, yet, for the Adams brothers, the problem was not merely a case of a few bad apples. In their view, the end result of this betrayal of traditional, republican individualism would be the installation of a dictatorship of impersonal corporate capitalism—which, ironically, would place undue influence in the hands of a single titan. The Wall Street conspiracies they reported on were at one and the same time highly idiosyncratic yet also part of a more systemic reorganization of American political economy: "The stock exchange revealed itself as a haunt of gamblers and a den of thieves; the offices of our great corporations appeared as the secret chambers in which trustees plotted the spoliation of their wards; the law became a ready engine for the furtherance of wrong, and the ermine of the judge did not conceal the eagerness of the partisan."[15] Their analysis repeatedly combined a focus on individual agency and impersonal structure, and they developed a form of conspiracy rhetoric that went beyond the typical accusation of a hidden hand behind what might otherwise have seemed to be baffling financial events. It is thus not surprising that the Adams brothers were uncertain as to how to represent what they had uncovered. "It is a new power," they asserted, "for which our language contains no name. We know what aristocracy, autocracy, democracy are; but we have no word to express government by moneyed corporations."[16]

Populism and the Paranoid Style

If, from their lofty position, the Adams brothers were not quite able to name the problem, other, more demotic voices a generation later were less circumspect. Many Populist and other radical authors from the 1880s onward (reaching a crescendo in the run up to the presidential election of 1896) denounced what they saw as a conspiracy of the plutocratic class. In *The New Plutocracy*, for example, the Socialist writer John C. Reed warned that "while our people are nominally and seemingly self-governing, they are in reality governed by the private corporations mentioned, who fleece them on a most gigantic scale without their knowing it."[17] Reed presented a totalizing picture of the power of the plutocracy, asserting that, from the legislature to the press, and from the clergy and the universities, everything is under their control. He was concerned, however, not merely to depict an abstract system of power, but to expose the actual conspirators who, in his view, had been manipulating events behind the scenes. "At the proper place in this work," he warned, "we must drag these lurking wirepullers into the sunlight."[18] Like other Populist and radical writers, Reed found the key for much of what was wrong with contemporary America in the convoluted details of postbellum monetary policy. For Reed, as for so many other writers of that period, all present-day woes were ultimately traced back to the "crime of '73," in which the forces of plutocracy had supposedly conspired to bring about the demonetization of silver.

The endlessly repeated accusation was that the Coinage Act of 1873—which had uncontroversially confirmed in law the everyday reality that silver coins had dropped out of circulation—had, in fact, been part of a larger, secret plan by the vested interests of eastern capital to return the United States to the gold standard after its temporary experiment with fiat notes (greenbacks) during the Civil War. The story usually revolved around the rumor that British banker Ernest Seyd—in some versions, at the behest of imagined arch-conspirators, such as the Rothschilds, in particular, or the so-called international Jewish banking cabal, in general—had arrived in the United States with a briefcase full of dollars to bribe congressmen into passing this piece of legislation.[19] In the eyes of many Populist commentators, the crime of '73 ultimately had the effect of promoting the interests of wealthy eastern capitalists at the expense of the debtor class in the west. It was undoubtedly a conspiracy theory, and a fairly simple-minded one at that, but it was also connected to a wider, political-economic analysis of the relationship between class power and the technocratic details of monetary policy:

> Thus did the plutocrats of finance demonetize silver. Now that they have in the last two presidential elections struck down finally, as it seems to them, all serious popular resistance, they but sneer and scoff when one mentions the crime of 1873. That does not wipe it out. It is the blackest forgery, the basest example of *crimen falsi* in human annals. The perfidy and turpitude of those who deliberately deceived congress and the president in consummation of their plot of years to sell their own countrymen to foreigners are matched only in Benedict Arnold and Iago. It behooves all who love the right and the land of their fathers to keep this most gigantic of all the many monetary treacheries in the unfading and unforgiving memory of the American people.[20]

For Reed, as for other Populist and radical agitators, bringing to light the details of this supposed primal act of financial conspiracy was vital to any Progressive project. Even if the specific details of the allegation turned out to be false, the conspiratorial focus on individual decisions made by bankers and politicians that shaped the market to benefit a particular class provided an important counterweight to the laissez-faire insistence that economic arrangements were immutable states of nature.

As Reed's diatribe makes clear, those who would expose what they believed to be a conspiracy were well aware that their critics would "sneer and scoff" at them. In his seminal analysis of the "paranoid style in American politics," Richard Hofstadter famously viewed such Populist denunciations of conspiracy as the sign of a delusional mindset that crops up repeatedly in American history, albeit only among the poorly educated and ill-informed on the margins of power, who fail to understand what he regarded as the strength of the American political system's "usual methods of political give-and-take," in contrast to the more bitter and bloody ideological conflicts in Europe.[21] For Hofstadter, conspiracy theorists are prone to seeing the world in Manichean, apocalyptic, suspicious terms, convinced that grand conspiracies provide the "motive force" of historical causation. At the same time, however, the heated rhetoric and lurid psychosexual projections of imagined enemies are, in this analysis, wedded to a pedantic obsession with the minutiae of spuriously footnoted evidence. According to Hofstadter, the tendency of the paranoid style to see individual causes behind impersonal historical processes means that conspiracy theorists are guilty of creating a simplistic and seductive appeal to the masses. Even allowing for the fact that conspiracism occurs repeatedly throughout American history, Hofstadter noted that "it remains true that Populist thought showed an unusually strong tendency to account for relatively impersonal events in highly personal terms."[22] There was "something about the Populist imagination," Hofstadter noted, "that loved the secret plot and the conspiratorial meeting. There was in fact a widespread Populist idea that all American history since the Civil War could be understood as a sustained conspiracy of the international money power." If only intellectuals are familiar with "impersonal explanations" for troubling events, then, for Hofstadter, it follows that the paranoid style will be popular among uneducated and suspicious farmers who are far from the centers of power: "Populist thought often carries one into a world in which the simple virtues and unmitigated villainies of a rural melodrama have been projected on a national and even an international scale."[23] Most controversially, Hofstadter saw in Populism the potential roots of modern mass political demagoguery, which had, at the time he first began to formulate these ideas in the mid-1950s, recently manifested itself in the form of McCarthyism. In making the implicit connection between Populism and McCarthyism (and, later, the rise of Goldwater conservatism), Hofstadter's analysis of the paranoid style served to delegitimize forms of radical dissent by tarring them with the brush of irrational—and mainly right-wing—extremism.[24] Significantly, Hofstadter also found many Populist exponents of the paranoid style guilty of knee-jerk "rhetorical antisemitism."[25] In sum, Hofstadter argued that the Populist and radical writers of the Gilded Age and the Progressive Era were too eager to blame easy scapegoats for economic woes that were more complex. And yet, before the emergence of the professional social sciences around the turn of the twentieth century, alternative explanations for financial calamities were not necessarily any more sophisticated or accurate than the Populist conspiracy theories.

Nevertheless, Hofstadter's focus on the symbolic dimensions of political rhetoric still has much to commend it, especially when reading classic texts such as the Omaha Platform of the Populist Party, written by Ignatius Donnelly, with its accusation that, with the demonetization of silver, a "vast conspiracy against mankind has been organized on two continents, and it is rapidly taking possession of the world."[26] Hofstadter's implicit dismissal of much of the Populist rhetoric as merely delusional, however, fails to understand the wider significance of conspiracy theory as a form of economic analysis during that period.[27] As we have seen, in the last quarter of the nineteenth century, conspiracist interpretations of corporate malfeasance that accounted for "relatively impersonal events in highly personal terms" were not confined to those from the backwaters, but were also deployed by Brahmin commentators such as the Adams brothers, whose genteel way of life and traditional sense of noblesse oblige seemed equally redundant in the brave new world of corporate conglomerations. Furthermore, it is arguable that conspiratorial antisemitism, although pervasive in much Populist writing, did not greatly influence American policy or action; it was often merely an unthinking evocation of centuries-old diatribes against usury. In many cases, the ultimate enemy is identified as the antidemocratic forces of the aristocracy in general and often, specifically, the British—with the Rothschilds scoring the trifecta of being Jewish, British, and aristocratic.[28]

Even some of the texts that serve as Hofstadter's main examples, such as Sarah Emery's *Seven Financial Conspiracies* and William H. Harvey's *Coin's Financial School*, are not as delusional as Hofstadter—and critics from their own era —accused them of being. Although Emery, for example, rehashes the old canard about Seyd's supposed plan to influence the passage of the Coinage Act of 1873, her analysis focuses more squarely on the underlying historical pattern of laws passed in the interests of the financial elite, underpinned by her conviction that the evidence is hidden in plain sight in the public record—if you know what you are looking for. In focusing on the broader legislative framework, rather than condemning individual bankers, her pamphlet thus constitutes more of a hybrid form of conspiratorial political economy than simply the delusional scapegoating of Jewish financiers and their stooges in Congress. Emery's starting point is the economic misery and increasing inequality that devastated the lives of many ordinary Americans in the 1870s and again in the 1890s, each time as a result of a financial collapse that began among the elite on Wall Street. For Emery, traditional explanations of hard times in terms of natural disaster, or the will of Providence, or immoral greed on the part of the bankrupt are inadequate, but so, too, is the emerging social scientific view of impersonal economic forces, such as overproduction or excessive competition. Instead, she traces the deep historical causation of class divisions to a systematic pattern of political corruption.[29] Unlike the incendiary accusations of the Omaha Platform, Emery's widely distributed and much reprinted pamphlet (at least 400,000 copies were produced) provides an account that is enormously detailed in its financial and legislative analysis, even if the ultimate conclusion readers took from it was that the nation's recent economic policies had served to promote the vested interests of the moneyed elite.[30] "Murder, insanity, suicide, divorce, drunkenness, and all forms of immorality and crime have increased from that day to this in the most appalling ratio," Emery insisted. "Every result is produced from certain causes, and it is certain that no more like begets like than that the increase of misery and crime in our country are the direct results of evil legislation."[31]

Like Emery's tract, *Coin's Financial School* (1894) is remarkably detailed in its discussion of technical monetary policy, which is somewhat surprising, given that this pamphlet was a wildly popular success, selling over a million copies.[32] A Mississippi congressman noted that "a little free silver book called 'Coin's Financial School' is being sold on every railroad train by the newsboys and at every cigar store."[33] Although the book is structured as a public lecture, with personalized, ad hominem ripostes to his audience, it is not a simple-minded attack on individual bankers per se, but on the *system* of capitalism that promoted greed and hard-wired economic injustice into society.[34] Even if "Coin" Harvey's interpretations of monetary theory are idiosyncratic at best, he provided a welcome rejoinder to the conventional laissez-faire wisdom that the market is a neutral and self-regulating ecosystem governed by the impersonal laws of economic competition. He insisted instead that the financial arrangements of a nation are always connected to class interests. Furthermore, his faith in the intrinsic value of silver is not, in itself, ultimately any more irrational than the goldbugs' unwavering addiction to the gold standard. In any case, his position on silver is based less on a metaphysical credo in the inherent properties of the metal than on a strategic recognition of its current political utility. Although a bimetallist at heart, he is willing to countenance the adoption of greenbacks.

Even if the details of some of Harvey's economic interpretation are ultimately misguided, what remains striking about the work is the way in which it brings together abstract analysis with a variety of representational modes aimed at making his points more concrete, personal, and, thus, comprehensible to a lay audience. For example, Harvey includes in his lecture a handy illustration of how many gold and silver coins fit into one cubic foot, to give his audience a rough handle on large numbers and thus make the financial abstraction imaginable on a human scale. In addition to the dialogical and dramatic nature of the imaginary lectures, the inclusion of cartoons is, as we saw in chapter 3, in keeping with many other popular attempts from that period to make finance intelligible to a nonspecialist audience. The metaphor of the invisible hand, for example, is given a literal twist in a cartoon depicting the hand of a banker pulling the string that winds up the mental cogs within the mind of the "average business man."[35] Although this satirical drawing provides a crude and conspiratorial suggestion that bankers control business, it also evokes a model of ideological influence and coordination that questions the naive faith in an invisible hand providing benevolent order to the selfish chaos of business activity.

The book contains other literalizations of economic metaphors, such as a cartoon personifying the assassination of silver; or a depiction of a massive hand with a sponge of debt soaking up the productive money of the west; or a drawing in which the invisible hand of supply and demand is made visible and tangible as it manipulates the ratio between gold and silver.[36] Following in the footsteps of Irving Fisher's 1892 dissertation on economics (though it is highly unlikely that Harvey was aware of it), *Coin's Financial School* also includes a diagram of free coinage as a pipe connecting two reservoirs of gold and silver, providing a hydraulic analogy for financial movements, albeit vastly less complex than Fisher's machine.[37] If Harvey's cartoon of the Rothschilds—as an octopus spanning the world—at first sight merely repeats the familiar anthropomorphic and antisemitic image of Jewish financial influence, it also suggests a slightly more nuanced interpretation of global economics in its depiction of the octopus's tentacles as arteries through which capital flows from the core to the periphery in the British Empire.[38] *Coin's Financial School* thus makes finance seem personal and homely, and yet, at the same time, presents it as an entire system. The book struggles to create a mode of presentation that can hold these two seemingly incompatible perspectives in one single view. This enormously influential tract therefore cannot be dismissed as merely delusional, not least because many of Harvey's opponents emulated his innovative approach to popular financial literacy.[39]

The Impossibility of Conspiracy

It was not only later commentators, such as Lippmann and Hofstadter, who dismissed the conspiratorial turn in popular accounts of the market. By the 1880s, Wall Street apologists and the emerging profession of economics had begun to insist that the vernacular view of market manipulation was outdated, because simple conspiracies were no longer possible. For example, in an article in the middle-class magazine *Arena*, which was more a public relations exercise than an objective portrait, the Wall Street grandee Henry Clews looked back with a certain nostalgia on the days of the daring exploits of the robber barons:

> The corners in Harlem, Hudson, Erie, and Northwest, in which Vanderbilt, Drew, and Gould achieved such successes for themselves and their associates, have passed into history as a conspicuous portion of the great events of Wall Street. Their interest is chiefly historical, because of late years no comprehensive corners have been organized. Share capitals are so large that it is difficult for one man to control any one of them, and a divided corner is apt to fail. But in their day and generation they have offered brilliant illustrations of genius and strategic skill in financial warfare.[40]

While conceding that market-manipulating conspiracies might have played a part in the more lawless era of Wall Street chicanery, Clews is keen to suggest that they are no longer even possible, because the market has now reached a high degree of complexity and professionalism. This position was, no doubt, self-serving and not a little hypocritical (Clews himself was accused of contravening NYSE rules by advertising for customers), but it captures an increasingly influential idea: the market was becoming too big to be moved by a lone trader or a small cabal, whether in secret or out in the open. In another editorial, Clews insists that it is impossible for such a large group of men to deal with one another on Wall Street on anything other than "principles of fair dealing and equity"; he observes that a "conspiracy to cheat must always be confined to a small number" (416), suggesting that popular fears that the entire financial system is to blame are misguided.[41] The stock exchange apologist William C. Van Antwerp likewise asserted sanguinely that the era of robber-baron skullduggery was long since gone, leaving the market to the "way of natural supply and demand":

> The questionable practices in Wall Street which started all this hubbub, and which were a natural and human accompaniment of the slowly developed technique of this or any other business, have now been effectually stopped. It has been a very long time, for example, since Jay Gould ran his printing-press for Erie certificates, and that incident cannot possibly happen again. The Keene type of manipulator has gone, never to return. "Corners," too, have seen their last day on 'Change, and so have other artificial impediments in the way of natural supply and demand. It has been years since the Cordage scandal, and the Hocking Coal incident marked the end of that form of manipulation. Yet there are persons who talk of these things as though they were daily occurrences, overlooking the fact that the New York Stock Exchange, by its own efforts, put a stop to the evils complained of, and will never tolerate their return.[42]

In a similar fashion, but from a different institutional perspective, Henry Emery, in his trail-blazing 1896 economics treatise on speculation, argued that the notion of the market being able to be controlled or cornered by a small conspiracy of powerful interests was fundamentally misguided, because share ownership was no longer confined to a handful of insiders. Emery sternly warns against "the greatest evil of speculation," namely, "the reckless participation in the market by the outside public." He admits, however, that widening participation in the stock market, in theory, is a good thing, because "the more buyers and sellers the less likelihood, in the long run, of wide fluctuations," and, more importantly, "manipulation in a wide and active market is probably more difficult than in a narrow market." The market now needed to be recognized as a vast aggregation of individual transactions, and it was becoming the impersonal mechanism for determining prices and allocating resources that theoretical economic models assumed. "Many of the most active securities represent capital of such enormous proportions, and so widely distributed, as to make individual control . . . impossible," Emery notes. "No corner . . . could occur in such securities."[43] Emery argues that, unlike the situation in medieval Europe, when it was actually possible for an individual or a clique to manipulate the price of a commodity by buying up and physically hoarding it, in the brave new world of futures trading in the Chicago pits, the speculator could only manage to corner a particular subset of contracts for future delivery, not the actual commodity. For Emery, small-scale manipulations are part of the normal and proper process of establishing the collective wisdom of prices in the market, and the vast accumulation of such trades on an hour-by-hour basis is precisely what makes large-scale manipulation impossible. "In a sense," he concludes, "all speculation is manipulation."[44] Although Emery does not state it in these terms, his underlying assumptions are that the market knows best, that the market cannot be beaten, and that prices will ultimately reflect fundamental values. While it has some similarities to the efficient market hypothesis that came to dominate academic discussions of finance from the 1960s on, the implication of Emery's analysis is that the knowledge and agency of the market itself trumps that of any individual, no matter how powerful. Although Emery and other probusiness commentators insisted that speculation was best left to professionals, who could correctly price and shoulder risk, they also recognized that the increasing democratization of stock market participation would, in theory, ensure that manipulation of the market by cliques of insiders was a thing of the past; therefore, Populist conspiracy theories were hopelessly misguided.

The foolishness of those who thought that they had found the secret to what was really going on in Wall Street is likewise given typically short shrift by Edwin Lefèvre in his short story, "The Tipster," which tells of a naive young man who is convinced that a mysterious "they" control the market:

> Shortly after he left Smithers he buttonholed another acquaintance, a young man who thought he knew Wall Street, and therefore had a hobby—manipulation. No one could induce him to buy stocks by telling him how well the companies were doing, how bright the prospects, etc. That was bait for "suckers," not for clever young stock operators. But any one, even a stranger, who said that "they"—the perennially mysterious "they," the "big men," the mighty "manipulators" whose life was one prolonged conspiracy to pull the wool over the public's eyes—"they" were going to "jack up" these or the other shares, was welcomed and his advice acted

upon. Young Freeman believed in nothing but "their" wickedness and "their" power to advance or depress stock values at will. Thinking of his wisdom had given him a chronic sneer.[45]

Although writers like Emery and Lefèvre decried the naivety of conspiracy interpretations of market movements, their own position was predicated on an equally dubious Panglossian faith that the market, if left to professionals rather than bungling amateurs, would miraculously regulate itself. They ignored not only the stark reality that individual manipulation of the market continued to play a part, but also the increasingly apparent conclusion that the operation of the stock and produce exchanges was skewed toward predictable class interests.

Some probusiness writers made similar arguments, positing that the socialization of ownership brought on by corporate shareholding gave the lie to muckraking accusations about powerful individuals manipulating the market behind the scenes. As we saw in chapter 3, in the postbellum period, both critics and apologists alike tended to identify particular corporations visually with the charismatic individuals who had created them, seeing either the visible hand of Napoleonic genius or the sinister hand of conspiracy. By the 1890s, early efforts at antitrust legislation had begun to warn of the danger of vast, superhuman entities crowding out small entrepreneurs and proprietors, with the impersonal corporations, not the charismatic proprietor, now constituting the real conspiracy. Yet those in favor of the Great Merger Movement argued that the dispersal of ownership through mass shareholding ensured that large industrial combinations and their influence over the market could no longer be regarded as a plutocratic conspiracy against the "little guy," because ordinary folk were now the collective owners. For example, in his testimony before the U.S. Industrial Commission's inquiry into trusts in 1900, Charles Flint insisted: "Never before was there such a wide distribution of manufacturing interests. The great bulk of the stock is held, not by the very rich, but by the moderately well-to-do. The control of the new system is not vested as it was under the old, in the hands of a few abnormally rich men, but it rests with the majority of stockholders, whose numerical strength is growing every day."[46] For Flint and other corporate advocates, the democratization of ownership—combined with what they saw as the increasing complexity of the channels of decision making and control within large, bureaucratic organizations—ensured that a simple model of market abuse under the sway of a conspiring robber baron no longer made sense. In this line of procorporate thinking, conspiracy theories were necessarily mistaken. Their opponents, however, insisted that the increasing size and complexity of corporate capitalism merely meant that conspiracies were far more dangerous, and far harder to detect.

Conspiracy in Restraint of Trade

Despite these emerging attempts to rethink the nature of individual agency in an era of increasingly collective organization, from the 1870s into the first decades of the twentieth century, large-scale combinations continued, for good or ill, to be viewed in both the popular and legal imaginations in terms of individual rights, sometimes as extensions of the will of singular "captains of industry." As Rudolph Peritz comments: "Trusts and other large business enterprises were not the faceless conglomerates we perceive them to be today. Rather, they were associated with names, faces, and industries. . . . And the personified corporation was not limited to popular culture. Among elites as well, bureaucratic institutions were imagined in human terms."[47] The central issue was whether, in an increasingly interconnected economy, agency was always the result of individual, intentional action or whether it emerged—in a way that was hard to explain or represent or find morally accountable—from the corporation itself, *as if* it were a single person, and (more problematic still) from the interacting components of the entire corporate system.[48]

This question was at the heart of legal debates over the definition of the crime of conspiracy in the Gilded Age and the Progressive Era. British common law, especially concerning labor combinations to raise wages, had traditionally viewed the very act of conspiring as illegal in itself, even if the planned actions (e.g., withdrawing one's labor) were not a crime if carried out by an individual. American jurists, at least up until the 1890s, rejected this common law approach, insisting instead that it was the criminality of the acts carried out by a conspiracy that made them wrong, rather than their origin in a conspiracy, a position that was articulated most notably by Massachusetts Supreme Court Justice Lemuel Shaw in the *Commonwealth v. Hunt* decision of 1842. Price fixing and other "combinations in restraint of trade" on the part of business owners had also traditionally been viewed under British common law as wrongful conspiracies, but in the United States—at least until the emergence of antitrust legislation in the late nineteenth century—they were not considered illegal in their own right. At any rate, secret but voluntary agreements to carry out a conspiracy to skew the market were not contracts that could be enforced at law, so members of a conspiracy could not sue one another for failing to keep their private agreements. In addition to being regarded as operating within the legitimate realm of individual freedom of contract, price-fixing pools, or cartels (in the industrial sector), and the corner, or the stock flotation syndicate (in the realm of finance), were seen by their participants as legitimate solutions to the problem of falling profits amid what businessmen began to blame as ruinous and chaotic competition. What was regarded as sensible cooperation by some, however, was viewed as potentially damaging collusion by others, with an uneasy convergence of prolabor, antimonopoly critics on the one hand, and defenders of traditional values of free-market competition on the other.[49]

  These modes of informal collusion were not formally regarded as criminal conspiracies, but the development of antitrust legislation, beginning with the Sherman Anti-Trust Act of 1890, meant—at first—that all combinations in restraint of trade, whether cartel or trust or union, were deemed to be inherently illegal. The act reflected the still-dominant laissez-faire assumption that any concentration was an interference with the natural laws of free competition, and monopolistic power was only achievable through conspiracy or some other illegitimate manipulation. For the more conservative, literalist position (still in the majority in the U.S. Supreme Court in the early part of the 1890s) the aim was to outlaw all forms of combination or conspiracy in restrain of trade as inimical to free competition and, therefore, illegal per se. These antimonopolist critics insisted that the need for the state to intervene in the market and curtail individual freedom of contract in order to ensure competition trumped the traditional principles of free-market liberalism. All fixed prices, whether they benefited the public or not, were deemed to be wrong, because the aim was to protect "small dealers and worthy men" (in the much-repeated phrase of Supreme Court Justice Peckham's opinion in the *United States v. Trans-Missouri Freight Association* case of 1897) from the unfair encroachment of big corporations. With the *Addyston Pipe & Steel Company* case (1899), however, the rule-of-reason faction began to dominate the judicial argument. The case before the U.S. Court of Appeals (Sixth Circuit) involved a deal among makers of cast-iron pipe not to bid competitively against one another in tendering for municipal business. Their defense was that such an agreement was necessary for them to make a reasonable profit. Judge Howard Taft rejected their case but made the important clarification that some restraints of trade should be permissible if they were reasonable and not the direct aim of the conspirators. Rather than forbidding all restraints of trade as necessarily a conspiracy, the rule-of-reason proponents were thus prepared to countenance the possibility that some form of combination in restraint of trade was reasonable, if it was necessary to provide a fair return on investment; or, through corporate reorganization that achieved a monopoly, a reduction in prices beneficial to the public; or, to a lesser extent, for labor to command a fair wage.

The existence of a conspiracy was thus no longer a crime in itself in the eyes of probusiness jurists.[50]

Despite the ascendency of the rule-of-reason faction, however, gentlemen's agreements and even more formalized cartels continued to come under the antitrust spotlight in the 1880s and 1890s.[51] If profits were falling because of "ruinous competition," as corporate apologists argued, the challenge for business was to find ways of cooperating that avoiding legal sanction and yet worked in practice. Even if a group of businessmen succeeded in establishing a conspiratorial agreement to fix prices or corner the market in the short term, the difficulty was that the collusion, unenforceable by legal contract, ultimately tended to break down. Given the antimonopoly attacks on business collusion from without and the inherent weakness of informal agreements from within, it soon became apparent to corporate lawyers that a different form of cooperative structure would be needed. Following the cartel, the next logical development, from the 1880s onward, was the trust, a legal ruse that was first instituted in 1882 by Samuel Dodd, a lawyer working for Rockefeller's Standard Oil Company. Owners of the constituent firms that were being amalgamated voluntarily assigned their voting rights—in secret—to the trustees, thus bypassing the need for formal incorporation, with all of the usual restrictions that would have brought with it. The trust format was thus designed to sidestep legal restrictions on ultra vires and foreign-ownership rules (i.e., operating beyond the particular state in which they were chartered) that pertained to corporations, quite simply because trusts were not corporations.

Antitrust legislation, however, soon targeted these new trusts as conspiracies by any other name, based on what would soon become the increasingly outmoded laissez-faire assumption that any concentration of business power that thwarted "natural" competition must be the result of conspiratorial manipulation. In 1892, for example, the Ohio Supreme Court ordered the breakup of Standard Oil of Ohio, although the larger Standard Oil entity continued to operate through interlocking directorships. The next phase of legal maneuvering saw the introduction of the corporation as a full-blown holding company, which came about with the passage of the New Jersey Corporation Law of 1889. New Jersey's free incorporation law (followed rapidly by other states that were forced to play catch-up) was initially designed to make the creation of trusts easier, but it had the effect of opening the floodgates to the creation of vast corporate conglomerates, in what became known as the Great Merger Movement, in the decade from approximately 1895 to 1905. Whereas corporate lawyers had justified the trust in terms of the natural property rights of the individual shareholders (transferred by proxy to the trust directors), they increasingly began to insist that the merged corporation, as a holding company, possessed a legal identity—a personality, in the jargon of the time—in its own right. This form of an unlimited corporation did away with a preponderance of the usual restrictions imposed on corporations, most notably by allowing the holding company to buy shares in other companies. Now that business entities were free to buy up a controlling interest in rival firms (without having to go to the enormous expense and hassle of outright ownership), corporations resulting from mergers became virtually immune to antitrust accusations of monopolistic, conspiratorial price fixing and other predatory activities, despite their increasing power and control of particular industrial sectors.

Indeed, one advantage of both trusts and mergers as legal entities was that they made the accusation of, say, a price-fixing conspiracy much harder to prove, because the original, separate firms were now, in theory, part of the same huge organization, so technically there were no two separate parties that could conspire with one another. Where once rivals within a particular sector of the economy had needed to actively conspire to bring about a restraint of trade, now they could voluntarily secede their intentions to a holding company that could not, logically, conspire with itself.[52]

Despite the increasing acceptance by both apologists and critics alike that economic concentration was inevitable, some commentators continued to rail against the dangers of conspiracy to the body politic. The muckraking journalist and political agitator Henry Demarest Lloyd, for example, feared that the logical endgame would be for all corporations to eventually consolidate into a single, giant combination that, despite its omnipotent, monopolistic reach, would nonetheless be able to avoid an accusation of conspiracy: "Under these kaleidoscopic masks [of the different legal forms of combination] we begin at last to see progressing to its terminus a steady consolidation, the end of which is one-man power. The conspiracy ends in one, and one cannot conspire with himself."[53] The final stage of this evolutionary arms race between regulators and corporate lawyers was the kind of "community of interest" pursued by Standard Oil (or, more accurately, this was how the company chose to present itself when the legal spotlight was on it). In the U.S. Supreme Court case of 1911 that led to its breakup, Standard Oil was accused of being the ringmaster of a cartel, illegally forcing its competitors to toe its line through predatory pricing and exclusionary transportation deals. Rockefeller's lawyers insisted, however, that the deals had been struck under an individual's freedom of contract, and that, instead of a conspiracy, there was merely a convergence of enlightened interests.[54]

It is thus arguable that the changing organizational and legal structure of industrial combinations during this period was not simply the inexorable progress of greater managerial efficiency (as many argued at the time, and since), but was instead part of a long-running, highly contested, intricate set of legal maneuvers designed to avoid antitrust legislation, or, at the very least, maneuvers entered into with the predictable consequence that they might avoid such scrutiny. At the same time, however, the new corporate forms enabled precisely the kind of collusive, coordinated activity that muckraking critics denounced as conspiracy. The vital question for critics trying to prove a conspiracy was whether a trust or a corporation could act with the same degree of coordination and purpose—and therefore culpability—as an individual. Trust advocates claimed that stockholders and corporate directors handed over control to the trustees, who made decisions for companies in which they had no direct involvement, often not through formal, recorded, decision-making processes, but merely through an unspoken, cartel-like harmony of purpose. The trustees were thus deemed not to be personally accountable—a state of affairs that was hard to combat under existing antitrust laws. The Brown University economist Elisha Andrews, for example, insisted that trusts were indeed capable of acting like a conspiracy. "Whatever the theory," Andrews argued, "whatever it states in law, the trust is, in actual fact, a solid, organic, efficiently centralized structure."[55]

The ebb and flow of the legal struggles surrounding trusts and corporations ended up redefining the very idea of conspiracy. Although not initially designed to do so, the legal notion of corporate personality (or corporate personification, as it was sometimes known) ended up being used to bypass trust-busting accusations of conspiracy by presenting these complex organizations as if they were a single being, almost with a life and a mind of their own. At the same time, however, muckraking opponents of the vast industrial and financial conglomerates used the familiar trope of personification to provide an easy target on which to focus their resentments, "piercing the corporate veil" (in the legal jargon of the time) to show the individual intention and culpability behind the legal euphemism of collective agency, coupled with limited liability for individual shareholders. Reading the market as a conspiracy was thus not the last refuge of the simple-minded, but an understandable response to the need to hold someone or something to account for the economic hardships that beset so many yet seemed either to be attributable to a faceless corporation or to merely emerge out of the nature of the economic system. In some muckraking novels and commentary, however, illegitimate power came to be imagined not as concentrated in a single hand, but dispersed throughout a network—all the while without lapsing back into the

Smithian fantasy of the benevolent coordination of the invisible hand. Indeed, antitrust agitation began to suggest that the *system* of corporate and financial capitalism itself constituted a conspiracy, rather than any specific aberration of it.

The second part of this chapter will consider in detail two particular attempts from the early decades of the twentieth century to come to terms with, and come up with terms for, the changing nature of corporate and financial conspiracy. Both cases push up against the limits of representation as they struggle to bring together an understanding of impersonal structure and personal agency. They also explore the possibility of a conspiracy that is organized not as a simple, hierarchical chain of command, but as a distributed system. The first case study is Frank Norris's naturalist novel, *The Octopus*, and the second is the work, in the U.S. House of Representatives, of the Pujo Committee's investigation into the existence of a purported money trust, focusing in particular on Exhibit 243, a diagram produced by the committee.

The Fiction of Corporate Personality

From the 1870s to the 1920s, legal debate returned repeatedly to the issue of what was known in legal jargon as the "fiction of corporate personality." Since the time of the U.S. Supreme Court's *Trustees of Dartmouth College v. Woodward* decision (1819) up to the 1880s, legal orthodoxy and common practice held that a corporation was a creature of the state, with its powers explicitly granted and limited by state charter. Corporations were thus deemed to be "artificial entities," whose property rights were derived from public authority through charters, grants, and concessions, rather than inhering in them naturally, as in the dominant Lockean model of private individuals contracting freely. In the last decade of the nineteenth century, however, the concession theory of corporate existence was undermined, as the development of free incorporation meant that, in reality, corporations no longer owed their existence to or could be controlled by the state charters that supposedly created them. In the eyes of both critics and apologists alike, industrial combinations and their efficiencies of scale were seen as part of the inexorable, evolutionary progress of business organization that would inevitably eclipse the age of small-scale, proprietorial, individual competition. Some conservative legal theorists in the 1880s and 1890s nevertheless attempted to account for the emergence of the new, freely incorporated combinations in terms of traditional individual property rights. Corporations, in this line of thinking, were merely agglomerations of individual corporators, and any rights that seemed to belong in a metaphysical fashion to the combination, as if it were a person, were ultimately derived from the unproblematic natural rights of the individual shareholders (even when signed over to trustees). Corporations, in effect, were little more than large partnerships, and thus required no new legal categories to explain their rights and qualities.[56]

In contrast to this contractarian approach, legal commentators, influenced by the German organicist tradition associated most famously with Otto Gierke and translated for an Anglo-American context by Frederic Maitland and Ernst Freund, began in the 1890s to theorize instead that a corporation—like other collective organizations and groups—had an identity, and thus a legal stature, in its own right, just like natural legal persons. In this model, corporate personality was not derived from an explicit state concession or from the rights of the individual members that supposedly made up the collective. By 1900, a corporation was no longer deemed to be an artificial creature of the state but was designated as a real, or natural, entity in its own right—a legal person, or, as Maitland put it, a "right-and-duty-bearing unit."[57] By 1911, for example, law professor Arthur Machen could confidently declare that "a corporation is an entity—not imaginary or fictitious, but real, not artificial but natural."[58] One important consequence of conceiving of the corporation as a real rather than an artificial entity was to make it less amenable to state regulation or scrutiny. Yet the idea of a collective organization having (nearly) the same legal status as individuals caused great difficulty for some commentators. As the pragmatist philosopher John Dewey complained in a famous article in 1926 (by which time the debate had come to seem archaic), the discourses about the legal fiction of corporate personality in the Gilded Age and the Progressive Era became bogged down in unnecessarily metaphysical discussions, often because commentators drew on nonlegal, philosophical notions of personhood in order to test their applicability to the corporate case, at times tying themselves in knots as they tried to identify the qualities of personality that could apply to both individuals and groups.[59]

Despite Dewey's dismissal of the pointlessness of much of this discussion, the debates in the legal sphere, as much as in the popular realm, nevertheless had to grapple with genuinely difficult questions about intentionality, agency, blame, and identity in the age of ever-larger corporate conglomerations. The idea that a corporation was merely a glorified partnership was increasingly untenable from the 1890s onward. For one thing, shares in the newly formed mergers began to be offered directly to the wider public, as investors, through the stock exchanges, rather than through a private subscription to a limited number of active owner-partners. Given the anonymity and complexity of the emerging market in industrial securities in which the ownership of shares could pass through many hands, courts in the early 1890s therefore understandably began to relax the "trust fund doctrine" that previously had, in theory, made the initial subscribers of subsequently failed companies liable for the full par value of the shares.[60]

Corporations were thus recognized as having a legal identity separate from the identity of the individual owners—even to the logical conclusion of immortality —in a way that partnerships (which were wound up with the demise of the partners) never could. Ownership was now simply too diffuse to make the idea of a corporation as a private partnership plausible, and the practical, day-to-day influence of the directors and managers was too powerful to maintain a fantasy of active control by a corporation's supposedly ultimate owners. Indeed, the real point of the corporate form of organization was precisely that it enabled limited liability for the shareholders, unlike the strict liability rules governing partnerships. Likewise, it was no longer possible, in any meaningful sense, to see corporate decisions as the unanimous expression of the conglomerated intentions of the individual corporators. Corporations were therefore described as having a will and an identity of their own that corresponded neither to the intentions of the shareholders nor even strictly to the intentions of the appointed directors and managers. Despite this convenient legal fiction of corporate will and personality, in reality, corporate activities and decision making were becoming too complex to be regarded as the product of unitary identity and intentionality, whether derived from the will of the shareholders, the directors, or the "corporate personality" itself. As we have seen, however, this did not stop Populist critics from continuing to try to hold individuals accountable or to identify—even if only for dramatic purposes—the real individual power behind the veil of corporate personality.

Given this situation, it comes as little surprise that novelists around the turn of the twentieth century were repeatedly attracted to the rhetoric and narrative logic of conspiracy as they grappled with the problem of representing the complexities of collective liability and complex causality through a traditional narrative form that privileged individual agency and responsibility. Ignatius Donnelly, for example, not only penned the Omaha Platform, as well as his truly bizarre conspiracist interpretations of the myths surrounding the lost continent of Atlantis and the authorship of Shakespeare's plays, but he also wrote *Caesar's Column* (1890), a macabre, dystopian imagining of class conflict as an all-out conspiracy.[61] Jack London's *Iron Heel* (1908) likewise presented a dystopian future in which a shadowy oligarchy of corporate trusts controlled the whole of society. Many of the fictional portrayals of finance from this period pandered to the public's insatiable appetite for revelations about the underhanded scheming carried out by the nation's robber barons. For example, in David Graham Phillips's muckraking novels— *The Master-Rogue* (1903), *The Cost* (1904), and *The Deluge* (1905)—everything that happens in Wall Street is shown to be the result of deliberate plotting by the Machiavellian princes at the heart of the nation's financial exchanges.[62] In *The Cost*, the narrator at one point suggests that the striking events on the stock exchange are like a force of nature: "The mysterious force which had produced a succession of earthquakes moved horribly on, still in mystery impenetrable, to produce a cataclysm. In the midst of the chaos two vast whirlpools formed—one where Great Lakes sucked down men and fortunes, the other where Woolens drew some down to destruction, flung others up to wealth."[63] By this point in the novel, however, the reader knows that the sudden downturn is not the result of natural, elemental forces, but of an individual enemy motivated by a love tussle. In a fairly heavy-handed way, *The Master-Rogue* and *The Deluge* allow readers to see market machinations from the inside, because they are presented as an unapologetic, first-person account: we learn, as all good conspiracy theorists believe, that nothing happens by accident, because everything is planned and plotted in advance.[64] Some novels, however, began to question what conspiratorial agency and moral accountability might mean in the era of vast, bureaucratic corporations and the complex, interwoven nature of modern economic life. As David Zimmerman has shown, Upton Sinclair's *The Moneychangers* (1908), a fictional account of the panic of 1907, destabilizes the traditional notion of conspiracy by suggesting that ordinary members of the public might be complicit in letting the financial panics happen, even if they have their origins in the sinister machinations of an oligarchy.[65]

Frank Norris's novels provide some of the most intriguing, but also the most contradictory, fictional engagements with financial conspiracy during this period. *The Octopus* (1901) and *The Pit* (1903), the first two portions of Norris's *Epic of the Wheat*, a projected trilogy of novels about the production, marketing, and consumption of wheat, revolve around the question of who, or what, is in control of the mighty economic systems at play. These works of literary fiction, immensely popular in their time, engage with the same issues that were animating the debate on the legal notion of corporate personality. The novels capture the conflicting desire to represent corporate capitalism and the manipulation of finance as both a simple, personal conspiracy and a complex, impersonal network. Like the octopus cartoons examined in chapter 3, at one and the same time they personalize financial conspiracy, and register the dispersal of power into the abstractions of the economic sublime, as they struggle to find a representational form that can bring together agency and structure. Both novels are shot through with awkward tensions as they try to square the circle of individual versus collective causation, but these formal contradictions reveal much about the problem of popular attempts to read the market around the turn of the twentieth century.[66]

In the eyes of its original readers, *The Octopus* presented a classic Populist portrait of the megacorporation at the turn of the twentieth century as an evil conspiracy against the common people, and it did much to popularize the image of the corporate financial system as a cephalopod with a sinister, human face.[67] The novel is mainly told from the perspective of Presley, a would-be poet from the east who wants to write a modern Homeric epic of the west. He eventually comes to realize that his true epic subject is the struggle of the farmers of the San Joaquin Valley in California against the might of the (fictional) Pacific and Southwestern Railroad. Early in the novel, Presley is out walking in the fields when a railroad locomotive thunders by, and it is described in the first of many such incantatory passages as a monstrous creature, part horse, part mythical being: "a locomotive, single, unattached, shot by him with a roar, filling the air with the reek of hot oil, vomiting smoke and sparks; its enormous eye, cyclopean, red, throwing a glare far in advance, shooting by in a sudden crash of confused thunder; filling the night with the terrific clamor of its iron hoofs."[68] Back home at Magnus Derrick's ranch, where he is staying, Presley then sees the locomotive—through a trope of what might be termed mechanical anthropomorphization—as a symbolic embodiment of the unstoppable power of the railroad trust itself:

> Then, faint and prolonged, across the levels of the ranch, he heard the engine whistling for Bonneville. Again and again, at rapid intervals in its flying course, it whistled for road crossings, for sharp curves, for trestles; ominous notes, hoarse, bellowing, ringing with the accents of menace and defiance; and abruptly Presley saw again, in his imagination, the galloping monster, the terror of steel and steam, with its single eye, cyclopean, red, shooting from horizon to horizon; but saw it now as the symbol of a vast power, huge, terrible, flinging the echo of its thunder over all the reaches of the valley, leaving blood and destruction in its path; the leviathan, with tentacles of steel clutching into the soil, the soulless Force, the iron-hearted Power, the monster, the Colossus, the Octopus. (1: 48)

The passage works its way through repetition and amplification, eventually alighting on the single image that sums up what the "soulless" corporation is to those whose livelihoods are shaped by it: the octopus.

The novel is loosely based on the Mussel Slough incident of 1880, in which a small group of Californian farmers tried to prevent the Southern Pacific Railroad from seizing their homesteads in a dispute over the price the railroad wanted to charge the settlers to buy the land they had worked on and improved for more than a decade. In Norris's version, however, the protagonists are not the dirt-poor tenant farmers of Mussel Slough, but are comparatively wealthy ranchers with large landholdings. Despite their relative affluence, in the logic of Norris's story they represent the increasingly outdated fantasy of a Jeffersonian yeomanry, coupled with an old-fashioned faith in the level playing field of a free-market exchange between equals. Magnus Derrick, the leader of the Farmers' League that is set up to fight the railroad's conspiratorial scheme, believes in the fantasy of rugged individualism. He prides himself on his supposedly unimpeachable virtue and, more than anything, wants to be firmly in control of his own destiny. In an image drawn from the world of railroads, Derrick refuses to take a vacation, because he believes that his firm and very visible hand is needed to control his ranch, imagined as an engine: "the machine would not as yet run of itself; he must still feel his hand upon the lever" (1: 57).

Derrick, however, is still a gold miner and a gambler at heart. His get-rich-quick attitude is at odds with the nostalgic ideal of careful husbandry of the land. He and the other farmers of the San Joaquin Valley are not immune to the spirit of financial speculation that, in most of the agrarian and Populist rhetoric of the period, was an anathema to the producerist fantasy of honest, self-reliant labor as the only true source of economic value. As Norris's trilogy aimed to show, however, both the seemingly self-reliant producers of wheat in remote corners of California and the distant consumers in the Far East are tied together in an intricate financial network, with the stock ticker as the symbol of the local presence of that abstract and deterritorialized market. Like the ticker fiends explored in chapter 2, Magnus and his son Harran "had sat up nearly half of one night watching the strip of white tape jerking unsteadily from the reel. At such moments they no longer felt their individuality. The ranch became merely the part of an enormous whole, a unit in the vast agglomeration of wheat land the whole world round, feeling the effects of causes thousands of miles distant—a drought on the prairies of Dakota, a rain on the plains of India, a frost on the Russian steppes, a hot wind on the llanos of the Argentine" (1: 51). With their large ranches, the farmers in *The Octopus* are described as practicing agriculture on an industrial scale that is as monumental and as rapacious as the railroad itself. Derrick, in particular, is seduced by the idea of establishing a vast (and presumably monopolistic) trust of producers that could exploit new global markets and stand up to the might of the railroad.

Despite the seemingly clear opposition between the evil of the trust and the good of the people, the novel makes the connections between the two sides apparent. The main story revolves around a supposed conspiracy orchestrated by the railroad: first, to raise its freight rates in order to drive those farmers to ruin, and then to sell off the tenanted lands at prices elevated to a level beyond the reach of the farmers, before installing its own dummy buyers in their place. In the eyes of the ranchers, the railroad is the very epitome of a cunning and ruthless conspiracy. We learn, for example, that in the eyes of Dyke, the locomotive engineer turned hop farmer, "the Trust was silent, its ways inscrutable, the public saw only results. It worked on in the dark, calm, disciplined, irresistible" (2: 60). Yet, pushed into a corner, the Farmers' League sets in motion—in Presley's dismissive term—its own "obscure conspiracy" (2: 161), employing Derrick's other son, Lyman, in a doomed attempt to fix the election of the railroad commission that will set the rates. For Derrick, resorting to bribery is an affront to his much-vaunted moral code, but other farmers, such as the hot-headed Annixter, see it merely as a way of fighting fire with fire. This necessary turn away from their republican faith in the impartiality of contract ironically returns them to a more old-fashioned and more personalized form of business, which is also in keeping with their conviction that the railroad trust had made a personal, contractual promise to them to honor the original valuation of the land.

This tension between a personal and an impersonal encounter with the trust and the larger financial market runs throughout the novel. On the one hand, in the eyes of the ranchers, the railroad is inhuman, a mixture of monster and machine. For example, Annie Derrick, Magnus's wife, "saw very plainly the galloping terror of steam and steel, with its single eye, cyclopean, red, shooting from horizon to horizon, symbol of a vast power, huge and terrible; the leviathan with tentacles of steel, to oppose which meant to be ground to instant destruction beneath the clashing wheels" (1: 173). On the other hand, the vast and seemingly anonymous trust is embodied for them in the all-too-solid person of its local agent and banker, S. Behrman. "There was no denying the fact," the narrator comments, "that for Osterman, Broderson, Annixter, and Derrick, S. Behrman was the railroad" (1: 64). Behrman's corpulent and repulsive frame, together with his ostensibly Jewish name, seems to the farmers to be the very personification of corporate greed and shady manipulation.[69] In the logic of the novel Behrman is, at one and the same time, an actual individual and a symbolic representation—a personification—of the corporation. In a very different sense to the one used in legal debates during that period, he is a literalized fiction of corporate personality. His all-too-human flesh, like a corporation, is seemingly immortal, impossible to kill off, despite Presley's would-be anarchist attempt to assassinate him with a thrown bomb and Dyke's last-ditch attempt to kill, with his bare hands, the man who, in his eyes, embodies all the duplicity of the railroad.[70] For Annie Derrick, it was futile to "grapple with the railroad—that great monster, iron-hearted, relentless, infinitely powerful. Always it had issued triumphant from the fight; always S. Behrman, the Corporation's champion, remained upon the field as victor, placid, unperturbed, unassailable" (1: 172). Behrman, who is both a man and a personification, eventually dies in a manner that is overloaded with symbolism: he is smothered by the wheat flowing into the hold of a cargo ship, until only his hand—the visible hand of invisible manipulation—is seen clutching in desperation above the rising tide of grain. If Behrman is the human representative of the vast trust, even he—as he contemplates the Niagara of wheat that will soon drown him in the hold of the cargo ship—believes that there is no single individual behind the entire system: "The place was deserted. No human agency seemed to be back of the movement of the wheat. Rather, the grain seemed impelled with a force of its own, a resistless, huge force, eager, vivid, impatient for the sea" (2: 350).

Although Behrman is the local stand-in for the railroad and the most immediate instrument of the conspiracy, the farmers are in no doubt as to who is really behind the trust and its plots. As Harran explains to his fellow ranchers: "S. Behrman manipulated the whole affair. There's a big deal of some kind in the air, and if there is, we all know who is back of it; S. Behrman, of course, but who's back of him? It's Shelgrim." The narrator picks up on this thought:

> Shelgrim! The name fell squarely in the midst of the conversation, abrupt, grave, somber, big with suggestion, pregnant with huge associations. No one in the group who was not familiar with it; no one, for that matter, in the county, the State, the whole reach of the West, the entire Union, that did not entertain convictions as to the man who carried it; a giant figure in the end-of-the-century finance, a product of circumstance, an inevitable result of conditions, characteristic, typical, symbolic of ungovernable forces. In the New Movement, the New Finance, the reorganization of capital, the amalgamation of powers, the consolidation of enormous enterprises—no one individual was more constantly in the eye of the world; no one was more hated, more dreaded, no one more compelling of unwilling tribute to his commanding genius, to the colossal intellect operating the width of an entire continent than the president and owner of the Pacific and Southwestern. (1: 99–100)

In the farmers' vernacular, Shelgrim is the puppet master who controls everything and is at the heart of the conspiracy. "He sits in his office in San Francisco," Annixter declares, "and pulls the strings and we've got to dance" (1: 100). Shelgrim is the hidden hand, rather than the invisible hand.

After a violent showdown in which many of Presley's rancher friends are killed, he finds himself in San Francisco, passing the building that houses the headquarters of the railroad trust. In an image of individual control that is repeated many times in the novel, Presley imagines Shelgrim as the locomotive engineer in charge of the entire machinery of the trust, albeit combined with a hint of the medieval feudalism of the robber barons: "Here was the keep of the castle, and here, behind one of those many windows, in one of those many offices, his hand upon the levers of his mighty engine, sat the master, Shelgrim himself" (2: 279). On a whim, Presley decides to enter the building and confront the legendary man who is the controlling intelligence behind the evil octopus conspiracy. The man he finds, however, is not monstrous, but human. Presley "had been prepared to come upon an ogre, a brute, a terrible man of blood and iron, and instead had discovered a sentimentalist and an art critic" (2: 284). Although not the ogre Presley had been expecting, Shelgrim is nevertheless a man of infinite capacities, larger than life, more than a mere individual. He was "not only great, but large; many-sided, of vast sympathies, who understood with equal intelligence, the human nature in an habitual drunkard, the ethics of a masterpiece of painting, and the financiering and operation of ten thousand miles of railroad" (2: 284).

Here, Presley at last penetrates behind the corporate veil, supposedly discovering the actual person behind the fiction of corporate personality. Like the revelatory moment in *The Wizard of Oz* (another novel with seemingly strong, agrarian, Populist sympathies, published a year before *The Octopus*), Presley presumes he has discovered the human figure pulling the levers of power behind the anonymous façade of the trust.[71] Although Shelgrim turns out not to be quite the cartoon octopus of the Populist imagination, Presley nevertheless presumes that he is the controlling intelligence at the peak of the vast pyramid of conspiracy that defeated the ranchers. Instead, in a disorienting moment that catches Presley completely off guard, Shelgrim conjures up an infinite regress of the origin of power, insisting that even he is not in control of the railroad trust:

"Believe this, young man," exclaimed Shelgrim, laying a thick powerful forefinger on the table to emphasize his words, "try to believe this—to begin with—THAT RAILROADS BUILD THEMSELVES. Where there is a demand sooner or later there will be a supply. Mr. Derrick, does he grow his wheat? The Wheat grows itself. What does he count for? Does he supply the force? What do I count for? Do I build the Railroad? You are dealing with forces, young man, when you speak of Wheat and the Railroads, not with men. There is the Wheat, the supply. It must be carried to feed the People. There is the demand. The Wheat is one force, the Railroad, another, and there is the law that governs them—supply and demand. Men have only little to do in the whole business. Complications may arise, conditions that bear hard on the individual—crush him maybe—BUT THE WHEAT WILL BE CARRIED TO FEED THE PEOPLE as inevitably as it will grow. If you want to fasten the blame of the affair at Los Muertos on any one person, you will make a mistake. Blame conditions, not men."

"But—but," faltered Presley, "you are the head, you control the road."

"You are a very young man. Control the road! Can I stop it? I can go into bankruptcy if you like. But otherwise if I run my road, as a business proposition, I can do nothing. I can not control it. It is a force born out of certain conditions, and I—no man—can stop it or control it. Can your Mr. Derrick stop the Wheat growing? He can burn his crop, or he can give it away, or sell it for a cent a bushel—just as I could go into bankruptcy—but otherwise his Wheat must grow. Can any one stop the Wheat? Well, then no more can I stop the Road." (2: 285–86)

As in *The Pit*, the vision of power that Shelgrim evokes is one in which human actors are mere conduits for the sublime, impersonal, and natural forces that flow through them. Other than the personified abstractions of the wheat and the railroad themselves, there is no individual at the top of the chain of command. Or, to put it another way, in Shelgrim's cosmogony, there is no hidden center from which the conspiracy originates, with the corporation and its actions appearing instead as blameless acts of nature:

> Presley regained the street stupefied, his brain in a whirl. This new idea, this new conception dumfounded him. Somehow, he could not deny it. It rang with the clear reverberation of truth. Was no one, then, to blame for the horror at the irrigating ditch? Forces, conditions, laws of supply and demand—were these then the enemies, after all? Not enemies; there was no malevolence in Nature. Colossal indifference only, a vast trend toward appointed goals. Nature was, then, a gigantic engine, a vast cyclopean power, huge, terrible, a leviathan with a heart of steel, knowing no compunction, no forgiveness, no tolerance; crushing out the human atom standing in its way, with nirvanic calm, the agony of destruction sending never a jar, never the faintest tremor through all that prodigious mechanism of wheels and cogs. (2: 286)

Much to his surprise, Presley finds himself swayed by Shelgrim's argument. The novel itself takes the possibility of the uncanny agency of corporations seriously, not least because it chimes in with the mystical sense of enlightenment that Presley's shepherd friend Vanamee has achieved in viewing human endeavor— as well as human tragedies, including the rape and death of his beloved—as insignificant in the face of cosmic energies, of which the fertility of the wheat and the might of the railroad trust are the most potent symbols. The final conclusion that the novel reaches, buoyed up by capital letters, as if trying to convince both the reader and Presley himself, is that individual human agency is insignificant in the face of seemingly cosmic forces:

> Men—motes in the sunshine—perished, were shot down in the very noon of life, hearts were broken, little children started in life lamentably handicapped; young girls were brought to a life of shame; old women died in the heart of life for lack of food. In that little, isolated group of human insects, misery, death, and anguish spun like a wheel of fire. BUT THE WHEAT REMAINED. Untouched, unassailable, undefiled, that mighty world-force, that nourisher of nations, wrapped in nirvanic calm, indifferent to the human swarm, gigantic, resistless, moved onward in its appointed grooves. (2: 360)

Both the railroad trust—the local symbol of global capitalism—and the irrepressible fertility of the wheat crop are presented as impersonal forces that operate on a plane far above mere mortal concerns and the traditional conceptions of individual agency: "Men were naught, death was naught, life was naught; FORCE only existed—FORCE that brought men into the world, FORCE that crowded them out of it to make way for the succeeding generation, FORCE that made the wheat grow, FORCE that garnered it from the soil to give place to the succeeding crop" (2: 343). At the same time, however, these inhuman forces are repeatedly personified in the novel. Like the use of prosopopeia in Greek mythology, the personification of abstract forces humanizes but also mystifies natural and social processes. "There, under the sun and under the speckless sheen of the sky," the description of the harvest rhapsodizes, "the wooing of the Titan began, the vast primal passion, the two world-forces, the elemental Male and Female, locked in a colossal embrace, at grapples in the throes of an infinite desire, at once terrible and divine, knowing no law, untamed, savage, natural, sublime" (1: 125–26).[72]

Although Presley is seduced by the vision of sublime natural and economic forces that cast into relief petty human concerns, he finds the implications of Shelgrim's speech troubling. He still feels an emotional need to find someone responsible for the tragic events at the ditch, and the final section of the novel vacillates between the two positions. Once away from Shelgrim's office, Presley qualifies the self-serving analysis provided by the railroad boss, recognizing instead the asymmetrical nature of power and suffering:

> The drama was over. The fight of Ranch and Railroad had been wrought out to its dreadful close. It was true, as Shelgrim had said, that forces rather than men had locked horns in that struggle, but for all that the men of the Ranch and not the men

of the Railroad had suffered. Into the prosperous valley, into the quiet community of farmers, that galloping monster, that terror of steel and steam had burst, shooting athwart the horizons, flinging the echo of its thunder over all the ranches of the valley, leaving blood and destruction in its path. Yes, the Railroad had prevailed. The ranches had been seized in the tentacles of the octopus; the iniquitous burden of extortionate freight rates had been imposed like a yoke of iron. The monster had killed Harran, had killed Osterman, had killed Broderson, had killed Hooven. It had beggared Magnus and had driven him to a state of semi-insanity after he had wrecked his honor in the vain attempt to do evil that good might come. (2: 359)

Unlike Shelgrim's insistence on the passive voice, this passage—focalized through Presley's consciousness—once again uses active verbs, although it is not the railroad boss himself that is the subject, but the abstract, collective personifications: "the Railroad," "the monster," "the Octopus."

As Presley reflects on the death of his friends, especially when he is sickened by the indifference of the haute bourgeoisie whose dinners he attends in San Francisco, he still feels an emotional pull to the dawning class consciousness fuelled by Populist and anarchist conspiracy rhetoric that had marked his final weeks at the ranch, leading up to the cataclysmic events at the ditch. He is dimly aware that Shelgrim's insistence that the trust creates and controls itself is an ideological naturalization of a political-economic arrangement, borne out in the way Shelgrim equates the sublime "financiering" of the trust with the uncontainable fertility of the wheat. Although the novel continues to push toward its final, mystical conclusion, Presley nevertheless registers a residual resistance to Shelgrim's all-too-convenient evasion of blame: "The Railroad might indeed be a force only, which no man could control and for which no man was responsible, but his friends had been killed" (2: 317).

Contemporary readers of the novel assumed that *The Octopus* was a straightforward attack on corporate trusts, pictured as a conspiracy against the common man. New Historicist critics, however, such as Walter Benn Michaels, have insisted that Norris's novel legitimates the procorporate position, because it naturalizes corporations by fetishizing the discourse of superhuman forces.[73] Nonetheless, it would be more accurate to read the novel as both a diatribe against the incorporation of America *and* an endorsement of it. Like many of the other Populist attacks on financial capitalism explored in this chapter, it combines the rhetoric of personalized conspiratorial agency with a quasi-structural analysis of distributed systems of power that operate as networks, rather than as simple, hierarchical chains of command. What makes the movement between the two more fluid, and thus more complicated, is that the portrait of impersonal power is often presented through the trope of personification. Far from an older, animistic tradition of thought giving way to a newer, more abstract mode of economic representation in the age of the corporation, *The Octopus* demonstrated that the abstract could only be made legible via new modes of personification. The naturalist writing thus attempted to make sense of collective agency and causality through the representational technology of the individual-centered novel. There is not a simple conspiracy behind the railroad, the novel implies, but an entire system of corporate trusts; nevertheless, that abstract system is endowed with monstrous will and envisioned as an octopus (which, in turn, is imagined as if it were endowed with human desires and intentionality). The rhetoric suggests that, on the one hand, the evil is intentional and centered in the "great bulk" (2: 283) of Shelgrim's body, yet, on the other hand, it is so infinitely distributed that it is scarcely recognizable as a coherent being: "Abruptly Dyke received the impression of the multitudinous ramifications of the colossus. Under his feet the ground seemed mined; down there below him in the dark the huge tentacles were silently twisting and advancing, spreading out in every direction, sapping the strength of all opposition, quiet, gradual, biding the time to reach up and out and grip with a sudden unleashing of gigantic strength" (2: 60–61). The image of the octopus enables Norris (and other radical critics of that era) to conceive of the dizzying complexity of financial capitalism as part of a single, coherent system, yet, at the same time, to imbue that abstract system with agency and will. In this way, *The Octopus* establishes a *mise en abyme* in the quest for the ultimate source of agency and causality.

The map of conspiracy the novel creates is not the usual one, in which power is conceived as a chain or a pyramid, or, at the very least, as having a center. When Presley visits the railroad headquarters in San Francisco (which is in keeping with the revelation about Shelgrim that he is about to discover), he at first is struck by the fact that the building is not "pretentious." He "must have passed it, unheeding, many times," yet despite being unremarkable from the outside, nevertheless "it was the stronghold of the enemy—the center of all that vast ramifying system of arteries that drained the life-blood of the State; the nucleus of the web in which so many lives, so many fortunes, so many destinies had been enmeshed" (2: 279). Presley's mental map of how power operates resembles the actual map of the railroad that Lyman Derrick studies in his office:

> It was a commissioner's official railway map of the State of California, completed to March 30th of that year. Upon it the different railways of the State were accurately

plotted in various colors, blue, green, yellow. However, the blue, the yellow, and the green were but brief traceries, very short, isolated, unimportant. At a little distance these could hardly be seen. The whole map was gridironed by a vast, complicated network of red lines marked P. and S. W. R. R. These centralized at San Francisco and thence ramified and spread north, east, and south, to every quarter of the State. From Coles, in the topmost corner of the map, to Yuma in the lowest, from Reno on one side to San Francisco on the other, ran the plexus of red, a veritable system of blood circulation, complicated, dividing, and reuniting, branching, splitting, extending, throwing out feelers, off-shoots, tap roots, feeders—diminutive little blood suckers that shot out from the main jugular and went twisting up into some remote county, laying hold upon some forgotten village or town, involving it in one of a myriad branching coils, one of a hundred tentacles, drawing it, as it were, toward that center from which all this system sprang. The map was white, and it seemed as if all the color which should have gone to vivify the various counties, towns, and cities marked upon it had been absorbed by that huge, sprawling organism, with its ruddy arteries converging to a central point. It was as though the State had been sucked white and colorless, and against this pallid background the red arteries of the monster stood out, swollen with life-blood, reaching out to infinity, gorged to bursting; an excrescence, a gigantic parasite fattening upon the life-blood of an entire commonwealth. (2: 4–5)

The map of the railroad both abstracts and vivifies a system. It is, at one and the same time, mechanical and organic, animal and vegetable, impersonal yet alive with its own malevolent volition. On the one hand, the passage suggests that the inanimate railroad is a living creature that has a single point of control, be it the "plexus" of a central nervous system or a beating heart, with its "ruddy arteries converging to a central point." At other moments, however, the "multitudinous ramifications" of the railroad are portrayed not as part of a being with a central location of control, but as a dizzying and decentered network out of which conspiratorial agency emerges, without there being any obvious commanding agent pulling the strings. Yet, just when it seems that the passage lapses into ideological obfuscation with its portrait of the railroad trust as a sublime phenomenon whose complexity and vast scale is beyond human comprehension, it invokes the uncanny possibility that there is agency and control *in the system itself.* The description also conjures up the master image of the novel as a whole: the map of the railroad resembles an octopus, with a centralized intelligence, yet with endlessly ramifying appendages that constitute a complex but organic whole ("a myriad branching coils, one of a hundred tentacles").

In its account of corporate and financial capitalism, the novel thus wavers between embracing a thoroughly posthuman notion of individual agency, viewed from a sublime distance, and remaining committed to a rabble-rousing, conspiratorial depiction of big business as the expression of a monstrous, parasitic will. These contradictory viewpoints within *The Octopus* are never ultimately resolved, either aesthetically or politically. In part this is a reflection of and engagement with the contemporary legal debates surrounding the nature of corporations. The novel does raise the possibility, however, of a synthesis between the two opposing poles of theories: traditional, individual agency versus newer, sociological models of structural causation. In the era of monopoly capitalism, *The Octopus* represents the system of class privilege *as* conspiracy.

"Unless You Have Got Actual Control, You Can Not Control Anything"

When antitrust legislation was not being used to attack unions, the cases brought forward tended to involve individual firms or clusters of firms working through a deliberate, yet secret, agreement to fix prices or force competitors out of business. I now want to examine in detail a case study in which the purported conspiracy not only involved an entire sector of the economy, but was imagined as operating almost without intentional agreement. What makes the case so arresting is that it pushes to the limit the very meaning of conspiracy and raises the question of how best to represent the system of high finance that was emerging around the turn of the twentieth century. Was there indeed a system, or was it merely a collection of individual, uncoordinated acts? Should finance be left to the experts, or should the state bring regulatory oversight and transparency to what bankers insisted were private agreements, governed by individual freedom of contract? Were bankers selflessly working in the national interest to maintain financial stability, or should the government be trusted to interfere in the natural organization of the market? If there was a panic on Wall Street, must there always be someone to blame? If there seemed to be evidence of what looked to all intents and purposes like coordination and control in the financial markets, must there necessarily be a hidden hand at work? Finally, was the financial system now too complex to be controlled by a small clique of powerful private bankers—and, if so, then who should be in charge of it?

Although J. P. Morgan was at first hailed as a popular hero for single-handedly saving the nation's financial system during the panic of 1907, some skeptical voices were troubled by the idea that an individual banker could wield such vast financial power, constituting a one-man lender of last resort, a function that, critics began to argue, should be the privilege and the responsibility of a central bank.[74] Following agitation by Senator Robert La Follette and Senator Charles Lindbergh Sr. (father of the future aviator hero), the U.S. House of Representatives established the Pujo Committee in 1912 to investigate monopolistic abuses of power in the banking sector: to discover whether, in short, there existed a secretive money trust. As the original House Resolution that established the investigation put it:

> It has been further charged and is generally believed that these same groups of financiers have so entrenched themselves in their control of the aforesaid financial and other institutions and otherwise in the direction of the finances of the country that they are thereby enabled to use the funds and property of the great national banks and other moneyed corporations in the leading money centers to control the security and commodity markets; to regulate the interest for money; to create, avert, and compose panics; to dominate the New York Stock Exchange and the various clearing house associations throughout the country, and through such associations and by reason of their aforesaid control over the aforesaid railroads, industrial corporations, and moneyed institutions, and others, and in other ways resulting therefrom, have wielded a power over the business, commerce, credits, and finances of the country that is despotic and perilous and is daily becoming more perilous to the public welfare.[75]

The working assumption of the investigation was not merely that a de facto banking conspiracy had a stranglehold on credit, but that a "money trust" had control of the industrial combinations they floated on the New York Stock Exchange. The investigation argued that the private bankers were drumming up new business by using the inside information and influence they obtained from each bank having one of their partners as a director on the board of a large number of companies. The suspicion was that a cluster of investment banks acted as both principal and agent, both underwriter and investor, in the enormous consolidation deals they brokered, which would mean that the nation's system of finance was hopelessly corrupt. At its heart, the Pujo Committee was concerned with the question of whether there should be democratic oversight of high finance, and whether there should be a limit to the influence—either explicit or implied—that an individual or a single bank could hold over the nation's economic institutions.

Despite the fiery rhetoric of the House Resolution, in practice the Pujo Committee was more circumscribed in its investigative remit, constrained at first by the need to avoid seeming partisan in the election season of 1912, and hampered by a reluctance on the part not only of the banking community, but also sectors of the government itself, to furnish relevant evidence.[76] Although denied access to the full accounts of most corporations, and even to the government's own records kept by the comptroller of the currency, the committee's lead counsel, Samuel Untermyer, nevertheless managed to amass a large amount of data about the extent of the interlocking corporate directorships of the biggest Wall Street investment banks and many of the largest industrial combinations in the country. In particular, Untermyer focused on the concentration of power and money in the hands of a small group of financial institutions, led by J. P. Morgan, that included the First National Bank; the National City Bank; Lee, Higginson, and Company; Kidder, Peabody, and Company; and Kuhn, Loeb, and Company. Among its many headlined conclusions (which were summarized and expanded in *Other People's Money*, a popular and influential book written by Louis Brandeis in 1914), the report concluded that industrial corporations and public utilities worth $22 billion were under the control or influence of this handful of financiers, who sat on the boards of countless corporations in a complex pattern of interlocking directorships and voting trusts, and participated as stockholders.[77] For example, George F. Baker, the president of the First National Bank, was a director in 58 companies, while Morgan, First National Bank, and National City and Guaranty Trust held over 300 directorships in 100 companies.

The volume of evidence was overwhelming, and it provided the American public with a damning insight into the murky world of high finance. Yet the evidence remained circumstantial, at best, without ever uncovering a "smoking gun" document or a moment of testimony that would prove the existence of a money trust as anything more than a muckraking metaphor. Morgan, for example, admitted in one cross-examination that he and Baker were old friends and had engaged in mutually beneficial associations and transactions, but there was no paper record of the agreements, and thus no chance of proving an actual conspiracy—a state of affairs befitting the genteel world of banking in which a gentleman's word was his bond.[78] Proof of a conspiracy was the sticking point. Although the original House Resolution—and certainly the popular view—was that a money trust indeed existed and was engaged in a "despotic" and "perilous" conspiracy, Untermyer and Brandeis came to a more diplomatic conclusion. In their eyes, even if there was not an actual document that could prove a conspiratorial agreement or intention behind the money trust, this small group of financiers nevertheless managed—through a "gentleman's agreement" or "banking ethics"—to eliminate competition in investment banking and thus constituted, in all but name, a monopolistic conspiracy in restraint of trade under the terms of the Sherman Anti-Trust Act.[79] For Untermyer, the terminology was crucial: "If, however, we mean by this loose, elastic term 'trust' as applied to the concentration of the 'money power' that there is a close and well-defined 'community of interest' and understanding among the men who dominate the financial destinies of our country and who wield fabulous power over the fortunes of others through their control of corporate funds belonging to other people, our investigators will find a situation confronting us far more serious than is popularly supposed to exist."[80] The Pujo Committee never managed to prove the conspiracy allegations conclusively, although it is arguable that they did manage to provide convincing evidence that high finance was run by a "community of interest"—even if they did not go so far as to name it class privilege. The changes to antitrust legislation that were passed by the U.S. Congress, however, were ultimately not very far-reaching or effective in tackling the problems the investigation had exposed. The committee concluded that banks were likely to fall prey to a conflict of interests, with their loyalties compromised between promoting the profitability of their own firm and securing the best deal for both their corporate clients and the investing public, and, more often than not, they abused their position of privileged access to inside information to speculate for easy profits. As a solution to the specific problem of conflicts of interest, the committee proposed the Clayton Act of 1914, which extended the Sherman Anti-Trust Act of 1890 by prohibiting directors from sitting on the boards of two companies competing in the same sector of the economy.

Despite the failure of the investigation to prove an explicit conspiracy, I want to argue that the Pujo Committee's struggle to explain and represent the nature of collusion in itself provides a significant insight into the public perception of finance during this period. Leaving aside the specific political wranglings, what this case reveals is a deep-seated ideological rift in the understanding of agency and causation. An older, more personal, individualistic way of thinking about business continued to hold sway in Wall Street long after the complexity of large, collective organizations became a reality. The case also brings home the difficulties that observers of finance had in finding an adequate way of representing the relationship between individual agency and structural causation in the new corporate era, with much of the debate revolving around the thorny issue of what counted as control and conspiracy, and where the dividing line between the two lay. The first section will look in detail at some of the thousands of pages of testimony from the Pujo hearings, while the following section will examine an individual diagram produced by the committee that maps the interlocking corporate and financial directorships.

The Pujo Hearings

The hearings were a fraught affair. Most notoriously, William Rockefeller evaded appearing before the committee, with his doctors insisting that he was too ill to give testimony, because a cough brought on by stress could kill him. He led the committee's lawyers, who were trying to serve a subpoena on him, on a merry dance as he retreated from public view into his mansion in North Tarrytown, New York. He gave the slip to the Pinkerton detectives watching out for him and escaped to his cottage on Jekyll Island in Georgia, where he eventually granted a brief and inconclusive interview, cut short by his supposedly life-threatening laryngitis.[81] In the actual hearings, Untermyer repeatedly tried to show that the coterie of bankers centered on Morgan acted covertly, in concert, to control the financial affairs of the nation. For his part, Morgan was adamant in arguing that he had no actual control over any of the companies he was associated with. He insisted that his private banking business (an unlimited partnership, rather than a limited liability corporation) should remain out of the scrutinizing gaze of the state. As far as he was concerned, his selfless patriotism and his gentlemanly code of banking ethics were ultimately a better guarantee that the interests of the nation would be served than any regulatory intrusion.

Untermyer clashed repeatedly with his witnesses, with the two sides differing not only in their fundamental political outlook, but also in the meaning of seemingly straightforward terms. At the heart of the matter was whether Morgan and the dense network of directors associated with him were actually in control of the corporate and trust boards they sat on. For example, when Untermyer quizzed William Sherer, the manager of the New York Clearing House Association, on whether the Security Bank and the Fourth National Bank were closely interwoven, Sherer replied that he had no direct, personal knowledge, only hearsay. Untermyer prodded him further, trying to pin him down over the meaning of the term "control," and the exchange ended in a stalemate:

UNTERMYER: Do you know that they have a number of directors in common?

SHERER: Yes. The bank is owned by a great many stockholders.

UNTERMYER: I am not talking about stockholders. We are talking about the people who control its practical affairs and its management, not about the stockholders. You know what control means, do you not?

SHERER: Yes.

UNTERMYER: You know that control of a bank, so far as its active management and direction and policy are concerned, is not dependent upon the stock ownership, and that the two have no relation, do you not?

SHERER: I do not want to answer that, because I consider the stockholders the
owners of the bank, and I do not want to say that the owners of the bank give up
control of it.

UNTERMYER: But you know the management is one thing and the stockholding is
quite another thing?

SHERER: Yes.

UNTERMYER: You know that the banks of this city, as a rule, are managed by men
who do not control the stock?

SHERER: No, I do not know that.

UNTERMYER: Do you know whether that is so or not?

SHERER: No.[82]

Untermyer then returns to the question of what counts as "control" in one
of his lengthy cross-examinations of Morgan. Untermyer tries to get Morgan to
admit that he favors combination over competition, and Morgan confesses that
while he likes "a little competition," he prefers cooperation (the term he insists
on using instead of the more damning "combination"). Morgan feels that he is
being misrepresented and makes a request to put his version across. The two
men dance around the meaning of the word "control," in a sequence of bizarre
and increasingly tautological exchanges:

MORGAN: This may be a sensitive subject. I do not want to talk of it. This is probably the only chance I will have to speak of it.

UNTERMYER: You mean the subject of combination and concentration?

MORGAN: Yes; the question of control. Without you have control, you can not do
anything.

UNTERMYER: Unless you have got control, you can not do what?

MORGAN: Unless you have got actual control, you can not control anything.

UNTERMYER: Well, I guess that is right. Is that the reason you want to control
everything?

MORGAN: I want to control nothing.

UNTERMYER: Then what sort of control is it that you want? You say, in order to
have complete control . . .

MORGAN: I do not want either—I do not want any control.

UNTERMYER: What is the point, Mr. Morgan, you want to make, because I do not
quite gather it?

MORGAN: What I say is this, that control is a thing, particularly in money, and you
are talking about a money control—now, there is nothing in the world that you
can make a trust on money.

Morgan interprets Untermyer's words in a literal fashion, arguing that money—understood simply as gold coin rather than as privileged access to credit—is impossible to monopolize. In another session, Untermyer returns to the question of control, and once again fails to get Morgan—arguably the most powerful and influential man in America at this point—to admit that he controls anything:

UNTERMYER: Some other man who might control might not take the view you have?

MORGAN: He would not have the control.

UNTERMYER: That is your idea, is it? Your idea is that when a man has got a vast power, such as you have—you admit you have, do you not?

MORGAN: I do not know it, sir.

UNTERMYER: You admit you have, do you not?

MORGAN: I do not think I have.

UNTERMYER: You do not feel it at all?

MORGAN: No; I do not feel it at all.[83]

Morgan's immediate argument is that a single, powerful man cannot control affairs because the board of directors can always outnumber him. What is more striking, however, is his steadfast refusal to acknowledge that, even if in a minority, the outsized influence of his firm in the financial community could still hold sway, or to even concede that he could, in any way, be considered powerful.[84]

On another occasion, Morgan begrudgingly accepts Untermyer's suggestion that his authority is *unconscious* for him, calling up the enigmatic notion that he possesses power over which he claims to have no personal knowledge or control. This raises the paradoxical possibility that a conspiracy might emerge unbeknownst to the conspirators:

UNTERMYER: You and Mr. Baker dominate the anthracite coalroad situation, do you not, together?

MORGAN: No; we do not.

UNTERMYER: Do you not?

MORGAN: I do not think we do. At least, if we do, I do not know it.

UNTERMYER: Your power in any direction is entirely unconscious to you, is it not?

MORGAN: It is, sir; if that is the case.

UNTERMYER: You do not think you have any power in any department of industry in this country, do you?

MORGAN: I do not.

UNTERMYER: Not the slightest?

MORGAN: Not the slightest.[85]

In one light, Morgan's prevarications spring from his conviction that he is merely *primo inter pares* on a board of trustees, a humble agent for the individual share-holders he represents, rather than the formally recognized principal driving the structural changes to the constituent businesses—a process that, unsurprisingly, became dubbed "Morganization." Read in a different light, however, these re-peated clashes around the definition of "control" get at the heart of the issue at stake in the Pujo hearings. If there is no actual conspiracy, is it possible for con-trol to emerge without straightforward intention or direct, personal knowledge? Is it possible that Untermyer is wrong to claim that there is a conspiracy, but, at the same time, that Morgan is wrong to deny having any influence over the nation's financial and industrial system?

For their part, the bankers insisted that there had been no conscious act of conspiracy, and no personal knowledge of one. They also therefore claimed that, if there happened to emerge a situation that, in an unfavorable light, resembled an illegal restraint of trade, it was not their primary aim—and this was key to the legal definition of conspiracy under the rule-of-reason interpretation of the Sherman Anti-Trust Act, which permitted restraints of trade as long as they were not the main intention of the business agreement. For example, Sherer defended the Clearing House Association's (CHA) practice of creating a virtual monopoly by forbidding members to deal with the Curb Exchange or the rival Consoli-dated Exchange, along with the stipulation that only members could clear checks through the CHA at the set rate. Like most of the witnesses, Sherer endlessly tried to claim no personal knowledge of any of the common rumors of sharp practices. He maintained that it was not a case of a deliberate restraint of trade, since the Clearing House was like a private club in which the members submit voluntarily to the rules that they endorse. In this case, however, as Sherer and others insisted, the agreement on rates did not happen through explicit, contrac-tual approval, but through a tacit, mutual accord on the principles of conservative banking. The CHA thus did not constitute a conspiracy, Sherer argued with a remarkable degree of chutzpah, any more than did a voluntary agreement by union members not to offer their labor below a certain wage. This voluntarist model obsessively cleaved to the principle of economic actors as autonomous individuals, operating on the level playing field produced by freedom of contract and competition. Sherer's denial of the existence of a money-trust conspiracy thus did not contravene the Sherman Anti-Trust Act on a very literal reading of the law. Nevertheless, it ignored the patently obvious facts exposed by the investigation: the CHA used its clout to reinforce the monopoly power and priv-ileges of an inner circle of elite bankers.

Like Sherer, Morgan repeatedly rebuffed the accusation that there was a formal money-trust agreement contravening existing law by likewise employing a very literalist interpretation of how conspiratorial agreements are made. He made clear, for example, that he did not personally know some of the directors with whom he was alleged to be colluding and thus could not be guilty of orchestrating a conspiracy. In a letter belatedly replying to the accusations and insinuations made by Untermyer in his cross-examination of Morgan, Morgan & Company's lawyers were adamant that the kind of all-encompassing money trust sketched out by the Pujo Committee was impossible, because it was contrary to the natural, immutable, impersonal laws of supply and demand: competition can never be totally suppressed. The letter challenged the "exceedingly mistaken inferences," drawn from the diagrams and tables prepared by the committee that showed interlocking directorships, that "this vast aggregate of the country's wealth is at the disposal of these 180 men." The letter noted that "such an implication rests solely upon the untenable theory that these men, living in different parts of the country, in many cases personally unacquainted with each other, and in most cases associated only in occasional transactions, vote always for the same policies and control with united purpose."[86] This face-saving letter presented a view of high finance operating solely through the impersonal, rational calculus of economic logic, rather than the actual mutual back-scratching of a clubbable coterie. It rejected out of hand the all-too-plausible idea that vested class interest indeed might lead to individual bankers always voting the same way, even if they did not explicitly agree to do so in advance—a possibility that, ironically, was pretty much exactly the defense offered by Sherer in his account of the Clearing House, operating, through tacit agreement, as a private members' club.

In his own testimony before the Pujo Committee, Morgan did not emphasize the modern, abstract, impartial nature of finance, as the letter from his counsel had done, but instead, like Sherer, repeatedly evoked a picture of banking dominated by the Old World values of personal trust and close-knit social connections. He was adamant, for example, that the decision to loan money ultimately rested not on an objective and strictly numerical analysis of credit history or financial worth, but on a much more subjective response to an applicant, based on a trust in personal character, rather than impersonal numbers:

MORGAN: I know lots of men, business men, too, who can borrow any amount, whose credit is unquestioned.

UNTERMYER: Is that not because it is believed that they have the money back of them?

MORGAN: No, sir; it is because people believe in the man.

UNTERMYER: And it is regardless of whether he has any financial backing at all, is it?

MORGAN: It is very often.

UNTERMYER: And he might not be worth anything?

MORGAN: He might not have anything. I have known a man to come into my office, and I have given him a check for a million dollars when I knew he had not a cent in the world.

[. . .]

UNTERMYER: Is not commercial credit based primarily on money or property?

MORGAN: No, sir; the first thing is character.

UNTERMYER: Before money or property?

MORGAN: Before money or anything else. Money can not buy it.

UNTERMYER: So that a man with character, without anything at all behind it, can get all the credit he wants, and a man with the property can not get it?

MORGAN: That is very often the case.

UNTERMYER: But that is the rule of business.

MORGAN: That is the rule of business. . . . Because a man I do not trust could not get money from me on all the bonds in Christendom.[87]

Morgan and the other bankers called before the Pujo Committee thus seemed to want it both ways. On the one hand, they stressed that business is a matter of impersonal, rational calculation and economic laws that would undermine any conspiracy theory of a cabal of bankers pulling the strings behind the scenes. On the other hand, they were keen to emphasize that personal relationships and trust are the key to the world of private banking. This contradiction was not merely the result of self-serving prevarication (although there is fair measure of that). Instead, it must be seen as a result of the wider difficulty that both critics and apologists alike had in accounting for the continuing relevance of individualism in an era of megalithic corporations operating in an increasingly complex financial landscape.

The financiers resolutely denied any kind of conspiratorial connection or monopolistic control, but it is still worth asking if there was any substance to the Pujo Committee's accusations. If there was not an actual conspiracy, then how can we explain the overwhelming influence of a small clique of private bankers —and of J. P. Morgan in particular—during the development of the great trusts and corporations? Following the lead of Alfred Chandler, many business and economic historians have argued that, unlike Britain and France, the United States and Germany followed a path to the "managerial revolution" that separated ownership from control. For Chandler, it was the persistence of "personal capitalism" (that is, both family ties in the ownership of corporations, and the close involvement of family owners in the management of their firms) that explains why Britain suffered an economic decline in the twentieth century. In this story, the United States had a far lower rate of interlocking corporate directorships than Britain and even Germany, thereby explaining its comparative economic success. The Pujo Committee, according to this line of thinking, saw the hidden hand of an evil conspiracy, whereas it should have seen the genius of what Chandler famously termed the "visible hand" of managerial efficiency.[88] Chandler's story of inevitable progress toward technological and economic efficiency has, however, been challenged from many quarters. Some historians have shown that "personal capitalism" persisted in some sectors of the American economy far longer than Chandler had imagined and, in the British case, was necessary to sustain trade across the vast distances of the Empire.[89] Even the basic premise of the American innovation of managerial capitalism has been questioned, with Leslie Hannah, for instance, demonstrating how, in 1900, Britain and France had a far more democratic spread of share ownership and corporate governance rules, with the United States far closer in reality to the picture of plutocratic control sketched out in the Pujo Committee's report and its diagrams.[90] It is arguable, therefore, that during this period, it was the United States, and not Britain, that was dominated by "personal capitalism" and dense interlocking networks of elite bankers, even if they were structured by mutual interests and social cohesion, rather than direct conspiracy.[91]

More recently, economists such as Bradford DeLong have revisited the issue, posing the question, if there was no monopoly, why did firms like J. P. Morgan & Company manage to sustain such extravagant profits from the mergers they created? DeLong starts with the presumption that there was no secret money trust. Therefore, he posits that both the corporations and the investors were willing to pay a premium for something they might have been able to get cheaper elsewhere. DeLong claims that using Morgan to handle the stock market flotations of newly formed corporate behemoths in effect added 30 percent to the value of a corporation's stock, in part because Morgan insisted on instituting sound managerial restructurings once he took his seat on the board. In essence, DeLong's argument is that in a "market for lemons," sound guidance is worth paying for, to even up the informational asymmetry.[92] DeLong's neoclassical economic analysis sees only rational economic agents, however, and ignores the possibility that forms of monopoly control exist that do not amount to a full-blown conspiracy, yet profoundly tilt the playing field in favor of the already powerful.

Susie Pak's study of the secretive world of private banking begins with a similar question to that of DeLong: "If the Morgans' network was not homogenous or collusive, and if their influence was not based on their monetary capital, as they claimed, what was the source of their power?"[93] Like DeLong, Pak starts from the position that there was no tightly knit conspiracy, at least in the way that the Pujo Committee and popular sentiment imagined. Her research into the Morgans' social networks suggests, however, that their influence was not solely a result of rational and impersonal economic factors. The kinship and community networks the Morgans cultivated were necessary in a business world in which information was hard to come by, because there was very little in the way of regulatory requirements for disclosure and the publication of accounts. In short, they provided the personal trust that was vital to doing business in an era without adequate mechanisms for impersonal trust, and this personal mode persisted far longer into the twentieth century than most economic theorists, either at the time or since, have countenanced. The underwriting syndicates the Morgans put together relied on—and in turn helped cement—social networks in Manhattan based on kinship ties, memberships in elite clubs, and the reciprocal exchange of favors, as well as the interlocking directorships identified by the Pujo Committee. As Edith Wharton's novels make clear, inclusion in a deal was as much the result of a social calculation as an economic one, and, vice versa, financial cooperation also helped advance social ambitions, albeit not always in fully reciprocated ways. Pak also demonstrates that although the Morgans maintained their elevated status by cultivating very exclusive and exclusionary social circles (they were undeniably racist and antisemitic), they nonetheless were willing to do business, when necessary, with German-Jewish bankers, such as the house of Kuhn-Loeb. The two groups moved on parallel social tracks but shared a commitment to the discretion and conservative values that formed the bedrock of "gentleman banking." It was precisely the flexibility of their networks that made them so durable, with their secretive world of insider dealing and the granting of favors lasting long into twentieth century. Simple-minded Populist conspiracy theories about the existence of a money trust may well have been mistaken in many of their claims, but their basic sense that finance was dominated by a plutocratic network was not so wide of the mark.

As Pak suggests, it was the invisibility of those ties—maintained more by tacit assumptions than actual agreements—that made it so difficult for the Pujo Committee to prove that there was a conspiracy. Progressive critics of high finance thus made the mistake of focusing solely on combating illegal, formal collusion, when, in fact, it was the informal social ties and shared mores that were more important in oiling the machinery of business during this period. The partners of J. P. Morgan & Company (Morgan himself died in 1913) reluctantly accepted the Clayton Act's prohibition on interlocking directorships, if only to avoid negative publicity, but in private they recognized that the social relationships would continue unabated, and, ironically, would become increasingly important if more-formal channels of economic cooperation were outlawed. Thus Jack Morgan (Pierpont's son) insisted in private that he was "absolutely confident that the present relationships are built on personalities rather than on stock ownership, and that they will continue unadulterated," while Benjamin Strong Jr. of the Bankers Trust acknowledged that "legislation won't bother us if we are surrounded by such good friends."[94]

Muckraking critics were thus wrong to focus fixatedly on the specific details of a single, vast, money-trust conspiracy. Their broader conspiratorial outlook on high finance, however, should not necessarily be rejected automatically as delusional or misguided. First of all, the Chandlerian dismissal of Progressive Era interpretations of business and economic development as a highly personal story of heroes and villains (associated most famously with *The Robber Barons*, Matthew Josephson's scathing look back at the Gilded Age from the anticapitalist perspective of the Great Depression) is in danger of throwing the baby out with the bathwater.[95] Chandler advocated a new approach to business history that would focus not on the individual skullduggery or the genius of the robber barons, but on the abstract economic, technological, and managerial factors that seemed to inevitably fuel industrial progress. By taking this line, however, the emergent discipline of business history downplayed the role of finance (and the particular compromises reached between Washington and Wall Street) in its Whiggish story of the triumph of the efficiencies of industrial capitalism. The preoccupation with modern structures of impersonal bureaucracy, economic rationality, and professional management blinded this research to the surprising persistence of personal connections, insider dealing, and a cultural milieu more suited to secretive collusion than transparent competition. In a similar fashion, Hofstadter's attack on the irrational elements of Populist and muckraking rhetoric ended up unfairly delegitimizing the desire to understand the way in which monopoly power worked: through personal networks and the unspoken assumptions of class privilege. Hofstadter might have been correct in dismissing Populist critics for their adherence to the "simple virtues and unmitigated villainies of a rural melodrama," but the alternative—seeing financial history as entirely the result of immutable economic laws—ignores the role of individual agency and the socially embedded networks of privilege in which those individuals operate.

If the Pujo Committee was wrong to claim that the money trust was a carefully orchestrated conspiracy, it was nevertheless correct to recognize that financial networks based on personal connection were central to the monopoly stage of industrial capitalism, especially before the banking reforms of the New Deal. What emerges from the surreal and frustrating exchanges in the Pujo hearings is a surprisingly complex picture of power that is both individual and structural, intentional and unconscious. The forms of collusion it reveals are sometimes conscious but more often are unspoken, merely taken for granted, part of the collective world view of gentleman banking. Muckraking attacks on high finance thus grappled with the problem of what to call the concatenation of influence they uncovered, how to make sense of it, and how to represent it. If it was not a conspiracy, what was it? The short answer is that it was the workings of the class interest of the moneyed elite, coupled with lax regulation, with all of it underpinned by a shared ideological outlook that made active, conscious conspiring unnecessary. But the language of class and ideology has usually been relegated to the fringes of American political life, as stigmatized as the talk of conspiracy. (Even Pak, for example, rarely identifies the exclusive social networks of the Morgans as part of class privilege.) As William Domhoff rightly notes in his exhaustive study of the way that America has historically been ruled by a small elite that, with the Occupy Movement, has recently come to be identified as "the 1%," there is no need for a conspiracy theory. The elite openly pursue their transparent goals of self-advancement, and it does not take a secret conspiracy of obscure plotters for them to be able to achieve this.[96] On the other hand, in the early decades of the twentieth century, in a situation with little accurate information on the workings of Wall Street, and in the absence of the analytical frameworks of sophisticated sociology, making sense of the invisible networks of high finance—figuring out whether Morgan was, like Shelgrim, the cunning spider at the center of the web—stretched to the limit the explanatory and representational models of the time.

Exhibit 243 and Other Diagrams

The tension between viewing power in terms of individual, secretive, intentional agency or seeing it as the result of an ideological collective structure is at its most extreme in a remarkable illustration that was included as an appendix to the Pujo Committee's report (fig. 5.1). The chart was submitted as Exhibit 243 and was one of a series of diagrams that provided a schematic representation of the links

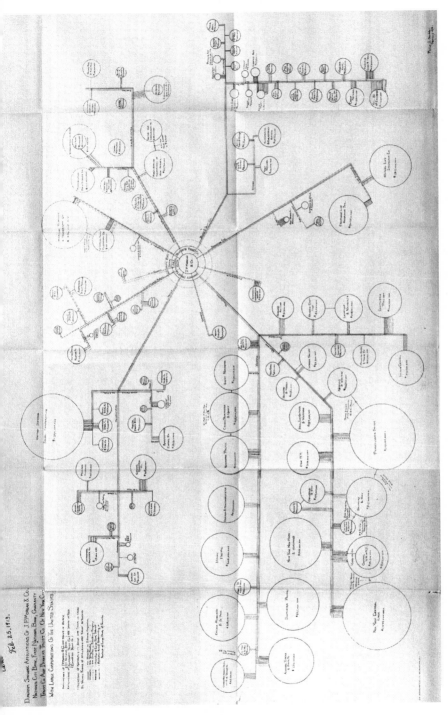

Figure 5.1 "Exhibit No. 243," Pujo Committee Report, 25 February 1913. The Pujo Committee was tasked with investigating the existence of a money trust that allegedly involved an illegitimate concentration of power in the hands of the nation's bankers. This illustration, prepared by the Committee, shows the affiliations of J. P. Morgan with other directors of banks and insurance firms. Image courtesy of FRASER [Federal Reserve Archival System for Economic Research, Federal Reserve Bank of St. Louis].

between the various bankers and institutions under investigation. The diagram was derived from a huge table that plotted all the interlocking directorships of the biggest financial firms with the largest industrial and transportation companies. The table and diagrams were prepared by Philip Scudder of the Investors' Agency, a New York firm of accountants and financial advisers. In his testimony to the committee, Scudder recounted how it took a team of twelve clerks, working day and night for three weeks solid, to gather the data and prepare the table and charts.[97] Exhibit 243 uses careful color-coding to show the various affiliations (black for those involving J. P. Morgan & Company, green for the National City Bank, and so on), along with different lines to indicate the precise nature of the relationship (e.g., a wiggly line for a voting trustee, dashes for a director in a subsidiary company). Finally, the size of the circles is in proportion to the capital worth of each firm.

It was important to Populist, Progressive, and Socialist critics alike to find a way of rendering visible the networks of power against which they were protesting. As Louis Brandeis put it: "Wealth expressed in figures gives a wholly inadequate picture of the allies' power. Their wealth is dynamic. It is wielded by geniuses in combination. It finds its proper expression in means of control. To comprehend the power of the allies we must try to *visualize the ramifications through which the forces operate*" (emphasis added).[98] Scudder no doubt would have received his instructions from Untermyer, but there is little in the historical record about where the latter derived the specifications for Exhibit 243. Although largely forgotten now, the diagram is fascinating, because it draws on a variety of different and quite contradictory representational traditions to create what is arguably one of the first attempts to provide a graphical mapping of the entire landscape of American financial capitalism.

We might begin by noting that the diagram has a family resemblance to the many satirical cartoons of the era, which picture corporations as octopuses. With its depiction of Morgan as the central financial intelligence, connected by numerous appendages to outlying parts of the national economy, Exhibit 243 resembles a structural circuit diagram of a cephalopod. Like the railroad map in *The Octopus*, the schematic conjures up the specter of a monster with flailing tentacles. The chart also recalls muckraking cartoons that depicted Morgan as a spider at the center of the web of "flim flam finance," trying to lure the public to their doom (see figure 3.4). The muckraking cartoons of the era and the Pujo diagrams share a desire to see a totality that is more than the sum of its parts, to visualize a coordinated pattern beneath the surface detail, and, above all else, to identify the individual—or at any rate, the individual firm—at the center of the web.

Unlike the satirical cartoons, however, the Pujo diagrams unsurprisingly eschew any direct personification or anthropomorphism, relying on corporate names, numbers, and color-coded lines to make their argument. Yet, as illustrations, they are not entirely mechanical and impersonal; they are painstakingly hand drawn, equally works of art as charts of accountancy.[99]

As much as the diagrams are geometric abstractions of anthropomorphic octopuses or spiders, they also draw their visual rhetoric from the corporate organizational charts that were pioneered by the engineer Daniel McCallum for the New York and Erie Railroad in the 1850s.[100] In McCallum's seminal drawing, the unprecedented organizational complexity of a large corporation was visualized as a series of branch and trunk lines, much like the ramifying structure of the railroad itself (fig. 5.2). What is striking, however, is that the more familiar pyramidal shape in twentieth-century organizational charts is here inverted: the managers are at the bottom, with the lowliest and remotest parts of the New York and Erie Railroad at the top. McCallum's chart is even more intriguing because its visual metaphor is organic, rather than machinic; it resembles a natural-history drawing of a fern or the display of a peacock's feathers (both favored decorational motifs in Victorian America), rather than an engineering drawing. Its schematic logic also draws on the much older visual trope of the family tree, which was beginning to be used in more systematic ways in the mid-nineteenth century, such as the one-time railroad lawyer Lewis Henry Morgan's schematic diagrams of comparative kinship structures derived from his study of Native Americans.[101]

Ironically, the Pujo Committee charts, which were designed to show the conspiratorial complicity of the corporate giants, drew on the very modes of organizational rationality that Chandler and Robert Wiebe argue contributed to the rise of corporations.[102] This irony is understandable if we remember that Untermyer was trying to make a case for a money trust that was less fevered than the Populist accusations, which not only had led to the establishment of the Pujo Committee, but were in danger of getting the investigation sunk before it could even begin. It must also be remembered that both Untermyer and Brandeis, before they turned to the antimonopoly cause, had made their fortunes as lawyers undertaking corporate reorganizations, particularly of railroads. It was, I want to suggest, precisely their training in the organizational efficiency of the railroads that allowed them to visualize financial corruption as a *system*. Exhibit 243 thus reveals insider dealing not as an occasional and incidental corruption of proper business, but as a structural component of it, part of a complete ecosystem.[103]

The Pujo diagrams have few direct antecedents, but they do share features with two other early twentieth-century visualizations of corporate interlocks.

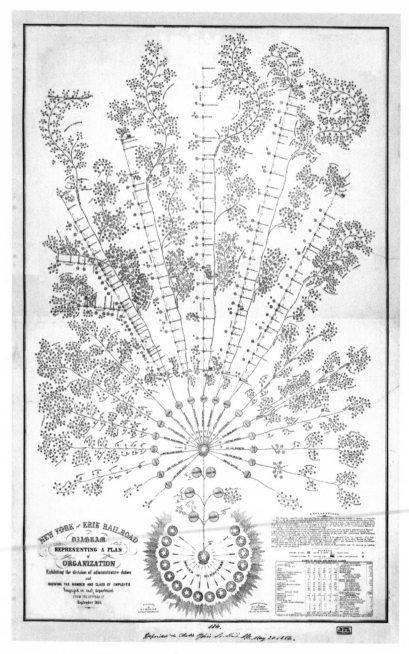

Figure 5.2 "Representation of a Plan of Organization," New York and Erie Railroad (1855).
Daniel McCallum's drawing of the organizational structure of the New York and Erie
Railroad in the 1850s is considered to be one of the forerunners of modern corporate
organizational charts. Geography and Map Division, Library of Congress.

Historians of social network analysis have identified the young British Fabian writer, John Atkinson Hobson, as the creator of one of the first visual depictions of corporate interlocks. Having gone to South Africa to report on the Boer War, Hobson was alarmed to discover that the jingoistic promotion of the war was being orchestrated by what he believed to be a conspiracy of newspapers in the control of financiers—and it was the financiers who were cynically promoting military intervention by the British, in order to provide themselves with protection for their business activities that they had no wish to pay for directly themselves. Hobson argued that there was a cabal of corporate and financial interests that were controlling events and, therefore, that the patriotic story of imperial conquest was just a smoke screen. Hobson also insisted that, apart from Cecil Rhodes, most of the significant financial players were Jewish.[104] Hobson's work on the supposed secret economic truths behind the fiction of imperialism influenced Lenin, and historians such as Niall Ferguson have lined up to dismiss Hobson's work as conspiracy-minded antisemitism.[105] In the revised edition of his *Evolution of Modern Capitalism*, however, published in 1906, Hobson began to develop a less ad hominem and more structural analysis of the relationship between German-Jewish financial interests, South African corporations, and the process of imperialism.[106] Like the Pujo Committee, Hobson was grappling with the problem of how to visualize financial capitalism at the moment of its dizzying global expansion. A similar convergence of a personal-conspiratorial and an impersonal-structural perspective can be seen in the diagram accompanying Hobson's text (fig. 5.3). Like the Pujo charts, it encapsulates the contradictory impulses of mapping structure and plotting conspiratorial agency.

In contrast, John Moody, the American financial analyst and founder of the bond-rating agency that still bears his name, produced diagrams of corporate interlocks around the turn of the twentieth century that were designed not to condemn the conspiracy of capitalism, but to celebrate the emergence of the trusts and corporate combinations as an inevitable stage in economic evolution (fig. 5.4). For Moody—as it was for Morgan—the problem of competition was to be solved through cooperation. "The modern trust," Moody asserts, "is the natural outcome or evolution of society conditions and ethical standards which are recognized and established among men today as being necessary elements in the development of civilization."[107] The charts are not mere illustrations, but are central to Moody's overall project of trying to understand and represent industrial combinations that have grown too big to be grasped by mere mortals.

Moody acknowledges that, because of the lack of publicly available documentation and the interconnectedness of the entity, "it is not possible to more than

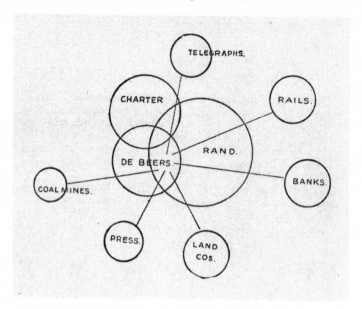

Figure 5.3 John A. Hobson, *The Evolution of Modern Capitalism: A Study of Machine Production*, 2nd ed. (London: Walter Scott, 1906), 272. The Socialist John Hobson adapted his original antisemitic interpretation of the Jewish mining interests in South Africa into a more schematic diagram of the interlocking vested interests propping up British imperialism. Harvard College Library.

attempt an approximate estimate of the entire Standard Oil industrial, financial, and commercial interests of the nation, as their ramifications are so varied and extensive that a clear line of demarcation could not be drawn which would absolutely distinguish the interests which are more or less dominated by them, from those which are not." Nonetheless, "the chart which we publish . . . gives a fairly accurate 'bird's eye view' of the immensity of their influence and importance as the leading factors in American financial and industrial affairs."[108] From this imaginary bird's-eye perspective, Moody is convinced that, beneath the melodramatic surface story of corporate skirmishes, the two sides constitute a single, vast entity: "It should not be supposed, however, that these two great groups of capitalists and financiers are in any real sense rivals or competitors for power, or that such a thing as 'war' exists between them. For, as a matter of fact, they are not only friendly, but they are allied to each other by many close ties, and it would probably require only a little stretch of the imagination to describe them as a single great Rockefeller-Morgan group."[109]

Whereas the Pujo Committee saw the "ramifications" of the banking-industrial complex as something akin to a conspiracy, Moody—like Presley in *The*

Octopus—marveled at the quasi-divine, sublime order that emerged beneath the mundane intrigue and infighting. He paints a picture of a vast corporate being whose life force circulates throughout the nation, and wasteful competition between rival firms is replaced by a new cooperative and symbiotic system:

> Therefore, viewed as a whole, we find the dominating influences in the Trusts to be made up of an intricate network of large and small groups of capitalists, many allied to one another by ties of more or less importance, but all being appendages to or parts of the greater groups, which are themselves dependent on and allied with the two mammoth or Rockefeller and Morgan groups. These two mammoth groups jointly (for, as pointed out, they really may be regarded as one) constitute the heart of the business and commercial life of the nation, the others all being the arteries which permeate in a thousand ways our whole national life, making their influence

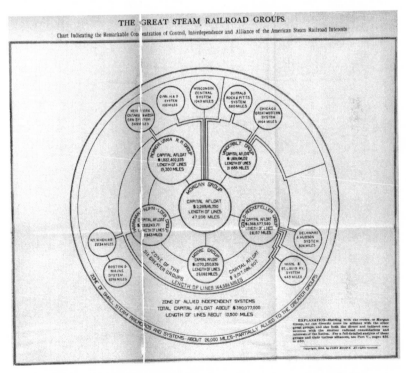

Figure 5.4 John Moody, "The Great Steam Railroad Groups," *Truth about the Trusts: A Description and Analysis of the American Trust Movement* (New York: Moody, 1904), insert after p. 432. The business analyst and statistician John Moody saw the development of industrial and transport conglomerations as the next inevitable step of economic evolution and attempted to portray visually the interlocking corporate interests as an orderly system. Harvard College Library.

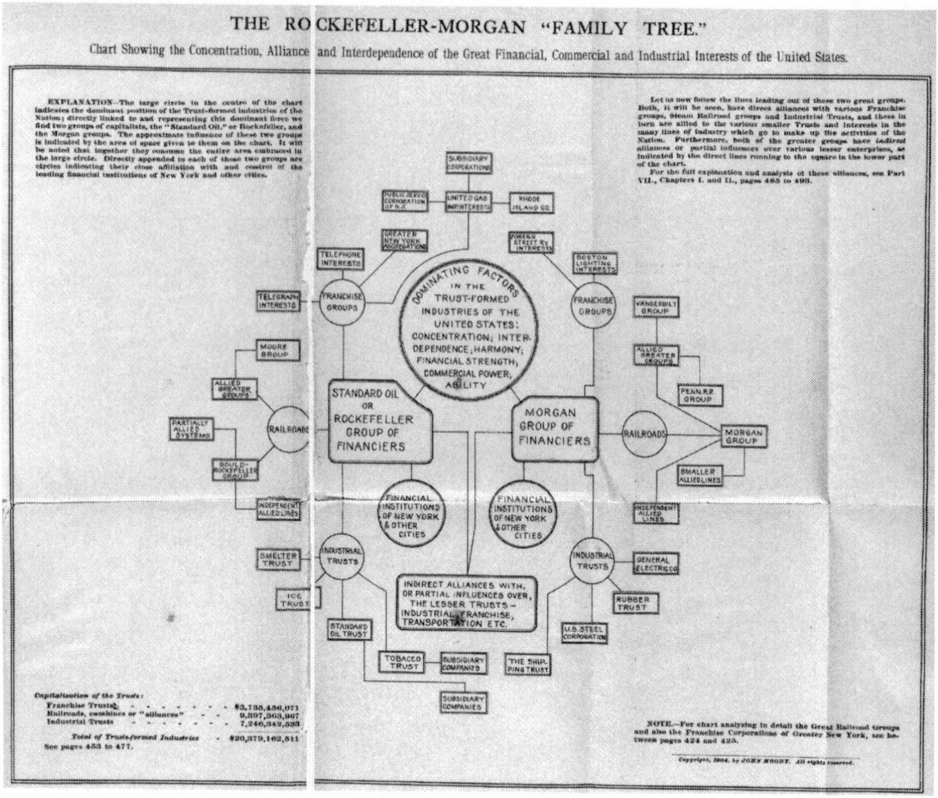

THE ROCKEFELLER-MORGAN "FAMILY TREE."

Chart Showing the Concentration, Alliance and Interdependence of the Great Financial, Commercial and Industrial Interests of the United States.

Figure 5.5 From John Moody, "The Rockefeller-Morgan 'Family Tree,'" *Truth about the Trusts: A Description and Analysis of the American Trust Movement* (New York: Moody, 1904), insert after p. viii. Where muckraking critics saw backstabbing competition or dubious collusion between Rockefeller's industrial concerns and Morgan's financial operations, Moody viewed them as a more harmonious "family tree." Harvard College Library.

felt in every home and hamlet, yet all connected with and dependent on this great central source, the influence and policy of which dominates them all.[110]

Moody's written description of the Rockefeller-Morgan group is couched in familiar biological terms (dating back to at least the Physiocrats) of a central heart supplying the economic life force to the whole body of industrial America. Although Moody's image is labeled a "family tree," the picture draws more from the visual rhetoric of machine diagrams than the organic language of biological or hereditary models (fig. 5.5). If the Pujo Committee perceived conspiratorial complicity and crushing size, Moody instead saw "interdependence, harmony, financial strength, commercial power, [and] ability." However, both the Pujo Committee and Moody were animated by a desire to create a panoramic overview of industrial capitalism as a coordinated *system*, albeit with very different intents. For the Pujo Committee, as for Hobson, what began to emerge from the diagrams was a picture of a system that acted like a conspiracy, or, at the very least, produced the kinds of effects *as if* there had been a deliberate plot.[111]

Conclusion: System as Conspiracy

Leaving aside the question of accuracy, the Moody and the Pujo diagrams presented an abstracted panorama of the entire corporate economy of the United States in a way that had not really been done before. Although they reached wildly different conclusions, they both signaled a significant departure from earlier ways of conceiving of the power structure of large organizations—and even the entire economy—as hierarchical. That traditional approach was embodied most clearly in some of the very few visual representations of power structures that were made before twentieth-century corporate organizational charts appeared, such as schematic diagrams from the eighteenth century depicting the Catholic Church, or illustrations from the 1790s revealing the supposed hidden channels of power of secret societies, such as the United Irishmen or the Bavarian Illuminati.[112] Like the Moody diagrams, the Pujo charts represent the financial-industrial complex not as a pyramid in which authority flows down from above, or as a simple web in which control radiates outward from the center, or even as a hub-and-spoke conspiracy, but as a circuit of flows in which power is dispersed throughout the entire, interconnected system.

In *Other People's Money*, Brandeis attempted to clarify what the Pujo Committee had uncovered. "A single example," he claimed, "will illustrate the vicious circle of control—the endless chain—through which our financial oligarchy now operates."[113] This is not the usual hierarchical chain of command favored by conspiracist denunciations of secret societies like the Illuminati. Instead, Brandeis describes an interwoven pattern of control in which, like poststructuralist theories of signification, the ultimate source of power and meaning is ultimately deferred: "The chain is indeed endless; for each controlled corporation is entwined with many others."[114] Viewed in isolation, Exhibit 243 might seem to show J. P. Morgan & Company as the controlling spider at the center of the web, or the central, octopus-like intelligence controlling the economy through its tentacles. It is important to note, however, that this was just one of several visualizations produced by Scudder from the master table of interlocking directorships, each viewing the network of relationships through a different filter. The individual Pujo diagrams edge toward identifying the commanding conspirator at the heart

of system, but, viewed as an entirety, they create a picture of power that is uncannily decentralized and cannot be easily put together into one overarching
figure. On the one hand, the individual diagrams present a level of detail that
is highly personalized: they name names and document in microscopic detail
the actual connections between particular capitalists. On the other hand, taken
together, they constitute an abstract and impersonal representation of the dense
and messy entanglement of familial, social, and financial ties.

In this regard, the Pujo charts have much in common with some recent works
of art that attempt to provide a visualization of financial capitalism. For example,
we can see a similar fusion of the abstract and the personal in the work of the
conceptual artist Mark Lombardi, who produced a series of elaborate drawings
in the 1980s and 1990s that provided a "cognitive mapping" of the conspiratorial
connections that emerged from his research into the financial and political scandals of the period. Lombardi drew the diagrams in order to make some sense
out of the 12,000 filing cards he had assembled in the course of his research.[115]
Looked at in one way, these drawings are not so different from the countless flow-
charts of conspiratorial association that clutter up the Internet. If we stand back
from Lombardi's drawings, however, what we see are works of sublime beauty,
geometric abstractions that resemble modern-day constellations. In a similar
fashion, there is the work of the French artist duo, Bureau d'Études, who produce "cartographies of contemporary political, social, and economic systems,"
with the aim of "revealing what normally remains invisible and contextualizing
apparently separate elements within a bigger whole."[116] Finally, *Griftopia*, William
Powhida's 2011 reworking of Lombardi's drawings, takes us back closer to the
muckraking spirit of the Pujo Committee's Exhibit 243, where all roads seem to
lead ultimately to Morgan, or, in Powhida's case, to Alan Greenspan.[117]

Viewed through the prism of these modern conceptual artists, we can see how
the Pujo diagrams not only combine conspiratorial agency and impersonal system, but represent system *as* conspiracy. They endow impersonal structures with
personal agency, in a similar way to the Gilded Age cartoons that personify financial corruption as a larger-than-life conspiracy. This may well still mean that they
ultimately fail to account for the structural processes at work, but they cannot be
dismissed as simple and naive conspiracy theories. Conspiracy theory has usually
been seen as the polar opposite of systems theory, a throwback to a humanist and
melodramatic fantasy of individual villainy as the hidden cause behind troubling
developments in society. Timothy Melley, however, in his account of the recurrent
"agency panic" in post–World War II American literature and culture, argues that
there is a "postmodern transference" at work.[118] Paranoically fearful of the loss

of individual agency through the controlling influence of vast organizations, networks, technologies, or systems, writers repeatedly imagine that those abstract and impersonal structures act *as if* they have the malign will of a conspiring individual. A faith in individual agency is thus ironically preserved by imaginatively transferring it onto a larger entity. The abstract structure is imbued with a sense of uncanny, almost supernatural agency, a ghost within the machinery of modernity. Melley suggests that this process is peculiar to the late twentieth century and is, at heart, a panicked reaction to the increasing complexity and interdependence of American life in the era of corporate globalization. Fredric Jameson makes a similar diagnosis, claiming that "conspiracy theory is the poor person's cognitive mapping in the postmodern age." It is, Jameson asserts, a "degraded attempt—through the figuration of advanced technology—to think the impossible totality of the contemporary world system."[119] Jameson reads conspiracy theory not as a mere symptom of a delusional mindset, but as an *allegory*, at the level of form rather than content, of the complex social and economic changes of globalization that cannot be understood in any straightforward way.

It is arguable that a similar rhetorical process was at work in the first Gilded Age, as it is in the current Gilded Age, for similar reasons. The sudden emergence of enormous corporate and financial entanglements in the late nineteenth century likewise undermined traditional ways of understanding personal and historical causation, not least because of the increasingly vast disparities of wealth. In his study of the breakdown of traditional societies in the nineteenth century, Robert Wiebe famously noted: "As men ranged farther and farther from their communities, they tried desperately to understand the larger world in terms of their small, familiar environment. They tried, in other words, to impose the known upon the unknown, to master an impersonal world through the customs of a personal society."[120] For Wiebe, though, as for Hofstadter and Lippmann, those who turned to older and more-personal ways of understanding the world— of which conspiracy theories are a prime example—were rural folk who failed to comprehend the changes that urbanizing modernity was bringing. Instead, we might follow Melley's insight: many writers turn to the rhetoric of conspiracy theory in order to account for the operation of the invisible hand of the market, because a more properly sociological analysis, in terms of class or ideology or political economy, is viewed with suspicion in the American scene. That was as true for the muckraking era as it is for our own.

Epilogue

There are times when reading the market trends and market psychology using specific metrics seems as effective as Roman soothsayers reading entrails. However, if you carefully pick the indicators, understand their limitations and use them in tandem, you will be much better positioned to spot the market's mood and adjust for what that mood means for your positions.

Jason Van Bergen, "How to Read the Market's
Psychological State," Investopedia

Brad and his team were building a mental picture of the financial markets after the crisis. The market was now a pure abstraction. It called to mind no obvious picture to replace the old one that people still carried around in their heads. The same old ticker tape ran across the bottom of the television screens—even though it represented only a tiny fraction of the actual trading. Market experts still reported from the floor of the New York Stock Exchange, even though trading no longer happened there.

Michael Lewis, Flash Boys: Cracking the Money Code *(2014)*

In the bull market leading up to the dotcom crash of 2000 and in the years since the global financial crash of 2007, amateur trading on the stock market has reached unprecedented levels.[1] This army of do-it-yourself day traders are, for the most part, self-trained, often relying on websites, blogs, and the rolling financial advice dished out on television channels such as CNBC. Despite the many changes in the technology and the media of finance over the course of the last century, instructions for the nonexpert on how to "read the market" tend merely to echo the fledgling financial advice from the (first) Gilded Age. The recommendation is still to carefully watch the prices coming over the ticker tape—now digital and symbolic, rather than analog and literal—in order to tune into the mind of the market and perceive the hidden patterns that are invisible to the untrained eye:

> Learn to follow the market's price action and read the signals it gives. This can become a strict discipline in itself and the result will be greater confidence that a trade is or is not working. . . . If we are watching a high, low, or opening price as a pivot point, we are watching to see whether there is any impulsive price action as the market approaches the point or moves further away from it. What is "impulsive action?" I like to call it a "whoosh." The market moves rapidly as if just coming to life for the first time. It is usually a series of ticks in one direction without a tick in the opposite direction. The market is tipping its hand.[2]

Despite most of these forms of technical analysis and chart reading having been shown by academic financial economists to be based on flawed statistical analyses, many of the old nostrums of tape reading continued to be trotted out as fact; indeed, in some cases the authors explicitly reference favorites from the turn of the twentieth century, such as Charles Dow and Richard Wyckoff.[3]

As with the vernacular financial advice explored in this book, the twenty-first-century equivalents insist that market reading involves intense discipline and watching. "By making it a habit to read the market every day, five days a week," one website advises, "you'll be able to make a good call on its health." The writer warns that "the market's health and direction could alter in the space of 24 hours, which is why you should remain vigilant at all times. If you take your eye off the market, you may miss out on the opportunity of getting in when a new uptrend has been established."[4] Yet the approach to be adopted is not simply becoming a hypervigilant and hyperrational watcher of the market's health, like a financial physician who is permanently on call. As we saw in the advice manuals for the lay investor from the turn of the twentieth century, market reading is still considered more an art than a science, more mystique than technique.[5] One blog notes that "regarding tape reading, it truly requires the 'gift of touch.'"[6] It is necessary to cultivate a peculiar habit of being in which the self is merged with the fluidities of the market in a quasi-mystical fashion: one website recommends "creating the perfect mindset that can handle unusual and uncertain liquid trading environments." Successful trading, according to this and other guides, involves moving beyond rational knowledge: "[It] is not about knowing. Trading is about acting on situations, patterns, and signals that you are familiar with. This all comes from experience, proper training, and something that you and I call *in-tuition*."[7] The appeal of such advice literature remains resolutely populist, selling the promise that the investor of small means can learn the tricks required to be able to compete with the big players, the insiders. One blog counsels that "it pays to watch what the big players are doing," and it is tape reading that can level the playing field: "Price and volume charts can help you to see what the professional investors are doing, allowing you the opportunity to follow in the large investors' footsteps."[8]

Another striking similarity between these autodidactic homilies and their forerunners from a century ago is the way in which they animate and personify the market, often as a divine being whose mood and intentions can be augured by its adepts. For those with the strict discipline to follow its signs, it is possible to see how the "market moves rapidly as if just coming to life for the first time," and, for those able to interpret this, the market is "tipping its hand." Electronic trading may now be completely anonymous, but the market that is created by this trading is considered to be a person.[9] One website giving advice on "How To Read The Market's Psychological State," for example, encourages its readers that, "if you carefully pick the indicators, understand their limitations and use them in tandem, you will be much better positioned to spot the market's mood." We have also become accustomed to hearing bankers, economists, and other sooth-sayers reading the entrails of financial data to interpret the whims and moods of the market god. This deity is usually portrayed as far more inscrutable than the more homely creature imagined by the day-trading gurus, sometimes seeming like a wrathful god, and at others as a "skittish" creature that might easily be spooked: "One reason the market acted so skittishly Monday is that it simply can't wait six weeks or so before the government is ready to start buying the first $250 billion worth of toxic securities from troubled firms. In normal times, this would seem blazingly fast. In these compressed times, it seems terribly slow. The markets want to know—right now—whether the bailout plan will work."[10] At times, it comes to seem as if the projected authority of the financial markets—simultaneously reified and personified, made to seem both impersonal and highly idiosyncratic—is dictating events, here hurrying the U.S. government into a huge bailout for troubled banks, or there demanding a hasty sacrifice from the Greek people in order to appease the inscrutable gods of finance.[11]

The techniques, rhetoric, and ideology of popular modes of "reading the market" have remained remarkably consistent across a century. Yet there are signif-icant differences. Most importantly, the very notion of "the market" has become a highly charged term. It no longer refers simply to a particular stock exchange, or even to the stock market in general. Instead, it is the preferred term of neoliberalism, which has fetishized the idea of an omnipotent, omniscient, ubiquitous market that is wiser than any individual, wiser, even, than any collective political consideration: the market knows best.[12] Second, at the turn of the twenty-first century, the lives of a much greater percentage of ordinary Americans have become caught up in the dramas of finance than those at the turn of the twentieth century: more than half the nation is invested in the stock market in some form (usually through their retirement pensions), while many more in the lead-up to the subprime mortgage crisis came to think of their homes as fungible investments.[13] Indeed, with the massive public bailouts of banks and corporations, and the ensuing Great Recession, there are few whose everyday lives have not been affected by the opaque world of global finance. Third, the scale and significance of finance has increased dramatically. After a high point of 4 percent in the 1920s, by 1940, only 2 percent of the overall gross domestic product came from finance; by 2000, it was 8 percent. These figures are more extreme if we consider the share of business profits. In the 1950s and 1960s, between 10 and 20 percent of total profits in the U.S. economy came from the financial sector, but by 2001, 40 percent of total profits originated there.[14]

As became clear in the wake of the 2007 crash, the world of shadow banking has grown to a scale that is hard to comprehend. In the eyes of many commentators, it is a crazed, self-replicating machine that has become uncoupled from the so-called real economy. By 2007, the international financial system was trading derivatives valued at one quadrillion dollars per year. This is ten times the total worth, adjusted for inflation, of all products made by the world's manufacturing industries over the last century.[15] Farmers in the late nineteenth century were mystified by how futures contracts for grain that were traded on the Chicago Board of Trade far exceeded the amount of wheat actually grown, but the scale and secrecy surrounding derivatives contracts now makes their fears about "wind wheat" seem quaint. (The popular political response to the 2007 crash and subsequent sovereign debt crisis at times contained direct echoes of the late nineteenth century, however, with calls to outlaw speculative practices such as short selling.[16]) The global financial system has now reached a level of abstraction and opacity that is hard to comprehend, let alone regulate. The market increasingly consists of complex mathematical formulas, embedded in computer code, caroming around the world at close to the speed of light. The development of algorithmic trading in general, and high-frequency trading (HFT) in particular, has opened up the specter of machines trading with other machines at a speed that mere humans are incapable of following or controlling.[17] In the "flash crash" of 6

May 2010, 9 percent of the value of the Dow Jones was wiped off within minutes as an exponential chain reaction of machine-generated selling caused the market to crash, only for it to rebound equally rapidly and inexplicably. As Michael Lewis explains in *Flash Boys: Cracking the Money Code*, trades are now conducted at a speed measured in nanoseconds (one-billionth of a second), far beyond the capability of humans—and even the investigatory powers of regulators—to comprehend. Lewis describes how members of the banking team he focuses on "were building a mental picture of the financial markets after the crisis": "The market was now a pure abstraction. It called to mind no obvious picture to replace the old one that people still carried around in their heads. The same old ticker tape ran across the bottom of the television screens—even though it represented only a tiny fraction of the actual trading. Market experts still reported from the floor of the New York Stock Exchange, even though trading no longer happened there."[18] It is arguable, however, that technological changes have always outstripped the ability of the popular imagination to make sense of the market, and the latest developments are not, in this regard, any different from previous ones. It has always been the case that speed gains you an advantage in the market. Despite the mantra of the efficient market hypothesis—that the market already knows any relevant information in advance and factors it into the current price—insiders have habitually attempted to rig the market in their favor. The stock exchange has never been the free, transparent, perfectly functioning market that its neoliberal champions have claimed.[19]

The idea that the market has reached a level of "pure abstraction" has now become commonplace. While there is some truth to this observation, it ignores the way in which the market—even a market created by high-frequency trading—continues to be depicted in popular rhetoric as an animal, person, god, or force of nature. The impersonal market, as we have seen in this volume, is repeatedly made intelligible by concretizing its abstractions. As Paul Crosthwaite argues, though, the effect of these anthropomorphic figurations is "paradoxically affirmative, because they imply that these autonomous and largely unregulated systems [of HFT], with the potential to generate devastating financial convulsions, should be treated not merely as lying outside the scope of human deliberation and intervention, but as 'natural' and unchangeable facts of life."[20] Likewise, presenting the stock market as a self-contained and self-regulating ecosystem—albeit one prone to cataclysmic natural disasters—fails to recognize the crucial role of the state in creating, sustaining, and subsidizing the free market.

When popular accounts of finance are not framed in terms of abstraction or anthropomorphization, they tend to focus on the individual human dramas of greed, fear, and contagion as ways of explaining the chaotic movements of the market. Rationales for the crash of 2007 thus tend to rely on a handful of basic narratives, which, at their heart, either blame the system or blame individuals. On the one hand, there are accounts that speak in terms of systems and processes: it was a "black swan" event that could not have been predicted, or it was the result of the structural flaws in the banking system that should have been foreseen. Other explanations point the finger at particular people or human characteristics: it was the recklessness of individual bankers, or the inevitable "madness of crowds," or the greed of the American public in wanting to live beyond their means. As in the first Gilded Age, however, some of the most compelling popular ways of making sense of the market in general, and financial crashes in particular, work by making the mystifying abstractions concrete and personal. Drawing on images and narratives whose pedigree dates back to the turn of the twentieth century, these vernacular modes of reading the market have never been so necessary, nor so fraught.

Introduction

1. Frank Norris, *The Pit: A Story of Chicago* (New York: Doubleday, 1903), 34. Subsequent references to this edition will be included in parentheses in the body of the text.

2. The opera takes place at the Auditorium Theater, which was built in 1889 by the architectural firm of Adler and Sullivan. As chapter 3 discusses in more detail, Sullivan also designed a significant number of financial buildings, including the Chicago Stock Exchange building (1894). As David Zimmerman observes in *Panic! Markets, Crises, and Crowds in American Fiction* (Chapel Hill: University of North Carolina Press, 2006), 123–49, by making comparisons with the scene at the opera, the novel draws attention to the theatricality of the trading pit at the Chicago Board of Trade.

3. Francis A. Walker and Henry Adams, "The Legal-Tender Act," in Charles F. Adams and Henry Adams, *Chapters of Erie and Other Essays* (1871; reprint, New York: Henry Holt, 1886), 316.

4. For details on the game of "Pit," see the leaflet accompanying the centenary facsimile edition, as well as Steve Fraser, *Every Man a Speculator: A History of Wall Street in American Life* (New York: HarperCollins, 2005), 247–48.

5. William Dean Howells, *The Rise of Silas Lapham* (Boston: Ticknor, 1885), 87; and Henry Clews, *Fifty Years in Wall Street* (1908; reprint, New York: John Wiley, 2006), 159.

6. Clear data on the level of popular participation in stock markets during this period is thin. Cedric B. Cowing, in *Populists, Plungers, and Progressives: A Social History of Stock and Commodity Speculation, 1890–1936* (Princeton, NJ: Princeton University Press, 1965), suggests that there were only 500,000 shareholders on the eve of World War I, while H. T. Warshow ("The Distribution of Corporate Ownership in the United States," *Quarterly Journal of Economics* 39 [1924]: 15–38) states that stock owning tripled between 1900 and 1922, from 5 percent of the population to 12 percent. See also Thomas R. Navin and Marian V. Sears, "The Rise of a Market for Industrial Securities, 1887–1902," *Business History Review* 29 (1955): 105–38. For a good summary of the varying evidence, see Julia C. Ott, *When Wall Street Met Main Street: The Quest for an Investors' Democracy* (Cambridge, MA: Harvard University Press, 2011), 2. There is also a growing body of scholarly literature on the question of whether the American securities market was comparatively underdeveloped in this period; for a summary of the debates, see Mary O'Sullivan, "The Expansion of the U.S. Stock Market, 1885–1930: Historical Facts and Theoretical Fashions," *Enterprise and Society* 8 (2007): 489–542.

7. On the changing historical significance of finance to the U.S. economy, see Greta Krippner, *Capitalizing on Crisis: The Political Origins of the Rise of Finance* (Cambridge, MA: Harvard University Press, 2011), 27–57.

8. On Liberty Bonds and the NYSE's public relations campaign, see Ott, *When Wall Street Met Main Street*. For the post–World War II story, see Janice M. Traflet, *A Nation of Small Shareholders: Marketing Wall Street after World War II* (Baltimore: Johns Hopkins University Press, 2013); and Edwin J. Perkins, *Wall Street to Main Street: Charles Merrill and Middle-Class Investors* (Cambridge: Cambridge University Press, 1999).

9. On the importance of regional exchanges, the New York Curb Exchange, and over-the-counter (OTC) trading in the late nineteenth century, see O'Sullivan, "Expansion of the U.S. Stock Market."

10. On bucket shops, see David Hochfelder, "'Where the Common People Could Speculate': The Ticker, Bucket Shops, and the Origins of Popular Participation in Financial Markets, 1880–1920," *Journal of American History* 93 (2006), 335–58; the revised version in Hochfelder, *The Telegraph in America, 1832–1920* (Baltimore: Johns Hopkins University Press, 2012), 101–37; and Jonathan Ira Levy, "Contemplating Delivery: Futures Trading and the Problem of Commodity Exchange in the United States, 1875–1905," *American Historical Review* 111 (2006): 307–35.

11. Hochfelder, *Telegraph in America*, 127.

12. John Hill, *Gold Bricks of Speculation* (Chicago: Lincoln Book Concern, 1904), 93.

13. On the redrawing of the boundary between investment, speculation, and gambling, see Ann Fabian, *Card Sharps, Dream Books, and Bucket Shops: Gambling in Nineteenth-Century America* (Ithaca, NY: Cornell University Press, 1990); Marieke de Goede, *Virtue, Fortune, and Faith: A Genealogy of Finance* (Minneapolis: University of Minnesota Press, 2005), 47–86; and Urs Stäheli, *Spectacular Speculation: Thrills, the Economy, and Popular Discourse*, trans. Eric Savoth (Stanford, CA: Stanford University Press, 2013), 19–92.

14. De Goede, *Virtue, Fortune, and Faith*, 19, 17.

15. Mary Poovey, *Genres of the Credit Economy: Mediating Value in Eighteenth- and Nineteenth-Century Britain* (Chicago: University of Chicago Press, 2008).

16. Andrew Milner, *Locating Science Fiction* (Liverpool, UK: Liverpool University Press, 2012), chapter 2, discussing Raymond Williams, *The Long Revolution* (London: Chatto & Windus, 1961).

17. My use of the term "vernacular financial advice" draws on but also differs from Alex Preda's account of a "popular 'science of the financial markets'" in *Framing Finance: The Boundaries of Markets and Modern Capitalism* (Chicago: University of Chicago Press, 2009). Preda documents how, in the eighteenth century, financial speculation was deemed to be outside the realm of rational calculation and knowability and, therefore, not part of the scope of Enlightenment scientific enquiry. Once socially respectable stockbrokers began to achieve a public voice in the nineteenth century (most noticeably in Britain and France in the middle part of the century), however, they were able to reposition financial knowledge as a form of scientific enquiry akin to the physical sciences (and here Preda draws on Philip Mirowski's influential analysis of the distorting use of mechanical metaphors in economic theory). Although Preda's exploration of the longer struggle for the legitimacy of financial knowledge is useful, *Reading the Market* investigates forms of financial writing (in both fictional and nonfictional genres) that were aimed at a more popular audience than the "self-styled 'scientific' manuals" that Preda concentrates on. For a more

detailed discussion of the possibility of a history of vernacular financial science, see Preda, "Informative Prices, Rational Investors: The Emergence of the Random Walk Hypothesis and the Nineteenth-Century 'Science of Financial Investments,'" *History of Political Economy* 36 (2004): 351–86; Franck Jovanovic, "Was There a 'Vernacular' Science of Financial Markets in France During the Late Nineteenth Century? A Comment on Preda's 'Informative Prices, Rational Investors,'" *History of Political Economy* 38 (2006): 531–45; and Preda, "Tracing the Boundaries between Vernacular Science and Academic Theories: A Reply to Franck Jovanovic," *History of Political Economy* 38 (2006): 547–54.

18. Lendol Calder, "Spending and Saving," in *The Oxford Handbook of the History of Consumption*, ed. Frank Trentmann (Oxford: Oxford University Press, 2012), 349.

19. John F. Kasson, *Rudeness and Civility: Manners in Nineteenth-Century Urban America* (New York: Hill & Wang, 1990), 77.

20. Arjun Appadurai coins the term "financescape" in "Disjuncture and Difference in the Global Cultural Economy," *Public Culture* 2 (1990): 1–24.

21. David Henkin, *City Reading: Written Words and Public Spaces in Antebellum New York* (New York: Columbia University Press, 1998), 137–66.

22. On the epistemological and social problems caused by the counterfeiting of banknotes, see Stephen Mihm, *A Nation of Counterfeiters: Capitalists, Con Men, and the Making of the United States* (Cambridge, MA: Harvard University Press, 2007).

23. Zimmerman, *Panic!*, 25.

24. Edward Tailer's diaries are held at the New-York Historical Society. They are discussed in Henkin, *City Reading*, 130–33; and Preda, *Framing Finance*, 133–35, 224–33.

25. Donald Mackenzie, *An Engine, Not a Camera: How Financial Models Shape Markets* (Cambridge, MA: MIT Press, 2006).

26. See Judith Butler, "Performative Agency," *Journal of Cultural Economy* 3 (2010): 147–61. The science and technology studies (STS) approach to performativity, epitomized by Michel Callon and Donald MacKenzie, has come under fire recently. On the one hand, political economists, such as Karel Williams and Philip Mirowski, have argued that the STS approach merely leads to attempts to produce more-accurate, technical models that confirm the myth of *Homo economicus*, rather than a broader investigation of the social and political dominance of particular narratives about financialization that are embedded in the technical models. See, for example, Mirowski and Edward Nik-Kah, "Markets Made Flesh: Callon, Performativity, and the FCC Spectrum Auctions," in *Do Economists Make Markets? On the Performativity of Economics*, ed. Donald MacKenzie, Fabian Muniesa, and Lucia Siu (Princeton, NJ: Princeton University Press, 2007), 190–224.

27. For a discussion of Wall Street as a synecdoche for finance, see Fraser, *Every Man a Speculator*. Although, in the legislative inquiries and legal disputes with the bucket shops around the turn of the twentieth century, the NYSE was keen to distance itself from what it saw as less-reputable financial practices, in its nascent public relations campaign in the 1910s, it began to seem suitable to be identified in the public's mind as the center of finance. See also Steven H. Jaffe and Jessica Lautin, *Capital of Capital: Money, Banking, and Power in New York City* (New York: Columbia University Press, 2014).

28. Audrey Jaffe, *The Affective Life of the Average Man: The Victorian Novel and the Stock-Market Graph* (Columbus: Ohio State University Press, 2010), 15.

29. In *The Pit*'s variation on the real-life incident of Joseph Leitner's attempted corner in 1898, the invisible hand of the market trumps the once-mighty hand of the individual

speculator. In Norris's quasi-mystical accounting, the elemental forces of supply and demand are fuelled by the irrepressible fertility of the wheat itself. Yet *The Pit* also makes clear that the high prices for wheat are not purely the result of the iron laws of nature, but are artificially elevated by scheming traders. The novel thus fluctuates uneasily between portraying the market as a human construct and as a state of nature.

30. De Goede, *Virtue, Fortune and Faith*, xiii–xxvii.

31. Justin Fox, *The Myth of the Rational Market: A History of Risk, Reward, and Delusion on Wall Street* (New York: HarperBusiness, 2009).

32. On the self-referentiality of price data, as constructed by the EMH, see Paul Crosthwaite, *Speculative Investments: Finance, Feeling, and Representation in Contemporary Literature and Culture* (forthcoming).

33. Charles Dow, editorial, *Wall Street Journal*, 20 July 1901; reprinted in Samuel A. Nelson, *The ABC of Stock Speculation* (New York: Nelson, 1902), 44.

34. Randy Martin, *The Financialization of Daily Life* (Philadelphia: Temple University Press, 2002).

35. Jonathan Levy, *Freaks of Fortune: The Emerging World of Capitalism and Risk in America* (Cambridge, MA: Harvard University Press, 2012).

36. On the financial turn in recent historiography, see Noam Maggor's review essay, "David R. Farber, *Everybody Ought to Be Rich: The Life and Times of John J. Raskob, Capitalist*; and Susie Pak, *Gentlemen Bankers: The World of J. P. Morgan*," *Business History Review* 88 (2014): 187–94; and Jeffrey Sklansky, "Labor, Money, and the Financial Turn in the History of Capitalism," *Labor* 11 (2014): 23–46.

37. Jeffrey Sklansky, "The Elusive Sovereign: New Intellectual and Social Histories of Capitalism," *Modern Intellectual History* 9 (2012): 243.

38. For a polemical overview of the changing historical role of finance, see Per H. Hansen, "From Finance Capitalism to Financialization: A Cultural and Narrative Perspective on 150 Years of Financial History," *Enterprise and Society* (2014), doi:10.1093/es/khu047.

39. Richard White, *Railroaded: The Transcontinentals and the Making of Modern America* (New York: Norton, 2011).

40. As showcased in Martha Woodmansee and Mark Osteen, eds., *The New Economic Criticism: Studies at the Intersection of Literature and Economics* (London: Routledge, 2000), New Economic Criticism has investigated the commonalities between literature and economics as systems of symbolic representation and has made important contributions to the fields of literary, cultural, and historical studies. The key homological insight animating much of this work, however—that metaphors and money function as twin forms of the "general equivalent" of fungible exchange—has, at times, become merely an ahistorical truism that loses critical purchase on the varied moments of representational and/or financial crisis and is in danger of creating an uncomfortably close connection between poststructuralist theory and financialization itself. On the latter point, see, for example, Michael Tratner, "Derrida's Debt to Milton Friedman," *New Literary History* 34 (2004): 791–806; and Joshua Clover, "Value | Theory | Crisis," *PMLA* 127 (2012): 107–14.

41. One of the most compelling studies of cultural reactions to the dangerous volatility of value in nineteenth-century America is by Andrew Lawson, *Downwardly Mobile: The Changing Fortunes of American Realism* (New York: Oxford University Press, 2012). Joseph Vogl provides a useful summary of the historical stages of finance and the intellectual un-

derpinnings of neoliberalism in *The Specter of Capital* (Stanford, CA: Stanford University Press, 2014).

42. William James, *Pragmatism: A New Name for Some Old Ways of Thinking* (New York: Longmans, Green, 1907), 207–8. James Livingston, in *Pragmatism, Feminism, and Democracy: Rethinking the Politics of American History* (New York: Routledge, 2001), interprets this passage dialectically, suggesting that the dire situation of economic fluidity actually produced intellectual innovations that embraced the potential in that fluidity.

43. For a more detailed discussion of the notion of the "fictions of finance," see Peter Knight, "Introduction: Fictions of Finance," *Journal of Cultural Economy* 6 (2013): 1–11; Zimmerman, *Panic!*, 1–14; special issue on "The Fictions of Finance," *Radical History Review* 118 (2014); and Anna Kornbluh, *Realizing Capital: Financial and Psychic Economies in Victorian Form* (New York: Oxford University Press, 2013).

44. Karl Polanyi, *The Great Transformation: The Political and Economic Origins of Our Time*, foreword by Joseph E. Stiglitz (1944; reprint, Boston: Beacon Books, 2001). Polanyi's focus is primarily on Britain, but he asserts—unconvincingly—that the self-regulating market did not emerge in the United States until after 1890, because of the abundance of available land.

45. E. P. Thompson, "The Moral Economy of the English Crowd in the Eighteenth Century," *Past & Present* 50 (1971): 76–136.

46. Roy Kreitner, *Calculating Promises: The Emergence of Modern American Contract Doctrine* (Stanford, CA: Stanford University Press, 2007), 229.

47. Sir Henry Sumner Maine, *Ancient Law: Its Connection with the Early History of Society and Its Relation to Modern Ideas*, 10th ed. (1906; reprint, Boston: Beacon Press, 1963). On the double-edged sword of contractarianism, see Brook Thomas, *American Literary Realism and the Failed Promise of Contract* (Berkeley: University of California Press, 1997). Rudolph J. R. Peritz, in *Competition Policy in America, 1888–1992* (New York: Oxford University Press, 1996), describes how, in the twentieth century, the epistemological model of the American economy shifted from the ideal of individual contractual freedom, based on pure competition, to a "depersonalized, systemic paradigm of markets understood in abstract, functional terms" (62). I argue instead that the tensions between an individual and a depersonalized way of understanding contracts remained far into the twentieth century.

48. Niklas Luhmann, *Trust and Power* (Chichester, UK: Wiley, 1979).

49. Rowena Olegario, *A Culture of Credit: Embedding Trust and Transparency in American Business* (Cambridge, MA: Harvard University Press, 2006).

50. Wayland A. Tonning, "The Beginnings of the Money-Back Guarantee and the One-Price Policy in Champaign-Urbana, Illinois, 1833–1880," *Business History Review* 30 (1956): 196–210.

51. On anxieties about identification, see Scott A. Sandage, *Born Losers: A History of Failure in America* (Cambridge, MA: Harvard University Press, 2005); and Michael Pettit, *The Science of Deception* (Chicago: University of Chicago Press, 2013). Mihm, in *Nation of Counterfeiters*, documents how various institutions and anticounterfeiting technologies gradually made banknotes safer in the postbellum years, replacing the earlier need for personal confidence in the person holding the paper money with impersonal trust in the veracity of the note itself. Michael O'Malley, in *Face Value: The Entwined Histories of Money and Race in America* (Chicago: University of Chicago Press, 2012), argues that in the late

nineteenth century, many conservative Americans turned to a twin faith in racial essentialism and the intrinsic value of precious metal as a counterweight to what they perceived as the dangerous instability of money that was not backed up by gold as a signifier of value.

52. See, for example, Karen Halttunen, *Confidence Men and Painted Women: A Study of Middle-Class Culture in America, 1830–1870* (New Haven, CT: Yale University Press, 1982).

53. Georg Simmel, *The Philosophy of Money*, ed. David Frisby, 2nd ed. (London: Routledge, 1990), 124.

54. Giovanni Arrighi, *The Long Twentieth Century: Money, Power, and the Origins of Our Time*, 2nd ed. (London: Verso, 2009). Ian Baucom, in *Specters of the Atlantic: Finance Capital, Slavery, and the Philosophy of History* (Durham, NC: Duke University Press, 2005), provides an important adaptation of Arrighi's narrative in his account of the "insurantial imaginary" that, he argues, emerged in the eighteenth century with the slave trade's treatment of people as fungible and abstractable commodities. Although Baucom is drawn to Fredric Jameson's account ("Culture and Finance Capital," *Critical Inquiry* 24 [1997]: 246–65) of the "culture of finance capital," he is struck by the fact that the "speculative epistemologies and value forms" of our contemporary "hyperfinancialized" moment represent an uncanny repetition and intensification of late eighteenth-century finance capitalism, when "capital seems to turn its back entirely on the thingly world, sets itself free from the material constraints of production and distribution, and revels in its pure capacity to breed money from money—as if by a sublime trick of the imagination" (27).

55. Poovey, *Genres of the Credit Economy*.

56. Sandage, *Born Losers*, 99–128. See also Josh Lauer ("From Rumor to Written Record: Credit Reporting and the Invention of Financial Identity in Nineteenth-Century America," *Technology and Culture* 49, no. 2 [2008]: 301–24), who argues that, while most Foucauldian studies have concentrated on *state* biodisciplinarity, in the United States in the nineteenth century, credit-reporting agencies constituted an enormous realm of *private* surveillance.

57. Elias St. Elmo Lewis, *Financial Advertising: For Commercial and Savings Banks, Trust, Title Insurance, and Safe Deposit Companies, Investment Houses* (Indianapolis: Levey Bros., 1908), 178–79.

58. Lewis, *Financial Advertising*, 180; and Roland Marchand, *Creating the Corporate Soul: The Rise of Public Relations and Corporate Imagery in American Big Business* (Berkeley: University of California Press, 1998).

59. Anthony Giddens, *The Consequences of Modernity* (Cambridge: Polity, 1990), 83–91.

60. Viviana A. Zelizer, *The Social Meaning of Money* (Princeton, NJ: Princeton University Press, 1997).

61. In this broad claim I am drawing on Margot Finn's work on the discourse and practice of credit and debt in eighteenth-century and nineteenth-century Britain. Finn argues against modernization theorists, demonstrating instead how, even with the growth of consumerism and the cash nexus, there was a continuity with older forms of personalized gift exchange and a reliance on notions of character and social standing in the realm of credit. Finn posits not merely that gift exchange persisted alongside market exchange, but that it was part and parcel of market exchange; indeed, modern consumerism did not so much replace traditional networks of credit and obligation as it was fueled by them. See Finn, *The Character of Credit: Personal Debt and English Culture, 1740–1914* (Cambridge: Cambridge University Press, 2003).

62. Mark Seltzer, *Bodies and Machines* (New York: Routledge, 1992).

63. Elaine Freedgood, *Victorian Writing About Risk: Imagining a Safe England in a Dangerous World* (Cambridge: Cambridge University Press, 2000), 3.

64. Robert Wiebe, *The Search for Order, 1877–1920* (New York: Hill & Wang, 1967), 12. Stuart Banner, in *Anglo-American Securities Regulation: Cultural and Political Roots, 1690–1860* (Cambridge: Cambridge University Press), likewise argues that, although the first emergence of financial capitalism in the middle of the nineteenth century may have introduced new institutions and ideas, usually these were brought into the fold of intelligibility (and legislation) by an analogy to existing practices and discourses.

Chapter 1 · Market Reports

1. The intermingling of personal and business news continued in brokers' correspondence, even into the 1870s, as a way of cementing personal relationships and conferring authority on the price information, but the stock ticker, with its mechanization of trust, made this kind of communication less relevant. There are examples of correspondence from this period between clients and brokers in the Warshaw Collection of Business Americana, Archives Center, National Museum of American History, Smithsonian Institution, Washington, DC. On the changes brought about by the stock ticker, see also Alex Preda, *Framing Finance: The Boundaries of Markets and Modern Capitalism* (Chicago: University of Chicago Press, 2009), 121–22.

2. See John J. McCusker, "The Demise of Distance: The Business Press and the Origins of the Information Revolution in the Early Modern Atlantic World," *American Historical Review* 110 (2005): 295–321. See also Larry Neal, "The Rise of a Financial Press: London and Amsterdam, 1681–1810," *Business History* 30 (1988), 163–78; and John J. McCusker and Cora Gravesteijn, *The Beginnings of Commercial and Financial Journalism: The Commodity Price Currents, Exchange Rate Currents, and Money Currents of Early Modern Europe* (Amsterdam: NEHA, 1991).

3. The inclusion of financial columns in mainstream newspapers happened first in Britain in the 1820s; see Mary Poovey, ed., *The Financial System in Nineteenth-Century Britain* (Oxford: Oxford University Press, 2003). But by the end of the nineteenth century, British newspapers were self-consciously following the American development of the "new financial journalism" that adopted a more personal tone and also helped popularize speculation; see Dilwyn Porter, "City Editors and the Modern Investing Public: Establishing the Integrity of the New Financial Journalism in Late Nineteenth-Century London," *Media History* 4 (1998): 49–60. For accounts of nineteenth-century business and financial journalism, see David P. Forsyth, *The Business Press in America, 1750–1865* (Philadelphia: Chilton, 1964); Wayne Parsons, *The Power of the Financial Press: Journalism and Economic Opinion in Britain and America* (Aldershot, UK: Edward Elgar, 1989); and Alfred D. Chandler Jr., *Henry Varnum Poor: Business Editor, Analyst, and Reformer* (Cambridge, MA: Harvard University Press, 1954). For an insider's account of the development of financial journalism in the latter part of the nineteenth century, see Edwin Lefèvre, "The Newspaper and Wall Street," *Bookman* (April 1904), 136–48.

4. Wash sales involved simultaneous buying and selling by one person or group, in order to create the appearance of market activity in a particular stock. Stocks that were watered were believed to be overcapitalized (i.e., priced unreasonably in excess of the actual worth of the firm's assets). See Lawrence Mitchell, *The Speculation Economy: How Finance Triumphed over Industry* (San Francisco: Berrett-Koehler, 2007). For a discussion of muck-

raking journalism and the stock market, see Cedric B. Cowing, *Populists, Plungers, and Progressives: A Social History of Stock and Commodity Speculation, 1890–1936* (Princeton, NJ: Princeton University Press, 1965), 27–38.

5. A Wall Street "Piker," "Confessions of a Stock Speculator," *Independent* (21 March 1907), 671.

6. Henry Clews, *Fifty Years in Wall Street* (New York: Irving, 1908), 203–4. Frank Norris, in *The Pit: A Story of Chicago* (New York: Doubleday, 1903), has Sam Gretry, Curtis Jadwin's right-hand man, declare that "'I've fixed the warehouse crowd—and we just about own the editorial and news sheets of these papers.' He threw a memorandum down upon the desk" (336). Lefèvre, in his *Bookman* article, asserts unconvincingly that these practices were far less common in the United States than in Britain. On advertorial puffery in British newspapers, see Porter, "City Editors."

7. The story of Lawson is told by David Zimmerman in *Panic!: Markets, Crises, and Crowds in American Fiction* (Chapel Hill: University of North Carolina Press, 2006), 81–122.

8. See James H. Bridge, ed., *The Trust: Its Book (Being a Presentation of the Several Aspects of the Latest Form of Industrial Evolution)* (New York: Doubleday, Page, 1910).

9. U.S. Congress, House of Representatives, *Report of the Committee Pursuant to House Resolutions 429 and 504 to Investigate the Concentration of Control of Money and Credit*, H.R. Rep. No. 1593, 62nd Cong., 3d Sess. (1913), 115. Although "blue sky" laws designed to protect the investing public by compelling transparency in corporate financial information were enacted in some western states in the 1910s, many of the recommendations for national securities reform failed to gain purchase; instead, the trusts were busted by increasing the possibilities for competition through antimonopoly legislation, such as the Clayton Act of 1914. For a history of the political struggles over the democratization and regulation of shareholding, see Cowing, *Populist, Plungers, and Progressives*, 25–74; and Ott, *When Wall Street Met Main Street*, 9–54.

10. State of New York, *Report of Governor Hughes' Committee on Speculation in Securities and Commodities, June 7, 1909* (n.p.: 1909), 4. On the history of Justice Holmes's decision, see pp. 351–52 in David Hochfelder, "'Where the Common People Could Speculate': The Ticker, Bucket Shops, and the Origins of Popular Participation in Financial Markets, 1880–1920," *Journal of American History* 93 (2006): 335–58.

11. Although the old guard in the New York Stock Exchange rejected outright any of the Progressive calls for governmental regulation and continued to see themselves as essentially a private club, a younger, reformist group on the Committee on Library engaged in a public relations exercise to embrace the idea of the small investor as an American Everyman who should be allowed, just like the wealthy insider, to trade securities on the "free and open market" without paternalist interference from the government. They likewise promoted the activities of the NYSE as fulfilling a public service by setting prices and allocating capital. Despite the rhetorical appeal to the mythical small investor, in practice the governors of the NYSE thought it better not to attract bad publicity and tried to dissuade members from dealing with outside investors of limited means by restricting retail brokerages and outlawing advertising, in part to distinguish themselves from fraudulent firms and bucket shops (on the latter point, see Ott, *When Wall Street Met Main Street*, 39).

12. Mary Poovey, *Genres of the Credit Economy: Mediating Value in Eighteenth- and Nineteenth-Century Britain* (Chicago: University of Chicago Press, 2008), 32. James Taylor has a different take on the ideological function of the Victorian financial press, arguing that

although the press saw itself as the moral watchdog against commercial fraud, in times of financial panic it tended to rely on psychological explanations of the madness of crowds. A focus on the foolish gullibility of investors, rather than on the fraudulent practices of the financial institutions, diverted attention from a quest for regulatory reform of structural failings in the banking system. See Taylor, "Watchdogs or Apologists? Financial Journalism and Company Fraud in Early Victorian Britain," *Historical Research* 85 (2012): 632–50.

13. Alex Preda, in *Framing Finance: The Boundaries of Markets and Modern Capitalism* (Chicago: University of Chicago Press, 2009), argues that the stock ticker likewise demanded new modes of economic epistemology, a disciplining of the economic subject into habits of rational calculation and unceasing concentration on the endless flow of prices (132–35). Although evidence is scarce on how far thinking about the market was part of participants' daily lives, Preda cites the diaries of Edward Neufville Tailer, a clerk in New York City, in which Tailer obsessively monitors not only the rise and fall of stock prices, but also his own investment behavior.

14. On the idea of the stock market graph as a projection and introjection of stock prices that are themselves a representation of aggregated desire, see Audrey Jaffe, *The Affective Life of the Average Man: The Victorian Novel and the Stock-Market Graph* (Columbus: Ohio State University Press, 2010). Jaffe provides a very suggestive argument about the imaginative power of the stock market graph as a representational technology. She tends to exaggerate the significance of the graph form in the Victorian period, however, and she likewise gives too much credit at an early historical moment to the marginalist understanding of prices as a numerical expression of the aggregation of individual utility preferences. Certainly, in the American case, many lay observers of the stock market continued to think of prices as embodying the value of the firm's assets, and any deviation from a warranted price could only be explained in terms of secret manipulation by insiders or (toward the end of the century) the madness of crowds. David Henkin, in *City Reading: Written Words and Public Spaces in Antebellum New York* (New York: Columbia University Press, 1998), makes a similar argument to Jaffe about the uneasy relationship between projection and introjection, noting the habit of Edward Tailer in his diaries of deriving his sense of self not so much through interior reflection but through his reading of reports in the newspapers of social events and stock market activities in which he is involved (130–33).

15. *Wall Street Journal*, 8 July 1889, 1. For a history of Charles Dow and his paper, see Lloyd Wendt, *The* Wall Street Journal: *The Story of Dow Jones and the Nation's Business Newspaper* (Chicago: Rand McNally, 1982). On the ideological, performative work achieved by impersonal statistical reporting, such as the Dow Jones Industrial Average, see Marieke de Goede, *Virtue, Fortune, and Faith: A Genealogy of Finance* (Minneapolis: University of Minnesota Press, 2005), 87–120; and Preda, *Framing Finance*, 155–71.

16. Although Charles Dow emphasized the need for objective, impersonal market reporting, in practice the *Wall Street Journal* was not always averse to a more human-centered approach to financial journalism. Amid the usual talk of bulls and bears battling it out on the floor of the NYSE, the reporters for the *Wall Street Journal* would emphasize their closeness to the action, mentioning individual brokers by name, although they often used the impersonal voice to give at least a rhetorical semblance of objectivity, coupled with a cautiousness not to confuse a rumor with fact: "Distillers *was regarded as* drifting into a deadlock, where there would not be much movement until after the reorganization was complete" (6 April 1895, 2; emphasis added). Likewise, although the paper condemned

gossip and rumor as such, it was not averse to insisting that its information (from the horse's mouth) was simply more accurate than that of the popular press: "There seems to be a good deal of misunderstanding in regard to the Electric situation due to reports and rumors circulated by ill-informed people and newspapers" (6 April 1895, 2).

17. For a detailed account of this periodical, see Douglas W. Steeples, *Advocate for American Enterprise: William Buck Dana and the* Financial and Commercial Chronicle (Westport, CT: Greenwood Press, 2002).

18. Elizabeth Hewitt, "Romances of Real Life; or, The Nineteenth-Century Business Magazine," *American Periodicals: A Journal of History, Criticism, and Bibliography* 20 (2010): 1–22.

19. Edwin Lefèvre, "The Newspaper and Wall Street," *Bookman* (April 1904), 139.

20. Ibid.

21. Ibid., 148.

22. *New York Herald*, 11 May 1835, 3.

23. *New York Herald*, 28 February 1838, 1. For a detailed intellectual biography of Bennett and his paper, see James Crouthamel, *Bennett's* New York Herald *and the Rise of the Popular Press* (Syracuse, NY: Syracuse University Press, 1989).

24. The following examples are based on a random sampling of the *Herald's* money page over the period 1870–1910. Although it is tempting to concentrate solely on moments of high drama in the markets, my reading (of all three case studies) takes in both the days of excitement and the many days of "dullness," in order to examine the proposition that watching the market became a quotidian activity, rather than a matter of concern merely in times of financial panic.

25. As if to emphasize that it was even closer to the action, the market reports in the *Wall Street Journal* gave a near-hourly breakdown of the day's activities.

26. *New York Herald*, 22 April 1883, 26; and 25 April 1883, 13.

27. *New York Herald*, 6 July 1883, 8.

28. *New York Herald*, 13 July 1883, 8.

29. *New York Herald*, 17 November 1882, 8.

30. *New York Herald*, 19 April 1883, 5.

31. *New York Herald*, 23 April 1883, 8.

32. *New York Herald*, 26 June 1882, 11.

33. *New York Herald*, 18 November 1882, 8.

34. *New York Herald*, 23 April 1883, 8.

35. *New York Herald*, 10 July 1883, 8.

36. *New York Herald*, 22 April 1883, 26.

37. *New York Herald*, 2 December 1890, 12.

38. *New York Herald*, 8 July 1879, 9.

39. *New York Herald*, 26 February 1881, 3.

40. *New York Herald*, 22 April 1883, 26.

41. *New York Herald*, 25 June 1882, 21. With hindsight, we can recognize the dullness of the market as part of the economic crisis of 1882–1884, itself part of the deflationary depression of 1873–1896. See David Glasner and Thomas F. Cooley, "Depression of 1882–1885," in David Glasner, ed., *Business Cycles and Depressions: An Encyclopedia* (New York: Routledge, 1997), 149–51.

42. *New York Herald*, 22 April 1883, 26; 24 April 1883, 8; 25 April 1883, 13; and 26 April 1883, 5.

43. *New York Herald*, 6 July 1883, 8; 7 July 1883, 12; 8 July 1883, 15; 9 July 1883, 7; and 12 July 1883, 8.

44. *Harper's Weekly* (11 November 1899), 1151. Faith in publicity (preferably voluntary financial disclosure by the corporations themselves, coupled with the threat of the harsh light of journalistic scrutiny), rather than external governmental regulation, was the creed of most conservative commentators; compare, for example, the *Wall Street Journal*: "There is nothing like publicity as a remedy for corporation abuses and as a protection to investment interests" (8 October 1907, 1). As Mary Poovey notes in "Writing about Finance in Victorian England: Disclosure and Secrecy in the Culture of Investment," *Victorian Studies* 45 (2002): 17–41, a contradiction was at the heart of the financial page in the nineteenth century. On the one hand, there was a desire to create transparency in the otherwise murky world of business in an age before the legal requirement of disclosure, thus making it seem honest and open, in order to legitimize the "philosophy of commercial affairs." On the other hand, business had a strong competitive imperative to keep its activities secret, based on the common assumption that business was actually not part of the public realm but belonged instead to the private sphere of individual freedom of contract and the self-regulation of the market, away from governmental interference.

45. *Harper's Weekly* (7 October 1899), 1023.

46. *Harper's Weekly* (19 December 1900), 1275.

47. *Harper's Weekly* (1 August 1908), 28.

48. *Harper's Weekly* (12 August 1899), 805. See Mitchell, *Speculation Economy*, for a detailed account of how fears about overcapitalization came to dominate the discussion about the evils of the stock market at the time of the Great Merger Movement.

49. *Harper's Weekly* (9 May 1908), 9.

50. *Harper's Weekly* (23 May 1908), 9.

51. *Harper's Weekly* (15 March 1902), 351.

52. *Harper's Weekly* (12 February 1902), 457; and (25 January 1901), 101.

53. *Harper's Weekly* (11 November 1899), 1151.

54. *Harper's Weekly* (8 March 1902), 293.

55. *Harper's Weekly* (7 December 1901), 1214.

56. *Harper's Weekly* (1 February 1902), 132.

57. Although *Harper's* seems not to have been flooded with promotions for suspicious corporations and brokerages in the way that the Sunday newspapers were in the late nineteenth century, there is a noticeable shift in the advertisements on the money page, away from the magazine's stock-in-trade of ladies underwear, liquor, and patent medicines to financial services of a seemingly respectable kind.

58. *Harper's Weekly* (22 February 1902), 229.

59. *Harper's Weekly* (28 March 1903), 533.

60. Andy Logan, *The Man Who Robbed the Robber Barons* (London: Victor Gollancz, 1966), 14–15. Unless otherwise indicated, information about Mann in subsequent paragraphs is from Logan's biography. See also the brief summary of *Town Topics* in Maureen Montgomery, *Displaying Women: Spectacles of Leisure in Edith Wharton's New York* (New York: Routledge, 1998), 143–47.

61. Although high for a weekly magazine, these figures must be seen in comparison with the main New York newspapers, such as the *New York Herald*, the *New York World*, and the *New York Times*, which, by the 1880s, all had whole-page spreads on society gossip in their Sunday editions. The *Herald* sold 190,000 copies and the *World*, 350,000. See Montgomery, *Displaying Women*, 191, n12.

62. On the history of society journalism, see Logan, *The Man Who Robbed*; Montgomery, *Displaying Women*; and Eric Homberger, *Mrs. Astor's New York: Money and Social Power in a Gilded Age* (New York: Yale University Press, 2002), 204–19.

63. "Saunterings," *Town Topics* (17 December 1891), 1.

64. "Mann Would Reform the Four Hundred," *New York Times*, 1 August 1905, 7.

65. Edwin Post Jr., *Truly Emily Post* (New York: Funk & Wagnalls, 1961), 143. In Edith Wharton's *The Custom of the Country* (New York: Scriber's, 1913), parvenu Undine Spragg is instructed in the ways of society by Mrs. Heeny, the society manicurist and masseuse, who brings in clippings from *Town Talk*, Wharton's thinly disguised version of *Town Topics*. The same title also appears in Wharton's *The House of Mirth* (New York: Scribner's, 1905).

66. Montgomery, in *Displaying Women*, notes that Gilded Age society magazines and newspaper columns afforded leisure-class women greater publicity for their displays of fashionable activities, such as balls, sporting competitions, and other entertainments, but, at the same time, enforced greater surveillance of female morality. Montgomery makes extensive use of *Town Topics* in her study.

67. Homberger, *Mrs. Astor's New York*, 202–19. For a more wide-ranging account of the self-conscious formation of the New York bourgeoisie as a distinct class, see Sven Beckert, *The Monied Metropolis: New York City and the Consolidation of the American Bourgeoisie, 1850–1896* (Cambridge: Cambridge University Press, 2001).

68. *Town Topics* (20 January 1887), 16. Montgomery, in *Displaying Women*, notes that the same heroic military metaphors are used to describe the doings of society matrons like Mrs. Bradley-Martin (152).

69. *Town Topics* (6 January 1887), 14. On the idea of the charismatic speculator, see Preda, *Framing Finance*, 198–212.

70. For details about the restricted membership of the NYSE and its resistance to regulation, see Robert Sobel, *The Big Board: A History of the New York Stock Market* (New York: Free Press, 1965); and Ott, *When Wall Street Met Main Street*, 9–54.

71. See Hochfelder, "Common People"; and Preda, *Framing Finance*, 113–43.

72. *Town Topics* (3 February 1887), 20.

73. *Town Topics* (20 January 1887), 15.

74. *Town Topics* (3 February 1887), 19.

75. *Town Topics* (2 January 1890), 20. By the 1900s, even the *Wall Street Journal* had begun to include a column offering conservative investment advice, in the form of "Answers to Inquirers."

76. *Town Topics* (14 January 1892), 17.

77. *Town Topics* (2 January 1890), 16.

78. *Town Topics* (9 February 1893), 15.

79. *Town Topics* (20 January 1887), 15.

80. *Town Topics* (13 January 1887), 1. Edith Wharton takes the trope of the rise and fall of a woman's stock to the extreme in *The House of Mirth* (1905).

81. *Town Topics* (6 January 1887), 1.

82. *Town Topics* (27 January 1887), 1.

83. *Town Topics* (27 January 1889), 15.

84. "Ebb and Flow," *Town Topics* (16 June 1892), 16.

85. On the trope of anthropomorphized coins and notes, see Poovey, *Genres of the Credit Economy*, 145–47.

86. *Town Topics* (3 February 1887), 20. In the legal struggle over the bucket shops' access to price information from the ticker, the NYSE was understandably accused of operating a cartel, setting minimum rates for commissions and restricting which stocks could be listed. See Hochfelder, "Common People."

87. *Town Topics* (17 February 1887), 12. In his interpretation of Frank Norris's *The Pit* (1903), Zimmerman, in *Panic!*, argues that mesmerism was a recurrent trope in accounts of the market during this period. The novel's stock-manipulating hero, Curtis Jadwin, attempts to wrest control of the invisible hand of the market with the force of his magnetic personality and economic might, but in the end he is mesmerized by the economic sublime of the market itself (123–50).

88. "The Golden Calf: High-Class Bunco Steering," *Town Topics* (24 February 1887), 14. The most shocking thing of all, the article concludes, is that Clews ropes women into speculating in the market by employing particularly enticing promoters.

89. *Town Topics* (17 February 1887), 13.

90. *Town Topics* (13 March 1890), 17.

91. *Town Topics* (13 January 1887), 15.

92. *Town Topics* (14 January 1892), 16.

93. *Town Topics* (24 February 1887), 17.

94. *Town Topics* (13 January 1887), 15.

95. *Town Topics* (17 January 1907), 22.

96. For details of the court case, see Logan, *The Man Who Robbed*, chapters 2–3, 8–10; and Montgomery, *Displaying Women*, 145–47. Lefèvre, in his article in *Bookman*, piously claimed that such practices might happen in England, but not America.

97. Jaffe, *Affective Life*, 15.

Chapter 2 · *Reading the Ticker Tape*

1. Thomas Mortimer, *Every Man His Own Broker; or, A Guide to Exchange-Alley; In Which the Nature of the Several Funds, Vulgarly Called the Stocks, Is Clearly Explained, and the Mystery and Iniquity of Stock Jobbing Laid Before the Public in a New and Impartial Light; Also the Method of Transferring Stock, and of Buying and Selling the Several Government Securities, without the Assistance of a Broker, Is Made Intelligible to the Meanest Capacity; And an Account Is Given of the Laws in Force Relative to Brokers, Clerks at the Bank, &c.* (London: S. Hooper, 1761).

2. For a contemporaneous list of more-respectable sources, including books, magazine articles, legal treatises, and cases, see S. S. Huebner, "Bibliography on Securities and Stock Exchanges," special issue on "Stocks and the Stock Market," *Annals of the American Academy of Political and Social Science* 35 (1910): 217–32. In addition to these sources (many of which have now been digitized), I have consulted some of the more-ephemeral items in the Warshaw Collection of Business Americana, Archives Center, National Museum of American History, Smithsonian Institution, Washington, DC.

3. George G. Foster, *New York by Gaslight, with Here and There a Streak of Sunshine*

(New York: Dewitt & Davenport, 1850); and George Francis Train, *Young America in Wall Street* (New York: Derby & Jackson, 1857). For an overview of nineteenth-century cultural responses to Wall Street, see Steve Fraser, *Every Man a Speculator: A History of Wall Street in American Life* (New York: HarperCollins, 2005), 30–105.

4. Freeman Hunt, *Worth and Wealth: A Collection of Maxims, Morals, and Miscellanies for Merchants and Men of Business* (New York: Stringer & Townsend, 1856); and Edwin T. Freedley, *A Practical Treatise on Business; or, How to Get, Save, Spend, Give, Lend, and Bequeath Money; With an Inquiry into the Chances of Success and Causes of Failure in Business* (Philadelphia: Lippincott, Grambo, 1852).

5. See Richard Weiss, *The American Myth of Success: From Horatio Alger to Norman Vincent Peale* (New York: Basic Books, 1969); and Judith Hilkey, *Character Is Capital: Success Manuals and Manhood in Gilded Age America* (Chapel Hill: University of North Carolina Press, 1997).

6. James D. Mills, *The Art of Money Making; or, The Road to Fortune; A Universal Guide for Honest Success* (New York: International, 1872), vi.

7. James K. Medbery, *Men and Mysteries of Wall Street* (Boston: Fields, Osgood, 1870); William Worthington Fowler, *Ten Years on Wall Street* (New York: Burt Franklin, 1870); Matthew Hale Smith, *Twenty Years among the Bulls and Bears of Wall Street* (Hartford, CT: J. B. Burr & Hyde, 1871); Henry Clews, *Twenty-Eight Years on Wall Street* (New York: J. S. Ogilvie, 1887); and Clews, *Fifty Years on Wall Street* (New York: Irving, 1908).

8. Smith, *Twenty Years*, iv.

9. Tumbridge & Co., *Secrets of Success in Wall Street* (New York: self-published, 1875), 3. In addition to its annual guide, Tumbridge & Co. also put out a weekly newsletter, touting Russell Sage's share promotions. See Paul Sarnoff, *Russell Sage: The Money King* (New York: Obolensky, 1965), 242.

10. In an effort to avoid governmental regulation designed to protect outside investors, the NYSE prohibited advertising by its members (the Hughes Commission, for example, thought that one of the most serious problems bedeviling the public reputation of stock brokering was mailing prospective clients fraudulent circulars that were advertised in the Sunday papers). The brokers advertising in the *New York Times*, then, were members of other, less restrictive exchanges, such as the Consolidated Exchange.

11. Haight & Freese, *Guide to Investors* (New York: self-published, 1898), 24–25.

12. John H. Davis & Co., *The Business Methods and Customs of Wall Street; or, How Stocks and Bonds Are Dealt In for Investment or on a Margin* (New York: self-published, 1888), 8–9.

13. "Hoyle" [William E. Forrest], *The Game in Wall Street, and How to Play It Successfully* (New York: J. S. Ogilvie, 1898), iii.

14. Ibid., 26–27.

15. Ibid., 34–35.

16. Ibid., 33.

17. Ibid., 6.

18. A. N. Ridgely, *The Study and Science of Stock Speculation* (New York: self-published, 1909), 1.

19. Lewis C. Van Riper, *The Ins and Outs of Wall Street* (New York: self-published, 1898), 7–8.

20. Ibid., 11.

21. "Broker Charles W. Morgan Assigns," *New York Times*, 7 December 1900. Charles

W. Morgan advertised regularly in the Sunday edition of the New York newspapers, offering the booklet "How to Speculate Successfully in Wall Street." As well as John B. MacKenzie and Van Riper, he also mailed out 100,000 circulars a week, encouraging recipients to invest at least $200 in his discretionary-account scheme. Despite promises to make prodigious profits, the three fraudsters pocketed most of the money sent to them (it seems they paid out to existing investors from funds received from new clients, in what was, in effect, a Ponzi scheme). On discretionary-account frauds, see also John Hill Jr., *Gold Bricks of Speculation: A Study of Speculation and Its Counterfeits, and an Exposé of the Methods of Bucketshop and "Get-Rich-Quick" Swindles* (Chicago: Lincoln Concern, 1904).

22. "Oil Fraud Suspect Faces New Charge," *New York Times*, 26 June 1920.

23. J. Overton Paine, *Speculating in Wall Street in Margins: A Simple and Complete Treatise on the Buying and Selling of Bonds, Stocks, Grain, and Cotton on a Margin* (New York: self- published, n.d. [c. 1900]), 7, 4.

24. "J. Overton Paine in Court," *New York Times*, 1 September 1901. Paine continued in his trade of fraud and was again convicted, this time for suspect land deals, in 1937, at the age of 69.

25. Paine, *Speculating in Wall Street*, 6.

26. Henry Clews & Co., *Investment Guide* (New York: self-published, 1908), 12.

27. William Harman Black, *The Real Wall Street: An Understandable Description of a Purchase, a Sale, a "Short Sale," with Forms, Definitions, Rules, etc.* (New York: Corporations Organization, 1908).

28. H. M. Williams, *The Key to Wall Street Mysteries and Methods* (New York: M. W. Hazen, 1904).

29. "A New York Broker" [John F. Hume], *The Art of Investing* (New York: Appleton, 1888), 3–4, 147.

30. [John Moody and John. F. Hume], *The Art of Wise Investing* (New York: Moody, 1904), viii, 18–19, 23; and Thomas Woodlock, *The Anatomy of a Railroad Report and Ton-Mile Cost* (New York: Nelson, 1900).

31. [Moody and Hume], *Art of Wise Investing*, 43.

32. Thomas Gibson, *The Pitfalls of Speculation* (New York: Moody, 1906), 9.

33. Ibid., 146, 12.

34. Samuel A. Nelson, *The ABC of Wall Street* (New York: Nelson, 1900), 5.

35. Ibid., 32.

36. Ibid., 33.

37. Sereno S. Pratt, *The Work of Wall Street* (New York: Appleton, 1904); and Samuel A. Nelson, *The ABC of Stock Speculation* (New York: Nelson, 1902), 43.

38. Ibid., 44.

39. Roger W. Babson, *Bonds and Stocks: The Elements of Successful Investing* (Wellesley Hills, MA: Babson Statistical Organization, 1912). Since writing this chapter, I have learned much about Babson from Walter Friedman's *Fortune Tellers: The Story of America's First Economic Forecasters* (Princeton, NJ: Princeton University Press, 2013), 12–50.

40. A selection of these publications includes Charles A. Conant, *Wall Street and the Country* (New York: G. P. Putnam's Sons, 1904); Francis L. Eames, *The New York Stock Exchange* (New York: Thomas G. Hall, 1894); Henry Crosby Emery, *Speculation on the Stock and Produce Exchanges in the United States* (New York: Macmillan, 1904); E. C. Stedman, *History of the New York Stock Exchange* (New York: Stock Exchange Historical Company,

1904); and William C. Van Antwerp, *The Stock Exchange from Within* (New York: Double-day, 1913).

41. For a detailed account of the work of the Committee on Library and the arguments surrounding corporate financial transparency, see Julia C. Ott, *When Wall Street Met Main Street: The Quest for an Investors' Democracy* (Cambridge, MA: Harvard University Press, 2011), 9–54. On the Industrial Commission and the Hughes Committee, see Ott, *When Wall Street Met Main Street*, 22–29; Cedric B. Cowing, *Populists, Plungers, and Progressives: A Social History of Stock and Commodity Speculation, 1890–1936* (Princeton, NJ: Princeton University Press, 1965), 38–42; and Lawrence Mitchell, *The Speculation Economy: How Finance Triumphed over Industry* (San Francisco: Berrett-Koehler, 2007), 86–88, 124–28, 177–80.

42. Van Antwerp, *Stock Exchange from Within*, 162.

43. [Moody and Hume], *Art of Wise Investing*, 36.

44. Charles Duguid, *How to Read the Money Article*, 4th ed. (London: E. Wilson, 1902). Huebner, in "Bibliography on Securities," lists an American edition put out by Babson.

45. Henry Hall, *How Money Is Made in Security Investments; or, A Fortune at Fifty-Five*, 3rd ed. (New York: De Vinne Press, 1908), viii, x; Van Riper, *Ins and Outs*, 10.

46. Black, *Real Wall Street*, 3.

47. Nelson, *ABC of Stock Speculation*, chapter 9.

48. Alex Preda, *Framing Finance: The Boundaries of Markets and Modern Capitalism* (Chicago: University of Chicago Press, 2009), 131. A first step in the process of abstraction was the standardization of agricultural commodities. William Cronon describes how, in the decades following the Civil War, the innovation of standardized grain grading allowed produce of roughly the same grade to be stored communally in grain elevators, with the farmer receiving a paper receipt for the amount deposited (in place of having a specific grain stored in separate bags for each farmer). Not only did grain become abstracted into a generalized and fungible commodity, but the grain-elevator receipts could now be traded themselves as financial instruments, producing a further abstraction: going from trading the physical produce to buying and selling the idea of the produce. Along with the telegraph's ability to transmit real-time prices nationally, the standardized grading of grain enabled a national futures market in agricultural produce to emerge, transforming the solidity and local idiosyncrasy of individual farmers' crops into an abstraction, like the universal equivalent of money itself. See Cronon, *Nature's Metropolis: Chicago and the Great West* (New York: Norton, 1991), 109–42.

49. See David Hochfelder, "'Where the Common People Could Speculate': The Ticker, Bucket Shops, and the Origins of Popular Participation in Financial Markets, 1880–1920," *Journal of American History* 93 (2006), 335–58; and Preda, *Framing Finance*, 113–43.

50. *Magazine of Wall Street* 40 (25 August 1927), 753; Edmund Clarence Stedman, ed., *The New York Stock Exchange: Its History, Its Contribution to the National Prosperity, and Its Relation to American Finance at the Outset of the Twentieth Century* (New York: New York Stock Exchange Historical Company, 1905), 441. For a discussion of the figures, see Preda, *Framing Finance*, 127, and Hochfelder, "Common People," 340.

51. See Hochfelder, "Common People."

52. It is worth remembering, however, that as much as the tape created anonymous and mechanized forms of trust in trading, at the cutting edge on the exchange floor, the transactions were still very much based on face-to-face interactions, underpinned by a

communal sense of gentlemanly trust—after all, the trades were concluded with a mere nod or a wave of a hand, which were understood to constitute legally binding contracts. As Caitlin Zaloom explains in *Out of the Pits: Traders and Technology from Chicago to London* (Chicago: University of Chicago Press, 2006), even with the shift to electronic trading on the Chicago Board of Trade and the New York Stock Exchange in the late 1990s, traders maintain that they can recognize the individual style of other participants in the electronic marketplace, even if they don't know them personally.

53. Richard D. Wyckoff, *Studies in Tape Reading* (New York: Ticker, 1910), 12.

54. Thomas Gibson, "The Magazine as an Educator," *Ticker* 1, no. 5 (1908), 36.

55. Wyckoff, *Studies in Tape Reading*, 16.

56. Ibid., 6.

57. Van Riper, *Ins and Outs*, 16.

58. On Americans' conflicting attitudes toward unearned gains, see Jackson Lears, *Something for Nothing: Luck in America* (New York: Viking, 2003).

59. John B. McKenzie, *Bulls and Bears of Wall Street*, 3rd ed. (New York: self-published, 1899), 66.

60. Ibid., 24.

61. Wyckoff, *Studies in Tape Reading*, 10.

62. Ibid., 10–11.

63. Although *Reminiscences of a Stock Operator* was published in 1923 (New York: George H. Doran), much of the book refers to the period around the turn of the century, and its description of the mental attributes of the trader and its techniques for reading the tape are very much in tune with accounts written in that earlier period by Lefèvre and other authors. In the context of the ideas explored in this chapter, it is intriguing to consider how a ghost-written autobiography is an act of ventriloquism.

64. For a biography of Livermore that continues his story past the 1923 publication date of Lefèvre's book, see Richard Smitten, *Jesse Livermore: World's Greatest Stock Trader* (New York: John Wiley, 2001).

65. For details of how contemporary reviewers were not impressed with the book's meandering structure, see Todd Doyle, "Artists and Financiers in Wall Street Fiction: The Work of Edwin Lefèvre," PhD diss., University of Toledo (2001), 70–75.

66. Edwin Lefèvre, *Reminiscences of a Stock Operator* (1923; reprint, New York: John Wiley, 1994), 9. Subsequent references to this edition are included in parentheses in the body of the text.

67. [Moody and Hume], *Art of Wise Investing*, 56.

68. For an account of the considerable effects that financial writing could have on the market, see David Zimmerman's discussion of Thomas Lawson in *Panic!: Markets, Crises, and Crowds in American Fiction* (Chapel Hill: University of North Carolina Press, 2006), 81–122.

69. Wyckoff, *Studies in Tape Reading*, 17.

70. It is worth remembering that the prices Livingston encounters in the NYSE-affiliated brokerages are more "alive" than those he was used to in the bucket shops, because they respond to the buying and selling of shares by himself and other traders, whereas in the bucket shop his betting on a particular rise or fall in prices did not materially affect the market.

71. Wyckoff, *Studies in Tape Reading*, 17.

72. On the depiction of financial fortune as feminine, see, for example, J. G. A. Pocock, *The Machiavellian Moment: Florentine Political Thought and the Atlantic Republican Tradition* (Princeton, NJ: Princeton University Press, 1975), 423–61; and Marieke de Goede, *Virtue, Fortune, and Faith: A Genealogy of Finance* (Minneapolis: University of Minnesota Press, 2005), 21–46. For accounts of Adam Smith's metaphor, see Mark C. Taylor, *Confidence Games: Money and Markets in a World without Redemption* (Chicago: University of Chicago Press, 2004), 77–89; Zimmerman, *Panic!*, 131; and Syed Ahmad, "Adam Smith's Four Invisible Hands," *History of Political Economy* 22 (1990): 137–44.

73. See Sarah Burns, "Party Animals: William Holbrook Beard, Thomas Nast, and the Bears of Wall Street," *American Art Journal* 30 (1999): 9–35; and Paul Crosthwaite, Peter Knight, and Nicky Marsh, "Imagining the Market: A Visual History," *Public Culture* 24 (2013): 601–22.

74. Slavoj Žižek, *The Ticklish Subject: The Absent Centre of Political Ontology* (London: Verso, 1999), 339.

75. Anonymous, "On a Margin," *Continent* 6 (30 July 1884), 129.

76. Despite recognizing the prevalence of predatory practices (such as wash sales and false newspaper stories) during a period when the market was still "immature," Andrew W. Lo and Jasmina Hasanhodzic, in *The Evolution of Technical Analysis: Financial Prediction from Babylonian Tablets to Bloomberg Terminals* (New York: John Wiley & Sons, 2011), nevertheless assert that "what seems to have been lost in the annals of history is that technicians were the casualties, not the villains of pool operations, and their tools were honest means of detecting the danger in order to survive" (80). Although these authors are undoubtedly correct in noting that—in the popular investment manuals, at least—most tape reading was framed as a way for the ordinary investor to be able to second-guess the secret strategies of the market manipulators, it remains entirely plausible, as many of the fictional examples suggest, that those sharp operators could make the tape tell a false story, precisely because most of its readers regarded it as a transparent and unmediated form of communication.

77. A. N. Ridgely, *By Law of Might; or, The Campaign in Sunset; A Romance of the Real Wall Street* (New York: H. A. Simmons, 1908); and Ridgely, *Study and Science of Stock Speculation*, 11.

78. Edwin Lefèvre, *Sampson Rock of Wall Street: A Novel* (New York: Harper & Bros., 1907), 1. Subsequent references to this edition are included in parentheses in the body of the text.

79. One reviewer of the novel complained that its "four hundred pages of unrelieved tape and ticker, ticker and tape" render it a "dreary epic of barter in railway shares." See "Stories of Finance and Industry," *American Review of Reviews* (7 June 1907), 761, quoted in Doyle, "Artists and Financiers," 34.

80. Preda, in *Framing Finance* (207), also quotes this passage, but (as with several other quotations included in this chapter), I interpret it differently. In this case, Preda reads it as an example of how the ticker was able to "appresent" the market in a form of unmediated communication, but I think the novel betrays a skepticism about the ticker's tendency to work in the mode of realist representation, signaled here by a self-conscious focus on the romance and poetry of finance, not to mention the possibility that the story of the market that is legible on the tape has been deliberately manipulated by Rock.

81. *Ticker* 1, no. 4 (February 1908), 34.

82. Lefèvre, "The Tipster," *Wall Street Stories* (1901; reprint, New York: McGraw-Hill, 2008), 119.

83. Lefèvre, "The Break in Turpentine," *Wall Street Stories*, 60.

84. Lefèvre, "The Woman and Her Bonds," *Wall Street Stories*, 7.

85. McKenzie, *Bulls and Bears*, 66.

86. Lefèvre, "The Tipster," *Wall Street Stories*, 96–98.

87. As Steven Connor explains in *Dumbstruck: A Cultural History of Ventriloquism* (Oxford: Oxford University Press, 2000), despite many technical devices that reproduce distant speech (from Morse code to the telephone), people still find the idea of disembodied voices unsettling (364–86). One of the questions raised by Victorian encounters with disembodied voices and automatic writing during séances was whether they were evidence of a spectral agency at work, or (in the new, psychoanalytic terminology) the product of the unconscious mind of the medium. A similar dilemma haunts accounts of the ticker in particular, and market reporters in general: are they channeling the authentic voice or the otherworldly presence of the invisible hand itself, or is the market merely the aggregated voices of all the speculators, the collective unconscious of the crowd?

88. Lefèvre, "The Tipster," *Wall Street Stories*, throughout.

89. Lefèvre, "The Break in Turpentine," *Wall Street Stories*, 51.

90. Lefèvre, "The Tipster," *Wall Street Stories*, 101.

91. Ibid., 103, 107, 106.

92. Wyckoff, *Studies in Tape Reading*, 8; and Edwin Lefèvre, "James Robert Keene," *Cosmopolitan* (November 1902), 91.

93. Lefèvre, "Keene," 91.

94. Ibid., 92.

95. See Roger Luckhurst, *The Invention of Telepathy, 1870–1901* (Oxford: Oxford University Press, 2002); Pamela Thurschwell, *Literature, Technology, and Magical Thinking, 1880–1920* (Cambridge: Cambridge University Press, 2001); Laura Otis, *Networking: Communicating with Bodies and Machines in the Nineteenth Century* (Ann Arbor: University of Michigan Press, 2001); and Richard Menke, *Telegraphic Realism: Victorian Fiction and Other Information Systems* (Stanford, CA: Stanford University Press, 2008).

96. See, for example, Mark Seltzer, *Bodies and Machines* (New York: Routledge, 1992).

97. Fredric Jameson, "Culture and Finance Capital," *Critical Inquiry* 24 (1997): 251.

98. Lefèvre, "Pike's Peak or Bust," *Wall Street Stories*, 195.

99. Wyckoff, *Studies in Tape Reading*, 11, 18.

100. In his reading of Frank Norris's *The Pit: A Story of Chicago* (New York: Doubleday, 1903), Zimmerman, in *Panic!*, shows how the novel offers a depiction (in the person of the speculator Jadwin Curtis) of the confluence between the machinery of the mind and the machinery of the market, each under the control of a master manipulator yet always in danger of becoming out of control. The novel presents Jadwin as a hypnotist who is mesmerized by his own medium, while the market itself succumbs to the mass hysteria of panic. In both the novel and the late nineteenth-century discourse of New Psychology, Zimmerman argues, self-possession is considered to be a fiction, with identity an essentially imitative process that finds its most extreme example in market panics. As Zimmerman points out, Norris's novel, along with other financial and psychological writing from the period, focuses on the "signs and instruments of an agency lurking beneath or beside consciousness," which finds its tangible form in "spectral hands tapping at parlor organs

during séances, immaterial hands spelling out messages from the dead on planchette boards, [and] hysterics' hands mechanically scribbling out letters and novels while the patient slept or talked" (124).

101. See Molly McGarry, *Ghosts of Futures Past: Spiritualism and the Cultural Politics of Nineteenth-Century America* (Berkeley: University of California Press, 2008), 97; and T. J. Stiles, *The First Tycoon: The Epic Life of Cornelius Vanderbilt* (New York: Alfred A. Knopf, 2009), 501–5.

102. Quoted in Barbara Goldsmith, *Other Powers: The Age of Suffrage, Spiritualism, and the Scandalous Victoria Woodhull* (New York: Alfred A. Knopf, 1998), xi.

103. Amanda Frisken, *Victoria Woodhull's Sexual Revolution: Political Theater and the Popular Press in Nineteenth-Century America* (Philadelphia: University of Pennsylvania Press, 2004), 1.

104. Howard M. Wachtel, *Street of Dreams—Boulevard of Broken Hearts: Wall Street's First Century* (London: Pluto, 2003), 138. See also Ron Chernow, *The House of Morgan: An American Banking Dynasty and the Rise of Modern Finance* (New York: Simon & Schuster, 1991). E. L. Doctorow's novel, *Ragtime* (New York: Random House, 1975), features Morgan's occult tendencies.

105. On the residual fascination with fortune telling in the Gilded Age and the Progressive Era, see Lears, *Something for Nothing*, 250–57; Tammy Stone-Gordon, "'Fifty-Cent Sybils': Occult Workers and the Symbolic Marketplace in the Urban U.S., 1850–1930," PhD diss., Michigan State University (1998); and Jamie Pietruska, "Propheteering: A Cultural History of Prediction in the Gilded Age," PhD diss., Brown University (1995), chapters 7 and 8. In financial circles, the indulgence in occult forms of prediction continues to the present. See Lo and Hasanhodzic, *Evolution of Technical Analysis*; and Paul Crosthwaite, *Speculative Investments: Finance, Feeling, and Representation in Contemporary Literature and Culture* (forthcoming).

106. Ann Fabian, *Card Sharps and Bucket Shops: Gambling in Nineteenth-Century America* (New York: Cornell University Press, 1990), 137.

107. Ibid., 149.

108. This argument draws on Jackson Lears, *No Place of Grace: Antimodernism and the Transformation of American Culture, 1880–1920* (New York: Pantheon Books, 1981), whose book offers a correction to Robert H. Wiebe's argument, in *The Search for Order, 1877–1920* (New York: Hill & Wang, 1967), that the coming of modernity in the United States was marked by a quest for certainty amid the chaos and unpredictability of a society that was rapidly changing. Pietruska, in "Propheteering," develops a similar argument: modernity involved not so much the replacement of premodern forms of superstition as their incorporation, when "producers and consumers of prediction together rationalized uncertainty and shaped a new cultural acceptance of the predictable unpredictability of modern life" (2).

109. For contributions to this history, see Lo and Hasanhodzic, *Evolution of Technical Analysis*; and William A. Sherden, *The Fortune Sellers: The Big Business of Buying and Selling Predictions* (New York: John Wiley & Sons, 1998).

110. See Erik D. Craft, "Private Weather Organizations and the Founding of the United States Weather Bureau," *Journal of Economic History* 59 (1999): 1063–71; John Cox, *Storm Watchers: The Turbulent History of Weather Prediction from Franklin's Kite to El Niño* (Hoboken, NJ: Wiley, 2002); James Rodger Fleming, *Meteorology in America, 1800–1870* (Balti-

more: Johns Hopkins University Press, 1990); Katharine Anderson, *Predicting the Weather: Victorians and the Science of Meteorology* (Chicago: University of Chicago Press, 2005); Gary Alan Fine, *Authors of the Storm: Meteorologists and the Culture of Prediction* (Chicago: University of Chicago Press, 2007); and Pietruska, "Propheteering."

111. See Preda, *Framing Finance*, 144–71; and Walter Friedman, "The Harvard Economic Service and the Problems of Forecasting," *History of Political Economy* 41 (2009): 57–88.

112. Theodore M. Porter, *Trust in Numbers: The Pursuit of Objectivity in Science and Public Life* (Princeton, NJ: Princeton University Press, 1995); Mary Poovey, *A History of the Modern Fact: Problems of Knowledge in the Sciences of Wealth and Society* (Chicago: University of Chicago Press, 1998); and Lorraine Daston and Peter Galison, *Objectivity* (New York: Zone Books, 2007). Ian Hacking, in *The Taming of Chance* (Cambridge: Cambridge University Press, 1990), offers an important corrective to the broad narrative of the nineteenth century's embrace of rationalization through quantification, arguing instead that toward the end of the century, the increasing acceptance of statistical probabilities undermined the deterministic causality of a purely positivistic science.

113. Samuel Benner, *Benner's Prophecies of Future Ups and Downs in Prices: What Years to Make Money on Pig-Iron, Hogs, Corn, and Provisions* (Cincinnati, OH: self-published, 1876), 121. Benner's book went through many editions in the last quarter of the nineteenth century.

114. Benner, *Benner's Prophecies*, 16–17. Preda, in *Framing Finance*, outlines how, in the early decades of the twentieth century, the emerging profession of market analysis endeavored to create a tradition for the "science" of market forecasting by harking back to Benner and others (158–60).

115. See Sandra J. Peart, "Sunspots and Expectations: W. S. Jevons's Theory of Economic Fluctuations," *Journal of the History of Economic Thought* 13 (1991): 243–65.

116. Lo and Hasanhodzic, *Evolution of Technical Analysis*, 60.

117. Burton G. Malkiel, *A Random Walk Down Wall Street: The Time-Tested Strategy for Successful Investing*, 10th ed. (New York: W. W. Norton, 2012). At first, technical analysis was challenged by the development of fundamental analysis, which argued that the only way to make money from the market was to identify prices that were out of line with their real underlying value, to which they would inevitably return; both technical and fundamental analyses, in turn, were rendered seemingly redundant by the "random walk" thesis.

118. The irony, however, is that in the wake of the financial crisis that began in 2007, many commentators are coming to view the EMH itself as a pseudoscience, a myth that has been dressed up in the arcane mathematical language of the quants (i.e., experts at analyzing and managing quantitative data) who are at the forefront of financial engineering. See, for example, Justin Fox, *The Myth of the Rational Market: A History of Risk, Reward, and Delusion on Wall Street* (New York: HarperBusiness, 2009). Malkiel, in the 2012 revised edition of *Random Walk*, includes a chapter that assesses the critiques of the EMH and concludes that rumors of its demise have been exaggerated, not least because of his overall hypothesis: in the long run, an investment held in an index-tracking fund always manages to outperform any actively managed portfolio (267–302). For Malkiel, the axiom that you can't beat the market is explained in large part because of the taxes and management fees required in actively managed funds; it makes more sense, therefore, to track the market, but with a diversified portfolio to hedge against risks.

119. Arjun Appadurai, "The Ghost in the Financial Machine," *Public Culture* 23 (2011): 527–29.

120. The popular legend is that all four of Noble's husbands had committed suicide (this version of the story is recounted in Smitten's biography, for example). However, a recent investigation by Matthew Hansen (*Omaha World-Herald*, 27 October 2015) suggests that only one of Noble's ex-husbands committed suicide.

Chapter 3 · Picturing the Market

1. For an account of the legal struggle over stock prices as private property, see David Hochfelder, "'Where the Common People Could Speculate': The Ticker, Bucket Shops, and the Origins of Popular Participation in Financial Markets, 1880–1920," *Journal of American History* 93 (2006): 335–58.

2. Matthew Hale Smith, *Sunshine and Shadow in New York* (Hartford, CT: Burr, 1869), 46–47.

3. Arjun Appadurai coins the term "financescape" in "Disjuncture and Difference in the Global Cultural Economy," *Public Culture* 2 (1990): 1–24. Although he uses the term to describe some of the distinctive features of postmodernity, it can also be applied to the way that the placeless market was increasingly coming to be organized around the turn of the twentieth century, even if, as the present study argues, it was still experienced and explained in more-traditional, human-centered ways.

4. For a brief introduction to the history of visual representations of finance, see Paul Crosthwaite, Peter Knight, and Nicky Marsh, eds., *Show Me the Money: The Image of Finance, 1700 to the Present* (Manchester, UK: Manchester University Press, 2014). For an example of research into the visual logic at play in the financial crisis that began in 2007, see Christian De Cock, Max Baker, and Christina Volkmann, "Financial Phantasmagoria: Corporate Image-Work in Times of Crisis," *Organization* 18 (2011): 153–72.

5. On the audience for satirical cartoons, see Eirwen C. Nicholson, "Consumers and Spectators: The Public of the Political Print in Eighteenth-Century England," *History* 81 (1996): 5–21.

6. Bruce G. Carruthers, *City of Capital: Politics and Markets in the English Financial Revolution* (Princeton, NJ: Princeton University Press, 1999).

7. Mary Poovey, *Genres of the Credit Economy: Mediating Value in Eighteenth- and Nineteenth-Century Britain* (Chicago: University of Chicago Press, 2008), 82.

8. Stephen Mihm, *A Nation of Counterfeiters: Capitalists, Con Men, and the Making of the United States* (Cambridge, MA: Harvard University Press, 2007). On banknotes as circulating texts, see David Henkin, *City Reading: Written Words and Public Spaces in Antebellum New York* (New York: Columbia University Press, 1998). For a discussion of the semiotics of the dollar, see Michael O'Malley, "Specie and Species: Race and the Money Question in Nineteenth-Century America," *American Historical Review* 99 (1994): 369–95; O'Malley, *Face Value: The Entwined Histories of Money and Race in America* (Chicago: University of Chicago Press, 2012); Bruce Carruthers and Sarah Babb, "The Color of Money and the Nature of Value: Greenbacks and Gold in Postbellum America," *American Journal of Sociology* 101 (1996): 1556–91; Michael Germana, *Standards of Value: Money, Race, and Literature in America* (Iowa City: University of Iowa Press, 2009); and Josh Lauer, "Money as Mass Communication: U.S. Paper Currency and the Iconography of Nationalism," *Communication Review* 11 (2008): 109–32.

9. For a broad overview of the historical relationship between debtors and creditors,

see Philip Coggan, *Paper Promises: Money, Debt, and the New World Order* (London: Allen Lane, 2011).

10. On the trompe l'oeil painters, see Lawrence Weschler, *Boggs: A Comedy of Values* (Chicago: University of Chicago Press, 1999); and Walter Benn Michaels, *The Gold Standard and the Logic of Naturalism* (Berkeley: University of California Press, 1987). Michaels argues that, despite their seemingly satirical or critical intent, late nineteenth-century trompe l'oeil paintings by artists such as Harnett and John Haberle merely repeat the goldbug insistence on the value of the representational medium itself (with gold-backed money viewed not as a symbol of value, but as naturally valuable in itself). But, in a series of dizzying, paradoxical elaborations that threaten to undermine his main point, Michaels goes on to argue that the modernist rejection of the illusionism of naturalism itself betrays an equivalent commitment to a goldbug mentality: the reaction against a view of money and art as being governed by intrinsic value, and in favor of an account that highlights the processes and slippages of signification, recreates a new kind of essentialism in the fetishization of the brute matter of the artistic material itself.

11. On representations of the panic of 1837, see Jessica Lepler, "Pictures of Panic: Constructing Hard Times in Words and Images," special issue on "Hard Times," *Common-Place* 10, no. 3 (April 2010), www.common-place-archives.org/vol-10/no-03/lepler/. For the panic of 1873, see Scott Reynolds Nelson, "A Financial Crisis in Prints and Cartoons," *Journal of the Gilded Age and the Progressive Era* 10 (2011): 425–33.

12. Molly Crabapple is discussed in Nicky Marsh, "Debt and Credit," in Crosthwaite, Knight, and Marsh, *Show Me the Money*, 22–23.

13. For a discussion of the changing social status of the speculator, see Alex Preda, *Framing Finance: The Boundaries of Markets and Modern Capitalism* (Chicago: University of Chicago Press, 2009), 53–81.

14. On Edmonds's painting, see Leo G. Mazow and Kevin M. Murphy, *Taxing Visions: Financial Episodes in Late Nineteenth-Century American Art* (University Park: Palmer Museum of Art, Pennsylvania State University, 2010).

15. On the Standard Oil cartoon, see Steve Fraser, *Every Man a Speculator: A History of Wall Street in American Life* (New York: HarperCollins, 2005), 128–29. See also Robert Worth Miller, *Populist Cartoons: An Illustrated History of the Third-Party Movement in the 1890s* (Kirksville, MO: Truman State University Press, 2011).

16. For an overview of these tropes in economic imagery, see Mike Emmison and Alex McHoul, "Drawing on the Economy: Cartoon Discourse and the Production of a Category," *Cultural Studies* 1 (1987): 93–111. See also Paul Crosthwaite, "Animality and Ideology in Contemporary Economic Discourse: Taxonomizing *Homo economicus*," *Journal of Cultural Economy* 6 (2013): 94–109.

17. For details of these images, see Sarah Burns, "Party Animals: William Holbrook Beard, Thomas Nast, and the Bears of Wall Street," *American Art Journal* 30 (1999): 9–35.

18. See James K. Medbery, *Men and Mysteries of Wall Street* (Boston: Fields, Osgood, 1870).

19. W. A. Rogers, "Great Activity in Wall Street," *New York Herald*, March 19, 1908, 7.

20. What is noticeable about octopus cartoons from this period is that they appeared in both middle-class and working-class publications. On the use of conspiracy-minded cartoons in the radical press during the decades around the turn of the twentieth century, see Michael Cohen, "'The Conspiracy of Capital': American Popular Radicalism and the Politics of Conspiracy from Haymarket to the Red Scare," PhD diss., Yale University (2004).

21. See Robert MacDougall, "The Wire Devils: Pulp Thrillers, the Telephone, and Action at a Distance in the Wiring of a Nation," *American Quarterly* 58, no. 3 (2006): 715–41. MacDougall shows how, in the early decades of the twentieth century, corporate public relations for the Bell System telephone network succeeded in turning its size and reach into a positive feature.

22. See, for example, G. Frederick Keller, "The Curse of California," *Wasp* 9, no. 316 (19 August 1882), 520–21.

23. Udo J. Keppler, "Wall Street Bubbles: Always the Same," *Puck* 49, no. 1264 (22 May 1901), centerfold.

24. On the supposed obsolescence of proprietorial individualism in the era of corporate conglomeration, see Martin J. Sklar, *The Corporate Reconstruction of American Capitalism, 1890–1916* (Cambridge: Cambridge University Press, 1988), 16.

25. Udo J. Keppler, "Commercial Might versus Divine Right," *Puck* 51, no. 1316 (21 May 1902), centerfold.

26. Frank A. Nankivell, "The Central Bank," *Puck* 67, no. 1718 (2 February 1910), cover.

27. Luther Daniels Bradley, "Design for a Union Station," *Chicago Daily News*, 18 October 1907.

28. Udo J. Keppler, "Jack and the Wall Street Giants," *Puck* 54, no. 1402 (13 January 1904), centerfold.

29. Henry Adams, *The Education of Henry Adams: An Autobiography* (Boston: Houghton Mifflin, 1918), 500.

30. Harold Frederic, *The Market Place* (New York: American News, 1899); and Harold Frederic Papers, Library of Congress, Washington, DC, quoted in Bridget Bennett, *The Damnation of Harold Frederic* (Syracuse, NY: Syracuse University Press, 1997), 198.

31. On the problematic representation of responsibility, causality, and negligence in the age of the corporation, see Nan Goodman, *Shifting the Blame: Literature, Law, and the Theory of Accidents in Nineteenth-Century America* (Princeton, NJ: Princeton University Press, 1998).

32. For a discussion of the intellectual and cultural history of the legal notion of "piercing the veil," see Brook Thomas, *American Literary Realism and the Failed Promise of Contract* (Berkeley: University of California Press, 1997), 231–69.

33. "Get After the Substance, Not the Shadow," *Puck* 68, no. 1757 (2 November 1910), centerfold.

34. Steichen denied that it was his intention, but the lighting for the image was rehearsed in advance, with a janitor sitting in for Morgan. See Abigail Tucker, "J. P. Morgan as Cutthroat Capitalist," *Smithsonian Magazine*, January 2011, www.smithsonianmag.com/history-archaeology/J-P-Morgan-as-Cutthroat-Capitalist.html [accessed 2 August 2013].

35. Grant E. Hamilton, "'I Never Speculate'—Jay Gould," *Judge* 9 (9 January 1886), back cover. On Gould in the American public's imagination, see Richard R. John, "Robber Barons Redux: Antimonopoly Reconsidered," *Enterprise & Society* 13 (2012): 1–38.

36. John F. Muirhead, *The United States, with an Excursion into Mexico: Handbook for Travellers*, ed. Karl Baedeker (Leipzig: Karl Baedeker, 1893), 27.

37. Medbery, *Men and Mysteries*, 38.

38. Ibid., 25.

39. [John Moody and John F. Hume], *The Art of Wise Investing* (New York: Moody, 1904), 53.

40. Medbery, *Men and Mysteries*, 39.

41. The climactic scene of Frank Norris's *The Pit* is narrated from the perspective of Page Dearborn, who watches the drama uncomprehendingly from her vantage point in the spectators' gallery. On the way that Page "fetishizes the market's incomprehensibility," see David Zimmerman, *Panic!: Markets, Crises, and Crowds in American Fiction* (Chapel Hill: University of North Carolina Press, 2006), 148.

42. Medbery, *Men and Mysteries*, 38.

43. Ibid., 37–38.

44. *King's Views of the New York Stock Exchange* (New York: Moses King, 1898), 1.

45. "Modern Financial Institutions and Their Equipment," *Banker's Magazine* 74, no. 4 (April 1907), 613–14.

46. American National Bank of Indianapolis (1 September 1909), vertical file no. 326, Warshaw Collection of Business Americana, Archives Center, National Museum of American History, Smithsonian Institution, Washington, DC.

47. "Modern Brokerage Establishments," *Ticker* 1, no. 4 (February 1908), 7.

48. Haight & Freese, *Guide to Investors* (New York: self-published, 1898), 24.

49. For some examples, see "Bank Advertising Emblems," *Banker's Magazine* 79, no. 3 (August 1906), 299–302. Liz McFall and Francis Dodsworth, in "Fabricating the Market: The Promotion of Life Assurance in the Long Nineteenth Century," *Journal of Historical Sociology* 22 (2009): 30–54, argue that advertising life insurance in Victorian Britain was necessary, to help build a market for it in the face of public resistance, and that the buildings (and then the advertisements showing the buildings) contributed to the material fabrication of a market that embodied the values of liberalism: "The free market was not simply a product of intellectual argument, it had to be built, propagandized, and embedded in the urban infrastructure and culture" (51).

50. Catherine Ingraham, in "The Stock Exchange: Standing Upright, Idle," *Grey Room* 15 (2004): 80–101, discusses, in relation to the work of Louis Sullivan in particular, the origins of stock markets in animal stockyards and ancient temples, noting that in both cases there is a recurrent anthropomorphization in their architectural symbolism and structure, with, for example, classical columns constructed as figures, with feet, body, and a head. See also Ingraham, *Architecture, Animal, Human: The Asymmetrical Condition* (New York: Routledge, 2006), 261–86. For an insightful analysis of the way that the Chicago Board of Trade building helped to performatively structure the market it housed, see Caitlin Zaloom, *Out of the Pits: Traders and Technology from Chicago to London* (Chicago, University of Chicago Press, 2006), 25–58.

51. For details of Sullivan's life, see Louis Sullivan, *Autobiography of an Idea* (New York: Press of the American Institute of Architects, 1924); and Mervyn D. Kaufman, *Father of Skyscrapers: A Biography of Louis Sullivan* (Boston: Little, Brown, 1969).

52. The building was torn down in 1972, but the interior of the trading floor was salvaged and a reconstruction is on display at the Art Institute of Chicago.

53. With declining health and fortune, in his later years Sullivan went on to design a number of small midwestern banks (called his "jewel boxes") that combine a sense of dependable, democratic functionality with elements of aesthetic richness. Sullivan's reputation waned after his death, and many of his landmark buildings were demolished in the 1960s and 1970s, including the Stock Exchange building (that had, in any case, long since ceased to serve as the location of the Chicago Stock Exchange). Protests by a few fans

kick-started a revival of interest in the architect, one result of which was that the trading room and the entrance arch of the Stock Exchange building were salvaged and later put on prominent display in the Art Institute of Chicago. See Ingraham, "Stock Exchange."

54. Unlike later, more brutalist versions of modernism, Sullivan's buildings are rich in the arts and crafts style of decoration, suggesting that by "form follows function," he meant that because of technical developments like the steel frame, architecture could be liberated from traditional styles. Forms of ornamentation should therefore neither be haphazardly applied nor removed entirely, but instead should serve to provide a visible expression and harmonization of a building's inner structural composition by reference, for example, to organic forms, such as vines.

55. In contrast, the original Chicago Board of Trade Building (1885) was a heavy, neo-Gothic edifice, described by Frank Norris in *The Pit* (New York: Doubleday, 1903), and was more like a vaguely sinister mythical creature than a temple of modernity: "The lighted office buildings, the murk of rain, the haze of light in the heavens, and rised against it the pile of the Board of Trade Building, black, grave, monolithic, crouching on its foundations, like a monstrous black sphinx with blind eyes, silent, grave—crouching there without a sound, without sign of life under the night and the drifting veil of rain" (41). The Auditorium Theater, in fact, ended up being constructed in heavy stone, and the foundations designed by Adler and Sullivan were unable to support the increased weight, with the result that one corner of the building sank and warped.

56. See Janet Cecilia Marstine, "Working History: Images of Labor and Industry in American Mural Painting, 1893–1903," PhD diss., University of Pittsburgh (1993); and Bailey Van Hook, *The Virgin and the Dynamo: Public Murals in American Architecture* (Athens: Ohio University Press, 2003). Van Hook concludes that Gilded Age and Progressive Era murals were figural and mainly allegorical (and usually personified). Their ideology was conservative, favoring stability, the rule of law, and the education of the immigrant masses and was a defense of the corporate order.

57. James L. Yarnall, *John La Farge, a Biographical and Critical Study* (Farnham, UK: Ashgate, 2012), 242.

58. William Walton, "Recent Mural Decorations by Mr. E. H. Blashfield," *Scribner's Monthly* 37 (March 1905), 384, quoted in Van Hook, *Virgin and the Dynamo*, 115.

59. See Roland Marchand, *Creating the Corporate Soul: The Rise of Public Relations and Corporate Imagery in American Big Business* (Berkeley: University of California Press, 1998), 64–65; and MacDougall, "The Wire Devils."

60. This motif is still used to illustrate news reports of market activity, despite the relative decline of face-to-face, open-outcry trading. For a witty take on the iconography of brokers as a visual stand-in for the market as a whole, see "The Brokers with Hands on Their Faces Blog," http://brokershandsontheirfacesblog.tumblr.com [accessed 10 March 2012].

61. As Zimmerman notes in *Panic!*, many of the artists who illustrated Wall Street novels also drew images for adventure stories. W. R. Leigh, the artist for many of Lefèvre's stories, left his life as a commercial illustrator in New York to pursue a successful career as a painter of canvases of western life and natural scenes.

62. Medbery, *Men and Mysteries*, 41.

63. On the trope of financial drowning, see Andrew Lawson, *Downwardly Mobile: The Changing Fortunes of American Realism* (New York: Oxford University Press, 2012), 62–85.

64. David Graham Phillips, *The Deluge* (Indianapolis, IN: Bobbs-Merrill, 1905); and Phillips, *The Cost* (New York: Grosset & Dunlap, 1904), 399.

65. "Your Own Brains, versus Brain Bought, Begged, or Borrowed," *Ticker* 1, no. 6 (1908), frontispiece.

66. On the notion of an alternative economy of expenditure, see Georges Bataille, *The Accursed Share: An Essay on General Economy*, 3 vols., trans. Robert Hurley (New York: Zone, 1991–1993); Bataille, "The Notion of Expenditure," in *Visions of Excess: Selected Writings, 1927–1939*, ed. and trans. Allan Stoekl, with Carl R. Lovitt and Donald M. Leslie Jr. (Minneapolis: University of Minnesota Press, 1985); Paul Crosthwaite, "Blood on the Trading Floor: Waste, Sacrifice, and Death in Financial Crises," *Angelaki: Journal of the Theoretical Humanities* 15 (2010): 3–18; and Crosthwaite, "What a Waste of Money: Expenditure, the Death Drive, and the Contemporary Art Market," *New Formations* 72 (2011): 80–93.

67. Richard D. Wyckoff, *Studies in Tape Reading* (New York: Ticker, 1910), 17.

68. Edwin Lefèvre, *Sampson Rock of Wall Street: A Novel* (New York: Harper & Bros., 1907), 53.

69. Zimmerman, *Panic!*, 25. See also Urs Stäheli, "Watching the Market," in *Economic Representations: Academic and Everyday*, ed. David F. Ruccio (New York: Routledge, 2008), 242–56.

70. John Maynard Keynes, *The General Theory of Employment, Interest, and Money* (New York: Harcourt Brace, 1936), 156. In theory, according to the Nash Equilibrium, an infinite process of second-guessing will lead rational players of the game (in which the beauty contestants are ranked from 0 to 100) to converge eventually at 0. Although Keynes acknowledges that there are those who "practice the fourth, fifth, and even higher degrees," empirical studies have shown that usually players reach only the second or third level. See Rosemarie Nagel, "Unraveling in Guessing Games: An Experimental Study," *American Economic Review* 85 (1995): 1313–26.

71. Zimmerman, *Panic!*, 142.

72. Henkin, in *City Reading*, 137–66, documents how the profusion of legible texts circulating in antebellum New York (commercial signs attached to buildings, temporary advertisements and posters plastered to walls, daily mass-market newspapers, and banknotes and their accompanying counterfeit detectors) created a public sphere that, in contrast to Habermas's virtual community of like minds in polite society, inhabited actual public space and was both more democratic yet more anonymous than its eighteenth-century predecessor. Like Henkin, I am arguing here that tape reading, in the bucket shops at least, was a concrete and would-be democratic activity of public reading, which nevertheless has much in common with Habermas's idea of an abstract, virtual, and invisible community of solitary readers. (In the eighteenth century, the readers were resolutely bourgeois; although many ticker readers in nineteenth-century America were equally members of the elite, bucket shops promised to democratize participation in speculative investment.) The claim that ticker reading constitutes a form of "street reading" becomes still stronger later in the twentieth century with the advent of technological developments such as the Trans-Lux Movie Flash Ticker in the 1920s, which enabled projection of the ticker tape onto a screen in banks and brokerages. See Preda, *Framing Finance*, 131. From 1928 on, an electric scrolling tape on the façade of the New York Times building in Times Square provided a news and ticker feed, and the image of the masses staring at a scrolling electronic ticker

remains a visual shorthand for public reaction to the changing fortunes of the stock market. The title of this section nods toward Richard H. Brodhead, *Cultures of Letters: Scenes of Reading and Writing in Nineteenth-Century America* (Chicago: University of Chicago Press, 1993), albeit in a very different spirit from Brodhead's study of the social hierarchies of reading and writing practices in the nineteenth century.

73. George Rutledge Gibson, *Stock Exchanges of London, Paris, and New York: A Comparison* (New York: G. P. Putnam's Sons, 1889), 83–84, quoted in Hochfelder, "Common People," 339. Gibson marvels at the superiority of the American ticker service, compared with that in France or Britain.

74. Jonathan Crary, *Techniques of the Observer: On Vision and Modernity in the Nineteenth Century* (Cambridge, MA: MIT Press, 1990); and Preda, *Framing Finance*, 132–35.

75. For a Lacanian reading of investors' affective identification with securities, see Karin Knorr Cetina and Urs Bruegger, "The Market as an Object of Attachment: Exploring Postsocial Relations in Financial Markets," *Canadian Journal of Sociology* 25 (2000): 141–68.

76. Wyckoff, *Studies in Tape Reading*, 11.

77. *Ticker* 1, no. 4 (February 1908), 34.

78. H. M. Williams, *The Key to Wall Street Mysteries and Methods* (New York: M. W. Hazen, 1904), 70; and Lewis C. Van Riper, *The Ins and Outs of Wall Street* (New York: self-published, 1898), 72.

79. Roger Ward Babson, *Actions and Reactions: An Autobiography of Roger W. Babson* (New York: Harper, 1935). Other than Preda's *Framing Finance*, there has been little discussion of Babson and other chartists in the literature on the cultural history of finance. Walter Friedman's fine study, *Fortune Tellers: The Story of America's First Economic Forecasters* (Princeton, NJ: Princeton University Press, 2013) appeared after I had completed this chapter.

80. In the video installation *Black Narcissus* (https://vimeo.com/132643744/), the artists Matthew Cornford and David Cross have produced a compelling reworking of the familiar trope of financial peaks and troughs, with their CGI rendition of financial data from 2004 to 2014 as an otherworldly mountainscape. For an account of Cornford and Cross's work, see Alistair Robinson, "Booms and Busts: End of Season Thought," in Crosthwaite, Knight, and Marsh, *Show Me the Money*, 131–51.

81. Audrey Jaffe, *The Affective Life of the Average Man: The Victorian Novel and the Stock-Market Graph* (Columbus, OH: Ohio State University Press, 2010), 64–65.

82. Jean-Joseph Goux, in *The Coiners of Language*, trans. Jennifer Curtiss Gage (Norman: University of Oklahoma Press, 1994), makes an intriguing case for a homology between the rise of modernism and the demise of the gold standard. Although Goux oversimplifies some of the historical specificities of the collapse of the international gold standard in the interwar years, his argument (in this book and other works, such as his article on the "stock market mentality") remains important because it points toward the surprising affinities between cultural experimentation and market rationality.

83. Preda, *Framing Finance*, 150.

84. *Wall Street Journal*, 8 July 1889, 1.

85. De Goede, *Virtue, Fortune, and Faith*, 101.

86. On the introduction of the scientific method into economics, see Mary Morgan, *The History of Econometric Ideas* (Cambridge: Cambridge University Press, 1990).

87. On the turn to graphs in economics, see Harro Maas and Mary S. Morgan, "Tim-

ing History: The Introduction of Graphical Analysis in 19th Century British Economics," *Revue d'histoire des sciences humaines* 7 (2002): 97–127; Judy Klein, "Reflections from the Age of Economic Measurement," *History of Political Economy* 33 (2001): 111–36; and Klein, *Statistical Visions in Time: A History of Time Series Analysis, 1662–1938* (Cambridge: Cambridge University Press, 1997). Klein argues that practical techniques preceded academic, abstract modes of analysis. On the history of data visualization more generally, see Daniel Rosenberg and Anthony Grafton, *Cartographies of Time: A History of the Timeline* (New York: Princeton Architectural Press, 2010); Manuel Lima, *Visual Complexity: Mapping Patterns of Information* (New York: Princeton Architectural Press, 2011); Edward R. Tufte, *The Visual Display of Quantitative Information*, 2nd ed. (Cheshire, CT: Graphics Press, 2001); and Michael Friendly and Daniel J. Denis, "Timeline," Milestones in the History of Thematic Cartography, Statistical Graphics, and Data Visualization, www.datavis.ca/milestones/ [accessed 14 October 2011].

88. Alfred Marshall, "The Graphic Method of Statistics," in *Memorials of Alfred Marshall*, ed. A. C. Pigou (London: Macmillan, 1925), 175, quoted in De Goede, *Virtue, Fortune, and Faith*, 93.

89. There has been very little research on the ways in which economic knowledge has been presented visually for lay audiences. One foray into this uncharted field is a study of post–World War II economic textbooks, by Loïc Charles and Yann Giraud, "Economics for the Masses: The Visual Display of Economic Knowledge in the United States (1910–45)," *History of Political Economy* 45 (2013): 567–612.

90. Philip Mirowski, *More Heat than Light: Economics as Social Physics, Physics as Nature's Economics* (Cambridge: Cambridge University Press, 1989). Mirowski points out how the analogy between the conception of energy in physics and that of utility in economics does not hold.

91. Fisher details the development of his model in *Mathematical Investigations in the Theory of Value and Prices* (New Haven, CT: Yale University Press, 1925). It is important to note that the machine did not present a view of the stock market in particular, or even the entire economy in general, but instead modeled an isolated aspect of the wider economy. Fisher's device relied on the input from other economic subsystems remaining constant. In the middle decades of the twentieth century, economists began to develop more-dynamic "models," informed by systems theory, cybernetics, and ecology, with more-complicated feedback loops between the various processes. The economic accuracy of Fisher's model as a working theory of equilibrium has recently been attested to in William C. Brainard and Herbert E. Scarf, "How to Compute Equilibrium Prices in 1891," *American Journal of Economics and Sociology* 64, no. 1 (2005): 57–83. On the wider question of the use of models, both real and virtual, see Mary S. Morgan, *The World in the Model: How Economists Think and Work* (Cambridge: Cambridge University Press, 2012). For an intriguing account of a later construction of an actual mechanical model of the economy, see Alissa G. Karl, "Rhys, Keynes, and the Modern(ist) Economic Nation," *Novel* 43 (2010): 424–42. Oddly reminiscent of Fisher's hydraulic machine, one of the favorite visual metaphors for explaining the complex structure of collateralized debt obligations (CDOs) in the financial crisis that began in 2007 was the idea of each tranche of residential mortgage-backed securities (RMBSs) acting as a bucket that was topped up by the steady flow of repayments. See, for example, "What's a CDO?" *Upstart Business Journal*, http://upstart .bizjournals.com/multimedia/interactives/2007/12/cdo.html [accessed 2 May 2010].

92. Daniel Breslau, in "Economics Invents the Economy: Mathematics, Statistics, and Models in the Work of Irving Fisher and Wesley Mitchell," *Theory & Society* 32, no. 3 (2003): 379–411, posits a three-stage process involving abstraction, homogenization (of economic phenomena into commensurable units), and sedimentation, by which mathematically influenced economic ideas helped construct the idea of "the economy." Breslau's focus is mainly on the third stage, in which ideas became sedimented in the changing social milieu of academic economics in the early years of the twentieth century.

93. In fact, even though the econometricians of the Cowles Commission talked of the "economic system," it was really only with Keynes's *General Theory of Employment, Interest, and Money* (1936) and the institutionalization of macroeconomics that the term "the economy" began to gain any purchase. In addition to Breslau ("Economics Invents the Economy"), see Timothy Mitchell, "Fixing the Economy," *Cultural Studies* 12 (1998): 82–101; and Susan Buck-Morss, "Envisioning Capital: Political Economy on Display," *Critical Inquiry* 21 (1995): 434–67. Buck-Morss argues that a process of cognitive mapping was required to bring "the economy" into being: "The economy is now seen to act in the world. Because the economy is not found as an empirical object among other worldly things, in order for it to be 'seen' by the human perceptual apparatus it has to undergo a process, crucial for science, of representational mapping. This is doubling, but with a difference; the map shifts the point of view so that viewers can see the whole as if from the outside, in a way that allows them, from a specific position inside, to find their bearings. Navigational maps were prototypical; mapping the economy was an outgrowth of this technique" (440).

94. Mary Poovey, "Expanding the Domain of the Calculable: From Fair Valuation to Risk Management," *New History of American Capitalism*, ed. Sven Beckert and Christine Desan (forthcoming).

Chapter 4 · Confidence Games and Inside Information

1. Herman Melville, *The Confidence-Man: His Masquerade* (1857; reprint, London: Penguin 1990), 51. Subsequent references to this edition will be cited in parentheses in the text, with the abbreviation *CM* where necessary.

2. In contrast to the prevailing critical orthodoxy that viewed Melville's novel as a transcendent critique of a market economy, Wai Chee Dimock argues for a kinship between the book and market logic through an economic model of selfhood, which she terms "personified accounting." In doing so, Dimock follows Jean-Christophe Agnew, who sees this novel not as an attack on, but as an embodiment of the problem of the placeless market. See Dimock, *Empire for Liberty: Melville and the Poetics of Individualism* (Princeton, NJ: Princeton University Press, 1989), 176–214; and Agnew, *Worlds Apart: The Market and the Theater in Anglo-American Thought, 1550–1750* (Cambridge: Cambridge University Press, 1986), 195–203.

3. On the development of an everyday semiotics of commercial culture, see John F. Kasson, *Rudeness and Civility: Manners in Nineteenth-Century Urban America* (New York: Hill & Wang, 1990), 70–111.

4. The details of the original episodes are documented in Johannes Dietrich Bergmann, "The Original Confidence Man," *American Quarterly* 21 (1969): 560–77.

5. Michael Paul Rogin, *Subversive Genealogy: The Politics and Art of Herman Melville* (New York: Knopf, 1983), 242. See also Lara Langer Cohen, *The Fabrication of American*

Literature: Fraudulence and Antebellum Print Culture (Philadelphia: University of Pennsylvania Press, 2011), 162–76.

6. As Sianne Ngai suggests in *Ugly Feelings* (Cambridge, MA: Harvard University Press, 2009), *The Confidence-Man* is resolutely antirealist, refusing to cash in on, in any consistent way, the Black Guinea's (one of the many identities of the central character) promise of a single identity underpinning the various guises of the confidence man, coupled with the peculiar way in which feelings, like money, seem to float free from the characters who supposedly experience them. In *Empire for Liberty*, Dimock likewise identifies a peculiar impersonality at the heart of the novel: "If one could speak of the Invisible Hand as the ultimate capitalist fantasy, *The Confidence-Man*, in its inhuman, superhuman reign of words, would seem to enact that fantasy at its most extravagant, and most fantastic" (209).

7. Karen Halttunen (*Confidence Men and Painted Women: A Study of Middle-Class Culture in America, 1830–1870* [New Haven, CT: Yale University Press, 1982]) and others have noted the way that republican notions of masculine self-possession were evoked as a bulwark against the dangerous figure of the market-oriented confidence man. Kathleen De Grave, in *Swindler, Spy, Rebel: The Confidence Woman in Nineteenth-Century America* (Columbia: University of Missouri Press, 1995), argues that, unlike the con man, the emerging figure of the con woman has nothing to sell and instead manipulates the stereotype of womanhood, rather than playing on notions of rugged, manly independence.

8. Halttunen, *Confidence Men and Painted Women*.

9. *New York Herald*, 8 July 1849, quoted in Bergman, "Original Confidence Man," 561–62.

10. This interpretation is highlighted in Steve Fraser, *Every Man a Speculator: A History of Wall Street in American Life* (New York: HarperCollins, 2005), 30–32; and Amy Reading, *The Mark Inside: A Perfect Swindle, a Cunning Revenge, and a Small History of the Big Con* (New York: Random House, 2012), 24–26. In some subsequent versions of the scam reported in the newspapers, the confidence man offers his own, seemingly expensive watch as collateral on a loan temporarily given, with the watch turning out to be worthless and the con man long since gone. It is worth noting that in its different tellings, the primal scene of the Original Confidence Man always seemed to revolve around a watch. Over and above its obvious value (or lack of value) as a piece of portable property, the symbolism of a watch introduces the notion of time into the transaction. A gift, in effect, is a loan that has no time limit; in several cases the con man would protest his innocence by claiming that he had just not got around to paying back the loan, claiming that he was no more guilty than others who were late in paying back credit. If interest on a loan creates a commodification of time, then the con man's request for a watch as a symbol of trust produces a confusion between the timeless rhythms of a gift economy and the regular accounting of an exchange economy.

11. On the American dream of getting rich without effort, see Jackson Lears, *Something for Nothing: Luck in America* (New York: Viking, 2003).

12. The confusions that Melville's widow experienced between older nonmarket and newer monetary forms of value are part of a wider pattern in the nineteenth century. Viviana Zelizer, in *Morals and Markets: The Development of Life Insurance in the United States* (New York: Columbia University Press, 1979), discusses how the development of life insurance in nineteenth-century America was comparatively slow, as a result of the difficulty

in getting people to accept the idea of putting a price on something sacred. The acceptance of life insurance as a form of rational risk management also involved a shift in social attitudes toward caring for widows and orphans, going from relying on charity to relying on the market. See also Susan M. Ryan, "Misgivings: Melville, Race, and the Ambiguities of Benevolence," *American Literary History* 12, no. 4 (2000): 685–712.

13. "The Original Confidence Man in Town," *Albany Evening Journal*, 28 April 1855, quoted in Bergmann, "Original Confidence Man," 571–73.

14. It is also worth remembering, however, that popular anti-Masonry sentiment in antebellum America was based on the idea that the secret ties of Freemasonry would endanger the transparent bonds of citizenship by bringing back a form of status-based aristocratic privilege into a supposedly open, democratic, mobile American society.

15. Most victims of confidence tricks were reluctant to go to the police, for fear that their shameful encounter would be exposed to publicity. It is arguable that what had been violated was not their innocence, but the social fantasy of manly independence and, more worrying still, the fact that they had been a willing participant in their own seduction.

16. As scholars of nineteenth-century history have noted, for all its benevolent talk of selflessness, charity served to reinforce, in part, the imbalance of power inherent in the traditional hierarchies of society. The con man is appealing to a more modern form of charity, which comes with no strings of humiliation attached.

17. Stephen Mihm, *A Nation of Counterfeiters: Capitalists, Con Men, and the Making of the United States* (Cambridge, MA: Harvard University Press, 2007), 12–13.

18. Evert Duyckink, article in *Literary World* 5 (18 August 1849), 133, quoted in Bergmann, "Original Confidence Man," 566.

19. "'The Confidence Man' on a Large Scale," *New York Herald*, 11 July 1847, quoted in Bergman, "Original Confidence Man," 562–65.

20. Reading, *The Mark Inside*, 27.

21. On this argument, see Jens Beckert, "Imagined Futures: Fictional Expectations in the Economy," *Theory and Society* 42 (2013): 219–40.

22. On the relationship between these figures, see Susan Kuhlmann, *Knave, Fool, and Genius: The Confidence Man as He Appears in Nineteenth-Century Fiction* (Chapel Hill: University of North Carolina Press, 1973); Warwick Wadlington, *The Confidence Game in American Literature* (Princeton, NJ: Princeton University Press, 1975); Jay Robert Nash, *Hustlers and Con Men: An Anecdotal History of the Confidence Man and His Games* (Philadelphia: M. Evans, 1976); John G. Blair, *The Confidence Man in Modern Fiction* (London: Vision, 1979); Gary Lindberg, *The Confidence Man in American Literature* (New York: Oxford University Press, 1982); William Lenz, *Fast Talk and Flush Times: The Confidence Man as Literary Convention* (Columbia: University of Missouri Press, 1985); Judy Hilkey, *Character Is Capital: Success Manuals and Manhood in Gilded Age America* (Chapel Hill: University of North Carolina Press, 1997); Ann Fabian, *Card Sharps, Dream Books, and Bucket Shops: Gambling in Nineteenth-Century America* (Ithaca, NY: Cornell University Press, 1990); James Cook, *The Arts of Deception: Playing with Fraud in the Age of Barnum* (Cambridge, MA: Harvard University Press, 2001); Joshua D. Rothman, *Flush Times and Fever Dreams: A Story of Capitalism and Slavery in the Age of Jackson* (Athens: University of Georgia Press, 2012); and Walter A. Friedman, *Birth of a Salesman* (Cambridge, MA: Harvard University Press, 2005).

23. Lawrence Friedman, *Crime and Punishment in American History* (New York: Basic Books, 1994), 193–210.

24. Fabian, *Card Sharps*, 57.

25. Luc Sante, introduction, in David W. Maurer, *The Big Con: The Classic Story of the Confidence Man and the Confidence Trick* (London: Arrow, 2000), xi.

26. For a discussion of the changing cultural assumptions concerning the innocence of the con man's victims, see Michael Pettit, *The Science of Deception* (Chicago: University of Chicago Press, 2013), 21–48.

27. Maurer, *Big Con*, 3–4. See also the gloss provided by Amy Reading, "The Nine Stages of the Big Con," Amy Reading, www.amyreading.com/inside-the-book/the-nine-stages-of-the-big-con/.

28. On the green-goods game, see Timothy J. Gilfoyle, *A Pickpocket's Tale: The Underworld of Nineteenth-Century New York* (New York: W. W. Norton, 2007), 204–22.

29. George S. McWatters, *Forgers and Confidence Men*, Pinkerton Detective Series 3 (Chicago: Laird & Lee, 1891), 772–92.

30. Arthur Train, "The Last of the Wire-Tappers: The True Story of the Famous Felix Case," *American Magazine* 62 (June 1906), 149.

31. Anthony Comstock, *Frauds Exposed; or, How the People Are Deceived and Robbed, and Youth Corrupted* (New York: J. Howard Brown, 1880), 14. On the anonymity, promiscuity, and intimacy of mass-mailing swindles, see also David Henkin, *The Postal Age: The Emergence of Modern Communications in Nineteenth-Century America* (Chicago: University of Chicago Press, 2008), 56, 156.

32. Comstock, *Frauds Exposed*, 15.

33. Confirming the adage that there is no honor among thieves, there was not much confidence in evidence at the heart of Buckwalter's confidence game. Not trusting his clerks to deal with him squarely, Buckwalter placed more trust in the remarkably detailed legal contracts he had drawn up to establish the firm of Lawrence & Co. See Comstock, *Frauds Exposed*, 38–46.

34. John Hill, *Gold Bricks of Speculation* (Chicago: Lincoln Book Concern, 1904), 140.

35. The ruse of creating an entirely new exchange to enable and legitimize fraudulent practices is not so far from the situation described in Michael Lewis's *Flash Boys: Cracking the Money Code* (London: Allen Lane, 2014), which documents how new electronic trading exchanges were created in the 2010s to enable the more ethically and legally dubious forms of high-frequency trading to take place. The legal defense of bucket shops in the Supreme Court case of *Board of Trade v. Christie Grain & Stock Co.*, 198 U.S. 236 (1905), was, in essence, that they were no different from the official commodity exchanges (with speculators in both cases never expecting to actually take possession of the produce in which they were supposedly trading), coupled with the claim that price quotations were public information rather than private intellectual property. Although Hennig's schemes for the legitimization of bucket shops failed, Hill (*Gold Bricks of Speculation*, 80) reports that Hennig did manage to attain respectability in the upper echelons of Chicago society by offering extravagant prizes to the yacht club.

36. Comstock, *Frauds Exposed*, 111.

37. McWatters, *Forgers and Confidence Men*, 254. The printed letter McWatters cites makes the same appeal that Thompson used in his encounter with the jewelry store owner in Albany: "While conversing with a gentleman from your locality recently, you were named as a shrewd and reliable person, and one likely to enter into a business, the nature of which will be explained in this letter" (254–55). What is also remarkable, however, is

that, once the mark had been hooked by the template letters, many of the firms of discretionary brokers employed armies of clerks to create genuinely handwritten and personal letters, in a precise and persistent campaign tailored to take each victim for the maximum amount that could be extracted.

38. Hill, *Gold Bricks of Speculation*, 72.

39. Comstock, *Frauds Exposed*, 17.

40. Ibid., 58.

41. Ibid., 19.

42. Ibid., 33.

43. Hill, *Gold Bricks of Speculation*, 141.

44. New York [State] Committee on Speculation in Securities and Commodities, *Report of Governor Hughes' Committee on Speculation in Securities and Commodities* (7 June 1909), 5. On the Hughes Committee and debates about democratization, see Julia C. Ott, *When Wall Street Met Main Street: The Quest for an Investors' Democracy* (Cambridge, MA: Harvard University Press, 2011), 30–31; Cedric B. Cowing, *Populists, Plungers, and Progressives: A Social History of Stock and Commodity Speculation, 1890–1936* (Princeton, NJ: Princeton University Press, 1965), 39–41, 67–69; and Jerry W. Markham, *Law Enforcement and the History of Financial Market Manipulation* (Armonk, NY: M. E. Sharpe, 2014), 30–33.

45. [John Moody and John. F. Hume], *The Art of Wise Investing* (New York: Moody, 1904), 70.

46. Thomas Gibson, *The Pitfalls of Speculation* (New York: Moody, 1906), 11.

47. Richard D. Wyckoff, *Studies in Tape Reading* (New York: Ticker, 1910), 11.

48. Ibid., 74.

49. Henry Crosby Emery, *Speculation on the Stock and Produce Exchanges in the United States* (New York: Macmillan, 1904), 117.

50. Ibid., 178. Despite his misgivings about the use of inside information in the securities market, Emery insisted that the market in produce is governed by the economic laws of supply and demand.

51. Sereno S. Pratt, *The Work of Wall Street* (New York: Appleton, 1904), 69.

52. Jonathan Levy, *Freaks of Fortune: The Emerging World of Capitalism and Risk in America* (Cambridge, MA: Harvard University Press, 2012), 287.

53. "United States Steel Syndicate Transaction Memo," Box 7, "Material Prepared for Armstrong Hearing" Folder, George W. Perkins Papers, Columbia University Rare Book and Manuscript Library, New York, New York, quoted in Levy, *Freaks of Fortune*, 287. For a similar Gilded Age tale of a confusion of loyalties on the part of James Hazen Hyde (the Equitable Life Insurance Company heir), a story that involved the mixing of personal and business affairs, coupled with a patrician sense of acting for the greater good, see Patricia Beard, *After the Ball: Gilded Age Secrets, Boardroom Betrayals, and the Party that Ignited the Great Wall Street Scandal of 1905* (New York: HarperCollins, 2004).

54. See Stephen Bainbridge, *Securities Law: Insider Trading* (New York: Foundation Press, 1999), 8–10.

55. *Dirks v. SEC*, 463 U.S. 646 (1983), quoted in Bainbridge, *Securities Law*, 24.

56. H. L. Wilgus, "Purchase of Shares of Corporation by a Director from a Shareholder," *Michigan Law Review* 8 (1910): 267.

57. *Strong v. Repide*, 213 U.S. 149 (1909). On the significance of *People v. McCord*, 76

Mich. 200 (1871), see Train, "Last of the Wire-Tappers"; Gilfoyle, *Pickpocket's Tale*, 219–21; and Pettit, *Science of Deception*, 29–33.

58. See Edward J. Balleisen, "Private Cops on the Fraud Beat: The Limits of American Business Self-Regulation, 1895–1932," *Business History Review* 83 (2009): 113–60.

59. Richard White, "Information, Markets, and Corruption: Transcontinental Railroads in the Gilded Age," *Journal of American History* 90 (2003): 19.

60. Niklas Luhmann, *Trust and Power* (Chichester, UK: Wiley, 1979).

61. *The Life and Letters of Lafcadio Hearn*, ed. Elizabeth Bisland, 2 vols. (Boston: Houghton Mifflin, 1906), 2:182, quoted in Wayne W. Westbrook, *Wall Street in the American Novel* (New York: New York University Press, 1980), 78. On the sense of economic precariousness in the nineteenth century, for which the genre of realism provided an imaginary antidote, see Andrew Lawson, *Downwardly Mobile: The Changing Fortunes of American Realism* (New York: Oxford University Press, 2012).

62. Wai Chee Dimock, "The Economy of Pain: Capitalism, Humanitarianism, and the Realistic Novel," in *New Essays on* The Rise of Silas Lapham, ed. Donald Pease (New York: Cambridge University Press, 1991), 75.

63. The relationship between the love plot and the business plot is explored, for example, in Walter Benn Michaels, "Dreiser's *Financier*: The Man of Business as a Man of Letters," in *The Gold Standard and the Logic of Naturalism* (Berkeley: University of California Press, 1987), 61–83; and Howard Horwitz, "'To Find the Value of X': Speculation and Romance in *The Pit*," in *By the Law of Nature: Form and Value in Nineteenth-Century America* (New York: Oxford University Press, 1991), 146–67.

64. For an account of this trend in the contemporaneous reviews of the novel, see Patrick Dooley, "Nineteenth-Century Business Ethics and *The Rise of Silas Lapham*," *American Studies* 21 (1980): 79–93.

65. See, for example, Thomas G. Tanselle, "The Architecture of *The Rise of Silas Lapham*," *American Literature* 27 (1966): 430–57. The tension between the two plot lines is discussed further in Brook Thomas, *American Literary Realism and the Failed Promise of Contract* (Berkeley: University of California Press, 1997), 122–55.

66. Donald Pizer, *Realism and Naturalism in Nineteenth-Century American Literature* (Carbondale: Southern Illinois University Press, 1966), 125.

67. Dimock, "Economy of Pain."

68. Hildegard Hoeller, *From Gift to Commodity: Capitalism and Sacrifice and Nineteenth-Century American Fiction* (Hanover: University of New Hampshire Press, 2012).

69. Lewis Hyde, *The Gift: Imagination and the Erotic Life of Property* (New York: Vintage Books, 1983); and Jacques Derrida, *Given Time: 1. Counterfeit Money*, trans. Peggy Kamuf (Chicago: University of Chicago Press, 1992).

70. William Dean Howells, *The Rise of Silas Lapham* (1885; reprint, New York: Penguin, 1988), 68. Subsequent references to this edition will be cited in parentheses in the text.

71. Thomas, *American Literary Realism*, 122–23.

72. William Dean Howells, *A Hazard of New Fortunes* (1889; reprint, New York: Penguin, 2001), 396.

73. On the idea of the imaginary resolution of real social contradictions, see Fredric Jameson, *The Political Unconscious: Narrative as a Socially Symbolic Act* (Ithaca, NY: Cornell University Press, 1981).

74. Edith Wharton, *A Backward Glance* (New York: Appleton-Century, 1934), 176.

75. Richard White, *Railroaded: The Transcontinentals and the Making of Modern America* (New York: Norton, 2011), 100.

76. White, "Information, Markets, and Corruption."

77. White, *Railroaded*, 100–101.

78. Edith Wharton, *The House of Mirth* (New York: Scribner's, 1905); Wharton, *The Custom of the Country* (New York: Scriber's, 1913); and Wharton, *The Age of Innocence* (New York, Grosset & Dunlap, 1920). References to these editions will be included in parentheses in the text, with the abbreviations *HM*, *AI*, and *CC* where necessary.

79. Sven Beckert, *The Monied Metropolis: New York City and the Consolidation of the American Bourgeoisie, 1850–1896* (New York: Cambridge University Press, 2001), 31.

80. For an exploration of these ideas in Wharton, see Jennie Kassanoff, *Edith Wharton and the Politics of Race* (New York: Cambridge University Press, 2004).

81. Wai Chee Dimock, "Debasing Exchange: Edith Wharton's *The House of Mirth*," *PMLA* 100 (1985): 783–92.

82. We might compare how, in *The Rise of Silas Lapham*, the Coreys debate whether a dinner-party invitation to the Laphams repays their obligations to them.

83. Dimock, "Debasing Exchange," 784.

84. There is, however, one way in which the truth is "spoken," namely, endless blushing, which also serves to provide a graphic register of the shame it is designed to suppress.

85. See Richard White, "Friends," paper delivered at the "Reputation, Emotion and the Market" symposium, part of the Culture of the Market Network, Centre for Corporate Reputation, Saïd Business School, Oxford University, United Kingdom, 20 March 2010 (paper in possession of the author).

86. William Graham Sumner, *What Social Classes Owe to Each Other* (New York: Harper & Bros., 1883).

87. Wharton to Dr. Morgan Dix, 5 December 1905, *The Letters of Edith Wharton*, ed. R. W. B. Lewis and Nancy Lewis (New York: Scribner's, 1988), 98–99.

88. Hildegard Hoeller, *Edith Wharton's Dialogue with Realism and Sentimental Fiction* (Gainesville: University Press of Florida, 2000), 104–19.

89. Emily Broadman, Stephanie Chan, Killeen Hanson, and Richard White, "Tracing Railroad Directors, 1872–1894," Stanford University, Spatial History Project, www.stanford .edu/group/spatialhistory/cgi-bin/site/viz.php?id=115&project_id=0/ [accessed 14 November 2012].

Chapter 5 · *Conspiracy and the Invisible Hand of the Market*

1. For discussions of the way in which Americans in the earlier part of the nineteenth century tried to make sense of the vicissitudes of economic fortune in general, and financial panics in particular, see Ann Fabian, "Speculation on Distress: The Popular Discourse of the Panics of 1837 and 1857," *Yale Journal of Criticism* 3, no. 1 (1989): 127–41; Andrew Lawson, *Downwardly Mobile: The Changing Fortunes of American Realism* (Oxford: Oxford University Press, 2012); Jessica M. Lepler, *The Many Panics of 1837: People, Politics, and the Creation of a Transatlantic Financial Crisis* (Cambridge: Cambridge University Press, 2013); and Jonathan Levy, *Freaks of Fortune: The Emerging World of Capitalism and Risk in America* (Cambridge, MA: Harvard University Press, 2012). For an overview of the various panics, see Robert Sobel, *Panic on Wall Street: A History of America's Financial Disasters* (New York:

Beard Books, 1999); Charles R. Geisst, *Wall Street: A History, from Its Beginnings to the Fall of Enron* (Oxford: Oxford University Press, 2004); Scott Reynolds Nelson, *A Nation of Deadbeats: An Uncommon History of America's Financial Disasters* (New York: Random House, 2012); and Robert F. Bruner and Sean D. Carr, *The Panic of 1907: Lessons Learned from the Market's Perfect Storm* (Hoboken, NJ: John Wiley & Sons, 2008).

2. The origins of Adam Smith's trope of the "invisible hand" are multifold. In addition to the theological notion of Providence, the term also refers to the "Engineer of the Pit" who, invisible to the audience, orchestrates the theatrical machinery. See Syed Ahmad, "Adam Smith's Four Invisible Hands," *History of Political Economy* 22, no. 1 (1990): 137–44; and David Zimmerman, *Panic!: Markets, Crises, and Crowds in American Fiction* (Chapel Hill: University of North Carolina Press, 2006), 131. On the reworking of Adam Smith in nineteenth-century (British) literature, see Eleanor Courtemanche, *The "Invisible Hand" and British Fiction 1818–1860: Adam Smith, Political Economy, and the Genre of Realism* (New York: Palgrave Macmillan, 2011).

3. The development of American economic thought in the nineteenth century—in particular, the shift to a view of the market not merely as a mechanism of exchange, but as the source of value and identity—is discussed in Jeffrey Sklansky, *The Soul's Economy: Market and Selfhood in American Thought, 1820–1920* (Chapel Hill: University of North Carolina Press, 2002).

4. Martin J. Sklar, *The Corporate Reconstruction of American Capitalism, 1890–1916* (Cambridge: Cambridge University Press, 1988), 54–62.

5. On the development of New Psychology in general, and crowd psychology in particular, as a way of accounting for market mania, see Zimmerman, *Panic!*, 134–39; and Sklansky, *Soul's Economy*, 137–70.

6. The term "conspiracy theory" only came into popular use in the 1970s, following academic discussions by figures such as Karl Popper and Richard Hofstadter in the 1960s. There are recorded uses of the term from the late nineteenth century, but not in the same sense that we mean it today. See Andrew McKenzie-McHarg, "How Did Conspiracy Theories Come to Be Seen as Theories?" paper delivered at the Conspiracies Real and Imagined conference, University of York, United Kingdom, 8 September 2011.

7. Walter Lippmann, *Drift and Mastery: An Attempt to Diagnose the Current Unrest* (New York: Mitchell Kennerley, 1914), 2–3.

8. See Roland Marchand, *Creating the Corporate Soul: The Rise of Public Relations and Corporate Imagery in American Big Business* (Berkeley: University of California Press, 1998).

9. On the notion of "piercing the corporate veil," see Brook Thomas, *American Literary Realism and the Failed Promise of Contract* (Berkeley: University of California Press, 1997), 239–41.

10. This debate is discussed in Sklar, *Corporate Reconstruction*, 23–40.

11. For accounts of these stories, see Geisst, *Wall Street*; Kenneth Ackerman, *The Gold Ring: Jim Fisk, Jay Gould, and Black Friday, 1869* (New York: Dodd Mead, 1988); John Steele Gordon, *The Scarlet Woman of Wall Street: Jay Gould, Jim Fisk, Cornelius Vanderbilt, the Erie Railway Wars, and the Birth of Wall Street* (New York: Weidenfeld & Nicholson, 1988); and T. J. Stiles, *The First Tycoon: The Epic Life of Cornelius Vanderbilt* (New York: Knopf, 2009).

12. Richard R. John, "Robber Barons Redux: Antimonopoly Reconsidered," *Enterprise & Society* 13 (2012): 1–38.

13. Charles F. Adams and Henry Adams, *Chapters of Erie and Other Essays* (1871; reprint, New York: Henry Holt, 1886), 95–96.

14. Ibid., 98.

15. Ibid., 95.

16. Ibid., 96.

17. John C. Reed, *The New Plutocracy* (New York: Abbey Press, 1903), vii.

18. Ibid., viii.

19. This story has been dismissed by most commentators, such as Irwin Unger, *The Greenback Era* (Princeton, NJ: Princeton University Press, 1964), 331; and Milton Friedman, "The Crime of 1873," *Journal of Political Economy* 98 (1990): 1159–94. For a recent reexamination of the Seyd story, however, see Samuel DeCanio, "Populism, Paranoia, and the Politics of Free Silver," *Studies in American Political Development* 25 (2011): 1–26.

20. Reed, *New Plutocracy*, 214.

21. Richard Hofstadter, *The Paranoid Style in American Politics and Other Essays* (London: Jonathan Cape, 1966), 29.

22. Ibid.; and Richard Hofstadter, *The Age of Reform* (New York: Knopf, 1956), 73.

23. Hofstadter, *Age of Reform*, 70, 73.

24. The political implications of Hofstadter's stance have been dissected by a number of scholars recently. See, for example, Mark Fenster, *Conspiracy Theories: Secrecy and Power in American Culture*, revised ed. (Minneapolis: University of Minnesota Press, 2008), 23–51.

25. Hofstadter, *Age of Reform*, 81. Hofstadter, however, goes on to note that "the Greenback-Populist tradition activated most of what we have of modern antisemitism in the United States. . . . There has been a persistent linkage between antisemitism and money and credit obsessions" (81).

26. Ignatius Donnelly, "Omaha Platform," *The World Almanac, 1893* (New York: Press [*The New York World*], 1893), 83–85.

27. Although I disagree with the overall conclusions reached by Joseph E. Uscinski and Joseph M. Parent in *American Conspiracy Theories* (New York: Oxford University Press, 2014) about the waning influence of conspiracy theories in the age of the Internet, their innovative investigation of the changing rhetoric of conspiracy is instructive. In an analysis of letters to the editor written to two national newspapers, they discovered that almost one-third of the conspiracy talk from 1890 to 1896 fixated on the influence of "business," with those across the political spectrum viewing monopolies and trusts as a threat to American democracy.

28. For revisionist arguments about Populist antisemitism, see Gretchen Ritter, *Goldbugs and Greenbacks: The Antimonopoly Tradition and the Politics of Finance in America, 1865–1896* (Cambridge: Cambridge University Press, 1997); and Jeffrey Ostler, "The Rhetoric of Conspiracy and Formation of Kansas Populism," *Agricultural History* 69 (1995): 1–27.

29. As DeCanio ("Populism") argues, although the Seyd story is a red herring (not least considering that Seyd published a work in favor of bimetallism), the idea that political corruption—in the form of bribery on behalf of bankers—lay behind the passage of the Coinage Act of 1873 is supported by the discovery (in the Bancroft Library at the University of California, Berkeley) of letters from William Ralston, of the Bank of California, to Treasury Department bureaucrats.

30. Ostler, "Rhetoric of Conspiracy," 5–6.

31. Sarah E. V. Emery, *Seven Financial Conspiracies Which Have Enslaved the American People* (Lansing, MI: Robert Smith, 1894), 54. See also Pauline Adams and Emma S. Thorn-

ton, *A Populist Assault: Sarah E. Van De Vort Emery on American Democracy, 1862–1895* (Bowling Green, OH: Bowling Green State University Popular Press, 1982).

32. William H. Harvey, *Coin's Financial School*, ed. and introd. Richard Hofstadter (Cambridge, MA: Belknap Press of Harvard University Press, 1963), 5.

33. J. C. Catchings to Daniel L. Lamont, 6 April 1895, quoted in James Livingston, *Origins of the Federal Reserve System: Money, Class, and Corporate Capitalism, 1890–1913* (Ithaca, NY: Cornell University Press, 1989), 90.

34. On the political complexity of William "Coin" Harvey, see Livingston, *Origins of the Federal Reserve System*, 55.

35. Harvey, *Coin's Financial School*, 116.

36. Ibid., 109, 213, 118.

37. Ibid., 126.

38. Ibid., 215.

39. On the influence of Harvey's pamphlet, especially the way in which it was emulated by his opponents, see Hofstadter's comments in Harvey, *Coin's Financial School*, 1–81; and Livingston, *Origins of the Federal Reserve*, 90–96.

40. Henry Clews, "Wall Street, Past, Present, and Future," *Arena* 18, no. 92 (July 1897).

41. Henry Clews, "Delusions about Wall Street," *North American Review* 145, no. 371 (October 1887): 410–21.

42. William C. Van Antwerp, *The Stock Exchange from Within* (New York: Doubleday, Page, 1913), 30.

43. Henry Crosby Emery, *Speculation on the Stock and Produce Exchanges in the United States* (New York: Macmillan, 1904), 174, 182. Emery is forced to recognize, however, that insider manipulation might still happen in cases of outright fraud; he also believes that reforming the stock market so that only those who are "best qualified for speculation" to set prices is a pipe dream, because the big players actively welcome "outsiders" to help maintain an active market. In his view, democratization therefore brings as many evils as benefits.

44. Emery, *Speculation*, 176.

45. Edwin Lefèvre, "The Tipster," *Wall Street Stories* (1901; reprint, New York: McGraw-Hill, 2008), 108.

46. Charles R. Flint, "What Combination Has Done for Capital and Labor" in *The Trust: Its Book*, ed. James H. Bridge (New York: Doubleday, Page, 1902), 158.

47. Rudolph J. R. Peritz, *Competition Policy in America, 1888–1992* (New York: Oxford University Press, 1996), 55. In the section below, I discuss in greater detail the more technical, legal notion of "corporate personality."

48. Legal cases involving negligence made manifest the difficulties of establishing the parameters of legal responsibility as corporate organizations became more complex. Many of the cases revolved around the agent-principal problem, with corporate lawyers arguing that the traditional idea—that masters were responsible for the torts of their servants, or that principals could enable and were liable for the actions of their agents—no longer applied. Instead, corporate lawyers argued that, in the increasingly complex world of large organizations, there was no longer a direct personal connection between principal and agent and, therefore, no guarantee that expressly willed authority had been given. Large corporations thus necessitated a thorough-going rethinking of the nature of causation and individual agency. As Morton Horwitz notes in *The Transformation of American Law*,

1870–1960 (New York: Oxford University Press, 1992), "the gradual acceptance of the reality of multiple causation was one measure of recognition that a more complex and interdependent society had emerged by the turn of the century" (65). On the limits of corporate intentionality and responsibility during this period, see also Nan Goldman, *Shifting the Blame: Literature, Law, and the Theory of Accidents in Nineteenth-Century America* (Princeton, NJ: Princeton University Press, 1998). As the section below explains in more detail, one of the main debates about the nature of corporations was whether their rights derived from the individual corporators who owned them, or whether corporations constituted a species of legal person in their own right.

49. *Commonwealth v. Hunt*, 45 Mass. 111 (1842). On the development of conspiracy law in the United States, see Horwitz, *Transformation of American Law*; and Herbert Hovenkamp, *Enterprise and American Law, 1836–1937* (Cambridge, MA: Harvard University Press, 1991).

50. *United States v. Trans-Missouri Freight Ass'n*, 166 U.S. 290 (1897); and *Addyston Pipe & Steel Co. v. United States*, 175 U.S. 211 (1899). For details of the legal debates surrounding antimonopoly policies, see Peritz, *Competition Policy in America*; and Horwitz, *Transformation*.

51. In general, as Horwitz points out in *Transformation*, the U.S. Supreme Court lagged behind corporate theory and practice (in ultra vires cases and in recognizing corporate personhood, for example) as it tried in vain to uphold an older, conservative faith in individual competition in the face of ever-larger conglomerations.

52. The legal development of the different corporate structures is documented by Jack Blicksilver in *Defenders and Defense of Big Business in the United States, 1880–1900* (1955 PhD diss.; New York: Garland, 1985); Hovenkamp, *Enterprise and American Law*, 241–65; William G. Roy, *Socializing Capital: The Rise of the Large Industrial Corporation in America* (Princeton, NJ: Princeton University Press, 1999), 144–75; and Charles Perrow, *Organizing America: Wealth, Power, and the Origins of Corporate Capitalism* (Princeton, NJ: Princeton University Press, 2002), 197–212.

53. Henry Demarest Lloyd, *Wealth against Commonwealth* (New York: Harper, 1894), 511.

54. In *Standard Oil of New Jersey v. United States*, 221 U.S. 1 (1911), even though Standard Oil was ordered to be broken up, the basic defense—that there had been no conspiracy—was accepted by the court. As Benjamin Klein argues, however, Standard Oil was engaged in what would later come to be called a "hub-and-spoke conspiracy." Rockefeller and his agents enforced the conspiracy from the hub, albeit informally and without the kind of tightly knit, single-minded "breathing together" that is usually thought of in conspiracy theories. According to Klein, a networked monopoly thus emerged from the uneasy collusion between all the parties, with no single individual being able to dominate and pursue his own particular plans. See Klein, "The Hub-and-Spoke Conspiracy That Created the Standard Oil Monopoly," *Southern California Law Review* 85 (2012): 459–96.

55. E. Benjamin Andrews, "Trusts According to Official Investigations," *Quarterly Journal of Economics* 3 (1889): 133.

56. *Trustees of Dartmouth College v. Woodward*, 17 U.S. 518 (1819). As Horwitz points out in *Transformation*, the Supreme Court's decision in *Santa Clara County v. Southern Pacific Railroad Co.*, 118 U.S. 394 (1886)—which has often been cited as introducing the doctrine of corporate personality by granting an equal protection to corporations as that for individuals, under the logic of the Fourteenth Amendment—was actually predicated

instead on the still-dominant assumption that corporate rights derived from the rights of the individual corporators. Although it had far-reaching consequences, the original *Santa Clara* decision was barely noticed by the newspapers at that time (see Roy, *Socializing Capital*, 152), and it was not until the early 1900s that corporations were viewed by the U.S. Supreme Court as having legal personhood. In *Organizing America*, Perrow therefore warns against conspiracy-theory interpretations (most famously proposed by Charles and Mary Beard in the 1930s) that the change in the law was cooked up as part of a corporate conspiracy: "A zealot might cry 'conspiracy,' but that is going too far; it is enough to say that it was the result of obvious organizational interests in market control and empire building" (211).

57. Frederic Maitland, "Moral Personality and Legal Personality," in *The Collected Papers of Frederic William Maitland*, vol. 3, ed. H. A. L. Fisher (Cambridge: Cambridge University Press, 1911), 307.

58. Arthur W. Machen, "Corporate Personality," *Harvard Law Review* 24 (1911): 261–62.

59. John Dewey, "The Historical Background of Corporate Legal Personality," *Yale Law Journal* 35 (1926): 655–73. See also Gregory A. Mark, "The Personification of the Business Corporation in American Law," *University of Chicago Law Review* 54 (1987): 1441–83.

60. The courts also began to relax the common law doctrine, dating from the era of the corporation as a state concession, that required unanimous consent from shareholding owners to any extension beyond the explicitly chartered corporate purpose—initially by exploiting the rule that only a majority decision was needed to sell the assets of a firm if it was failing, a loophole that was then used to allow the buying and selling of constituent concerns within a holding company at the behest of its directors, rather than through the explicit unanimous consent of all owners.

61. Ignatius Donnelly, *Caesar's Column: A Story of the Twentieth Century* (Chicago: F. J. Schulte, 1890). On the conspiracy aesthetic of Ignatius Donnelly, see Alexander J. Beringer, "The Pleasures of Conspiracy: American Literature 1870–1910," PhD diss., University of Michigan, 2011. Beringer argues that the predilection for conspiracy theories in the Gilded Age and the Progressive Era is not merely because they offer a halfway house on the road to a proper, rational understanding of socioeconomics, but also because they provide their own compensations in terms of outrageous and sublime mystery. On the literary representation of conspiracy and terrorism in this period of American history, see Jeffory A. Clymer, *America's Culture of Terrorism: Violence, Capitalism, and the Written Word* (Chapel Hill: University of North Carolina Press, 2003).

62. Jack London, *Iron Heel* (New York: Macmillan, 1908); David Graham Phillips, *The Cost* (New York: Grosset & Dunlap, 1904); Phillips, *The Master-Rogue: The Confessions of a Croesus* (New York: McClure, Philips, 1903); and Phillips, *The Deluge* (Indianapolis: Bobbs-Merrill, 1905).

63. Phillips, *The Cost*, 395.

64. On the fundamental principles of conspiracy theories (nothing happens by accident; nothing is as it seems; and everything is connected), see Michael Barkun, *A Culture of Conspiracy* (Berkeley: University of California Press, 2003), 3–8.

65. Upton Sinclair, *The Moneychangers* (New York: B. W. Dodge, 1908); and Zimmerman, *Panic!*, 151–90. Zimmerman also provides a masterly reading of Norris's account of market panics in *The Pit* (New York: Doubleday, 1903) as an example of the "mesmeric sublime" (123–50).

66. Walter Benn Michaels famously argued that American naturalist fiction did not ultimately provide a critique of corporate consolidation during this period, because it relied on the same assumptions about corporate personhood that were used to justify the Great Merger Movement. In Michaels's account of the convergence between naturalist fiction and legal writings in the late nineteenth century, the scandal is not that corporations are like people, but that people are like corporations. The implication is that the genre of naturalism did not challenge the doctrine of corporate personality, but reinforced it, because naturalism's model of personhood was predicated on the same separation of material body and immaterial identity that, according to Michaels, was at the heart of legal cases defining corporate rights. While Michaels's discussion is frequently compelling, he overstates the extent to which legal theorists took the notion of legal personhood literally, with many continuing to rely on the individual rights at the heart of the partnership theory of corporations, or (like Arthur Machen, in "Corporate Personality") insisting that while corporations were natural entities prior to the law, they were not the same as real persons. Michaels also tends to turn the naturalists' engagement with the problem of individual collective agency into a philosophical insight about the fundamental nature of human identity, rather than a historically specific problem. Finally, in pushing toward his conclusion that naturalism constituted a single, overarching "logic" that was in tune with corporate capitalism, Michaels fails to acknowledge the contested nature of the debate. In his discussion of Michaels, Brook Thomas makes the intriguing suggestion that, "rather than conclude by saying that in naturalism all fictions are corporate fictions, we might be wiser to note that, so far, our literature has failed to produce any truly satisfying corporate fiction." See Thomas, "Walter Benn Michaels and Cultural Poetics: Where's the Difference?" in *The New Historicism: And Other Old-Fashioned Topics* (Princeton, NJ: Princeton University Press, 1991), 150.

67. On the original reception of *The Octopus*, see Christophe Den Tandt, *The Urban Sublime in American Literary Naturalism* (Urbana: University of Illinois Press, 1998), 70–96.

68. Frank Norris, *The Octopus: A Story of California*, 2 vols. (Garden City, NY: Doubleday, 1901), 1: 46. Subsequent references to this edition will be included in parentheses in the text.

69. On antisemitism in the novel, see Donald Pizer, "A Note on S. Behrman as a Jew in Frank Norris's *The Octopus*," *Studies in American Naturalism* 6, no. 1 (2011): 88–91.

70. On the immortality of the railroad trust in the novel, see Daniel J. Mrozowski, "How to Kill a Corporation: Frank Norris's *The Octopus* and the Embodiment of American Business," *Studies in American Naturalism* 6, no. 2 (2011): 161–84.

71. L. Frank Baum, *The Wonderful Wizard of Oz* (Chicago: George M. Hill, 1900). There is a long-running dispute on whether Baum's book is an allegory of the gold-standard debates of the 1890s. For a summary of this question, see Gretchen Ritter, "Silver Slippers and a Golden Cap: L. Frank Baum's *The Wonderful Wizard of Oz* and Historical Memory in American Politics," *Journal of American Studies* 31 (1997): 171–202; and Ranjit S. Dighe, ed., *The Historian's Wizard of Oz: Reading L. Frank Baum's Classic as a Political and Monetary Allegory* (Westport, CT: Greenwood, 2002).

72. On the cultural logic of personification in economics, see Campbell Jones, "What Kind of Subject Is the Market?" *New Formations* 72 (2011): 131–45.

73. See note 66.

74. Conspiracy theories about the panic of 1907 became increasingly popular once the

initial sense of relief diminished. See Zimmerman, *Panic!*, 151–57. The political debates leading up to the establishment of the Federal Reserve are dissected by Livingston in *Origins of the Federal Reserve System*.

75. U.S. House of Representatives, House Resolution 504, 62nd Cong., 2d Sess., 1912.

76. For an account of the political struggles of the Pujo Committee, see Lawrence E. Mitchell, *The Speculation Economy: How Finance Triumphed over Industry* (San Francisco: Berrett-Koekler, 2009); and Vincent P. Carosso, *Investment Banking in America: A History* (Cambridge, MA: Harvard University Press, 1970), 137–55. In a nice historical irony, Lindbergh Jr. married the daughter of one of the J. P. Morgan & Co. partners.

77. It has been estimated that this amount is the equivalent, proportionately, of $7.5 trillion today. See J. Bradford DeLong, "Did J. P. Morgan's Men Add Value? An Economist's Perspective on Financial Capitalism," *Inside the Business Enterprise: Historical Perspectives on the Use of Information*, ed. Peter Temin (Chicago: University of Chicago Press, 1991), 205–50.

78. See U.S. House of Representatives, Subcommittee of the Committee on Banking and Currency, *Investigation of the Financial and Monetary Conditions in the United States under House Resolutions Nos. 429 and 504*, 2 vols. (Washington, DC: Government Printing Office, 1912–1913), 1034–35.

79. Louis Brandeis, *Other People's Money: And How Bankers Use It* (New York: Stokes, 1914), 4.

80. Samuel Untermyer, "Is There a Money Trust? An Address Delivered Before the Finance Forum in the City of New York, Dec. 27th, 1911," quoted in Susie J. Pak, *Gentlemen Bankers: The World of J. P. Morgan* (Cambridge, MA: Harvard University Press, 2013), 28.

81. The details of this escapade are told in William Barton McCash and June Hall McCash, *The Jekyll Island Club: Southern Haven for America's Millionaires* (Athens: University of Georgia Press, 1989), 127–31.

82. U.S. House of Representatives, *Investigation of the Financial and Monetary Conditions*, 193.

83. Ibid., 1952.

84. Some later historians have taken Morgan's defense at face value: the bank directors did not operate in concert, it is argued, as there was plenty of disagreement and competition between them; and even if they had such a plan, they would not have been able to impose their will on the boards of directors, as they were rarely in a majority. This view is put forth forcibly by Carosso, *Investment Banking in America*, 139, 151. Some commentators (e.g., Thomas Huertas and Harold van B. Cleveland, *Citibank: 1812–1970* [Cambridge, MA: Harvard University Press, 1987]) have even characterized Untermyer as a self-serving, aspiring politician, deliberately and cynically throwing out accusations that he knew to be false.

85. U.S. House of Representatives, *Investigation of the Financial and Monetary Conditions*, 1061.

86. Letter from Messrs. J. P. Morgan & Co., in response to the invitation of the Sub-committee (Hon. A. P. Pujo, chairman) of the Committee on Banking and Currency of the House of Representatives, New York City, 25 February 1913 (New York: n.p., 1913), 8.

87. U.S. House of Representatives, *Investigation of the Financial and Monetary Conditions*, 1084.

88. Alfred Chandler, *The Visible Hand: The Managerial Revolution in American Business* (Cambridge, MA: Belknap Press of Harvard University Press, 1978).

89. Alfred Chandler, *Scale and Scope: The Dynamics of Industrial Capitalism* (Cambridge, MA: Harvard University Press, 1990), 235–334; P. J. Cain and Anthony G. Hopkins, *British Imperialism, 1688–2000* (Harlow, UK: Longman, 2002); and Geoffrey Jones, *Merchants to Multinationals* (Oxford: Oxford University Press, 2000).

90. Leslie Hannah, "The 'Divorce' of Ownership from Control from 1900 Onwards: Re-Calibrating Imagined Global Trends," *Business History*, 49, no. 4 (2007): 404–38.

91. See, for example, Mark S. Mizruchi, *The American Corporate Network: 1904–1972* (Beverly Hills, CA: Sage, 1982); David Bunting, "Origins of the American Corporate Network," *Social Science History* 7, no. 2 (1983): 129–42; Paul Windolf, *Corporate Networks in Europe and the United States* (Oxford: Oxford University Press, 2002); and Windolf, "Coordination and Control in Corporate Networks: United States and Germany in Comparison, 1896–1938," *European Sociological Review* 25, no. 4 (2009): 443–57.

92. DeLong, "Did J. P. Morgan's Men?"

93. Pak, *Gentleman Bankers*, 11.

94. Cited in Pak, *Gentleman Bankers*, 38. As Richard White notes in *Railroaded: The Transcontinentals and the Making of Modern America* (New York: Norton, 2011), "friend" was a key euphemism during this period (100–101).

95. Matthew Josephson, *The Robber Barons: The Great American Capitalists, 1861–1901* (New York: Harcourt, Brace, 1934).

96. G. William Domhoff, "There Are No Conspiracies," Who Rules America?, www2 .ucsc.edu/whorulesamerica/theory/conspiracy.html [accessed 1 October 2011].

97. U.S. House of Representatives, *Investigation of the Financial and Monetary Conditions*, 979–80.

98. Brandeis, *Other People's Money*, 30. The word "ramification" crops up repeatedly in discussions of corporate entanglement, with its connotations of branching that include associations with both family trees and railway/telephone branch and trunk lines.

99. Brandeis's articles in *Harper's Weekly*, which were later collected to form *Other People's Money*, were accompanied by muckraking cartoons, although the cartoons were not included in the book version. See University of Louisville, Louis D. Brandeis School of Law Library, http://louisville.edu/law/library/special-collections/the-louis-d.-brandeis-col lection/other-peoples-money-by-louis-d.-brandeis/ [accessed 1 October 2011].

100. Chandler, in *Visible Hand*, credits McCallum with being the first to produce corporate organizational charts (103). What is surprising, however, is that Chandler never actually saw the chart itself, basing his description instead on a detailed advertisement in the *American Railroad Journal*. Business historians have presumed that the original was lost, but (without knowing Chandler's difficulties in locating the original) I came across a version on the Library of Congress website, and copies of the original image have since been found. See Alfred Chandler, "Origins of the Organization Chart," *Harvard Business Review* 66 (1988): 156–57; and Caitlin Rosenthal, "Big Data in the Age of the Telegraph," *McKinsey Quarterly* 1 (March 2013): 13–18.

101. Lewis Henry Morgan, *Systems of Consanguinity and Affinity of the Human Family* (Washington, DC: Smithsonian Institution, 1870). On the history of the tree as a visual metaphor, see Manuel Lima, *The Book of Trees: Visualizing Branches of Knowledge* (New York: Princeton Architectural Press, 2014).

102. Chandler, *Visible Hand*, and Robert Wiebe, *The Search for Order, 1877–1920* (New York: Hill & Wang, 1967). Although, in theory, Morgan and his fellow financiers were try-

ing to remake the messy world to fit the spirit of rationalization embodied in the diagrams of corporate organization, in practice they were more likely to rely on personal networks and their first-hand knowledge of the competency of particular managers, rather than an abstract organizational structure as such.

103. The British Ecological Society was formed in the same year as the Pujo Committee diagrams were produced (although the term "ecosystem" was not fully explicated until 1935, with the publication of Arthur Tansley's "The Use and Abuse of Vegetational Concepts and Terms," *Ecology* 16, no. 3 [1935]: 284–307). As Adam Curtis argues in *All Watched Over by Machines of Loving Grace* (BBC Two, 2011), some of the spurious foundational claims of ecology were taken up by Chicago economists, who were attracted to the notion of benign, self-regulating, cybernetic systems.

104. John A. Hobson, *Imperialism: A Study* (London: J. Nisbet, 1902).

105. Niall Ferguson, *Empire: How Britain Made the Modern World* (London: Allen Lane, 2003), 280–82. A more nuanced view is offered by Peter Cain, *Hobson and Imperialism: Radicalism, New Liberalism, and Finance 1887–1938* (Oxford: Oxford University Press, 2002).

106. Linton C. Freeman, *The Development of Social Network Analysis: A Study in the Sociology of Science* (Vancouver, BC: Empirical Press, 2004). A version of the diagram first appeared in John A. Hobson, "The Structure of South African Finance," *Speaker* 12, no. 291 (29 April 1905), 117–18.

107. John Moody, *Truth About the Trusts* (New York: Moody, 1904).

108. Ibid., 491–92.

109. Ibid., 492–93.

110. Ibid., 493. Compare a far more conspiratorial interpretation in H. L. Barber, *Making Money Make Money; or, A Primer of Investing* (Chicago: A. J. Munson, 1916): "What we see is that two small groups of men, classed as the 'Rockefeller Group' and the 'Morgan Group,' are directly or indirectly interested vitally in about every large business enterprise in this country. . . . We will see later that when it [the reader's investment dollar] goes to one of these two groups it goes under conditions where the 'clique' who comprises it gets nineteen-twentieths of its earning power, and you get but one-twentieth. We will see that there is a perfected financial system that, by and through the magazines and newspapers, by and through the banks, by and through the reportorial agencies, leads, coaxes, and drives the dollars of the masses to this 'clique' of the classes as assuredly and as certainly as if these dollars were wrenched from them by force" (166–67).

111. It is worth comparing the discussion of "the System" in Thomas Lawson's *Frenzied Finance: The Crime of Amalgamated* (New York: Ridgeway, 1905). Lawson was a stock promoter who then turned to muckraking journalism and novel writing. In *Frenzied Finance*, he mounts a lengthy accusation against the stock-underwriting syndicate that had put together the Amalgamated Copper combination in 1899, which then spectacularly failed amid stories of massive corruption. At first sight, it seems as though Lawson is presenting system as conspiracy, in the way I have been describing the work of the Pujo Committee. In Lawson's case, however, "the System" is merely his designation for a tightly knit cabal involving many of the leading figures of Standard Oil, of which Lawson himself was initially a member. Lawson's depiction of "the System" has little to do with the discovery of an abstract and impersonal system underpinning the work of Wall Street and is, instead, more a litany of personal grievances and self-justification for his wayward actions. Although Lawson shared with Progressive critics a concern for the systematic corruption

of high finance, the plots of both *Frenzied Finance* and his novel, *Friday, the Thirteenth* (New York: Doubleday, 1907), are motivated by a very personal desire for revenge. For more on the Lawson story, see Zimmerman, *Panic!*, 81–122, esp. 94.

112. Robert Clifford, *Application of Barruel's* Memoirs of Jacobinism *to the Secret Societies of Great Britain and Ireland, by the Translator of That Work* (London, 1798), xiii, cited in Michael Taylor, "British Conservatism, the Illuminati, and the Conspiracy Theory of the French Revolution, 1797–1802," *Eighteenth-Century Studies* 47, no. 3 (2014): 293–312.

113. Brandeis, *Other People's Money*, 51.

114. Ibid., 54–55.

115. See Robert Hobbs, ed., *Mark Lombardi: Global Networks* (New York: Independent Curators International, 2003).

116. Bureau d'études, http://bureaudetudes.org/about/ [accessed 21 October 2011].

117. On the *Griftopia* image, see Paul Crosthwaite, Peter Knight, and Nicky Marsh, eds., *Show Me the Money: The Image of Finance, 1700 to the Present* (Manchester, UK: Manchester University Press, 2014), 49–51.

118. Timothy Melley, *Empire of Conspiracy: The Culture of Paranoia in Postwar America* (Ithaca, NY: Cornell University Press, 2000). See also Peter Starr, "We the Paranoid," American University, College of Arts and Sciences, www.american.edu/cas/wtp/.

119. Fredric Jameson, "Cognitive Mapping," in *Marxism and the Interpretation of Culture*, ed. Cary Nelson and Lawrence Grossberg (Basingstoke, UK: Macmillan, 1988), 356.

120. Wiebe, *Search for Order*, 12.

Epilogue

1. There are no clear statistics on numbers, but in 2000, the Electronic Trading Association estimated that there were only about 45,000 full-time day traders in the United States. That figure, however, is dwarfed by the 23 million "amateurs" who had opened their own brokerage accounts. See "Impact of Online Trading, Part 2," NOVA, www.pbs.org/wgbh/nova/stockmarket/online2.html. For a profile of the return to day trading after the 2007 crash, see David Segal, "Day Traders 2.0: Wired, Angry, and Loving It," *New York Times*, 27 March 2010. One of the most thoughtful explorations of the enticements of the stock market for the ordinary investor in the dotcom years is David Denby's memoir, *American Sucker* (New York: Little, Brown, 2004).

2. Linda Bradford Raschke, "Tape Reading," Traderslog, www.traderslog.com/tape-reading/ [accessed 21 May 2012].

3. See, for example, the "Richard D. Wyckoff Tape Reading Course," offered for $570 from the Wyckoff Stock Market Institute, https://wyckoffstockmarketinstitute.com/course_tape_reading.htm [accessed 20 December 2014].

4. Stephen Sutherland, "Why Reading the Market Every Day Makes Sense," ISACO, www.isaco.co.uk/blog/bid/181705/Why-reading-the-market-every-day-makes-sense/ [accessed 21 May 2014].

5. As Paul Crosthwaite demonstrates, even professional traders tend to think of the market as much as a supernatural force as a natural and rational one. See Crosthwaite, "Phantasmagoric Finance: Crisis and the Supernatural in Contemporary Finance Culture," in *Criticism, Crisis, and Contemporary Narrative: Textual Horizons in an Age of Global Risk*, ed. Paul Crosthwaite (New York: Routledge, 2011), 178–200.

6. Alton Hill, "Tape Reading (Time and Sales Window)," TradingSim Day Trading Blog, http://tradingsim.com/blog/tape-reading/ [accessed 21 May 2012].

7. "The Art of Reading the Tape: Part One," iBankCoin, http://ibankcoin.com/chart_addict/2010/01/12/the-art-of-reading-the-tape-part-one/ [accessed 21 May 2012].

8. Sutherland, "Why Reading the Market." Unfortunately, at most, only 20 percent of day traders make a consistent profit (and the figure is quite likely much lower); the vast majority are no match for a system that is dominated by the big banks, hedge funds, and specialist high-frequency trading firms. See Brad M. Barber, Yi-Tsung Lee, Yu-Jane Lieu, and Terrance Odean, "Do Individual Day Traders Make Money? Evidence from Taiwan," working paper, University of California, Berkeley (May 2004), http://faculty.haas.berkeley.edu/odean/papers/Day%20Traders/Day%20Trade%20040330.pdf; and Douglas J. Jordan and J. David Diltz, "The Profitability of Day Traders," *Financial Analysts Journal* (2003): 85–94.

9. Moreover, as Alex Preda demonstrates, the world of online day trading is a profoundly *social* one, despite the anonymity and abstraction of the data on the screen. See Preda, "Tags, Transaction Types, and Communication in Online Anonymous Markets," *Socio-Economic Review* 11 (2013): 31–56.

10. Jason Van Bergen, "How to Read the Market's Psychological State," Investopedia, www.investopedia.com/articles/trading/03/010603.asp; and Joe Nocera, "A Day (Gasp) Like Any Other," *New York Times*, 6 October 2008, www.nytimes.com/2008/10/07/business/07nocera.html. See also Paul Crosthwaite, "Animality and Ideology in Contemporary Economic Discourse: Taxonomizing *Homo economicus*," *Journal of Cultural Economy* 6 (2013): 94–109.

11. On the rhetoric and logic of personification in contemporary financial talk, see Campbell Jones, *Can the Market Speak?* (Winchester, UK: Zero Books, 2013); and Jones, "What Kind of Subject Is the Market?" *New Formations* 72 (2011): 131–45.

12. Mark C. Taylor, in *Confidence Games: Money and Markets in a World without Redemption* (Chicago: University of Chicago Press, 2004), discusses how the market has not merely become personified as God, but has, in effect, become a substitute for God.

13. Randy Martin, *The Financialization of Daily Life* (Philadelphia: Temple University Press, 2002); and Gerald F. Davis, *Managed by the Markets: How Finance Re-Shaped America* (Oxford: Oxford University Press, 2009).

14. These figures are taken from Greta Krippner, *Capitalizing on Crisis: The Political Origins of the Rise of Finance* (Cambridge, MA: Harvard University Press, 2011), 27–57. It also needs to be remembered that for firms in the financial sector, profit is measured after bonuses have been paid. If those bonuses were viewed properly as part of the firms' profits, rather than as part of their salary expenditures, then the figure for profits within the financial sector would be significantly higher. Furthermore, even seemingly straightforward manufacturing firms, such as the Ford Motor Company, increasingly derive the majority of their profits from financial products (i.e., selling loans to buy their cars, rather than from the cars themselves).

15. Ian Stewart, "The Mathematical Equation That Caused the Banks to Crash," *Guardian*, 12 February 2012.

16. See, for example, Graeme Wearden, "European Debt Crisis: Markets Fall as Germany Bans 'Naked Short-Selling,'" *Guardian*, 19 May 2010.

17. The possibility of an artificial-intelligence, high-frequency trading algorithm coming to life is given full gothic treatment in Robert Harris's compelling novel, *The Fear Index* (London: Hutchinson, 2011).

18. Michael Lewis, *Flash Boys: Cracking the Money Code* (London: Allen Lane, 2014), 52–53.

19. The problem with Lewis's book is not merely that it focuses on a few bad apples in its portrait of HFT as a temporary perversion of the otherwise smooth running of the stock market. Rather, its real flaw is that it suggests that the only ones smart enough to do anything about the problem are insiders like Brad Katsuyama (the hero of Lewis's tale), whose free-market solution is not better and more-democratic regulation, but the creation of a new electronic exchange that is intended to level the playing field and undermine the HFT firms' advantage.

20. This rhetorical strain is dissected in Crosthwaite, "Animality and Ideology," 106.

Page numbers in italics refer to illustrations